MIGRATION

MIGRATION

Immigration and Emigration
in International Perspective

EDITED BY
LEONORE LOEB ADLER AND UWE P. GIELEN

Foreword by
Robert J. Kleiner, Barnabas I. Okeke, and Tom Sorensen

Westport, Connecticut
London

Library of Congress Cataloging-in-Publication Data

Migration: immigration and emigration in international perspective / edited by Leonore Loeb Adler and
    Uwe P. Gielen; foreword by Robert J. Kleiner, Barnabas I. Okeke, and Tom Sorensen
      p. cm.
    Includes bibliographical references and index.
    ISBN 0–275–97666–1 (alk. paper)
    1. Emigration and immigration.   I. Adler, Leonore Loeb.   II. Gielen, Uwe P. (Uwe Peter),
    1940–
JV6035.M5415   2003
304.8'2—dc21   2002070927

British Library Cataloguing in Publication Data is available.

Library of Congress Catalog Card Number: 2002070927
ISBN: 0–275–97666–1

First published in 2003

Praeger Publishers, 88 Post Road West, Westport, CT 06881
An imprint of Greenwood Publishing Group, Inc.
www.praeger.com

Printed in the United States of America

The paper used in this book complies with the
Permanent Paper Standard issued by the National
Information Standards Organization (Z39.48–1984).

10 9 8 7 6 5 4 3 2 1

Contents

Dedication to Bruce Bain

We dedicate this volume to Bruce Bain, who died as a result of a tragic accident.

Bruce Bain was born in Montreal, Quebec, Canada. He was brought up in a multilingual and multicultural setting, where he developed the foundation for learning languages. He received his bachelor's degree at Sir George Williams University, his master's degree and doctorate at the University of Alberta, all in the area of psychology. At the time of his death, he was Professor in the Department of Educational Psychology, University of Alberta where he taught for 28 years. His main research interests were cross-cultural studies on language and cognition, bilingualism, human development, ethnographic studies, and histories of psychology. He had researched and lectured in universities all over the world, including China, the Czech Republic, Denmark, the Dominican Republic, France, Germany, Hawaii, Hong Kong, Japan, Korea, the Philippines, Russia (Siberia), Singapore, and South Africa. He had shown a penchant for cross-cultural studies in his undergraduate years, with an interest in Africa, where he got his first teaching post at the University of Makerere in Uganda. His research interests expanded to Europe in his earlier professorial years, and Southeast Asia in the later years, with a special interest in Hong Kong and China where he had spent extensive study leaves. His coresearcher in that part of the world was his Hong Kong-born wife, Dr. Agnes Yu.

He was in the midst of a 20-year longitudinal study on language, cognition, bilingualism, and personality development spanning several countries at the time of his untimely death. He believed that in research one never reaches the last word, one just continues the quest for knowledge and validation. In his field-work and ethnographic studies, Dr. Bain became immersed in the daily lives of the local residents. To him, that was the most valuable part of his research—experiencing the reality of the local inhabitants' daily lives and learning to see and feel as they did. Out of these experiences he developed a fierce sense of human rights and dignity and became active in various international organizations in these pursuits.

Besides being a dynamic speaker and an inquisitive researcher, Dr. Bain was a dedicated teacher and was well loved by his students for his dedication to teaching, support for their research, and unquenchable search for knowledge. He was an internationalist who devoted much of his life to social equality and justice. His life's passions were family, dogs, friends, books, music, opera, travel, and gardening. He passed away on January 24, 1999, among family and friends.

Each of us has to look into our Self and fear failure, fear death, fear inadequacies of various kinds and come out on the other side wiser, healthier, and prepared to share with others what is important in life. You have made the voyage: and now you must give back to those who have yet to complete the journey.

–Bruce Bain, in a letter to a friend, December 1998

Foreword

Robert J. Kleiner, Barnabas I. Okeke, and Tom Sorensen

It is refreshing to see a book that deals with the dynamic aspects of migration and its impact on mental health and psychological adjustment and that is not afraid to demonstrate the intervening complex dynamic interaction needed to explain the total migration experience and its effects. It is even more difficult when we put together a group of studies concerned with a wide range of different cultures and different countries. It is tragic that Bruce Bain, a long-term colleague, teacher, and researcher should have passed away so suddenly, but it is fortunate that one of the chapters was coauthored by him. It illustrates in so many ways the new directions that migration research must go and illustrates as well the need to deal consciously with the issues raised here.

A book with these dimensions indicates that we cannot depend on simple correlational studies of early empirical research where migration was defined in such terms as birthplace and was correlated with a wide range of variables also simply defined. In a book with a scope such as this one, it may help to provide the reader with some guidelines for reading and integrating the material. With such guidelines, it is hoped that we may better appreciate the richness and challenge of the material presented. The first set of issues is more abstract or meta-theoretical in nature, and it deals with the value of the book as the product of a group of scholarly efforts. The second set of issues is more concrete in nature and deals with the way the various authors approach the particular substantive issues of their chapters. Clearly, the authors dealt with these issues in various ways, and collectively they clarify the need for such efforts to make the problem of migration and its effects better understood.

In approaching the problem of migration and its effects, one is already dealing with a very complex task that requires considering it from many points of view and drawing on the contributions of many disciplines. Therefore, one needs to determine the degree to which the explanatory or "causal" theories emanating from these different disciplines are made use of in a holistic manner.

No single theory can deal with the integration of data taken from different levels of analysis. Descriptive data alone cannot provide us with any explanatory understanding of the phenomenon.

The complexity of the phenomenon also requires us to make use of and draw on the empirical findings that have been generated by the different disciplines that bear on the task at hand. Of course the quality of the data emanating from different disciplines also vary in their precision and validity but the question is the degree to which the different data sets "ring true" in the explanations they provide.

Migration as a phenomenon requires us to consider the place and influence of macrolevels of analysis (e.g., institutional influences), microlevels of analysis (e.g., the structure of the personal social networks), associated symbol systems (e.g., values, motives), and their interactive effects as well. With such considerations, it needs to be kept in mind that levels of analysis in different disciplines require examining different variables and different aspects of the total social nexus being studied. Thus, holistic or integrated analyses are quite demanding.

Because different investigators have written the following chapters, the reader will encounter a variety of theoretical frameworks and methods. In this context, it is not easy to ascertain the extent to which the authors' conclusions about the nature of the emigration and immigration experience may prove similar or dissimilar from country to country.

In the preceding points, we have emphasized the complexities and difficulties that need to be dealt with and anticipated at a more abstract level, but the issues of the complexities and the difficulties also inhere in the phenomenon itself. As the various chapters illustrate so well, the insights gained for dealing clinically or otherwise with migration of any kind depend on a number of crucial considerations. One must consider the influence of the migrants' experience and socialization in the ethnic and ecological environment of the community from which they came (i.e., the "community of origin"), the worldview and expectations of the sociocultural environment to which they migrate (i.e., the "community of destination"), and the nature of their transition or movement experience.

When we turn to the task of understanding migration specifically and its effects, research in recent years has shown increasingly that such research can no longer deal with the individual or interactive effects of a few operationally defined variables like education, social status, income, urban-rural origins, or communities and countries of destinations. And this is shown here as well. Such operational/statistical methods may be "precise" and "accurate," but the research itself is too conceptually simplistic, and it usually fails to comprehensively take into account the total holistic experience.

We are impressed with the breadth of the sociocultural variables that are included in the analyses presented by the different chapter authors and with their efforts to integrate them meaningfully in their various discussions.

In addition, there is the emerging recognition of the need to deal with sociocultural variables at the proximal level (i.e., in terms of how such variables exert their influence through the social networks to which individuals belong, interact with, and are influenced by). There is also the emerging awareness that the many concrete aspects and dialectical properties of the communities of origin, the communities of destination, and the transition experience are part of the migration experience and must be included in any analysis of it.

It should also be clear that analyses dealing with the integration of both distal and proximal variables, and of macrolevels and microlevels of analysis are difficult to accomplish and there are few models in the literature to show the way. We need to develop such models.

Similarly, there is a growing recognition that the individual and interacting effects of multiple cultural and subcultural influences are equally complicated and difficult. Prevailing statistical models may be tempting to use but more often than not they fail to satisfy the assumptions that such studies require. We, as clinicians and researchers, need innovative models for this task as well.

Finally, these analyses show the necessity of always considering the nature of the psychological realities of the individuals being studied, their experiences within a variety of social networks, and the objective realities that determine the limits or boundaries to what can occur within the examined psychosocial realities.

As these studies develop, it must become increasingly obvious that one is always faced with new demanding and provocative problems that require solution. Collectively however, the studies included in this volume break new ground, use different strategies from those that were used in the past (and continue to be used), which is indeed interesting, productive, and provocative.

Preface

Migration has been an inherent part of human existence ever since our protohuman and human ancestors left Africa to populate the rest of the world. Although we can reconstruct these early migrations only in their rough outlines, it is likely that then as now human migration was accompanied by anticipation, excitement, fear, the fracturing of long-standing social relationships, heartaches, tensions, and even bloodshed between the migrants and the local populations, and the willing or unwilling exchange of ideas, skills, attitudes, and genes. Today, more than ever, migration forms a central part of the global flow of persons, goods, practices, and ideas.

The historical origins, underlying processes, and psychosocial consequences of migration need to be investigated in all their complexities. Because migration has so frequently been the result of population pressures, political disasters, and powerful economic forces, demographers, political scientists, historians, sociologists, and economists have most often studied it. In contrast, many of the psychocultural and psychosocial processes that both drive and accompany migration are less well understood because they tend to fall into the areas of expertise of psychologists–and most psychologists have so far shown little or no interest in migration.

To help remedy this situation, we developed this volume to add the voices of a prominent international group of cross-culturally oriented psychologists to the worldwide debate on migration. The book provides an overview of emigration from and immigration into selected countries located around the globe. The countries in question include poorer countries such as the Philippines, Mexico, Egypt, and Ireland (in former times) that have "exported" millions of migrants as well as the rich and industrialized countries that have traditionally been the recipients of immigration. Interestingly, many of the European nations that used to send waves of emigrants to the new worlds in North and South America, Australia, and South Africa have in recent years become the reluctant receiving countries for numerous immigrants. However, as the chapters on Norway and Germany suggest, most European countries have now such low birthrates that they must either face rapidly declining population numbers or open their doors to immigrants from Eastern Europe, Africa, the Near East, and elsewhere. Psychologically, however, Western European societies remain unprepared for the waves of immigrants and refugees that are knocking on their doors.

Throughout the book, the reader will encounter an astonishing variety of migrants: Hong Kongers skillfully adjusting their immigration and emigration plans to the whims of Communist leaders, Filipino maids celebrating their day off in a Hong Kong park, Kazakhstani *Aussiedler* of Polish or German background returning to the lands of their ancestors, Egyptians traveling to rich oil-producing countries located on and near the Arabian peninsula, successful politicians of Irish background in the United States, Armenians fleeing from Turkish genocide, Brazilian "U-turn workers" of Japanese descent facing the problems of readaptation to a tight-laced Japanese society, the ingathering of Jews in the new State of Israel, desperately poor contract laborers coming to the Republic of South Africa to work in mines, successful Caribbean immigrants moving up the economic ladder in New York City, undocumented Mexican laborers trying to cross the U.S. border with false papers or no papers at all, and so many others. This volume is, literally, about the destinies and fates of a steadily growing segment of the world's population.

Both of the editors are immigrants who left Germany for the United States: one fleeing the Hitler regime and the other escaping from poverty and the prospects of a limited professional future. As such we were hardly alone: In the 1990 census, some 50 million Americans traced their own background or that of their ancestors to Germany—more than to any other country. These ancestors brought with them an astonishing amount of "psychocultural capital" to the New World. By psychocultural capital we mean the social and technical skills, knowledge, personality traits such as courage, openness to new experiences, curiosity, readiness to take risks, perseverance, and willingness to endure relentless hard work, attitudes, consumption habits, and endlessly varied ways of life that migrants bring with them to their new social surroundings. In the long run, this psychocultural capital is often worth more than trainloads of gold because it contributes to the prosperity and long-term vitality of the receiving societies.

Immigrants from German-speaking countries and their descendants, for example, introduced superior agricultural methods; helped to shape and reshape the American educational system from the kindergarten level to the graduate level; manned the ubiquitous marching bands; founded, directed, and played in symphony orchestras and opera companies; emphasized gymnastics; built such bridges as the Brooklyn Bridge; established newspapers; painted everybody and everything from Native Americans to Yosemite Park; wrote books on almost every conceivable subject; won numerous Nobel prizes; introduced Christmas trees and other Christmas customs; fought in the American Revolutionary War; led American armies in World War I, World War II, and the Gulf War; helped to build atom bombs; established breweries whose products would wean many of their fellow Americans from hard liquor; and made innumerable other contributions to American society. Today, these contributions have been inextricably woven into America's many-hued cultural quilt together with the contributions of countless immigrants from the other regions of the globe.

In recent years, most immigrants to the United States have come from Asia, Latin America, and the Caribbean regions rather than from Europe. Not only are they helping to reshape American society into a multiracial, multicultural society incorporating influences from every corner of the world, but they are also bringing with them new psychocultural capital that is lending American society a special kind of vitality and dynamism. Similar trends may be observed in other immigration societies such as Canada and Australia.

However, migrants bring with them not only psychocultural capital but also psychocultural liabilities. Consider, for instance, the Spanish *conquistadores* who in the 16th century began to arrive in the New World to wreak havoc on the native societies. They brought with them diseases such as smallpox, malaria, measles, and influenza that killed large proportions of the native population, cannons, guns, armory, and horses to gain rapid military superiority, an especially brutal and fanatical version of Christianity, a disdain for manual labor, and a general outlook on life that favored the ruthless exploitation of both the native people and the land's resources. Because they wished to exploit the land and those representing to them other, seemingly inferior "races," the *conquistadores* bequeathed to many parts of Latin America a general outlook on life that would help to retard their economic development for centuries to come.

Migration, then, can have both positive and negative consequences. In today's world of relentless and ever accelerating change, we need to understand both. To achieve this goal, this volume contains a broadly conceived sequence of chapters that taken together present a broad overview of the psychosocial origins and consequences of migration in selected countries around the world. We dedicate this volume to all those migrants who are already beginning to change our world in the new century and to Bruce Bain, an internationally minded student of migration whose life was tragically cut short by an accident.

Preparing this volume has been a pleasure because so many people supported our efforts. We would like to thank Petra Bernard, Oksana Chumachenko, Natasha Carty, and Oraine Ramoo who contributed their considerable typing, proofreading, and computer skills while helping to prepare the book manuscript. St. Francis College, through the Institute for International and Cross-Cultural Psychology, provided much appreciated institutional and financial support.

The editors express appreciation to the University Seminars at Columbia University for assistance in the preparation of the manuscript for publication. Material drawn from this work was presented to the University Seminar on Moral Education.

I

Patterns of Migration

1

Human Migration and Immigration: An Overview

Anthony J. Marsella and Erin Ring

HUMAN MIGRATION AND IMMIGRATION IN HISTORICAL PERSPECTIVE

The impulse to migrate is inherent in human nature—an instinctual and inborn disposition and inclination to wonder and to wander in search of new opportunities and new horizons. Indeed, the separation of the human species into its myriad ethnic, cultural, linguistic, and racial groups was—and remains—an outcome of migration. It has also been the basis of gene and cultural transmission and accommodation.

Early Migration Waves

Migration has been a major source of human survival, adaptation, and growth across the centuries and millennia. This was true in the earliest days of human existence, when hunters and gatherers roamed as individuals and bands across Africa to Eurasia and then across the Bering Straits to North America and South America. This was true as early sea voyagers followed coastlines and then crossed oceans to unknown worlds, and as nations colonized new lands in pursuit of power and wealth moving citizens, servants, and slaves around the globe. This was also true during that great period of migration when Europeans left their homes for the promise and possibilities of America—for freedom, hope, and identity. And it is also true today as new migrants from Asia and Central and South America move to North America, Europe, and Australia (Castles & Miller, 1993; Diamond, 1999; Kraut, 1994; Sowell, 1996).

Diamond (1999), in his critically acclaimed book on the origins and determinants of human societies, contended that early migration waves occurred in the following patterns: Approximately 7 million years ago protohumans (e.g., *Australopithecus africanus, Homo erectus*) developed in Africa. By 1 million years ago, early humans (*Homo sapiens*) had migrated to China and Southeast Asia, and by 500,000 years ago, to northern Europe. Then, around 40,000 years ago, there was human migration to Australia, and subsequently to the South Pacific

Islands. This was a followed around 20,000 years ago by migration into Siberia and then into North America (by about 12,000 years ago). By 10,000 years ago, human migration had proceeded into South America, as far as Patagonia, Argentina. The last major migration of ancient times to uninhabited lands occurred between A.D. 100, when Polynesians sailed to Hawaii, and A.D. 1000, when Polynesians sailed to New Zealand.

As Diamond (1999) constantly pointed out, these dates must all be considered approximations; however, they are supported by strong archaeological evidence. Thus, according to Diamond, from the beginnings of human evolution in Africa around 7 million years ago, to around A.D. 1000, all habitable lands in the world had been occupied by human beings. This global migration has had profound and irreversible consequences for both the human species and the world's physical environment, and the early migration waves set the stage for the migration waves that continue today.

In all instances, the lives of both the migrants and those who arrived before them are changed by migration, for migration is an interactive process—both migrant and host are permanently altered by the encounter. A new social and environmental ecology emerges. Values, ideas, and diseases are exchanged, and eventually so are genes. Migration has been responsible for the fall of civilizations and the rise of others, as was the case with the Roman Empire, which fell before migratory waves of eastern and northern European tribes—Cimbri, Huns, Goths, Visigoths, Ostrogoths, and Vandals. We can ignore neither the historical importance of the vast and sweeping Islamic migrations of the Ottoman Turks, nor the northern European migrations of the Anglo-Saxons and Jutes that shaped Ireland and the United Kingdom, nor those of the Celtic people who preceded them by thousands of years.

Colonization and Migration

In North and South America, indigenous civilizations and cultures fell before Spanish, English, and French settlers. And, of course, there is that most brutal period in history when millions of sub-Saharan Africans were captured and sold as slaves in the New World. No strains of Dvorak's Symphony no. 9, "From the New World," played in the background as African tribespeople were forcefully herded onto ships to be sold into slavery. In the history of human migration, perhaps no other event is filled with such tragedy and brutality. The magnitude of this horror remains inscribed on Black and White minds even today and serves as a constant reminder of the consequences of forced migrations. Zolberg (1978) wrote:

The need for vast quantities of cheap labor in the Americas was satisfied by the importation of West Africans as slaves. Trans-Atlantic slave trade was brutal. Numbers of live arrivals grew from an estimated 1,800 a year for the period 1451–1600, to 13,400 for 1601–1700, and 55,000 annually for the period 1701–1810, a total of about 7.7 million altogether. (p. 245)

Forced migration was also imposed on American Indian tribes, who were compelled to surrender by conquering settlers and soldiers, who then moved surviving Indians to barren and disease-filled lands unwanted by others. Later even these desolate lands were taken from the Indians (e.g., Stannard, 1992).

Migration in the 19th and 20th Centuries

The upsurge in human migration continued vigorously into the 19th and 20th centuries. Jews migrated by the thousands facing the programs of 19th-century Russia and devastation in Europe between 1930s and the post-World War II period. These waves of migration sustained a pattern throughout their history as a people beginning with their historic exodus from Egypt in ancient biblical times to the terrors of the Inquisition in 15th-century Spain. And there was, of course, the most sizable migration in human history as more than 50 million people left Europe between 1850 and 1930 for life in the United States, Canada, and South America. They came from scores of countries—Ireland, Italy, Russia, Poland, Hungary, Slovakia, and the Scandinavian nations (Hoerder & Knauf, 1992). In his account of migration to America, Kraut (1982) wrote:

Twenty-three and a half million people arrived in the United States between 1880 and 1921, mostly from southern and eastern Europe, but also from parts of Asia and Latin America. In their wake, these restless people shattered the economic and social patterns of communities they left behind. What caused all this movement? Many of the changes that had affected western Europe in the middle of the nineteenth century were now moving east. In southern and eastern Europe, a rapidly increasing population, the decline of an aging agrarian system, and the emergence of the industrial revolution fractured traditional political, economic, and social relationships. When people lost confidence that long respected political institutions and social customs could stabilize their lives, they sought change; many chose emigration. (pp. 8–9)

And what of the millions of displaced and deported people—Poles, Czechs, Latvians, Estonians, Germans, Hungarians, and others—who were uprooted and relocated in World War II and the years that followed? And how can the world forget the millions of Pakistanis and Indians forced to move as Britain yielded colonial rule of India in 1948? And what of the millions of Mexicans who have crossed the Mexican-U.S. borders in search of work and freedom from poverty and destitution, making Spanish the second most frequently spoken language in the United States (e.g., Sowell, 1996).

Massive migration waves also occurred among Chinese, Japanese, and other East and Southeast Asian groups. Chinese laborers, imported by the tens of thousands helped build the American West, and Japanese laborers worked the sugar and pineapple fields of Hawaii from dawn to dusk for a pittance. Eventually, by the 1920s, the Japanese became the largest single population group in Hawaii and anti-Asian legislation was passed to stem the tide of the "yellow horde" (Nordyke, 1989). According to Kraut (1994), the Japanese migration to Hawaii—officially sanctioned by a government agreement between Japan and Hawaii—brought 26 ships carrying 28,691 Japanese to Hawaii between 1885 and 1894.

And so it is today in nations across the world, in Kosovo, Bosnia, Sudan, Guatemala, Kurdistan, Zambia, Rwanda, Cambodia, Ethiopia, Vietnam, China, Tibet, and a hundred more places. The current migrants are victims of ethnic cleansing and genocide. In many instances, past and present, entire populations have approached extermination, saved only by migration to new lands often filled with as much risk as the lands they left behind them. Migration has saved lives and destroyed others. And so it is that migration furthers human evolution by posing new demands, creating new opportunities and choices, opening the human mind and body to new possibilities and risks (e.g., Diamond, 1999; Kraut, 1994; Sowell, 1996).

THE UNITED STATES: NATION OF IMMIGRANTS

Immigration has made the United States the most ethnically and racially diverse nation in the world. Its history is a history of immigrants, and its current position as the most powerful and influential economic and political nation in the world is testimony to the contributions immigrants have made. This statement neither endorses nor justifies the tragic circumstances surrounding the decimation of the indigenous American Indian and Native Hawaiian populations (Stannard, 1992), or the African slave trade on which much of the early American economy was built (Zolberg, 1978). These stains on American history are permanent and irreversible, and the only moral response can now be an unrelenting determination to fulfill the promise of the Bill of Rights and to create a nation of equality and opportunity for all.

The current population of the United States is approximately 288 million people. Of this number, its is estimated that about 13% are of African American ancestry, 11% are of Hispanic origin, 4% are of Asian Pacific ancestry, and 1% are of American Indian/Native Alaskan ancestry. A quick accounting indicates that approximately 30% of all residents of the United States are now of non-European ancestry or origin. Of even more interest is the fact that more than 26 million people in the United States today are foreign born—about 1 in 10 people. More than one fourth of these foreign-born residents are from Mexico. Other nations contributing sizable numbers to the U.S. population are the Philippines, China/Hong Kong, Cuba, Vietnam, India, Dominican Republic, El Salvador, Great Britain, and Korea (Reimers, 1992). It is no surprise that New York City, Los Angeles, Miami, Chicago, and Washington, DC, are the cities with the largest annual immigrant populations (*The World Almanac*, 1999). The immigration laws of the United States provide for a variety of immigration options based on immigration quotas. In 1997, the immigrant quota was 675,000, excluding refugees. This number includes visas granted for immediate relatives (family immigrants), employment-based immigrants (e.g., priority workers, professionals, skilled workers, and investors), and diversity immigrants.

EUROPE AND IMMIGRATION

In Europe, immigration has been a problematic reality since the end of World War II. In the last decade, national borders that once clearly defined different cultures, languages, and ways of life have yielded to a new multiculturalism that is posing many challenges for migrant and resident alike (Coleman, 1995; Collinson, 1993). In a report on the status of migration in Europe, the World Health Organization (WHO, 1991) European Regional Office in Denmark stated:

Since World War II, European countries have experienced a vast international movement of persons: political refugees, labor migrants, immigrants from the (former) colonies. The overwhelming majority of this migrant population, in any country, has a different cultural background than the autochthonous population. This migration has proved to be a permanent phenomenon in Europe. In fact, the migrant population, as a result of migration and birth, is steadily increasing in numbers. European countries, therefore, are becoming increasingly multicultural, multiethnic societies. (p. 1)

Outside of Russia, which has a population of approximately 146 million people, the most populous nation in Europe is Germany with a population of approximately 82 million people (*The World Almanac*, 1999). Today, according to Sowell (1996), Germany has more than 7 million foreigners living within its borders, one third of all the foreigners living in Europe. But all countries in Europe are now multicultural because of the broad spectrum of racial and ethnic groups within their borders. Coleman (quoted in Sowell, 1996) stated:

The largest number of migrants in Europe come form poor countries. More than a million were from Morocco, nearly a million and a half from Iran, more than a million and a half from Italy, and well over two million from Turkey. Italians were more than one-fourth of the foreigners living in Belgium and one-third of the foreigners living in Switzerland but they were only a tenth of the foreigners living in West Germany, where Turks were nearly one-third of the foreign born population. In the Netherlands, Italian immigrants are outnumbered ten to one by Moroccans, even though there were more Italians than Moroccan immigrants in Europe as a whole. (p. 38)

The European response to this situation has not always been pleasant. Marsella (1997) pointed out that hate crimes against immigrants and refugees have become commonplace in European countries. The following headlines tell the story: "Illegal Immigrants' Plight Dividing France" (Cue, 1996), "Europe Besieged by New Ripple of Ethnic Hatred" (Koring, 1991). In Germany, hate groups have bombed, burned, and beaten Turks, Kurds, and Afghans with impunity. In France, more than 10,000 foreigners were deported in one year on highly publicized flights to Africa and the Middle East. One French political leader, Jean Marie Le Pen, called for expelling 3 million immigrants, and a poll showed one in three Frenchmen agree with his position (Cue, 1996). In England, influxes of Indians, Pakistanis, Chinese, Africans, and Black Caribbeans have led to endless race riots in the streets and schools and to cries for a return to "ye olde England." Jean Philbert (quoted in Cue, 1996), the chairman of the

French Parliamentary Commission on Immigration, stated: "We have to be careful because France is a country that is slowly becoming racist. If we don't do something, the situation will become worse. France cannot integrate its 5 million legal foreigners if the government doesn't crack down on illegal immigrants" (p. A–22).

FEAR OF IMMIGRANTS AND RISING XENOPHOBIA

Citizens of many Western countries fear that immigrants will take jobs, start alternative economies (e.g., drug subcultures), and engage in sexual relations with, and even marry, their children. They fear the immigrants will introduce "alien" ideas and lifestyles that may challenge, undermine, or overwhelm existing ways of life. The fear is the same around the world: "They are not like us, and they do strange things." "I don't trust them, they are different from us." The element of difference is important, because there are generally not complaints about immigrants who possess similar racial, cultural, or historical characteristics (e.g., White English people migrating to the United States) (Marsella, 1997). It is clear that the responses to many of the recent arrivals from the Middle East and sub-Saharan Africa have been racist and xenophobic. For example, Riding (1991) wrote:

Throughout Western Europe, there is a perception that immigrants—Arabs in France, Turks in Germany, Pakistanis in Britain, and so on—are "taking over" schools, housing complexes and neighborhoods. That has become a major factor contributing to rising opposition to new immigration. Whether in Birmingham, Frankfurt, Florence, or Marseille, third-world communities have become the target of simmering xenophobia and occasionally racist violence, with some ultranationalist groups even trying to court popularity by demanding that poor foreigners be forcibly repatriated. They [new immigrants] continually run the risk of unemployment, of having to accept the worst housing and of facing disproportionate difficulties in schools. They run the risk of becoming marginalized and remaining marginalized. (p. 3)

Marsella (1997) suggested that part of the fear of the new immigrants may be related to the widespread fear of uncertainty in our world. Perhaps there is something within the "primitive" reflexive areas of our brain that arouses fear when we encounter those who are different. It is possible that there is survival value in avoiding or dominating people who are different. However, it is also clear that these differences can be overcome when people feel secure and when they are faced with common challenges. In addition, one cannot help but wonder if the pressures of rapid social change and the breakdown of familiar institutions and moralities have spawned national psyches that are fearful of our uncertain times. Our world seems to be unraveling and things seem out of control, and under these circumstances, all changes are suspect.

THE MIGRATION EXPERIENCE

The Roots of Migration

Migration arises from forces that both push and pull—the push of discontent and adversity, and the pull of new possibilities and rewards. In most instances, the decision to migrate seems to arise from a sense of danger, discontent, and boredom. The decision to migrate can be felt and experienced consciously and unconsciously. It can occur amid a full and complete awareness of present dangers, threats, and risks. It can occur, also, amid an unconscious or preconscious awareness of dread or impending doom, or the decision may simply arise from a need to move beyond the present circumstances to new possibilities. Migration can be a move away from adversity, but it can also be a move toward a felt sense of possibility and hope. This is the beauty, the mystique, and the wonderment of the human impulse to migrate. Massey (1994) reviewed theories of international migration. Unfortunately, most of the existing theories are linked to economic, geographic, and demographic factors and fail to incorporate psychological variables. This is largely because psychologists and psychiatrists have tended to ignore the topic; however, this appears to be changing and future views on migration and immigration will likely include more considerations of psychological (e.g., values, hope, fear) and psychosocial (e.g., identity) variables.

Migration and Stress

Migration is stressful. The stress begins in the earliest phases of the push and pull of forces leading to migration and extends to the later phases of migration: departure, transit, arrival, and resettlement. Migration is hazardous to life, limb, and psyche. The events and experiences of migration, even under the most positive experience, remain an indelible imprint of words, images, and emotions. The sights, sounds, and smells of the journey are all retained, to be retold years later again and again to all that will listen. There is an old Sicilian saying: "When you leave home, you know what you leave behind, but not what you will find." There are similar phrases in all ethnic groups—words to remind the migrant of the dangers and possibilities of their journey. Migration, regardless of its motives, is a challenge to human resiliency and resourcefulness from the beginning to the end. Ultimately migration is about the most human of needs and motives including hope, rootedness, and identity. Sowell (1996), in his book on culture and migration, wrote: "For what migrations have meant has been not merely a relocation of bodies but, more fundamentally, a redistribution of skills, experience, and other 'human capital' across the planet. It is the process of cultural change that has transformed nations and continents" (p. 38).

Humans have migrated as individuals and as population waves from their earliest days. But, unlike past centuries, when the world's population was small, and when lands were sparsely settled, the human population today has risen to more than 6 billion people, and most habitable lands are now densely populated and covered with major urban centers. Still immigrants come—by choice or chance, forced or free. As was true in the past, the immigrants of today are the educated and the wealthy, the ignorant and the poor, the young and the old. They leave and they arrive as welcomed guests or as intruders, whether the authorities admit them legally or whether they cross borders illegally in the silence and dark of night.

Today, migration, whether forced or voluntary, involves new constraints and impositions on migrant and host. Most national borders are now well defined and guarded against unwelcome intruders (but cf. Chapter 18 on the South African experience). National immigration laws and policies control who may enter and when. Responses to new migrants by host residents populations have never been free of rejection, anger, or concern; but today there is a widespread resentment and antipathy among populations in developed nations. (This is true in spite of the fact that the very people harboring the resentment are either immigrants or descendants of immigrants themselves—so much for human memory and so much for human empathy.) There is too little recognition, acceptance, or sympathy for the fact that all human beings have come to their place of residence through migration, that the impulse and act of migration is common throughout the species, and that it offers everyone an opportunity for a shared experience. The ancient words of the Book of Leviticus of the Old Testament are revealing: "And if a stranger sojourn with thee in your land, ye shall not vex him. But the stranger that dwelleth with you shall be unto you as one born among you, and thou shalt love him as thyself; for ye were strangers in the land of Egypt" (Leviticus 19: 33–34).

TERMS OF REFERENCE

Concern for Migration

Migration has become a major concern of government officials, political leaders, policymakers, and scholars, and numerous books and journal articles have been published on a variety of topics related to migration including cultural change (e.g., Sowell, 1996), health (e.g., Loue, 1998), law (e.g., Weiner, 1995), mental health (e.g., Marsella, Bornemann, Ekblad, & Orley, 1994), population movements and demographics (e.g., Castles & Miller, 1993), politics (e.g., Arditis, 1994), urbanization (e.g., Muller, 1993), and the survival of human society (e.g., Diamond, 1999). Popular journals on the topic include *International Migration Review, Asian-Pacific Migration,* and *Journal of Refugee Studies.*

The International Organization for Migration (IOM) is perhaps the most visible international organization concerned with migration. However, the International Federation of Red Cross and Red Crescent Societies, the UN High Commission for Refugees (UNHCR), and the World Council of Churches, Refugees and Migration Services also have high visibility as policy, service, and research agencies. Other private agencies that have high visibility include Amnesty International, International Rescue Committee, Doctors Without Borders, Human Rights Watch, and the U.S. Committee on Refugees.

Migration and Immigration. The term *migration* refers to the act or process by which people, especially as a group, move from one location (city, country, region) to another. The term *migrant* has no legal status. Thus, many nations now use the terms *immigrant* or *emigrant*. These terms have legal status, and they are carefully defined in various national and international legal codes. *Immigration* typically refers to the process of people leaving one nation for permanent residence in another. *Emigration* typically refers to the process of people leaving a nation.

Migratory Workers and International Workers. Related terms such as *migratory workers, international workers, aliens, illegal immigrants,* and *asylum seekers* have gained much currency in the popular media. The language of migration has also given rise to a number of qualifiers that proceed the term *immigrant* such as "forced versus voluntary," "legal versus illegal," and "temporary versus permanent." In addition, there are new terms for international workers arising out of the rapid growth of multinational corporations, such as *skilled transients, multinational transferees,* and *capital assisted migrants* (Marsella, 1997). Migratory workers and international workers have become major global problems because of the abuses and exploitation they experience. As sources of cheap labor, they endure many indignities and mistreatment. John Steinbeck's *The Grapes of Wrath* provided one of the earliest literary accounts of the terrible circumstances surrounding the migratory workers who left Oklahoma to work the fruit and vegetable fields of California. Typically, the pay of migratory workers is low, their housing is dilapidated, and their health risks are high from pesticides. In spite of these conditions, governments have done little to improve the lot of the migrant farmworker. (For an example of the conditions faced by migrant workers in South Africa, see Chapter 18.)

This is also the case for international workers. They come from China, Bangladesh, the Philippines, and Vietnam, lured to developed countries by promises of high wages and good employment only to be kept as virtual slaves behind locked doors sewing garments for name brands. They work 12 to 15 hours per day in closed guarded rooms that reach 90-degree temperatures. They cannot escape, and if they try they may be assaulted or killed. Many are illegal immigrants, and as such they have no one to turn to for assistance. Recently, a lawsuit was filed by a Manhattan law firm against some of the leading apparel companies purchasing clothing from foreign-run companies in Saipan, a U.S. territorial island. The suit is seeking $1 billion in unpaid wages and damages (Yaukey, 1999). But this lawsuit may be too little and too late for the countless workers whose lives have been traumatized by their experiences of modern-day slavery.

Pressures for migration have led to new multimillion-dollar illegal industry—"immigrant smuggling." A 1996 *Honolulu Stan Bulletin* article described a huge pipeline of illegal Asian immigrants into the United States that went from Russia to Cuba to Central America:

Chinese, Indian, and Pakistani migrants paid up to US $28,000 each to smugglers for a grueling clandestine journey that climaxed in this border city where teenagers ferried them across the Rio Grande to a muddy flood plain south of McAllen, Texas. In December, a federal study of alien trafficking estimated that some 100,000 Southeast Asian and Chinese immigrants pass through Central America and Mexico each year on their way to the United States. (*Asian-Immigrant*, 1996, p. A–8)

According to Morganthau (1993), it is estimated that 600,000 illegal immigrants enter the United States each year and there are no "natural forces" that seem to be able to stem the tide. Cue (1996) estimated that France presently has somewhere between 250,000 and 600,000 illegal immigrants. The IOM estimated that 70,000,000 persons, mostly from developing nations, are working legally or illegally in other countries as migrants or aliens, stating, "The isolation, even open hostility, to migrant workers and their families is widespread in host countries, despite the fact that few host-country workers would undertake the kinds of menial tasks performed by these foreigners" (quoted in United Nations, 1995, p. 53).

Refugees: Definitions. Perhaps the most controversial term associated with migration is *refugee*. History is replete with examples of those forced to migrate because of religious, political, or ethnic persecution. According to Marrus (1985), the term *refugee* was first applied to French Protestants driven from their country at the end of the 17th century. He stated:

Those who departed France in the wake of the French Revolution because of their monarchial predilections preferred the term emigrés, a term most recently used by journalists to describe remnants of Russian nobility returning to the motherland they left earlier this century and, occasionally, to Russian Jews taking advantage of the *glasnost* spirit of moderation to depart the Soviet Union. Only after 1870 did terms such as *heimatlos* or *staatenlos* come to designate certain kinds of stateless refugees in Germany. After World War I, the term *Flüchtling* became a comprehensive designation for those seeking new homes. (p. 9)

The Geneva Convention Related to the Status of Refugees defined in Article 1.A (2) a specific and narrow category of refugee as an individual who:

As a result of events occurring before 1 January 1951, and owing to well-founded fear of being persecuted for reasons of race, religion, nationality, membership of a particular social group or political opinion is outside the country of his nationality and is unable or, owing to such fear, is unwilling to avail himself of the protection of that country; or who, not having a nationality and being outside the country of his former habitual residence as a result of such events, is unable or, owing to such fear, is unwilling to return to it. (UNHCR, 1979, p. 29)

Both this geographical limitation and the time limit in Article 1 were, however, discarded in the additional protocol relating to the Status of Refugees promulgated in 1967. Thus amended, the Geneva Convention remains the primary basis for the granting of refugee status. However, this has posed new problems because the wave of anticolonial wars in the so-called Third World was unleashing a new set of forced migrants, clearly deserving of international protection, but scarcely able to prove individual persecution, and much less welcome in the rich states of the north (Marsella et al., 1994).

The U.S. Immigration and Nationality Act of 1980 (1980) used the following definition of refugee:

A refugee, for our purpose, is any person who is outside any country of such person's nationality or, in the case of a person having no nationality, is outside any country in which such person last habitually resided, and who is unable or unwilling to return to, and is unable or unwilling to avail himself or herself of the protection of that country because of persecution on account of race, religion, nationality, membership in a particular social group, or political opinion. (p. 12)

In 1989, more than 50 countries throughout the world, many of them first-asylum countries, agreed to support and implement the State Department's Comprehensive Plan of Action (CPA). The CPA established a uniform agreement that persons in first-asylum countries would be subjected to a "status determination" process that determined whether there is a legitimate claim to refugee status based on the criteria of persecution. The CPA asserted that those persons who fail to meet the criteria and who are not candidates for resettlement "should return to their country of origin" (quoted in Marsella et al., 1994).

The Scope of the Refugee Problem. Although figures vary according to the different agencies monitoring the international refugee situation, it is estimated that there are more than 20 million international refugees in the world today. To this amount must be added approximately 20 million internally displaced people who are "refugees" within their own countries (U.S. Committee on Refugees, 2000). Thus, there are at least 40 million refugees and internally displaced people in the world today. According to the World Refugee Survey 2001 (U.S. Committee on Refugees, 2001), the most recent figures on refugees indicate that the countries that have produced the greatest number of refugees and internally displaced persons are Palestine, Afghanistan, Sudan, and Iraq. Some worldwide information about refugees and internally displaced persons is displayed in Tables 1.1, 1.2, and 1.3.

And far too often, the violence of the refugee camps replaces the violence they fled. Because of mounting domestic problems, many in North America and Europe that formerly welcomed refugees are now closing their doors to further entry. For those few refugees fortunate enough to be admitted, there are the new problems to be overcome—problems of acculturation, racism, language, work, housing, health, and personal safety. For many refugees, the process of rebuilding their lives often proves to be as traumatic as the dislocation process from which they sought refuge (Marsella et al., 1994).

Migration in the Age of Globalization

In a recent address, Taran (1999) suggested that our age of globalization is now generating a new configuration of forces promoting migration. Globalization is that process and product by which the lives of all human beings on our planet are drawn into greater interdependency and consequence. The driving forces of globalization are global communications, global transfer of wealth and

Table 1.1
Principal Sources of Refugees at End of Year

	2000	1999
Palestinians	4,000,000	3,931,000
Afghanistan	ª3,600,000	2,560,000
Iraq	450,000	568,000
Sierra Leone	400,000	460,000
Somalia	370,000	425,000
Sudan	460,000	420,000
Yugoslavia	190,000	390,000
Angola	400,000	340,000
Croatia	315,000	340,000

Note: From United States Committee on Refugees (2001).
ªThese figures do not include the 2001 situation. It is esimated that the new number may exceed 5 million, making Afganistan the unfortunate leader in this category.

Table 1.2
Principal Sources of Internally Displaced Persons

	2000	1999
Sudan	4,000,000	4,000,000
Angola	1,100,000–3,800,000	1,500,000–2,000,000
Colombia	2,100,000	1,800,000
Indonesia	750,000–850,000	—
Congo-Kinshasha	1,800,000	800,000
Iraq	700,000	900,000
Afghanistan	375,000	500,000–750,000
Burma	600,000–1,000,000	500,000–1,000,000
Turkey	400,000–1,000,000	500,000–1,000,000
Bosnia/Hercegovina	518,000	830,000
Burundi	700,000	800,000
Azerbaijan	575,000	568,000
Sri Lanka	600,000	560,000
Total (end of the year)	21 million plus	

Note: From United States Committee on Refugees (2001).

money, and global political and natural events (terrorism, trade, global warming, etc.). This situation has an impact on migration. Taran advanced seven reasons for migration including: (a) increasing armed violence, (b) ethnic and racial conflict, (c) aspects of globalization such as unemployment and culture conflict, (d) environmental degradation, (e) development-induced migration, (f) denial of democracy, and (g) large-scale corruption.

It is essential to understand that the decision to migrate is related to both pushes and pulls that constitute a complex calculus of decision making. This is true for both forced and voluntary migration; however, in forced migration, a single event such as the invasion of one's land by threatening armies or forces

Table 1.3
Refugees and Asylum Seekers by Region

	2000	1999
Africa	3,346,000	3,147,000
Americas	562,000	737,000
East Asia and Pacific	792,000	657,000
Europe	1,153,000	1,909,000
Middle East	6,035,000	5,849,000
South Asia	2,656,000	1,779,000
Central Asia	14,544,000	14,078,000

Note: From United States Committee on Refugees (2000, 2001).

can simply override all other reasons. In a world in which there are more than 70 low-intensity wars and conflicts occurring (e.g., Sri Lanka, Chechnya, Afghanistan, Iraq), it is certain that forced migration will be increasing. A complicating factor in all of this is the growing number of "illegal" migrants showing up throughout the world and requesting asylum. The recent situation in Australia in which the prime minister rejected the entry of hundreds of illegal migrants who sought asylum via Indonesia typifies what we can expect in the future. Still, it is clear that the challenges before us are far more than legal—they are moral and humanitarian as well. In a world in which the poor outnumber the rich by such sizable numbers, the question of our responsibilities to others remains the most pressing issue of our time.

SOME CLOSING THOUGHTS ON MIGRATION AND IMMIGRATION

Migration and Immigration Will Increase

Migration and immigration will continue unabated in the future, in waves and numbers that will be as great as waves of the past. The reasons for this are clear.

- The world population is increasing and is likely to surpass 10 billion by the year 2050.
- World poverty is also increasing, and this, in combination with television programs showing the wealth of the Western world, will result in ever increasing migrations of the poor toward the developed nations.
- Continuing abuses and exploitation of women in their own nations will encourage women to seek economic opportunities abroad, even if the home and work situations are as destructive as those left behind.
- Political persecution and abuse will send people in search of freedom, even as it has in the past.
- Religious persecution and abuse will also send people in search of freedom.
- Natural disasters—earthquakes, volcanoes, hurricanes, drought, and floods—will

force people to migrate to new locations. For example, 40 million people were displaced by storms in Bangladesh in 1998. Although people have endured these storms for centuries, increasing knowledge of the opportunities and safety of other lands will increase migration.

- Man-made disasters—terrorism, war, nuclear accidents, toxic waste, pollution—will continue to occur with alarming frequency and impact. These cannot be avoided. Terrorist bombings may well yield to biological terrorism that will require the evacuation of entire cities.

- Growing resentment and antagonism toward immigrants from non-Western countries is likely to increase and become characterized by greater violence because of the availability of weapons of mass destruction. Immigrants may be forced to migrate several times before finding acceptability.

Commenting on some of the circumstances likely to lead to increased immigration, Desjarlais, Eisenberg, Good, and Kleinman (1995) stated:

Degraded living conditions in various regions may quite possibly force impoverished people to move to more prosperous regions in search of food, land, and housing. Along with the constant flow of political refugees, many of these "environmental refugees" will be at risk for economic exploitation, substandard living conditions, social isolation and psychological distress. One ominous development is the increase in anti-immigration sentiments in European and North American societies which are geared toward isolationist policies rather than efforts to deal directly with the roots and problems of dislocation. (pp. 27–28)

The new international migration waves will be from south to north, and from east to west. Immigration—legal and illegal—will follow economic opportunity and political freedom. Western Europe, North America, and Australia will continue to be the preferred destinations for the poor, persecuted, and professionally talented. The latter point should not be dismissed lightly. "Brain drain" is a serious problem because it takes talent from developing nations and transfers it to developed nations (see, e.g., Chapter 17 and 18, which deal with migration in Egypt and South Africa, respectively). This is especially true given the need for technical and professional employment (e.g., medicine, engineering, computers, nurses).

Arthur Schlesinger (1991) feels this is bad for the host country because it poses serious political problems for national unity. He wrote: "The contemporary ideal is shifting from assimilation to ethnicity, from integration to separatism" (p. 2), and "group separatism crystalizes the differences, magnifies tensions, intensifies hostilities" (p. 21). Schlesinger may be correct, but he ignores the contributions the immigrants make and the "fact" that immigrants eventually become accustomed to the comforts of the developed nations and lose their identification and attachment to their home country. They send money home, but few end up returning. In addition, a more serious problem may be global corporations that locate in developing nations because of cheap labor and resources. Their international employees often live in compounds with maids and servants and do little to contribute to the growth of the nation. The consequences can be seen in places such as Bhopal, India, or in the polluting industries, like mining, in Africa and South America.

For the United States, immigration has always contributed to the nation's strength and development. Each new wave of immigrants has brought new energy, determination, and ideas—an injection of talent and a renewal of purpose for the nation. A decade ago, Portes and Rumbaut (1990) wrote the following about immigration to the United States:

Immigrants and refugees will continue to come, giving rise to energetic communities, infusing new blood in local labor markets, filling positions at different levels of the economy, and adding to the diversity of sounds, sights, and tastes in our cities. The history of America has been to a large extent, the history of its immigrants—their progress reflecting and simultaneously giving impulse to the nation's expansion. Although problems and struggles are inevitable along the way, in the long run, the diverse talents and energies of newcomers will reinforce the vitality of American society and the richness of its culture. (p. 246)

Resentment and Rejection will Increase

The response to increased migration and immigration will be resentment and new restrictive legislation. This has always occurred and it has grown in frequency and severity in the past decade. Bouvier (1991) argued that limiting immigrants is necessary because the new immigrants create four major problems: (a) They take away resources from the existing American underclass, (b) they steer the economy toward an unskilled labor economy, (c) they make it difficult for new immigrants to adapt because the sheer numbers create self-contained societies, and (d) they add to the population and environmental problems. Bouvier suggested that developed countries cannot become "safety valves" for the burgeoning populations of developing countries but rather should assist these countries in their own development. A *Newsweek* national poll in the United States reported that 59% of Americans indicated that immigration was once a good thing for the country, 60% feel that it is now a bad thing, 62% feel immigrants take the jobs of U.S. workers, and 59% believe immigrants wind up on welfare roles and raise taxes for Americans ("Immigration Backlash," 1993, p. 19). Today, migration has become more controlled through highly national immigration laws that limit entrance to (a) national quotas from certain countries, (b) family members of citizens and former immigrants who are now citizens, and (c) certain desirable or needed occupational specialists or professions, and various refugee concessions (Marsella, 1997).

Reconciliation of Immigrant and Host Populations

Fear, Anger, and Grief. The resentment and rejection of immigrants is rooted in fear, anger, and grief. All of these are understandable responses given human nature. People initially fear what is different, and they initially feel anger toward those most readily identifiable because of differences. These groups often become scapegoats and targets of frustration. This was the case for Blacks in the United States, Jews in Germany and throughout Europe, Arabs in France, Asians in Uganda, Chinese in Indonesia, and Albanians in Kosovo. The sense of grief felt over the loss of traditions and defined history is also real among host populations. Furthermore, the inequities in opportunities can lead some immigrants to establish "alternative criminal economies," such as drugs, gambling, and robbery, adding to the host population's resentment and reinforcing their stereotypes of the immigrants. In brief, fear, anger, and grief are natural responses; however, they can be changed if new perspectives and values are fostered.

Ethnocultural Diversity. Foremost among these desired values is the prizing of ethnocultural diversity. Diversity is a key to human survival, but little has done by governments to promote this important idea. The Mexican Nobel Prize-winning poet and writer Octavio Paz (1978) recognized the importance of cultural diversity for human survival when he wrote:

What sets worlds in motion is the interplay of differences, their attractions and repulsions. Life is plurality, death is uniformity. By suppressing differences and peculiarities, by eliminating different civilizations and cultures, progress weakens life and favors death. The idea of a single civilization for everyone, implicit in the cult of progress and technique, impoverishes and mutilates us. Every view of the world that becomes extinct, every culture that disappears, diminishes a possibility of life.

Paz understood that ethnocultural variability, like biological variability, promotes and sustains life. To the extent that we insist on homogeneity, we are closing ourselves to needed options and alternatives. Successful evolution requires variability because variability creates the differences necessary for adaptation to changing environmental demands. The "unenlightened" society will continue to insist on "cultural homogeneity," and in doing so, will foster its own demise. The enlightened society will acknowledge and promote the "diversity" and in doing so, encourage its survival.

Ethnocultural diversity is not the source of the many national and international conflicts we face. Rather, the source of the problems resides in the prejudice, intolerance, bias, and hostility that our failing to cope with ethnocultural diversity generates. A society can tolerate and utilize extensive ethnocultural diversity if it is willing to provide members from different ethnocultural traditions with equal opportunity and freedom. Within this kind of society, diversity will thrive, but so will a commitment to national unity. This was, in fact, the dream of America. The United States never succeeded in erasing or eliminating its citizens' commitments to their ethnocultural heritage, contrary to the claims of the assimilationists. Old roots were never lost; new roots merely grew alongside them, making an ever stronger tree. When Arthur Schlesinger worries about the "disuniting of America," he only needs to be reminded that "pluralism" and "unity" are different sides of the same American coin (Marsella, 1994).

International Tribunals. The world is becoming a global community, but the laws necessary to function as a global community are still archaic and incapable of mediating the problems associated with the new problems that are arising. The obvious guilt of Slobodan Milosevic in Yugoslavia in the Kosovo conflict is a prime example of this failure. It is to be welcomed that this brutal and inhuman person is being tried in an international court in the Hague for ordering genocidal actions on a considerable scale.

World Citizenship. Increasingly, the question of world citizenship is becoming a topic of discussion. This is due to the conflicting loyalties that are arising between citizens and nations because of globalization, national policies favoring certain groups, and the recognition that human rights must be superordinate to national laws and policies. In 1948, the World Federation for Mental Health (WFMH) raised the issue of world citizenship.

The question must be faced as to whether survival is possible without adapting human institutions so that people can live as world citizens in a world community, in which local loyalties are rendered compatible with a wider allegiance to mankind as a whole. World citizenship means an informed, reflective, responsible allegiance to mankind as a whole. The movement toward world citizenship is one which fulfills, rather than goes counter to, the trend of history. It is possible to envisage a world community built on free consent and on the respect for individual and cultural differences. (Quoted in Brody, 1987, p. 4)

The magnificence of the idea of a global union committed to human rights and welfare has failed to move the United Nations toward resolving the international immigration problems of recent decades. The national interests of powerful countries continue to dictate global political, social, and economic dynamics and outcomes. But this cannot continue. Our leaders must rethink local, national, hemispheric, and global futures with a special concern for morality and humanitarian values.

Johnson and Williams (1993), in the introduction to their provocative *Illegal Aliens in the Western Hemisphere: Political and Economic Factors*, capture some of the dilemmas we face:

We believe in the natural right of all human beings to enjoy the physical and emotional inviolability of one's self. This includes the right to try to find a better life in another country; and it is instinctive for each person to violate that country's immigration laws, if necessary, in the quest for a better life. Obviously, the target nation has a countervailing juridical right to try to enforce its laws. The conflict of right against right in this process can, and should, be managed by the hemispheric community so that the human rights of all can be preserved. These include the right to decent space in which to live, enough food to eat, clean air to breathe, and a reasonable expectation that one's offspring can also find a life that is free of want, suffering, and oppression. It also means the natural right of human beings to have an opportunity to fulfill their talents and aspirations, not to be perpetually restrained by artificial political borders. (p. 4)

REFERENCES

Arditis, S. (Ed.). (1994). *The politics of East-West migration.* New York: St. Martin's Press.

Asian-immigrant smuggling ring busted. (1996, May 30). *The Honolulu Star Bulletin,* p. A–8.

Bouvier, L. (1991). *Peaceful invasions: Immigration and changing America.* Washington, DC: Center for Immigration Studies.

Brody, E. (1987). *Mental health and world citizenship.* Austin, TX: Hogg Foundation for Mental Health.

Castles, S., & Miller, M. (1993). *The age of migration: International population movements in the modern world.* New York: Guilford Press.

Coleman, D. (1995). International migration: Demographic and socioeconomic consequences in the United Kingdom and Europe. *International Migration Review, 24,* 155–180.

Collinson, S. (1993). *Europe and international migration.* London: Royal Institute of International Affairs.

Cue, E. (1996, April 21). Illegal immigrants' plight dividing France. *The Honolulu Advertiser,* p. A–22.

Desjarlais, R., Eisenberg, L., Good, B., & Kleinman, A. (1995). *World mental health: Problems and priorities in low income countries.* New York: Oxford University Press.

Diamond, J. (1999). *Guns, germs, and steel: The fates of human societies.* New York: Norton.

Hoerder, D., & Knauf, D. (1992). *Fame, fortune, and sweet liberty: The great European migration.* Bremen, Germany: Temmen.

Johnson, K., & Williams, M. (Eds.). (1981). *Illegal aliens in the Western hemisphere: Political and economic factors.* New York: Praeger.

Immigration backlash. (1993, August 9). *Newsweek,* 16–25.

Koring, P. (1991, November 28). Europe besieged by a new ripple of ethnic hatred. *The Honolulu Star Bulletin,* p. C–3.

Koring, P. (1991). *East Germany's jobless display their resentment of foreigners.* Honululu Star Bulletin.

Kraut, A. (1982). *The huddled masses: The immigrant in American society— 1880–1921.* Arlington Heights, IL: Harlan-Davidson.

Kraut, A. (1990). Historical perspectives on refugee movements to North America. In W. Holtzman & T. Bornemann (Eds.), *Mental health of immigrants and refugees* (pp. 16–50). Austin, TX: Hogg Foundation for Mental Health and University of Texas.

Kraut, A. (1994). Historical aspects of refugee and immigrant movements. In A. J. Marsella, T. Bornemann, S. Ekbald, & J. Orley (Eds.), *Amidst peril and pain: The mental health and well being of the world's refugees* (pp. 33–56). Washington, DC: American Psychological Association.

Loue, S. (Ed.). (1998). *Handbook of immigrant health.* New York: Plenum.

Marrus, M. (1985). *The unwanted: European refugees in the twentieth century.* New York: Oxford University Press.

Marsella, A. J. (1994). Ethnocultural diversity and international refugees: Challenges for the global community. In A. J. Marsella, T. Bornemann, S. Ekblad, & J. Orley (Eds.), *Amidst peril & pain: The mental health and well being of the world's refugees* (pp. 341–364). Washington, DC: American

Psychological Association.

Marsella, A. J. (1997). Migration, poverty, and ethnocultural diversity: A global perspective on immigrant and refugee adaptation. *Scandinavian Journal of Work, Health, and Environment, 23*, 28–46.

Marsella, A. J., Bornemann, T., Ekblad, S., & Orley, J. (Eds.). (1994). *Amidst peril & pain: The mental health and well being of the world's refugees.* Washington, DC: American Psychological Association.

Massey, D. (1994). Theories of international migration: A review and appraisal. *Population and Development Review, 19,* 431–466.

Morganthau, T. (1993, August 9). America: Still a melting pot? *Newsweek, 22*(6), 16–25.

Muller, T. (1993). *Immigrants and the American city.* New York: New York University Press.

Nanda, V. (Ed.). (1989). *Refugee law and policy: International and United States responses.* Westport, CT: Greenwood Press.

Nordyke, E. (1989). *The peopling of Hawaii.* Honolulu: University Press of Hawaii.

Paz, O. (1978). *The labyrinth of solitude.* New York, NY: Grove Press.

Portes, A., & Rumbaut, R. D. (1990). *Immigrant America: A portrait.* Los Angeles: University of California Press.

Reimers, D. (1992). *Still the golden door: The third world comes to America.* New York: Columbia University Press.

Riding, A. (1991, March 24). France sees integration as answer to view of immigrants as "taking over." *The New York Times International,* p. 3.

Schlesinger, A. (1991). *The disuniting of America: Reflections on a multicultural society.* New York: Whittle Books.

Sowell, T. (1996*). Migration and world cultures: A world view.* New York: Basic Books.

Stannard, D. (1992). *American holocaust.* New York: Oxford University Press.

Taran, P. (1999). *Seven causes of migration in the age of globalization.* Paper presented at the International Migration Policy and Law Conference, Bangkok, Thailand.

United Nations. (1995). *Notes for speakers: Social development.* New York: Author.

UN High Commissioner for Refugees. (1979). *Collection of international instruments concerning refugees.* Geneva, Switzerland: Author.

U.S. Committee on Refugees. (2000). *World refugee survey.* Washington, DC: Author.

U.S. Committee on Refugees. (2001). *World refugee survey.* Washington, DC: Author.

United States Immigration and Nationality Act of 1980, 8 *U. S. C.* §1158 (1980).

Weiner, M. (1995*). The global migration crisis: Challenges to states and to human rights.* New York: HarperCollins.

The world almanac and book of facts—1999. (1999). Mahwah, NJ: World Almanac Books.

World Health Organization. (1991). *Mental health and multicultural societies in the Europe of the nineties.* Copenhagen, Denmark: Author.

Yaukey, J. (1999, June 27). Top fashion companies sued for unpaid wages. *The Honolulu Advertiser,* p. A–3.

Zolberg, A. (1978). *Human migration: Patterns and policies.* Indianapolis: Indiana University Press.

2

Psychosocial Factors of Immigration and Emigration: An Introduction

Paul G. Schmitz

In many societies during the last decades, migration has become a central topic in public discussion. Although migration has always been an important phenomenon in the history of mankind, the number of migrants has never been as large as in this century. The enormous increase refers to all subtypes of migrants, such as tourists, overseas students, businesspeople, traders, diplomats, seasonal workers, immigrants, refugees, and so on. The enormity of migrations in the present becomes apparent when we take for comparison an example from European history in the time of the "Germanic migrations" that changed European history between ca. 200 B.C. and 500 A.D. When different Germanic tribes moved successively from their homelands in northeastern Europe toward the west, the causes of these movements were presumably climatic changes, overpopulation (in relationship to food resources), pressures by other tribes of the same or of different ethnic groups also moving south and westward, and the great attractiveness of the provinces of the Roman Empire with regard to their highly developed way of life and the fertility of the land (in particular those parts of the Roman Empire that are now France and Italy).

As it is in present-day history, the main motives underlying migration in those times were mostly of an economic and political nature as well as the search for a better and safer place to live. However, there are marked differences between the migration waves in the past and those in this century with regard to the time dimension and the number of migrants involved: The movements of the Germanic tribes were relatively slow and the number of persons involved was relatively small. The East Goths invading Italy in 476 A.D. numbered not more than about 150,000 persons; the population of Italy, however, was about 6 million at that time. The Franks, who in the 4th century founded the kingdom of the Franks in Gallia (the later France) by invading its northwestern regions, may have numbered about 80,000 persons (Braudel, 1986; Werner, 1989). In contrast, Gallia's population was about 10 million in the 4th century.

Comparing the number of Germanic migrants to "France" in the time of the so-called Germanic migration with today's number of migrants, differences in size become obvious. To give some examples: The number of foreigners living in the European Community in the year 1990 was 13.7 million (e.g., Germany 4.9 million, France 3.6 million, the United Kingdom 1.9 million). The number of asylum seekers increased from 13,000 in 1973 to ca. 600,000 in 1992 (e.g., Germany 322,800; France 27,600; the United Kingdom 22,400) as presented in reports published by the Organization for Economic Corporation and Development (OECD) in 1992/1993 and by the United Nation High Commissioner Refugees (UNHCR)–Regional Office Europe in 1994. The number of refugees worldwide was estimated at about 19.5 million: 7.2 million in Asia; 5.5 million in Africa; 4.3 million in Europe (Nuscheler, 1995). In addition, Hof (1993) discussed the long-term migration balances (immigration minus emigration) between 1950 and 1989 for the larger Western industrial countries (the United States: 22,133,000; Germany: 9,432,000; France: 4,195,000; Canada: 3,428,000; Italy: −1,264,000; Great Britain: −841,000). Although some statistical data on migration are based on estimations and the correct interpretation of the data is sometimes unclear (Nuscheler, 1995), the statistics illustrate the relevance of the migration issue both for those societies affected by the flux of migrants and for social scientists. The great number of refugees and asylum seekers during the last decades justifies our calling the 20th century the "century of refugees."

PSYCHOLOGICAL PUBLICATIONS ON MIGRATION

With regard to psychology, the question arises whether the increase of migrants during the last decades is accompanied by increased theoretical discussion and empirical research both in psychology in general and in cross-cultural psychology in particular. An appropriate way to gain information on migration research may be the analysis of publications included in the databases PsycLIT (American Psychological Association) and PSYNDEXplus (Germany). Table 2.1 depicts the number of publications between 1990 and 1998 on migration or immigration listed in PsycLIT. The left column in the table shows the total number of publications on migration/immigration found in PsychLIT. The remaining columns contain the number of publications on migration divided up with regard to specific issues typically discussed and investigated in cross-cultural psychology.

As can be seen in Table 2.1, the publication rate of contributions to the field of migration research increased from 1990 to 1997 and decreased slightly from 1997 to 1998. A similar trend can be observed for specific migration topics.

The increasing number of publications shows that psychologists have become more conscious about the importance of this field of research; however, in comparison to the enormous increase of migration during the last decade, that number remains small. The analysis of the abstracts also shows that migration is often discussed or investigated according to specific themes such as acculturation, identity, values, stress, and coping and adjustment. In general, these constitute central issues in cross-cultural psychology (see Berry, Poortinga, Segall,

Table 2.1
Publications Regarding Immigration / Migration, 1990–1998 (PsycLIT)

	Total	Immigration/Migration in Connection With							
		Acculturation	Identity	Value	Stress	Coping	Adjustment	Diseases/ Pathology	Psychopathy/ Criminality
1990	156	12	10	8	23	5	25	8	1
1991	176	8	19	10	14	4	23	7	1
1992	186	9	16	13	20	6	29	2	1
1993	213	18	19	14	26	12	39	9	—
1994	207	25	21	12	25	6	22	5	—
1995	184	23	24	12	29	8	26	7	1
1996	297	36	40	24	38	11	38	20	—
1997	308	30	37	20	34	18	52	4	—
1998	272	30	20	12	17	9	17	11	—
Total	1999 (100%)	191 (9.6%)	206 (10.3%)	125 (6.3%)	226 (11.3%)	79 (4.0%)	171 (8.6%)	73 (3.7%)	4 (0.2%)

25

& Dasen, 1992). However, research on migration/immigration focusing simultaneously on more than one of these specific topics is rare, although elaborated
models of processes underlying emigration and immigration reveal that all these
themes are necessary for a comprehensive understanding of migration (Berry,
1997). In most research on migration, however, only partial aspects are investigated and discussed.

Acculturation is an important specific topic in migration or immigration research, yet acculturation is frequently discussed without relating it explicitly to
the broader aspects of migration or immigration. Consequently, many articles on
acculturation did not contain the additional keywords migration/immigration. It
seemed therefore to be of interest to analyze the publications by searching for
the keyword acculturation (see Table 2.2). Between 1990 and 1998, we find 882
publications on acculturation listed in PsycLIT, but only 191 (21.7%) of them
are also listed under the keywords immigration/migration. Acculturation research can be described by referring to special topics of interest such as belief
systems about identities, beliefs about the culture of origin and that of the host
society, and individual and societal value systems, as well as the investigation of
the processes underlying both psychological and sociocultural adaptation. Such
psychosocial processes, in turn, are thought to be influenced by moderator variables including perceptions of stress, coping, and specific acculturation outcomes such as adjustment or maladjustment (e.g., lack of well-being, diseases,
psychopathy). Theoretical analysis and empirical research on acculturation focus
on all these specific topics; however, in most specific studies only a few variables belonging to these central issues are simultaneously taken into consideration.

As was found for literature listed under the keywords migration or immigration, we discover again an increasing interest in acculturation from 1990 until
1996–1997. When we compare publications on acculturation with those on migration, we find a clear preference for nomothetic-quantitative methods in acculturation research. In contrast, as part of migration/ immigration research
idiographic and case study approaches are also sometimes applied.

Table 2.3 summarizes data regarding articles, reports, and books published
in German-speaking countries that can be found in the German database PSYN-
DEXplus. The total number of publications on immigration for the period 1990
to 1998 is 624, or 31.2% of the number of publications on immigration found in
PsycLIT for the same period. Consequently, the amount of articles, reports, and
books referring to the keywords migration/immigration published in the German-speaking countries has to be considered as relatively very great. However,
there exist some differences between the publications listed in PsycLIT and
those referred to in PSYNDEXplus: A large part of the German publications
concern more educational and intervention-related issues, a more idiographic
approach is frequently preferred, the number of cases investigated tends to be
small, most empirical studies relate to only one ethnic minority group, and case
studies are frequent. The number of publications listed in PSYNDEXplus that
refer to acculturation issues is relatively small (29) when compared to the 882
citations listed by PsycLIT for the 1990–1998 period. As with English-language

Table 2.2
Publications Regarding Acculturation, 1990–1998 (PsycLIT)

	Total	Immigration	Identity	Value	Stress	Coping	Adjustment	Diseases/ Pathology	Psychopathy/ Criminality
					Acculturation in Connection With				
1990	71	12	6	5	9	3	9	2	—
1991	51	8	10	9	6	4	4	—	—
1992	76	9	13	11	11	4	10	2	—
1993	99	18	13	8	9	3	11	2	—
1994	106	25	25	19	19	3	13	3	—
1995	116	23	24	14	13	6	12	3	—
1996	139	36	26	19	23	6	17	6	—
1997	112	30	21	10	8	8	22	—	—
1998	112	30	25	15	8	2	5	—	—
Total	882 (100%)	191 (21.7%)	163 (18.5%)	110 (12.5%)	106 (12.0%)	39 (4.4%)	103 (11.7%)	10 (2.5%)	—

Table 2.3
Publications Regarding Acculturation, 1990–1998 (PSYNDEXplus)

	Immigration	Acculturation
1990	34	4
1991	56	1
1992	43	2
1993	91	2
1994	94	3
1995	101	3
1996	95	3
1997	70	8
1998	40	3
Total	624	29

publications on immigration, we observe an increasing interest in this research field until 1995, but a decrease between 1996 and 1998. This is true except for 1997. Publications on acculturation remain at about the same level (i.e., about three publications per year) except for 1997.

Although it is difficult to compare both databases, it is nevertheless clear that in the European Community also (including those countries that are now but were not formerly among the classical immigration countries), the interest in immigration issues is increasing and researchers are becoming more conscious about various psychological and social problems related to migration. The analysis of research conducted in Germany (and in some other European immigration countries) suggests that social scientists are interested in a better understanding of migration and immigration problems and in developing more efficient intervention strategies. Given this situation, it is understandable that immigration research frequently has a pedagogical background. Although quantitative and cross-culturally comparable data are only rarely included, idiographic research and case studies can help us understand better how an immigrant constructs his or her world cognitively and how he or she deals with specific situational demands. This type of information can help us develop testable hypotheses and construct reliable and valid assessment instruments. Whereas quantitative data based on the same instrument but collected with different ethnic groups in different immigration countries allow for valid comparisons of findings across ethnic groups and societies, qualitative data may help us interpret and understand the obtained cross-cultural differences.

The greater interest in acculturation issues in the English-speaking world has been supported by the existence of a relative complex taxonomy developed over the last 2 decades by the Canadian cross-cultural psychologist John W. Berry and his coworkers (Berry, 1997). His model includes numerous variables at the individual, group, and societal levels of analysis. Berry's work refers to different psychological approaches concerning psychological and sociocultural adjustment including various models of coping and social learning, and it attempts to integrate a large amount of empirical findings. The central feature of his model is acculturation attitudes and strategies that were originally discovered when trying to understand how immigrants adopt to a new culture. Based on numerous studies, Berry and his coworkers and students discovered that many types of variables, including contextual, intervening, and/or moderator variables, shape the acculturation process. His taxonomy of acculturation situations grew increasingly complex over time, and it is heuristically useful. In that sense, Berry's approach can be seen as being helpful in bringing structure to the diversity of pertinent variables and research findings. Follow-up studies, comparative studies including different ethnic groups in different societies, as well as critical discussions regarding Berry's model (Schönpflug, 1997; Ward, 1997) made acculturation research popular both within English-speaking and non-English-speaking countries (Georgas & Papastylianou, 1994, 1996; Neto, 1988; Sam & Berry 1995; Schmitz, 1994a, 1994b).

Acculturation processes are important for understanding different types of migrating people including immigrants, emigrants, seasonal workers, guest workers, refugees, exchange students, businesspersons, tourists, and others. However, before we discuss Berry's acculturation model, basic terms relating to migration have to be delineated because they are partially overlapping and because their connotations differ from one society to the next.

TYPES OF MIGRATION

Scientific investigations of migration began in sociology before they did in psychology. Sorokin (1925) introduced the term *migration* into sociology where it has been frequently discussed in demographic contexts as vertical and horizontal/regional mobility. *Vertical mobility* refers to upward and downward mobility within a societal classification system, whereas *horizontal mobility* means change within a social level that does not include a change in the social rank order (Sorokin, 1925). *Regional mobility* can be considered as a specific case of horizontal mobility. Migration in the context of immigration and emigration refers to this latter type of horizontal mobility, although other types of mobility, such as upward or downward vertical mobility, are also relevant (e.g., when discussing various motivational factors underlying immigration/emigration and adjustment problems connected to it). With regard to horizontal or regional mobility, Thomas and Znaniecki published in 1919 to 1920 a well-known book on the migration of Polish farmers to the United States that had a strong influence on sociological research concerned with mobility and migration. Migration was also systematically investigated in France by Mauco (1932) who wrote the book *Les étrangers en France* [Foreigners in France], and by Demageon and Mauco (1939). Nourissier and Pillepich (1952) discussed which factors are responsible for the efficient psychosocial adaptation of migrants. Of considerable interest is the work of Peterson (1955), which investigated the implications of migration for both the emigration and the immigration countries, a topic that remains of central interest in modern acculturation research. An early boom of publications on regional migration caused by political and war-related factors can be found in the late 1940s and 1950s. For instance, Kulischer (1949) and Paikert (1962) analyzed the migration of 8 million refugees in eastern Europe until 1944 and of 12 million German refugees from formerly German territories or settlement regions in Poland, the Soviet Union, and Czechoslovakia (Angenendt, 1997). Murphy (1955) referred to the mass exodus of Muslims and Hindus in India after 1947, whereas Eban (1958) discussed Arab refugees in Palestine after the foundation of the state of Israel. All these studies deal with the issue of migration from a more sociological viewpoint. Taft and Robbins (1955) give an early overview of research on migration.

The sociological classification of different migration types refers to the following descriptive criteria:

- Geographical distance within a community (interregional, interprovincial, crossing national borders, intercontinental)
- Spatial sequences (direct migration, migration through intermediate stages)
- Settlement type (rural, small towns, big cities, rural vs. industrial)
- Time factor/length of stay (periodical, seasonal, permanent)
- Motivations underlying migration (forced/involuntary vs. voluntary, organized vs. unorganized, needs and presses in Henry Murray's sense)
- Organizational levels (individuals, families, groups, whole ethnic groups or nations)
- Sociobiographical characteristics (gender, age, family status, religion, ethnicity, education, profession, intellectual, and professional qualities)
- Characteristics of the host society (new vs. traditional immigration country, ethnic homogeneity vs. heterogeneity, population density, gross national product, employment rates, etc.)

These criteria, which sociologists consider relevant when distinguishing different types of migration and when identifying various form of outcomes, psychological and social problems, challenges, and developments, are also considered important in cross-cultural psychology (Berry, 1997; Furnham & Bochner, 1989). Cross-cultural/psychological approaches to migration may be distinguished from sociological approaches with respect to the level of analysis favored by researchers: Psychologists focus more on the individual level, whereas sociologists are more interested in the societal level. Today, there is a tendency to take into consideration simultaneously variables at the society, group, and individual levels, thus making one's research more interdisciplinary in character. From a more cross-cultural and psychological viewpoint and with regard to the adaptation of individual migrants, the early work of Taft has to be mentioned (Taft, 1977; Taft & Doxzy, 1961–1962). It, in turn, influenced later acculturation research (Berry et al., 1992).

Once psychological interest in migration increased, the key term human migration was introduced into the *Psychological Abstracts* in 1973. It is defined as movement of residence from one place to another and it includes nomadism, labor or seasonal migration, and patterns of rural, urban, or suburban migration. The term refers to what is considered by sociologists to constitute horizontal/regional mobility.

Migration compromises different types of migrants: immigrants, emigrants, refugees, seasonal workers, guest workers, businesspersons, diplomats, and exchange students and specialists. The key word immigration in the *Psychological Abstracts* was also introduced in 1973 where it refers to permanent resettlement in a country other than the country of a person's origin. The term emigration is not used as a key word either in PsycINFO or in PSYNDEXplus. The terms *emigration* and *immigration* are often used interchangeably, and in some everyday as well as scientific language usage they are not always clearly distinguished from each other. The use of the terms depends on the viewpoint of the researcher: When migration is discussed from the viewpoint of the host society, it is called *immigration*; the term *emigration* is used from the viewpoint of the country of origin. In the German language, the term *emigration* is used when persons have left their "home country" (in particular, during the time of the Third Reich) and now live far away from their *Heimat*.

When analyzing the German PSYNDEX database with regard to publications on emigration between 1977 and 1999, the number of publications where the term *emigration* appears in the title or in the text of the abstract is 134. A preliminary inspection shows that 43 of these publications discuss German refugees from the Third Reich. Most of them are case studies based on psychoanalytic theories. Furthermore, many of the publications discuss psychoanalysts and psychiatrists who emigrated from Austria and Germany to the United States either before or during the early beginnings of the Third Reich. Only 11 publications relate to other migrant groups such as German migrants from the German Democratic Republic to the Federal Republic of Germany (Schwarzer & Jerusalem, 1990) or Italian migrants to Switzerland (Schuh, 1991a, 1991b). Most articles on emigration are retrospective in character and discuss the loss of one's identity as a function of breaks and discontinuities in one's biography (G. Bittner, 1994), loss of the "fatherland" (I. Bittner, 1994), and various negative outcomes of emigration. The latter include depressive reactions, loss of interest, hypersensitivity (Guennay & Haag, 1990), disturbances in identification processes, loyalty conflicts, psychosomatic problems (Schuh, 1991a, 1991b), the experience of culture shock (Ennenbach & Harrison, 1993), and retraumatization and decompensation in later life (Lansen, 1995). Emigration is associated with negative connotations including loss of sociocultural identity and rootedness, and immigrants are treated as a risk group. Positive outcomes such as achieving a higher quality of life, a more secure life, or perceiving emigration as a challenge are not much taken into consideration. This one-sided emphasis may reflect psychoanalytic thinking with its tendency to make generalizations from patient groups to the normal population.

Of interest in this context is a study conducted by Kruse and Schmitt (1998). The authors interviewed 248 Jewish emigrants and Holocaust survivors and showed that the intensity of negative reminiscences about past traumatic experiences increases with age but that there also exist marked individual differences in this regard. Some of the emigrants and survivors displayed depression, states of anxiety, guilt feelings, and retreat from social relations, but others became more involved in social relations while providing information about the Nazi era. They wanted especially to help the younger generation avoid discrimination, racism, and xenophobia. The research results show that coping strategies and forms of psychological adjustment differ from one person to the next, a finding which will be discussed later in the context of Berry's strategies of acculturation.

Only a few investigations relate to the emigration country itself or consider emigration in a more prospective context (i.e., report research with persons before they emigrated). Schwarzer and Chung (1996) collected data in Hong Kong with Chinese Hong Kong citizens and Chinese students with regard to their expectation about the time after the transition of power from British to Chinese rule. Hutchinson and Simeon (1997) analyzed demographic data in Trinidad and Tobago between 1978 and 1992 with regard to people's economic situation, social distress, suicidal tendencies, and emigration. Jasso (1996) included in her study migrants, "significant others" in their country of origin, and those in the country of destination, while also investigating the relationship between income distribution and the propensity to emigrate among both rich and poor migrants. Rao, Meinzer, Manley, and Chagwedera (1998) compared data on emigration plans of graduate students in medicine from India and Zimbabwe. Significant national differences were found: Sixty-five percent of the Indian students indicated that they had thought about emigration to the United States and 22% had definitive plans, whereas only 25% of the Zimbabwean students had thought about emigration and a mere 2% had concrete plans to emigrate to the USA. Neto (1988) wrote an interesting article in which he described the motivational structure of persons who planned to emigrate and showed how these motivational factors were relevant to their later adaptation in the host society. In a recent study by Strassmann and Clarke (1998), the census on marriage and reproduction in 19th- and 20th-century rural Ireland was studied. The data analysis showed that emigration increased when economic opportunities decreased in Ireland. But the data also illustrated that emigrants improved their chances for getting married by leaving Ireland and that the economic situation of the remaining family members became better. Positive economic effects were also observed when emigrants transferred money back home in that the economic situation of the remaining families became better. This may have led to new economic incentives for social, political, and economic development in the home country.

Migration also includes return migration whose influence on the country of emigration tends to be both positive and negative: positive with regard to the transfer of wealth and technological knowledge, enhancement of international communication and interactions, participation in exchange programs, and improved economic and political integration of the former emigration country into international communities. However, it can also be problematic and conflictual because traditional ways of life and value systems are altered. In addition, the returnees have to be reintegrated into their original society (Georgas & Papastylianou, 1994). Diem-Wille (1994) pointed out that returning to the country of origin can be experienced by a person as a new form of emigration (the use of the term *immigration* would probably be more appropiate in this context) and that this may be connected to all the potential adjustment problems of typical migrants. A case study by Zeul (1994) showed that negative experiences in the host society can make the process of remigration more complicated and risky. Such investigations illustrate that persistent discrimination and negative prejudices experienced during the time of emigration may have a negative effect on the migrant's self-esteem. Lowered levels of self-esteem and self-realization problems are frequently accompanied by difficulties in readaptation to relatively new situations, such as a person's return to his or her culture of origin after a long period of living abroad. This may lead to psychological problems, psychosomatic diseases, and psychiatric disturbances. But it has also been found that the majority of returnees readapt quite efficiently or do not show any problems at all, and it appears that a series of moderator and intervening personality as well as situational variables have to be taken into consideration when trying to explain these individual differences. To identify various individual and social determinants of readaptation, it is best to compare returnees adjusting well with those adjusting poorly.

Specific subgroups of migrants are seasonal workers, guest workers, and exchange students. Migrants belonging to these subgroups have been "invited" by the host society to work or study in the host country for a more or less limited time, but the host society also expects that they will return to their home country after the fulfillment of their duties or after having completed their education or training. Generally, only a minimal adaptation to the culture of the host society is expected, and perceived cultural differences are accepted by members of the host society as long as these do not interfere in a major way with the lifestyle of the host society. But such "guests" frequently become real immigrants over the years. For instance, the history of guest workers in West European countries shows that governments, as obligated by law, had to grant entrance on a long-term basis to spouses and children for the purpose of family reunification (Angenendt, 1997; Hof, 1993; Nuscheler, 1995). The majority of publications on migration/immigration in Europe relates to these former guest workers who are now frequently considered immigrants and, depending on the country, new citizens. The acculturation and sociocultural adjustment of these immigrants will be discussed later when we refer to Berry's model of acculturation.

Another special field of research on migration refers to refugees (a term used as a key word in the *Psychological Abstracts* since 1988). A *refugee* is defined as an uprooted, homeless, voluntary or involuntary migrant who flees his or her native country, usually to escape danger or persecution because of one's race, religion, or political views, and who no longer is protected by his or her former government. Although this definition is a classic one, it is frequently difficult to distinguish unequivocally between various subtypes of migrants such as refugees from immigrants. When asking persons arriving at a border why they request a residence permit, their answers often depend on their self-classification, their perception of the situation, and their motivation. Together these factors determine whether they present themselves as visitors, immigrants, sojourners, or refugees. If a country does not consider itself an immigration country, as for example the Federal Republic of Germany did in the past (this opinion seems now to be changing), and if a person does not hold or cannot prove the nationality of the host country, for example by presenting a document proving a migrant family's German ancestors, it is nearly impossible to get the permission to immigrate. To improve their chances of receiving a residence permit, migrants are driven to declare that they are political or war refugees, and they will try to prove this. For the migrant, a relatively long procedure of obtaining official acknowledgment of one's new status is about to begin, and the person must tolerate a long period of uncertainty regarding his or her future. Refugees from certain countries where war or military conflicts prevail may find it easier to be acknowledged as refugees, especially when the host country is directly or indirectly militarily involved. This applies, for example, to those countries of the European Community involved in the Balkan wars. Acknowledgment as a refugee is also facilitated if the country of origin belongs to the same geographical area and when international, political, cultural, and economic relations already exist. The situation of a refugee will always be stressful, because family members may remain behind in the homeland, one's own as well as one's family's future is uncertain, and the culture and lifestyles of the country giving asylum may be quite different (Furnham & Bochner, 1989). Psychological, sociocultural, and health problems will probably arise if the migrant experienced traumatic events before the flight and if the migration was unplanned and involuntary. It may also be assumed that situational factors in the host country as well as a variety of personality variables will play a crucial role in the various psychosocial adjustment processes.

With regard to processes of adaptation and adjustment to a new culture by migrants, it is interesting to see that in PsycINFO the keyword *cultural assimilation* is used exclusively. This is true, although in cross-cultural psychology different strategies of adaptation and acculturation are distinguished and assimilation refers only to one of them. The term *cultural assimilation* was introduced in 1973, and it is defined as "contact of at least two autonomous cultural groups resulting in change in one or the other, or both groups;" it includes "the process of a minority group giving up its own cultural traits and absorbing those of a dominant society." In PsycINFO, cultural assimilation is referred to as *acculturation*, which is more or less considered as a synonym. It should be added that acculturation has become a central topic in cross-cultural research on immigration (Berry et al., 1992; Segall, Dasen, Berry, & Poortinga, 1999; Triandis, 1994).

MODELS AND TAXONOMIES OF ACCULTURATION

Berry (1997), Furnham and Bochner (1986), Schmitz (2001), and Ward and Rana-Deuba (1999) give overviews of acculturation models and taxonomies. Although the majority of contributions published during the last 2 decades referred to acculturation research in North America (Berry, 1997), European researchers have become increasingly interested in this field. Many of their investigations refer to those dimensions of acculturation defined and described by Berry (1997), Furnham and Bochner (1989), and Taft (1977, 1986) as well as to Berry's structural model or taxonomy of acculturation styles: Typical examples include Abou (1978), George (1986), Oriol (1981) in France; Bagley (1968, 1969, 1971, 1993), Burke (1977), Cochrane (1977), Furnham and Bochner (1989), Gupta (1977), Hemsi (1967), Watson (1977) in Great Britain; Boker (1981); Schmitz (1994a, 1994b), Suzuki (1981) in Germany; Georgas and Papastylianou (1994, 1996) in Greece; Sam and Berry (1995) in Norway; Boski (1994) in Poland; and Neto (1986a, 1986b, 1988, 1989, 1993) in Portugal.

The term *acculturation* refers to cultural changes that result from cultural contact between different cultural groups. Acculturation is a phenomenon that groups or individuals experience when they are confronted with changes in their cultural surrounding (Berry et al., 1992), and it refers both to adaptive processes and to adaptation as an outcome. Psychological, social, and cultural aspects are all included as part of the acculturation process (Berry, 1992). It should not be understood merely as a simple process of reaction to changes in the cultural context but rather as an active and sometimes creative approach to challenges experienced by immigrants confronted with cultural change (Schmitz, 2001). In French-speaking countries, the term *interculturation* is more popular, which is defined as a series of interaction processes of individual persons and groups who define themselves as culturally different (Camilleri, 1990; Clanet, 1990). Whereas *acculturation* refers to adaptation to a new culture, the term *interculturation* seems to be used as a broader term. It includes adjustment processes of immigrants as well as continuous mutual adjustment processes of sociocultural groups living either in a country (the intranational aspect of interculturation) or in a community of states, for example, the European Community (the international aspect of interculturation). The processes and outcomes of acculturation can be circumscribed by different strategies of adaptation that are preferred by a society and by its members (Berry, 1988, 1997). The distinction between the group and individual levels of acculturation is important in so far as it allows us to investigate, first, the relationship between acculturation forms at both the societal and individual levels and, second, the nature of conflicts if beliefs about acculturation goals differ between acculturating individuals and their own ethnic group (Schmitz, 2001).

Adaptation is defined by Berry (1997) as "changes that take place in individuals or groups in response to environmental demands" (p. 13). Two subtypes are distinguished, namely psychological and sociocultural adaptation. Berry, Kim, and Boski (1987) defined *psychological adaptation* as the "process by which the individual changes his psychological characteristics, changes the surrounding context, or changes the amount of contact in order to achieve a better fit (outcome) with other features of the system in which he carries out his life." Sociocultural adjustment includes the acquisition of social communication and interaction skills as well as the competence to participate actively in civil and political activities. Ward (1997) distinguished between psychological adaptation, which relates to psychological satisfaction and well-being, and sociocultural adaptation based on the learning of social skills. She argued that both types of adaptation are interrelated, but that they are theoretically and empirically distinct. Ward's research findings (Ward, 1996; Ward & Kennedy, 1994; Ward & Rana-Deuba, 1999) demonstrated that both types can be distinguished empirically. The arguments speaking in favor of the theoretical distinctiveness of both terms are the following: She believed that two different psychological and sociocultural paradigms, namely the coping process model and the social learning model, explain the different acculturation outcomes of, respectively, psychological adaptation and sociocultural adaptation. Furthermore, she claimed that psychological adaptation is modeled by personality, social support, and life-change variables whereas sociocultural adaptation tends to be influenced by more sociological variables such as length of time in a host country, past experiences with cross-cultural relocations, and amount of interaction with members of the host society. There exists empirical evidence that both processes are related to different sets of explanatory variables. In addition, various personality variables such as basic personality variables (as described by Costa & McCrae, 1992; Eysenck & Eysenck, 1985; Zuckerman, 1994), cognitive styles and structures (e.g., Rokeach, 1960; Witkin, 1965), modes of coping (Endler & Parker, 1990; Lazarus & Folkman, 1984), and cognitive representations (Thomae, 1988) are involved in both processes; they may explain individual differences in both types of acculturation processes, namely those described in the stress-coping paradigm and those emphasized by the social learning paradigm (Schmitz, 1994a, 1994b, 1994c, 1996). These acculturative processes can lead to different forms of adaptation according to specific patterns of personality and situational variables. Adjustment or maladjustment appears to depend on a variety of variables that will now be discussed (Berry, 1997).

During the last 2 decades, Berry has developed a comprehensive conceptual framework for acculturation research that is based on his own and his coworkers' empirical research and on a wide range of acculturation studies he found in the literature (Berry, 1976, 1992, 1997; Berry, Trimble, & Olmedo, 1986). He integrated in his conceptual framework various theoretical process models of acculturation and included a wide range of moderator and intervening variables to explain the influence of situational factors on both the acculturation process and the short- and long-term acculturation outcomes. The central feature of his framework refers to the acculturation process of a group or of an individual migrant. According to the quality of changes as a consequence of acculturation processes, he distinguished different types, namely "behavioral shifts" (Berry, 1980), "cultural learning" (Berry, 1997; Brislin, Landis, & Brandt, 1983; Ward, 1997), and "social skills acquisition" (Berry, 1997; Furnham & Bochner, 1989; Ward, 1997). The acculturation process can be studied with regard to two different paradigms: Lazarus's model of coping (Lazarus & Folkman, 1984) and the social learning paradigm (which is not related to a specific learning theory). The first paradigm is applied when acculturative stress experience, coping, and psychological adaptation are involved, and the social learning paradigm is preferred when the acquisition of social skills is investigated. A weak point of Berry's model is that the two paradigms are not integrated in a general model of acculturation and those outcomes of acculturation showing a large variety of individual differences are not clearly explained. Additional empirical research with regard to both topics is needed to explain the large variety of individual differences found in empirical research. With regard to the role of intervening and moderating variables, the framework has grown very complex during the last 10 years: Group- and individual-level variables are distinguished, and the variables belonging to the latter level are subdivided into individual level variables that operate either prior to or during the process of acculturation. All these variables are assumed to have an influence on both acculturation processes and acculturation outcomes.

Berry's taxonomy of moderator variables is used in acculturation research because it helps researchers to develop precise research designs and to interpret their empirical findings. With regard to variables assumed to operate prior to the acculturation process at both the individual and the group (society of origin) levels, these variables are mostly assessed retrospectively. Consequently, some of the variables have to be interpreted as cognitive representations of the individual rather than as "actual facts." Probably, these cognitive representations or constructs are more relevant for the explanation of acculturation outcomes than real events experienced in the past. As already discussed, investigations beginning prior to emigration are less frequent and longitudinal studies are mostly missing (Schönpflug, 1997).

Table 2.4 provides an overview over those variables that are considered as theoretically relevant moderators and intervening variables and that have been shown empirically to influence acculturation processes and outcomes. The classification is based on Berry's (1997) framework. The analysis of empirical contributions in the field of acculturation research has shown that in most cases not more than two different classes of variables are studied at the same time. Contradictory research findings can often be explained by the fact that important variables (for example, age, gender, profession, personality, etc.) were not controlled in a given research design, and that insufficiently developed research instruments were applied (Ward & Rana-Deuba, 1999). It is hoped that in future research, more comparative studies using increasingly complex research designs and applying comparable instruments will be conducted. A taxonomy can help the researchers decide which variables should be included in such studies.

Among other moderator variables, Berry's framework contains a group of variables that are called acculturation attitudes and strategies. They are integrated in a model of acculturation styles and the specific acculturation styles are in turn influenced by a series of other variables that are also included in the above mentioned taxonomy (Schmitz, 2001). This is not surprising as these acculturation strategies are closely related to coping strategies which are constitutive elements of the stress-and-coping paradigm and which are influenced by personality and situational variables (Schmitz, 1992a, 1992b, 1994a). Berry, Kalin, and Taylor (1977) and Berry (1988) presented a conceptual framework of acculturation styles that can serve as the basis for describing different types of acculturation attitudes and behavioral strategies of persons belonging both to ethnic groups and to the mainstream society (Schmitz, 1992a). The model contains two continuous dimensions: Dimension I can be described as "cultural maintenance" and Dimension II relates to "contact and interaction." The former asks whether one's original cultural identity and customs are valuable and whether they should be retained. The latter asks whether positive relations with other groups are considered to be of value and whether they should be maintained. If for purposes of presentation the answers to both questions are restricted to the responses yes or no, four combinations representing different acculturation strategies are obtained. Answering both questions affirmatively describes the option of "integration," which Berry et al. (1986) defined as maintenance of the cultural integrity of a group, as well as the movement by the group toward becoming an integral part of a larger societal framework. *Assimilation* implies the abandonment of one's cultural identity and the maintenance of positive relations with the new group, while *separation* (when chosen by members of the nondominant group) or *segregation* (when required from members of the dominant group) signify the maintenance of one's cultural identity with no interest in building up positive relations with other groups. The fourth option is called *marginalization*. This option is defined by Berry as giving up one's own cultural identity and not being interested in positive relations to another cultural group.

Berry's model of acculturation is of great interest in cross-cultural psychology because it offers several advantages: First, it allows one to analyze acculturation processes at the societal, group, and individual levels while offering the opportunity to relate data collected at one level to data gathered at another (Berry et al., 1992). Second, the model serves as an excellent basis for categorizing and describing different types of acculturation attitudes and behavioral strategies of both persons belonging to a minority group and of those who are members of the mainstream society (Schmitz, 1992a). Third, concerning acculturation at the individual level, acculturation styles are clearly and consistently related to basic personality dimensions. Schmitz (1992a, 1994b, 1994c) found that different modes of acculturation are clearly related to a variety of individual differences such as basic personality dimensions, cognitive styles, and cognitive structures. Berry's model is frequently used in acculturation research (e.g., Georgas & Papastylianou, 1994, 1996; Neto, 1993; Sabatier & Berry, 1994; Sam & Berry, 1995; Schmitz, 1994a; Ward, 1996).

Immigrants have to cope with situations they experience as stressful. Each of the four acculturation strategies can be experienced by an immigrant as stressful if he or she has to strive hard to realize his or her aims regarding successful adaptation to a new culture. This is particularly the case when in the host society or in his or her own ethnic group a specific type of acculturation is not accepted (Berry, 1992; Berry & Sam, 1997; Schmitz, 1994a). As Schmitz (1992a) reported, the degree of acculturative stress experienced by a migrant and his or her acculturation style determine together the individual's well-being and health-related behavior. Regarding long-term outcomes, empirical evidence suggests that either integration or assimilation may serve as effective strategies in most cases. Both techniques lead to an arrangement with the host society and clarify

Table 2.4
Classification of Intervening and Moderator Variables of Acculturative Adjustment Processes with Migrants

Group-level variables

Characteristics of the society of origin and settlement
Social-political structures and ideologies
Economic situation
Geographical and demographic factors
Belief and value systems: Ideologies, multicultural ideology
Ethnic attitudes
Social support and health systems

Acculturative group characteristics
Physical characteristics
Biological characteristics
Social and organizational
Cultural factors

Individual-level characteristics

Personal characteristics prior to emigration
Age, gender
Social status
Migration motivation and expectations
Social contacts
Education
Professional situation

Immigration/Acculturation-related characteristics
Acculturation experiences (prior to acculturation)
Acculturation attitudes and styles
Acculturation-related coping strategies
Perception of one's ethnic group
Perception of the society of settlement
Perceived sociocultural distances
Perceived prejudice and discrimination
Perceived resources (social support, problem-solving capacities)
Phase (length of time)

General personality characteristics prior to and during acculturation (moderator variables)

Biophysiological characteristics
Basic personality dimensions
Identity structure
Generalized expectancies (locus of control, interpersonal trust)
Cognitive styles and structures (constructs, beliefs)
Intellectual capacities and knowledge
Value systems
Need systems
Reaction forms: Coping, defenses

the relationship with the migrant's ethnic group. When a migrant prefers integration, he or she is usually able to arrive at a compromise between those behavior patterns expected by the host society and those by his or her ethnic group. If the migrant chooses assimilation, then he or she must assimilate into mainstream society and also give up ties with his or her ethnic group. In the case where segregation is preferred, the relationship with members of the host society is perceived as negative and remains unclear (Berry & Kim, 1988; Berry et al., 1992; Schmitz, 1992a). For instance, if conflicts between the needs and expectations supported by the host society rather than by one's ethnic group remain frequently unresolved over long periods of time, the migrant will experience prolonged acculturative stress, and health problems may arise (Berry, 1988). Marginalization, unless it is a temporary phenomenon, is considered by most researchers as the worst strategy a migrant can choose, because marginalization frequently leads to major psychosocial disturbances (Berry, 1990; Schmitz, 1994a, 1994b, 1999).

PERSONALITY TRAITS: A NEGLECTED GROUP OF VARIABLES IN ACCULTURATION RESEARCH

Although personality variables are included in Berry's framework, individual differences are not taken into consideration in a systematic way. Variables such as self-identity, self-realization, self-concept, or locus of control appear in migration research, but they are mostly not related to elaborated theories and it may remain unclear how they are to be measured. In addition, personality variables related to elaborated theories of personality such as basic temperament traits, cognitive styles and structures, values, and motivational systems are only occasionally included in a research design to explain obvious individual differences in adaptation and adjustment.

Basic personality dimensions should be considered as factors that, in addition to situational factors, strongly influence social behavior (Costa & McCrae, 1992; Eysenck & Eysenck, 1985; Zuckerman, 1979, 1994). Personality dimensions belonging to Eysenck's "Giant Three model," Costa and McCrae's "Big Five factor model," or Zuckerman's "Alternative Big Five model," are called "basic" because they are said to possess a genetic-biological basis at the genotype level. Most personality researchers, however, agree that at the phenotype level these dimensions are mostly shaped by environmental factors (Bates & Wachs, 1994; Eysenck, 1967; Eysenck & Eysenck, 1985; Zuckerman, 1994). As Schmitz showed (1993), these basic traits are also closely related to coping styles and health behavior. Consequently, it may be assumed that basic personality dimensions are also related to motivational processes during migration, the degree of perceived acculturation stress, acculturative attitudes and strategies, psychological and sociocultural adaptation, and feelings of well-being and health (Schmitz, 1994a, 1994b). Empirical findings illustrate that migrants preferring integration are open-minded and flexible; able to break up traditional belief systems and behavior patterns; and find it less difficult to integrate elements belonging to different cultural beliefs, value structures, and behavior patterns into a complex and new behavioral system (Rokeach, 1960, 1973; Witkin, 1965). Emotional stability and a low degree of anxiety facilitate this process. Immigrants favoring either assimilation or segregation do not show this degree of flexibility and openness and probably are not able or willing to construe more complex behavior systems that combine elements of behavior patterns reflecting different cultural backgrounds. Research findings show that they attempt to avoid conflicts between their own traditional beliefs and value systems and those of the new society. In the case of assimilation, they identify themselves with the culture of the host society, while in the case of segregation they join the ethnic group and minimize contact with the majority culture. Persons preferring segregation have been found to be less extroverted and that makes it difficult for them to establish new social contacts. Their higher degree of aggression-hostility may be interpreted as defensive.

When acculturation efforts are experienced as stressful, individual differences depend on a series of variables such as cognitive structures and styles, coping-styles, and personality variables. Coping strategies in particular have to be considered as relevant variables moderating the relationship between acculturative stressors and stress outcomes (Berry et al., 1992; Schmitz, 1992a, 1992c; Taft, 1977; Zheng & Berry, 1991). Taft (1977), for instance, considered coping as a central variable in acculturation and adaptation processes. Berry et al. (1992) discovered close relationships between Taft's coping-styles and acculturation styles. There is some empirical evidence that Berry's acculturation strategies are related to a person's general coping-style system (Schmitz, 1992c). In this context, Schmitz considered Berry's acculturation strategies of integration, assimilation, segregation, and marginalization to represent situation-specific forms of the individual's general coping system.

The relevance of basic personality dimensions as moderator variables was discussed by the author at the Ninth Biennial Meeting of the International Society for the Study of Individual Differences (Schmitz, 1999). In his study, immigrants belonging to different ethnic groups and experiencing a high degree of acculturation stress received the Dimensional Assessment of Personality Pathology-Basic Questionnaire (DAPP-BQ), which measures personality pathology (Livesley, Jackson, & Schroeder, 1989). The questionnaire contains 18 subscales, of which 16 are listed in Table 2.5. The scales can be used with both normal and pathological samples. The study focused on relationships between the DAPP-BQ variables and Costa and McCrae's Big Five factor model (FFM), on the one hand, and between Livesley et al.'s scales and disorders from the third revised edition of the *Diagnostic and Statistical Manual of Mental Disorders* on the other. The obtained results were consistent and clear-cut. For instance, regarding the relationships between the Big Five personality dimensions, traits measured by the DAPP-BQ, and dimensions of acculturation style, a few findings will be mentioned: Neuroticism (FFM) correlates positively with anxiousness, affective lability, and identity problems; extroversion (FFM) with stimulus seeking; openness to experience (FFM) negatively with avoidance and identity problems; agreeableness negatively with suspiciousness and rejection, and conscientiousness (FFM) with compulsiveness.

Table 2.5
Correlations Between DAPP-BQ-Dimensions (Psychopathy) and
Acculturation (Correlations >.30) for Immigrants Experiencing
a High Degree of Acculturation Stress

	Integration	Assimilation	Segregation	Marginalization
Anxiousness	−.39	.42	.43	.31
Affective lability	−.42		.42	.31
Diffidence			.35	
Insecure attachment	−.30		.41	
Social avoidance			.45	
Identity problems	−.39		.38	
Narcissism		.31	.42	
Stimulus seeking		.35	−.33	.49
Restricted expression			.32	.31
Intimacy problems			.35	.40
Interpersonal "disesteem"	−.36	−.42		.51
Rejection		−.38	.35	.55
Suspiciousness	−.45	−.41	.40	.43
Conduct problems	−.31	−.49	.34	.48
Compulsiveness		.31	.30	−.31
Passive oppositionality			−.37	.45

Note: From Schmitz (1999).

The data in Table 2.5 illustrate that integration is negatively correlated with dimensions suggesting psychopathic tendencies (according to Livesley et al., 1989). Whereas migrants experiencing acculturation stress and applying integration strategies do not show psychopathic tendencies, persons preferring segregation and marginalization do exhibit such tendencies. Migrants choosing integration do not show anxiousness and do not report identity problems. Assimilators are anxious, but they are not rejecting and not suspicious; anxieties may have motivated these persons to look for social contact with members of the host society. Migrants choosing segregation tend to be anxious, experience identity problems, and are rejecting and suspicious. They also look for social support, and because they may possess little interpersonal trust they look for support in their own ethnic group rather than seek contact with institutions and members of the host society. Migrants scoring high on marginalization show a different profile from those preferring segregation. They are also anxious, show passive oppositionality, are stimulus seekers (this characteristic is frequently related to the abuse of drugs such as alcohol), and are less compulsive (this includes low conscientiousness). In general, it appears that psychopathic behavior may become manifest when migrants both experience a high degree of acculturation stress over a long period of time and also prefer segregation and marginalization as acculturation strategies. However, it has to be emphasized that although a high degree of acculturation stress does not inevitably lead to psychopathology, research indicates that personality variables have a crucial influence on the acculturative outcome.

SUMMARY AND CONCLUDING REMARKS

Our discussion of studies delineating various psychosocial factors influencing the adjustment and well-being of migrants suggests a number of conclusions:

- There is an increasing interest in migration problems because the worldwide number of migrants has been growing rapidly.

- Immigration issues are more frequently studied than emigration and return migration. Emigration is mostly studied from a retrospective viewpoint. Longitudinal studies are needed to understand the dynamic relationship between emigration and immigration.

- It is of great theoretical interest to integrate different models of acculturation that are based on different psychological theories and to develop a more general model that would allow one to predict acculturative behavior and outcomes more precisely.

- Past research has shown that acculturation processes are influenced by a large variety of moderator and intervening variables. In this context, Berry's taxonomy can help the researcher to develop more comprehensive and complex research designs.

- Research instruments have to be refined and applied in comparative research. It is highly desirable to conduct idiographic as well as nomothetic studies and to combine both approaches in the same study.

- Personality dimensions should be increasingly taken into consideration because it has been demonstrated that individual differences become manifest both in the preference for various acculturation strategies and in acculturation outcomes.

- More elaborate models and theories based on empirical research will help social scientists to provide migrants with social support and enable them to develop more efficient intervention strategies.

REFERENCES

Abou, S. (1978). Integration et acculturation des immigrés: Un modèle d'analyse [Integration and acculturation of immigrants: A model of analysis]. *Migrants-Formation, 29–30*, 35–39.

Angenendt, S. (1997). *Migration und Flucht. Aufgaben und Strategien für Deutschland, Europa und die internationale Gemeinschaft* [Migration and flight. Tasks and strategies for Germany, Europe, and the international community]. Bonn, Germany: Bundeszentrale für politische Bildung.

Bagley, C. (1968). Migration, race and mental health: A review of some recent research. *Race, 9*, 343–356.

Bagley, C. (1969). A survey of problems reported by Indian and Pakistani immigrants in Britain. *Race, 11*, 65–78.

Bagley, C. (1971). Mental illness in immigrant minorities in London. *Journal of Biosocial Science, 3*, 449–459.

Bagley, C. (1993). Mental health and social adjustment of elderly Chinese immigrants in Canada. *Canada's Mental Health, 41,* 6–10.

Bates, J. E., & Wachs, T. D. (Eds.). (1994). *Temperament: Individual differences at the interface of biology and behavior.* Washington, DC: American Psychological Association.

Berry, J. W. (1976). *Human ecology and cognitive style: Comparative studies in cultural and psychological adaptation.* New York: Sage/Halsted.

Berry, J. W. (1980). Social and cultural change. In H. C. Triandis & R. Brislin (Eds.), *Handbook of cross-cultural psychology: Vol. 5. Social* (pp. 211-279). Boston: Allyn & Bacon.

Berry, J. W. (1988). Acculturation and psychological adaptation: A conceptual overview. In J. Berry & R. Annis (Eds.), *Ethnic psychology: Research and practice with immigrants, refugees, native peoples, ethnic groups and sojourners* (pp. 41–52). Amsterdam: Swets & Zeitlinger.

Berry, J. W. (1990). Psychology of acculturation. In J. Berman (Ed.), *Cross-cultural perspectives: Nebraska Symposium on Motivation* (pp. 201–234). Lincoln: University of Nebraska Press.

Berry, J. W. (1992). Acculturation and adaptation in a new society. *International Migration, 30,* 69–85.

Berry, J. W. (1997). Immigration, acculturation, and adaptation. *Applied Psychology: An International Review, 46,* 5–68.

Berry, J. W., Kalin, R., & Taylor, D. M. (1977). *Multiculturalism and ethnic attitudes in Canada.* Ottawa, Ontario, Canada: Government of Canada.

Berry, J. W., & Kim, U. (1988). Acculturation and mental health. In P. R. Dasen, J. W. Berry, & N. Sartorius (Eds.), *Health and cross-cultural psychology: Towards applications* (pp. 207–238). Newbury Park, CA: Sage.

Berry, J. W., Kim, U., & Boski, P. (1987). Acculturation and psychological adaptation. In Y. Y. Kim & W. B. Gudykunst (Eds.), *International Communications Annual: Vol. 2. Current studies in cross-cultural adaption* (pp. 62–89). London: Sage.

Berry, J. W., Poortinga, Y. H., Segall, M. H., & Dasen, P. R. (1992). *Cross-cultural psychology. Research and applications.* Cambridge, England: Cambridge University Press.

Berry, J. W., & Sam, D. (1997). Acculturation and adaptation. In J. W. Berry, M. H. Segall, & Ç. Kagitçibasi (Eds.), *Handbook of cross-cultural psychology: Vol. 3. Social behavior and applications* (pp. 291–326). Boston: Allyn & Bacon.

Berry, J. W., Trimble, J., & Olmeda, E. (1986). The assessment of acculturation. In W. J. Lonner & J. W. Berry (Eds.), *Field methods in cross-cultural research* (pp. 291–324). Newbury Park, CA: Sage.

Bittner, G. (Ed.). (1994). *Biographien im Umbruch. Lebenslaufforschung und vergleichende Erziehungswissenschaft* [Changes in biographies. Life-course research and comparative educational science]. Würzburg, Germany: Königshausen & Neumann.

Bittner, I. (1994). Heimatverlust als psychisches Trauma? Erfahrungen aus psychoanalytischen Erfahrungen [Loss of the native country? Experiences derived from psychoanalysis]. In G. Bittner (Ed.), *Biographien im Umbruch. Lebenslaufforschung und vergleichende Erziehungswissenschaft* [Changes in biographies. Life-course research and comparative educational science] (pp. 104–114). Würzburg, Germany: Königshausen & Neumann.

Boker, W. (1981). Psycho(patho)logical reactions among foreign labourers in Europe. In L. Eitinger & D. Schwartz (Eds.), *Strangers in the world* (pp. 186–201). Bern, Switzerland: Huber.

Boski, P. (1994). Psychological acculturation via identity dynamics: Consequences for subjective well-being. In A. M. Bouvy, F. J. R. van de Vijver, P. Boski, & P. Schmitz (Eds.), *Journeys into cross-cultural psychology* (pp. 197–215). Amsterdam: Swets & Zeitlinger.

Braudel, F. (1986). *L'identité de la France: Les hommes et les choses* [The identity of France: Men and things]. Paris: Editions Arthaud.

Brislin, R., Landis, D., & Brandt, M. (1983). Conceptualization of intercultural behavior and training. In D. Landis & R. Brislin (Eds.), *Handbook of intercultural training* (Vol. 1, pp. 1–35). New York: Pergamon.

Burke, A. G. (1977). Family stress and the precipitation of psychiatric disorder: A comparative study among immigrant West Indian and native British patients in Birmingham. *International Journal of Social Psychiatry, 23,* 35–40.

Camilleri, C. (1990). Introduction. In C. Clanet (Ed.), *Linterculturel: Introduction aux approches interculturelles en éducation et en sciences humaines* [The intercultural: Introduction to intercultural approaches in education and human sciences] (pp. 1–23). Toulouse, France: Presses Universitaires du Mirail.

Clanet, C. (1990). *L'interculturel: Introduction aux approches interculturelles en éducation et en sciences humaines* [The intercultural: Introduction to intercultural approaches in education and human sciences]. Toulouse, France: Presses Universitaires du Mirail.

Cochrane, R. (1977). Mental illness in immigrants to England and Wales: An analysis of mental hospital admissions, 1971. *Social Psychiatry, 12,* 25–35.

Costa, P. T., Jr., & McCrae, R. R. (1992). *NEO-PI-R: Revised NEO Personality Inventory (NEO-PI-R)*. Odessa, FL: Psychological Assessment Resources.

Demageon, A., & Mauco, G. (1939). *Documents pour servir à l'étude des étrangers dans l'agriculture française* [Documents for the study of foreigners in French agriculture]. Paris: Hermann.

Diem-Wille, G. (1994). Zur Bedeutung der Emigration für die Identitätsentwicklung. Ein Beitrag zur biographischen Forschung aus psychoanalytischer Sicht [The significance of emigration for identity formation: A contribution to biographical research from the perspective of psychoanalysis]. In G. Bittner (Ed.), *Biographien im Umbruch. Lebenslaufforschung und vergleichende Erziehungswissenschaft* [Changes in biographies. Life-course research and comparative educational science] (pp. 83–193). Würzburg, Germany: Königshausen & Neumann.

Eban, A. S. (1958). *The Arab refugees problem: Need for candor* [Statement before the United Nations Special Political Committee, November 27, 1957]. Jerusalem: Ministry for Foreign Affairs, Information Division.

Eisenstadt, S. N. (1954). *The absorption of immigrants. A comparative study based on the Jewish community in Palestine and the state of Israel.* London: Routledge & Paul.

Endler, N. S., & Parker, J. D. (1990). The multidimensional assessment of coping: A critical evaluation. *Journal of Personality and Social Psychology, 58,* 844–854.

Ennenbach, W., & Harrison, R. M. (1993). Der Auszug aus der Kultur— Probleme der Emigration [Departure from one's culture: Problems of emigration]. *Zwischenschritte, 12,* 437–447.

Eysenck, H. J. (1967). *The biological basis of personality.* Springfield, IL: Thomas.

Eysenck, H. J., & Eysenck, M. W. (1985). *Personality and individual differences. A natural science approach.* New York: Plenum Press.

Furnham, A., & Bochner, S. (1986, repr. 1989). *Culture shock: Psychological reactions to unfamiliar environments.* London: Methuen.

Georgas, J., & Papastylinanou, D. (1994). The effect of time on stereotypes: Acculturation of children of returning immigrants to Greece. In A. M. Bouvy, F. J. R. van de Vijver, P. Boski, & P. Schmitz (Eds.), *Journeys into cross-cultural psychology* (pp. 158–166). Amsterdam: Swets & Zeitlinger.

Georgas, J., & Papastylinanou, D. (1996). Acculturation and ethnic identity: The remigration of ethnic Greeks to Greece. In H. Grad, A. Blanco, & J. Georgas (Eds.), *Key issues in cross-cultural psychology* (pp. 114–127). Lisse, the Netherlands: Swets & Zeitlinger.

George, P. (1986). *L'immigration en France* [Immigration into France]. Paris: Librairie Armand Colin.

Guennay, E., & Haag, A. (1990). Krankheit in der Emigration—Eine Studie an türkischen Patientinnen in der Allgemeinpraxis aus psychosomatischer Sicht [A study of female Turkish patients in general medical practice from a psychosomatic viewpoint]. *Psychotherapie, Psychsomatik und Psychotherapy, 40,* 417–422.

Gupta, Y. (1977). The educational and vocational aspirations of Asian immigrant and English school-leavers: A comparative study. *British Journal of Sociology, 28,* 199–225.

Hemsi, L. K. (1967). Psychiatric morbidity of West Indian immigrants. *Social Psychiatry, 2,* 95–100.

Hof, B. (1993). *Europa im Zeichen der Migration. Szenarios zur Bevölkerungs- und Arbeitsmarktentwicklung in der Europäischen Gemeinschaft bis 2020* [Europe under the sign of migration. Scenarios of the development of the population and labor market until 2020]. Cologne, Germany: Deutscher Instituts-Verlag.

Hutchinson, G. A., & Simeon, D. T. (1997). Suicide in Trinidad and Tobago: Associations with measures of social distress. *International Journal of Social Psychiatry, 43,* 269–275.

Jasso, G. (1996). Deriving implications of comparison theory for demographic phenomena: A first step in the analysis of migration. *Sociological Quarterly, 37,* 19–57.

Kruse, A., & Schmitt, E. (1998). Erinnerungen an traumatische Erlebnisse in der Zeit des Nationalsozialismus bei (ehemaligen) jüdischen Emigranten und Lagerhäftlingen [Reminiscence of traumatic experiences in National Socialist Germany in (former) Jewish emigrants and extermination camp survivors]. *Zeitschrift für Gerontologie und Geriatrie, 31,* 138–150.

Kulischer, E. M. (1949). Displaced persons in the modern world. *Annals of the American Academy of Political and Social Science, 262,* 166–177.

Lansen, J. (1995). Spätfolgen bei den Opfern der Shoah [Long-term consequences in Holocaust survivors]. In I. Attia (Ed.), *Multikulturelle Gesellschaft—monokulturelle Psychologie? Antisemitismus und Rassismus in der psychosozialen Arbeit* [Multicultural society—monocultural psychology? Antisemitism and racism in psychosocial work] (pp. 88–95). Tübingen, Germany: Deutsche Gesellschaft für Verhaltenstherapie.

Lazarus, R. S., & Folkman, S. (1984). *Stress, appraisal and coping.* New York: Springer.

Livesley, W. J., Jackson, D. N., & Schroeder, M. L. (1989). A study of the factorial structure of personality pathology. *Journal of Personality Disorders, 3,* 292–306.

Mauco, G. (1932). *Les étrangers en France* [Foreigners in France]. Paris: Librairie Armond Colon.

Münz, R. (1997). Phasen und Formen der europäischen Migration [Phases and forms of the European migration]. In S. Angenendt (Ed.), *Migration und Flucht. Aufgaben und Strategien für Deutschland, Europa und die internationale Gemeinschaft* [Migration and flight. Tasks and strategies for Germany, Europe, and the international community]. Bonn, Germany: Bundeszentrale für politische Bildung.

Murphy, H. B. M. (1955). *Flight and resettlement.* New York: Columbia University Press.

Neto, F. (1986a). Adaptação psico-social e regresso ao país natal dos migrantes portugueses em França [Psychosocial adaptation and return to the native country of Portuguese migrants in France]. *Psicologia, 5,* 71–86.

Neto, F. (1986b). Aspectos da problemática da segunda geração portuguesa em França [Aspects of second-generation problems of Portuguese living in France]. *Povos e cultura, 1,* 167–186.

Neto, F. (1988). Migration plans and their determinants among Portuguese adolescents. In J. Berry & R. Annis (Eds.), *Ethnic psychology: Research and practice with immigrants, refugees, native peoples, ethnic groups, and sojourners* (pp. 308–314). Amsterdam: Swets & Zeitlinger.

Neto, F. (1989). Représentation sociale de la migration portugaise. Le regard des jeunes [The social representation of Portuguese migration: The viewpoint of youths]. In J. Retschitzky, M. Bossel-Lagos, & P. Dasen (Eds.), *La recherche interculturelle* [Intercultural research] (Vol. 1, pp. 86–99). Paris: L'Harmattan.

Neto, F. (1993). *Psicologia da migração portuguesa* [Psychology of the Portuguese migration]. Lisbon, Portugal: Universidade Aberta.

Nourissier, F., & Pillepich, A. (1952). *Enracinement des immigrants* [Rootedness of immigrants]. Paris: Bloud et Gay.

Nuscheler, F. (1995). *Internationale Migration. Flucht und Asyl* [International migration. Escape and asylum]. Opladen, Germany: Leske & Budrich.

Oriol, M. (1981). *Bilan des études sur les aspects culturels et humains des migrations internationales en Europe Occidentale: 1918–1979* [Survey of studies on the cultural and human aspects of international migration in western Europe: 1918–1979]. Strasbourg, France: ESF.

Paikert, G. C. (1962). *The German exodus. A selective study of the Post-World-War II expulsion of German population and its effect.* Den Haag, the Netherlands: Martinus Nijhoff.

Peterson, W. (1955). *Planned migration. The social determinants of the Dutch-Canadian movement.* Berkeley: University of California Press.

Rao, N. R., Meinzer, A. E., Manley, M., & Chagwedera, I. (1998). International medical students´career choice, attitudes toward psychiatry, and emigration to the United States: Examples from India and Zimbabwe. *Academic Psychiatry, 22,* 117–126.

Rokeach, M. (1960). *The open and closed mind.* New York: Basic Books.

Rokeach, M. (1973). *The nature of human values.* New York: Macmillan.

Sabatier, C., & Berry, J. W. (1994). Immigration et acculturation [Immigration and acculturation]. In R. Bourhis & J. P. Leyens (Eds.), *Stereotypes, discrimination et relations intergroupes* [Stereotypes, discrimination, and intergroup relations] (pp. 261-291). Liège, Belgium: Mardaga.

Sam, D. L., & Berry, J. W. (1995). Acculturation stress among young immigrants in Norway. *Scandinavian Journal of Psychology, 36,* 10–24.

Schmitz, P. G. (1992a). Acculturation styles and health. In S. Iwawaki, Y. Kashima, & K. S. Leung (Eds.), *Innovations in cross-cultural psychology* (pp. 360–370). Amsterdam: Swets & Zeitlinger.

Schmitz, P. G. (1992b). Immigrant mental and physical health. Special Issue: Immigrant mental health. *Psychology and Developing Societies, 4,* 117–132.

Schmitz, P. G. (1992c). Personality, stress-reactions, and diseases. *Personality and Individual Differences, 13,* 683–691.

Schmitz, P. G. (1993). Personality, stress-reactions, and psychosomatic complaints. In G. van Heck, P. Bonaiuto, & I. Deary (Eds.), *Personality psychology in Europe* (Vol. 4, pp. 321–343). Amsterdam: Swets & Zeitlinger.

Schmitz, P. G. (1994a). Acculturation and adaptation process among immigrants in Germany. In A. M. Bouvy, F. J. R. van de Vijver, & P. G. Schmitz (Eds.), *Journeys into cross-cultural psychology* (pp. 142–157). Amsterdam: Swets & Zeitlinger.

Schmitz, P. G. (1994b). Personnalité et acculturation [Personality and acculturation]. *Cahiers Internationaux de Psychologie Sociale, 24,* 33–53.

Schmitz, P. G. (1994c). Se puede generalizar el modelo de culturacion de John Berry [Can John Berry's model of acculturation be generalized?]. *Revista de Psicologia Social y Personalidad, 10,* 17–35.

Schmitz, P. G. (1996, August). Cultural identity problems and solution strategies. In P. G. Schmitz & F. Neto (Chairs), *Sociocultural identity and adaptation.* Symposium conducted at the 13th Congress of the International

Association for Cross-Cultural Psychology, Montreal, Quebec, Canada.

Schmitz, P. G. (1999, July). *The influence of personality variables on acculturative adjustment.* Paper presented at the Ninth Biennial Meeting of the International Society for the Study of Individual Differences, Vancouver, British Columbia, Canada.

Schmitz, P. G. (2001). Psychological aspects of immigration. In L. L. Adler & U. P. Gielen (Eds.), *Cross-cultural topics in psychology* (2nd ed., pp. 229–243). Westport, CT: Praeger.

Schönpflug, U. (1997). Acculturation: Adaptation or development? Commentary on "Immigration, acculturation and adaptation" by Berry, J. W. *Applied Psychology: An International Review, 46,* 52–55.

Schuh, S. (1991a). Psychische und familiäre Ursachen von Leistungsstörungen von italienischen Kindern und therapeutische Behandlungsmöglichkeiten [Psychological and familial causes of achievement disorders in Italian children and therapeutic treatment possibilities]. *Der Jugendpsychologe, 17,* 15–20.

Schuh, S. (1991b). Süditalienische Emigrantenfamilien in der Schweiz: Leben im Provisorium zwischen Vergangenheit und Zukunft [Southern Italian emigrant families in Switzerland: Living temporarily between past and future]. *Familiendynamik, 16,* 37–48.

Schwarzer, R., & Chung, R. (1996). Anticipating stress in the community: Worries about the future of Hong Kong. *Anxiety, Stress, and Coping, 9,* 163–178.

Schwarzer, R., & Jerusalem, M. (1990). Psychische und körperliche Gesundheit von Übersiedlern aus der DDR [Mental and physical health of emigrants from the German Democratic Republic]. *Psychmed, 2,* 108–110.

Segall, M. H., Dasen, P. R., Berry, J. W., & Poortinga, Y. H. (1999). *Human behavior in global perspective: An introduction to cross-cultural psychology* (2nd ed.). Boston: Allyn & Bacon.

Sorokin, P. A. (1925). American millionaires and multimillionaires. *Social Forces, 4,* 1–123.

Strassmann, B. I., & Clarke, A. L. (1998). Ecological constraints on marriage in rural Ireland. *Evolution and Human Behavior, 19,* 33–55.

Suzuki, P. T. (1981). Psychological problems of Turkish migrants in West Germany. *American Journal of Psychotherapy, 35,* 187–194.

Taft, D. R., & Robbins, R. (1955). *International migration.* New York: Ronald Press.

Taft, R. (1977). Coping with unfamiliar cultures. In N. Warren (Ed.), *Studies in cross-cultural psychology* (pp. 121–151). London: Academic Press.

Taft, R. (1986). Methodological considerations in the study of immigrants' adaptations in Australia. *Australian Journal of Psychology, 38,* 339–346.

Taft, R., & Doxzy, A. G. (1961–1962). The assimilation of intellectual refugees in Western Australia with special reference to Hungarians. *R. E. M. P. Bulletin, 9*(4) & *10*(1-2).

Thomae, H. (1988). *Das Individuum und seine Welt. Eine Persönlichkeitstheorie* [The individual and his/her world: A personality theory] (2nd ed.). Göttingen, Germany: Hogrefe.

Thomas, W. I., & Znaniecki, F. (1919–1920). *The Polish peasant in Europe and America* (5 vols.). Boston: Badger.

Triandis, H. C. (1994). *Culture and social behavior.* New York: McGraw-Hill.

Ward, C. (1996). Acculturation. In D. Landis & R. Bhagat (Eds.), *Handbook of intercultural training* (2nd ed., pp. 124–147). Newbury, CA: Sage.

Ward, C. (1997). Culture learning, acculturative stress, and psychopathology: Three perspectives on acculturation. *Applied Psychology: An International Review, 46,* 58–62.

Ward, C., & Kennedy, A. (1994). Acculturation strategies, psychological adjustment during cross-cultural transitions. *International Journal of Intercultural Relations, 18,* 329–343.

Ward, C., & Rana-Deuba, A. (1999). Acculturation and adaptation revisited. *Journal of Cross-Cultural Psychology, 30,* 422–442.

Watson, J. L. (Ed.). (1977). *Between two cultures: Migrants and minorities in Britain.* Oxford, England: Blackwell.

Werner, K. F. (1989). *Les origines (Avant l'an mil)* [The origin of France until the year 1000]. Paris: Fayard.

Witkin, H. A. (1965). Psychological differentiation and forms of pathology. *Journal of Abnormal Psychology, 70,* 317–336.

Zeul, M. (1994). Rückreise in die Vergangenheit. Zur Psychoanalyse spanischer Arbeitsemigrantinnen [Return to the past: On the psychoanalysis of Spanish female migrant workers]. *Psyche, 48,* 529–562.

Zheng, X., & Berry, J. W. (1991). Psychological adaptation of Chinese sojourners in Canada. *International Journal of Psychology, 26,* 451–470.

Zuckerman, M. (1979). *Sensation seeking: Beyond the optimal level of arousal.* Hillsdale, NJ: Erlbaum.

Zuckerman, M. (1994). *Behavioral expressions and biosocial bases of sensation seeking.* New York: Cambridge University Press.

3

The Hong Kong Immigrant Ethos on the Eve of the Handover in 1997

Bruce Bain and Agnes Yinling Yu

Because it is a rare event that speaks of the finer human achievements, the peaceful handover of sovereignty of land and people should occasion joy. In the case of the handover of Hong Kong from Great Britain to the People's Republic of China, however, there was joy for some, whereas others saw it as an opportunity for mischief making and political propaganda.

This chapter has a simple objective: To explore the ethos of Hong Kongers on the eve of the handover and to shed light on Hong Kong as a center of immigration and emigration.

History has decreed that for many Hong Kong is an immigrant way station, a revolving door to better things in Africa, America, Australia, Great Britain, Canada, Indonesia, and other nations around the world. The direction is always outward toward to the world, not inward toward China. After 2 millennia of experience, the revolving-door ethos of immigration into Hong Kong, with some staying, and some moving on to extraterritorial Hong Kongs around the world, is an integral part of the Hong Kong mind. It represents the bitter memories of Hong Kong's colonial past, the unified present with China, and the uncertain future as a special administrative region of China governed by the "one country, two systems, one citizenship" policy. It also reflects the pragmatic and entrepreneurial attitudes of most Hong Kongers–that Hong Kong is a "golden cow" to be milked to the last drop. Historically, Hong Kong had always been a way station for migration to different parts of the world for its inhabitants, particularly in times of economic or political turmoil. This chapter traces the pattern of migration from Hong Kong's distant past to the present. By exploring the forces which shaped the Hong Kongers' ethos, we will be better able to understand the immigrant mind.

Before presenting Hong Kong emigration patterns on the eve of its Handover, it behooves us briefly to describe the geography and making of Hong Kong. There are wonderfully learned volumes about the history of China and Hong Kong; especially noteworthy is Hsü (1995). Scholarly works of that impeccable order will flesh out many fascinating details and events noted in this brief overview.

GEOGRAPHY

Hong Kong is located in the Pearl River estuary, some 30 kilometers south of Guangzhou (Canton), and geographically located in the Xin'an District, Guangdong Province, China. It is made up of the main island of Hong Kong, 235 outlying islands, and a small spit of land called the New Territories, the promontory of which is Kowloon.

The overall landmass is 1,084 square kilometers, but only the island of Hong Kong, the New Territories, and the Kowloon Peninsula are heavily inhabited. The majority of the islands have no inhabitants at all. The 1997 population of the New Territories, Kowloon, and Hong Kong island is approximately 6.5 million, making for a density ratio of 116,000 persons per square kilometer in the urban areas, which represents one of the highest population density ratios in the world. Apart from the very wealthy who can afford a little more space in this unbelievably expensive real estate market, Hong Kongers live cheek-by-jowl in innumerable highrise apartment buildings, many "engineered" (rather than designed) and built in the 1960s and 1970s. The growing population required more land as resettlement area in the New Territories, claiming land that was once farmland. In the late 1900s, some outlying islands were developed to accommodate the more affluent and upscale lifestyle.

FROM YU TO MAO TSE-TUNG

Hong Kong has been inhabited since the Middle Neolithic period, ca. 3000 B.C.E. The original inhabitants were the Yu clans of southern China. Chinese chronicles indicate that the Yu and the Hong Kong regions were brought under central sovereignty about 220 B.C.E.

During this period, one bay on the island of Hong Kong, Tuen Mun, was used as the terminus of the Pearl River trading traffic. Tuen Mun Bay was also the original Chinese international trading port, with ships plying the seas to Southeast Asia, and as far away as India, Persia, and Egypt. The old trader docks and godowns are long gone, and today Tuen Mun is one of the many overcrowded working-class neighborhoods in Hong Kong.

By the time of the Tang (618–907 C.E.) and Song (960–1279 C.E.) dynasties, Hong Kong was established as an exporter of locally produced salt and incense. The population, estimated at less than 2,000 people, remained relatively small during these dynasties, probably because the inhabitants were constantly being raided by Chinese bandits by land and by Japanese, Korean, and Malaysian pirates by sea. The Hong Kongers' ethos of packing up and moving on a moment's notice has a long history.

A more stable Hong Kong community emerged during the Song dynasty, precipitated by large-scale Han Chinese migration to the Kowloon peninsula. Among these Cantonese-speaking people were Han Chinese families that settled in Hong Kong. These families were of the Tang, Hua, Lau, Ma, and Pang clans.

Reminiscent of the Native Indians in North, Central, and South America, remnants of these Punti (local) people are still around today, claiming special rights by virtue of being first on the land. To the revolving door mentality of Hong Kongers this appears as quaint, and to be ignored as quickly as possible.

Between the end of the Ming dynasty (ca. 1644) and the arrival of the first Britishers (ca. 1750), Hong Kong evolved from a small, self-regulating community of approximately 2,000 people, far from the Imperial Throne in Beijing, under regular attack by Chinese bandits and international pirates, to a substantial community of some 5,000 people.

A centuries-long trickle of migration into Hong Kong by the Hakka (boat) people augmented the Punti. These two ethnic groups made up the bulk of Hong Kong's population until 1949. Prompted by the People's Liberation Army, numerous people, most from Guangdong and some from Shanghai, "emigrated" to Hong Kong.

THE BRITISH GOD AND OPIUM

In the 17th to 19th centuries, "European colonialism" was not a dirty concept, at least not to the colonizers. The British colonial empire at its zenith was a mammoth enterprise, including Australia, Canada, India, and scores of smaller outposts around the world.

In the wake of the Asian missionary work of Francis Xavier, who became St. Francis of Jesuit fame, the Portuguese missionaries and traders were China's window on the "outer world of the barbarians." The Portuguese represent a warm spot in the Chinese collective memory, not only for their good educational works but also for what they did not do; namely, they did not bring the opium plague to China. A significant mark of Chinese affection, especially for a nation sometimes too proud of itself, was to name the old court language, Mandarin, after the Portuguese word *mandar*, meaning to rule. China's collective memory of the British, however, is very different.

As part of the British colonial enterprise, British religious missionaries and opium traders, sometimes supportive, sometimes antagonistic, one offering other-world spirits, the other offering this-world spirits, started arriving in Hong Kong in the 1750s. China was colonized by the Mongolian-Siberian Manchu-Ching Dynasty at the time.

For nearly a century there were many machinations and altercations between the British and the Manchus: one side trying to get their God and opium in and tea out of China and the other side trying to restrict the foreign God and especially British opium to the up-river city of Canton.

Based on a report of their "troubles" with the Chinese by the British opium traders, namely, the unwillingness of the Manchus to permit free trade in opium, a British expeditionary force was dispatched to Hong Kong in 1840, to "encourage" the Chinese to become free traders. The Chinese Army and Navy were no match for the Imperial British troops. The price the Manchus paid for peace was unrestricted British freedom to sell opium in China. To ensure its drug dealers security from Chinese law, the British also demanded and were ceded the island of Hong

Kong, on January 26, 1841.

UNTOLD TALES AND MENTAL HEALTH

It is crucial to have an understanding of 19th and 20th century British, Chinese, and world histories to recognize at least seven consequences of Hong Kong becoming Britain's economic crown jewel in East Asia:

- A monumental drug problem was foisted on China by Queen Victoria's government.

- The British Army, who were the 19th century "hit men" of the British drug dealers, set the standards for subsequent armies of drug thugs that plague the world today.

- The British legitimized a horribly cruel form of laissez-faire capitalism in East Asia, and the Chinese became fast adherents.

- The profits from the official British drug trade helped pay for Britain's worldwide colonial enterprise.

- An accounting of the official British profits, and the profits of British Hong and Chinese co-Hong private entrepreneur families remains to be presented.

- By their actions, the British and their Chinese co-Hong collaborators reduced a proud and productive people to a desiccated rabble under the curse of opium.

- To the Chinese, never keen to acknowledge participation of some of their own, Hong Kong represents a long-standing reminder of this British evil.

Much of the overt and covert acrimony surrounding the handover stemmed from the bitter memory of the devastation wrought upon China by the opium evil. What is obscured by this anguish is that that evil has to be understood in the terms of the times. To do otherwise is to use a standard of historical absolutism that is unwise.

It is not only irrational to eternally damn the British and their descendants, it is historically inaccurate. Chinese co-Hong families (prominent family associations based on business) were just as active collaborating in the drug trade. Inflicting the opium evil on one's own people is surely no less a crime. However, the descendants of the co-Hong families seem more praised than damned by today's worshipers in the temple of avarice.

To Mao's eternal credit, the opium dens in China were shut down, the drug dealers dispatched to any God of their choice, millions of addicts were reeducated, and the nation started to heal itself. Unfortunately, the drug dealers who escaped Mao's wrath moved on to do their evil in other countries. But that was not Mao's concern.

THE EARLY YEARS OF BRITISH RULE

Excluding the British garrison, in 1841 the population of Hong Kong was approximately 5,000, about 2,000 of whom were Hakka; about 2,800 were Punti; and the remainder were British traders, missionaries and their families, and the Parsee and Jewish merchants and their families.

Prompted by the rumor of work, however, Chinese peasants from Guangdong, mostly male, moved into Hong Kong. Because of this wave of immigrants, by 1844, the population had increased to approximately 20,000. Unfortunately, as is so often the case when human supply exceeds demand and there is no community or family support, many of these peasants, initially hoping for employment as laborers, became criminals of one stripe or another. In the mid-1840s, day-to-day conditions in Hong Kong were quite dangerous.

An unfortunate legacy of the 1840s is that Hong Kongers today still insist that the criminal elements among them are immigrants from China. Undeniably some of the traditional and contemporary criminal elements were and are immigrants from China. There exists also ample evidence, however, that Hong Kong has grown a fair number of its own villains. But in Hong Kong as elsewhere, when fact and fiction collide, fiction too often wins.

DARK HOLES

The xenophobic notion of "foreign devils" who are the cause of all misfortune, while hardly unique to China, nonetheless has a long history in that nation. Some 5,000 years ago, Chinese chronicles already wrote of the "need for eternal vigilance against foreigners."

One of the longest living myths among the Chinese is that they are the rightful rulers of the Middle Kingdom, whose manifest destiny is to civilize the barbarians, (i.e., everyone else). The T'aiping Rebellion (ca. 1851–1863) later served as a model for Mao's Cultural Revolution, with its anti–foreign devil overtones. Historical and contemporary attitudes toward Tibetans, Central Asians, Mongolians, and other minorities on the frontiers of China are a product of this Great-Wall-against-the-foreign-devils mentality. The future of this dark spot in the Chinese soul with regard to the numerous foreign devils in Hong Kong will be a test of China's willingness to exorcise its own cultural devils.

The background to the traditional non-Chinese population of Hong Kong is itself a fascinating tale. The T'aiping Rebellion brought a huge wave of refugees to Hong Kong. They were mostly Cantonese-speaking Chinese from Guangdong. Although a few were escaping China because of their role as collaborators with the British opium traders, most simply tried to escape the turmoil rampaging across China in the 1860s. Unlike the peasant immigrants of the 1840s, these refugees were of a wide range of social class, racial, and professional backgrounds. By 1863, they had swollen the Hong Kong population to approximately 120,000.

One little known consequence of the turmoil of the 1850s and early 1860s is that along with British opium traders, traders of other merchandise, missionary families, and a number of mostly Shanghai-based East Indian Parsee and Jewish families were among the refugees escaping to Hong Kong. They joined up with the already established Parsee and Jewish families in Hong Kong, making for a multiracial, multireligious legacy that continues to this day.

As is often the case in colonial contexts, reasonably harmonious social relations have existed regardless of race or religion. Moreover, following international trends, to the chagrin of some and the joy of others, interracial and inter-religious marriage became common in Hong Kong by the 1960s and 1970s.

Based on their collective experiences with geographically fixed and extraterritorial way stations, interracial marriage, bilingualism, international religions, revolving door immigration, and colonial administration Hong Kongers have evolved a unique way of life.

COOLIES AND GOLD MOUNTAIN

The biggest rotation of Hong Kong's revolving door came about during the last decades of the 19th century and the early decades of the 20th century. This was due to the turmoil in China brought on by the end the Manchu-Ching Dynasty.

This enormous wave of refugees, adventurers, and the dispossessed included mostly Cantonese-speakers from Guangdong. By 1930, Hong Kong's population had increased to approximately 900,000. Although the absolute number remained fairly constant during those decades, Hong Kong was little more than a waystation to other places for thousands who entered and left on the first available ship.

Over a 50-year period, from 1880 to 1930, approximately 1.5 million coolie laborers passed through Hong Kong. Some immigrated and emigrated as indentured laborers, others went as adventurers, and all were compelled by the siren call of the "Gold Mountain."

True to the genre of myth, it was never clear where the Gold Mountain was: in Africa, Australia, Canada, Central and South America, Japan, Korea, every country in Southeast Asia, the United States, or scores of smaller countries. Nonetheless, the myth seekers pursued the quest in search of fortune, though few found it.

The destiny of most was backbreaking manual labor on virtually every major construction project around the world in the pre–Great Depression years. The Suez and Panama Canals, the Canadian Pacific and Trans-Australian railways, the deep water harbors in Korea and Japan, the huge land reclamation projects in Central and South America, the highways up and down the West Coast of North America, and numerous other mammoth construction projects are a legacy of Hong Kong coolie labor. In addition, the thousands of large and small China-towns around the world, resembling extraterritorial Hong Kong's, are by-products of the wanderings of the coolie laborers of the 1880s to 1930s.

Because of illness or frustration with low pay and long hours of hard, dirty work, the coolies began to drop out of the no-gain labor game. Initially, they set up Chinese hand laundries, small grocery stores, or restaurants. By the pre–World War II years, some of these Chinatowns, including those in Amsterdam, Buenos Aires, Cape Town, Dar es Salaam, Havana, Honolulu, Jakarta, Johannesburg, Kuala Lumpur, London, Melbourne, Mexico City, Montreal, Port-of-Spain, New York, Panama, Perth, San Francisco, Seoul, Sydney, Toronto, Tokyo, Paris, Vancouver, and Victoria, became significant cultural enclaves.

There have been many changes in the size and purposes of these extraterritorial Hong Kongs over the years. The native-born ethnic Chinese in Canada and elsewhere, who were born after the 1960s, have frequently refused to live in the local Chinatown, preferring to integrate with the rest of the population. Following the pattern of immigrants everywhere, the next generations simply moved into other lifestyles, other enterprises, and the professions. Still, there remains a sense that, should something go wrong, or should one be a Chinese newcomer, Chinatown is where one goes to reconnect with one's essence.

During the 1880s to 1930s coolie labor was also used to reclaim what is now the Central District of Hong Kong. A number of other major construction projects also used coolie labor, although the pay and working conditions were usually no better than abroad. These coolies married locals and blended into the Hong Kong community.

THE HORROR OF HONG KONG

Peace and prosperity came to an abrupt halt in the 1930s. The Japanese invaded China in 1931, claiming Manchukuo (Manchuria) as their own. After 6 years of Mao Tse-tung versus Chiang Kai-shek turmoil, and Chiang and Mao versus the Japanese turmoil, the Japanese declared open war on China in 1937. Canton fell in 1938.

Two battalions of Canadian cannon fodder (the first author's uncle among them) were shipped to Hong Kong, arriving 3 weeks before the Japanese assault, on December 8, 1941. The Canadians were mostly raw recruits, serving in the Royal Rifles of Quebec and the Winnipeg Grenadiers. Canada's own experience as a British colony left some with a certain ambivalence about defending a part of Britain's colonial empire far from home and interest.

The Hong Kong militia, the small British garrison, and the Canadians nonetheless did their duty with valor. But they were no match for the well-trained, better armed, and numerically superior Imperial Japanese troops. They were forced to surrender on Christmas Day, in 1941.

The following 3 years and 8 months of Japanese occupation were a horror. One of the first acts of the Japanese was the mass deportation of some 100,000 Chinese Hong Kongers to work in the Japanese war industry. The working conditions rivaled the European Nazi slave labor camps for sadism and brutality. Many Hong Kongers were tortured or died at the hands of the Japanese.

The interned Canadian troops fared no better. Five hundred fifty Canadians died in battle or in prison camps or from being used as guinea pigs in drug warfare laboratories in Manchukuo. A statue of one of the Winnipeg Grenadiers, Sergeant Major John Osborne, VC, standing in Hong Kong Park, serves as a reminder of the Canadian sacrifice.

During this time, some Hong Kongers escaped to more secure areas in Guangdong (the second author's father among them). Attempts were made to bring food and medical supplies back to family and friends. But this too was a dangerous game, and many Hong Kongers died in futile attempts to avoid the Japanese troops. As in Korea, the Philippines, and Malaysia, the Japanese considered Hong Kong women to be "comfort women." Food was in short supply, medical treatment was virtually nonexistent, and life was exceedingly dangerous during these horrific years. Prior to Japanese occupation, the population of Hong

Kong was approximately 1.6 million. By the time the Japanese finally left, the population of Hong Kong was down to approximately 600,000.

Near the end of World War II in the Pacific and the start of the cold war, the British reclaimed Hong Kong on August 14, 1945. China had to wait another 52 years before counter claiming it for itself.

THE POSTWAR YEARS

During 1945 to 1949, the rate of immigration into Hong Kong exceeded that of the 1880–1930 period. A year and a half after the Japanese departure, the Hong Kong population was already approximately 1.85 million, well in excess of the prewar years. At the same time, during the immediate postwar years the number of those that moved on is estimated at 2.25 million. Some went to the Americas or Europe, a few went to the Philippines, and most went to various countries in Southeast Asia, everywhere joining up with previous generations of wandering Hong Kongers.

The postwar resident population of Hong Kong included those who had not left during the "horror years" of Japanese occupation; the British, Chinese, Jewish, and Parsee returnees; and Sikh and Moslem members of the British forces who were discharged in Hong Kong. But the largest group was represented by Chinese refugees escaping the rampages of the Mao versus Chiang civil war in China.

Much of this dramatic population increase was due to the British colonial administration's open-border policy. Anyone who crossed into Hong Kong was considered for right of domicile. This policy continued to 1949 when the border was closed. However, from 1949 to 1981, the cold war–motivated administration allowed that anyone who escaped from China and "touched base" in Hong Kong would be considered for right of domicile. The policy succeeded better than expected, with legal and illegal immigrants arriving daily during those years.

The Red Guard Cultural Revolution of the 1960s brought scores more to the colony. The Gang of Four turmoil of the late 1970s brought still more. In 1984, the Sino-British Joint Declaration on the future of Hong Kong was signed, and the "touched base" policy was rescinded. By then, however, the population had reached a phenomenal 5.8 million and the Hong Kong of present fame and notoriety had arrived.

FROM LION TO DRAGON

In the negotiated Sino-British Joint Declaration (signed on December 19, 1984), it was agreed that there would be no change in the way Hong Kong was governed under British rule, only that Hong Kong's sovereignty would change from Britain to China. As is often the case in the transfer of a sovereignty to its legitimate motherland, especially in cases where both parties have reason to remember the unsavory origins of the sovereignty being transferred, there seems more posturing than a genuine willingness to act with compassion for all. In the case of Hong Kong, there seemed little willingness to look at the Sino-British Joint Declaration as anything more than a document that each side had to sign to get on with their respective agendas.

From the time of its "gunboat diplomacy" acquisition in 1841, London-picked governors aided by London-picked advisers have ruled Hong Kong. This tradition of Hong Kong's being ruled by a nonelected chief executive aided by nonelected advisers suited Beijing's current political philosophy just fine. In 1991, some 151 years after its colonial acquisition of Hong Kong, for puzzling reasons (perhaps end-of-colonial-rule guilt or playing to domestic British politics), London allowed that some but not all members of a Hong Kong legislative council could be elected by universal suffrage. According to Beijing, this pseudoattempt at ballot-box democracy contravened both the Joint Declaration and the future Basic Law of Hong Kong, passed by the Seventh People's Congress in Beijing (Basic Law, 1990). London argued that the Basic Law applied only to posthandover Hong Kong, and the implementation of however limited a democratic process in Hong Kong was in agreement with the Joint Declaration. Beijing argued it was not.

HONG KONG SOCIETY ON THE EVE OF THE HANDOVER

Hong Kong's history in the 19th and 20th centuries has no doubt been deeply affected by Western involvement. It led to many changes in economic, social, and cultural policies, and when the handover to China took place, Hong Kong society had evolved unique patterns of adjustment in which family strategies of immigration and emigration played a central role.

Over the millennia Hong Kong has served as China's principal emigration entrepot to the world. By the 1990s, it also became an important commercial entrepot. Its traditional function, however, has been as a safety valve for waves of immigrants, refugees, and victims of seemingly endless turmoil and oppression in China. The tradition became one of using Hong Kong as a place for the family to stop off for a while and for some family members to move on to wherever opportunity beckoned. In this manner, over the centuries, Hong Kongers weaved many commercial, educational, family, and social threads into numerous communities around the world.

Paralleled only by the Jewish experience in modern history, Hong Kongers created geographically fixed and extraterritorial family communities in numerous Chinatowns around the world. With the new wealth among the Chinese Hong Kongers in recent years, they have also moved into upscale industrial, professional, and cultural enterprises around the world.

As it was on the eve of the British-Israel-Palestine handover in 1948, being a Hong Konger on the eve of the British-China-Hong Kong handover in 1997 was as much a state of mind as it was a geofamily reality. It is as true with Jews, Israelis, and extraterritorial Israelis as it is with Hong Kongers and Hong Kong and extraterritorial Hong Kongs that there is a real historical need for such geofamily arrangements. Under these auspices, national loyalties can sometimes be wrenching, but the alternative is psychological or even physical oblivion, and that sacrifice cannot be asked of anyone.

Hong Kong possesses a frenetic laissez-faire capitalist work ethic that has made it a modern international financial entrepot. For some, it is a temple of entrepreneurial success. As is the case everywhere, the working class more or less gets by. The middle class, aided by the ubiquitous underpaid and overworked Filipino maids, does very well financially. If need be, the middle class can easily move through the revolving door and live the good life in Canada or elsewhere.

Hong Kong has one of the world's best public and private transportation systems; an international communications network nonpareil; and a love of cuisine rivaled only by the European French. But everyday life in crowded Hong Kong is not for the faint of heart.

The Hong Kong that China reacquired July 1, 1997, has endemic problems, including massive industrial and automobile pollution, inadequate health and sanitation resources, rapidly declining educational standards, inadequate quality and quantity of housing, no minimum-wage legislation, obscene disparities of wealth and poverty, and constant pressure from legal and illegal immigrants for faster access to the many udders of Hong Kong's "golden cow." The post handover presence of the People's Liberation Army, with its reputation for corruption, is another potential problem of potent significance.

These problems are colored by Hong Kongers' jaded attitudes about Hong Kong. As long as they can make lots of money and be able to get themselves and their money out of Hong Kong before the golden cow dries up, Hong Kongers tolerate the problems. Any civic-minded authority that tries to raise taxes in an attempt to correct the problems is treated as the devil incarnate or is given "gifts" to encourage "clear thinking."

A potentially nasty human rights brouhaha is also in the offing concerning Hong Kongers of East Indian origins, such as the old Hong Kong Parsee and Jewish communities, and the more recent Muslim and Sikh communities. Many of these Hong Kongers are employed in commerce or the professions. Ironically, for what is basically a Chinese community, East Indian Parsees and Jews are among the very few whose roots in Hong Kong go back more than a generation or two.

Rights-of-domicile considerations being determined by China's national priorities could also impact expatriate British and other foreign-born Hong Kongers. Many in this latter group are employed in government and in universities. Some of the British expatriates have been in Hong Kong for decades.

For years, the Senior Common Room of the University of Hong Kong has resembled a British rumpus room in a colonial outpost of the empire. Some sentimental Brits even have a genuine affection for the place, perhaps motivated by generous salaries and working conditions they definitely would not enjoy in Britain.

Echoing the tortured emotions of racists everywhere, to some Chinese and Hong Kong zealots the presence of these non-Chinese foreigners is an anathema. Whether purposefully or not, this xenophobia is encouraged by China's supercharged policy of "one country, two systems, one citizenship." To the zealots, the popular slogan "Rule of Hong Kong by Hong Kongers" does not include people with names such as Daliwal, Cohen, or Robertson-Jones.

CHINESE OR HONG KONGERS?

Often missed in discussions about Hong Kong, including among the Chinese in the People's Republic of China (hereafter China), is the fact that there is a recognizable and vibrant Hong Kong culture. Each new wave of immigrants through the revolving door adds to the mores, but the essence has remained the same for centuries. Hong Kong is a very old community, with a history that extends back nearly 5,000 years and a way of life that is multilayered and complex.

Outsiders consider Hong Kong to be a Chinese community, but Hong Kongers see themselves as being very different from mainland China Chinese. This difference in cultural perception was captured vividly in a recent report by the Hong Kong Psychological Society. In its survey of 532 Hong Kongers, the researchers found that Hong Kongers believe China's Chinese to be "dirty, lazy, and dishonest" (Hong Kong Psychological Society, 1997).

Hong Kong culture is replete with reflective and colorful statements about the differences between Hong Kongers and China's Chinese, with the China Chinese typically being portrayed as rubes, thieves, or other things one does not say in polite company. Students of social history recognize archetypal prejudices about outsiders. Similar negative sentiments were spoken about European displaced persons, refugees, and Jews who, like Hong Kongers, for centuries had to migrate here, there, and everywhere. The China Chinese immigrants might take heart by noting that the same persons originally denigrated by the ignorant of North, Central, and South America went on to become comfortably integrated into their respective communities.

Given the historically tenuous nature of the Hong Kong experience, Hong Kongers have had a traditional need to be ready to flee, and money was necessary to survive the journey. Today, however, the middle- and especially the upper-class Hong Kongers have long since surpassed the need for emigration survival money. Today, avarice has become an ugly thread in the Hong Konger's web of geofamily arrangements.

The way of life for China's Chinese, on the other hand, is profoundly centered in a geographically fixed China, with a predominantly monoracial and monolingual population, predominantly indigenous religions, limited outside world contact, and an omnipresent and ominous cultural suspicion of foreigners. Hong Kongers and the China Chinese perceive the meaning of life through very different cultural spectacles, filtered by profound darkness on certain topics.

PROBLEM SOLVERS OR PART OF THE PROBLEM?

As a reflection of their own vision of the future of Hong Kong as a special administrative region of China, Hong Kong's chief executive designate and his advisers were chosen from Hong Kong's successful entrepreneurial class and other true believers in the "temple of avarice." Their mandate is clear: Continue the entrepreneurial success of Hong Kong. The danger is not that they will not, but that they will.

An indication of the extent of the reversal of principle in China of recent years is that Mao Tse-tung would have sent these same entrepreneurs to "reeducation camps." In contrast, the current China leadership hails them as heroes of the new revolution and as standard-bearers of China's new "capitalism with a Chinese character."

The rulers in Beijing, wise in the ways of authoritarian statecraft, wobbly in the ways of piranhaic entrepreneurship, may have welcomed back a piece of the motherland whose inhabitants are more than they bargained for. The problem is not that China will impose its brand of communism-corruption on Hong Kong but that Hong will impose its brand of laissez-faire-capitalism-corruption on China. What would Mao Tse-tung have said?

Yet this does not fully justify why so many people left Hong Kong just before the handover. It could have been due to the uncertainty of the future: What did China have in store for these people and what might be some of the outcomes of China's future policies?

HONG KONG NUMBERS

Despite modern methods of census taking, Hong Kong population figures are part head count, part informed guess. What is known with greater precision, however, is that between 1981, the year of the start of the negotiations between Britain and Hong Kong concerning the handover, and the end of 1996, 6 months before the handover, 503,800 Hong Kongers emigrated.

Between 1981 and 1996, 61% of all Hong Kong emigrants left for Canada, their most popular destination. Although the money to be made in Canada is, by Hong Kong standards, unimpressive, many Hong Kongers believe that the Canadian way of life is healthier for their families and children. It is North American without being American, and it is safe and comfortable. The winters are unattractive, but there are worse things, and Canada has a long and treasured relationship with Hong Kong.

The joint declaration wave includes the now famous hordes of Hong Kong "astronauts." These are the frequent-flyer Hong Kongers who, having acquired a foreign passport, leave their families in their adopted countries, and return to work in Hong Kong. They commute between Hong Kong and their adopted countries with a regularity that is second only to airline pilots.

Because some of these astronauts kept their Hong Kong identity cards, and they know Hong Kong ways, they can easily pass themselves off as resident Hong Kongers. Estimates are that approximately 400,000 native-born Hong Kongers now in possession of a Canadian or other foreign passport have returned to work in Hong Kong and may have been counted as Hong Kong residents. The questions of immediate concern to authorities are, How many included in the Joint Declaration wave intend to remain Canadians (or citizens of other countries), and how many intend to become Chinese citizens following the handover? A reasonable related technical question is, Why do Hong Kong authorities not know the specific number of those in the colony who hold foreign passports?

TO BE OR NOT TO BE

All Hong Kongers who acquired foreign passports had to give up their British national (overseas) passport. But in the mysterious ways of Hong Kong, they did not necessarily have to give up their Hong Kong identity cards.

China has repeatedly declared that citizens of China may not hold dual citizenship, and this includes residents of its Special Administrative Region of Hong Kong. China's often repeated position is that anyone who was born in Hong Kong and does not declare his or her foreign citizenship will be treated as a citizen of China. Such a prospect would cause palpitations among others, but Hong Kongers have a 2,000-year history of dealing with matters of migration and distant rulers. Not being keen to divulge their status to Chinese authorities until absolutely necessary, they remain Canadians while in Canada or nationals of other countries while in other countries, but count themselves in Hong Kong census administrations as Hong Kong residents. These problems continue to date and there does not seem to be an easy solution.

Authorities in China, Canada, and other countries wait with interest to know precisely who is one of theirs and who is a citizen of the new Hong Kong. The day of reckoning is coming soon for nationalists, intellectuals, academics, and Communist purists who rail against "bourgeois liberalism," colonialism, opium, vulgar laissez-faire capitalism, and neglect of open political process.

IMMIGRATION INTO HONG KONG
ON THE EVE OF THE HANDOVER

Hong Kong under China sovereignty officially is "one country, two systems"—capitalist in Hong Kong, but communist in the rest of the nation. There is grousing in China—among nationalists, intellectuals, academics, and communist purists who rail against "bourgeois liberalism"—about the need for different treatment for citizens of the same country. But this China-but-not-China, this wonderland on the southeast coast remains a prized immigration goal for the vast population of China.

Although Hong Kongers' feelings about a return to Chinese sovereignty were mixed, the feelings among China's Chinese were euphoric. Patriotic assertions such as "At last! A return of Hong Kong to the Motherland" were commonly heard in public in China. In private, however, talk frequently centered around beliefs that Hong Kong is a combination of Vancouver and Hollywood, with toilets and telephones that work, including a little spice provided by its long contact with the "foreign devils" and a standard of living that can only be dreamed about in contemporary China.

Getting to Hong Kong is the dream of many China Chinese today. Hong Kong is our own Gold Mountain, they say with envy and hope. As with many things in China, however, getting through the omnipresent cultural baggage and the notorious bureaucracy to Hong Kong is not for the faint of heart.

RACE

Under the Joint Declaration there are a number of regulations pertaining to immigration into Hong Kong. One of these China-sponsored regulations agreed to by the British speaks to one of the not-so-fine human achievements.

Continuing an odious practice of some millennia, in public documents and common practice, China equates "Chinese" with "race." Official immigration documents refer to those eligible for migration into Hong Kong as "Chinese nationals and former Hong Kong residents who are of the Chinese race." This clearly excludes former Hong Kong residents who are not of the Chinese "race." Should traditional practice prevail, it will exclude anyone not of the correct "race."

China's official statements about race, if contained in official documents of, for example Canada, would justly occasion outrage by decent people everywhere. Yet China continually gets away with such inanities.

Nonsensical notions of race from an uninformed past have no place in modern societies. The crude message sent to Chinese and non-Chinese alike does not augur well for self-understanding or for respectful regard of others.

TWO-WAY OR ONE-WAY VISAS?

Nationals of any nation, regardless of race, can apply for a two-way visa into Hong Kong; those of the correct nation or "race" also can apply for a one-way visa to Hong Kong. Those granted a two-way visa must return to their country of origin by the end of 90 days, whereas a one-way visa entitles its holders to remain in Hong Kong as permanent residents. The former are the most common; the latter are the most prized by the China Chinese.

Prior to the handover, the British colonial administration controlled who would or would not receive a two-way visa. China controlled who will and who will not receive a one-way visa. There were few restrictions on two-way visas. One applied, and if one could show a legitimate passport, a means of sustaining oneself while in Hong Kong, and a return ticket, these were granted rather expeditiously. One-way visas are another matter.

There were ongoing liaisons between Britain and China regarding one-way visa quotas: In 1979, the daily quota was 75; from November 1993 on, the daily quota was raised to 105; and in July 1995, the daily quota became 150. These quotas were always full, and the Hong Kong population is exploding exponentially. Today, one-way visas are based on the frequently changing policies on who should not receive such a visa from the Chinese administration.

On a fairly regular basis, the Hong Kong press carries stories about corruption among China's notorious government administrators. How much one has to pass under the table in order to get a one-way visa is a common topic. The truthfulness of many of these stories is moot. In the main, however, Hong Kongers simply nod their heads and acknowledge that China *is* the font of all corruption. Their own brand of corruption seems less serious to Hong Kongers.

HONG KONG'S CHANGING CHARACTER

The 1996 Hong Kong census reference moment was set at 3:00 at A.M. on March 15; at this point the population census estimate reached 6,016,974. This meant that between November 1993 and March 15, 1996, approximately 66,615 China Chinese immigrants moved into Hong Kong. Projections based on this census were that between November 1993 and June 1997, there would be 109,200 new Chinese immigrants from China moving into Hong Kong.

These figures do not include the 21,150 Vietnamese boat people refugees (referred to by the British and China authorities as "Vietnamese migrants"), or the 83,093 transients, or the 134,000 to 135,000 overseas Filipinos on work contracts, or the guesstimate of 100 to 1,000 illegal migrants from China, or the 130,000 children of Hong Kong parents now living in China that were eligible to rejoin their families after July 1.

Previous generations of immigrants used Hong Kong as part home and part way station to the world. Migration for previous generations was usually an uncomplicated matter. Following a perfunctory check by a foreign government, one got on a boat and went. But governments around the world today, for various internal and international reasons, have established well-defined standards and criteria for immigration.

Because those making up the latest wave of immigrants into Hong Kong have few skills that would make them attractive as prospective emigrants, they seem likely to remain permanent residents of Hong Kong for some time to come. As a result, the character of Hong Kong and its traditional relationship to the world will change, at least in the short run.

Where everyone would live, go to school, receive medical care, and all the other necessities of life is another worthy challenge facing the chief executive designate. Educating Hong Kongers to be more respectful and supportive of the immigrants may be an even more difficult challenge.

HUSBANDS, WIVES, AND CHILDREN

Among one group of Hong Kongers, mostly working-class or small entrepreneurial-class males with limited English and/or education, it is not unusual to have one's legal domicile in Hong Kong but work part time in Hong Kong and the other part in China. It is not uncommon for some in this group to find a wife in China. In some case it works out that the wife and children remain in China, or some of the children remain in Hong Kong while others live in China, with the wife residing in one place or the other. These convoluted family arrangements come about because the China wife can visit Hong Kong on a two-way visa to see her husband, have her baby in Hong Kong (thereby making it a legitimate citizen of Hong Kong), leave the baby with the Hong Kong husband, and return to China to try for a one-way visa to Hong Kong for herself. Of course, there also exist the inevitable cases of a wife in Hong Kong, another in China, and children in China and Hong Kong. Recent cases of wives visiting their husbands and finding an unknown second wife on the scene have resulted in scandal and the occasional husband felled with a bludgeon.

In recognition of the human problems faced by separated spouses and families, China has a daily quota within the overall one-way visa quota framework: Thirty are reserved for spouses of Hong Kong residents who have been separated for more than 10 years; 45 are reserved for children who have the right of abode in Hong Kong because one of their parents is Hong Kong born; the additional 75 are an open category, which may include applicants in either of the other two categories.

Between 1991 and 1996, the numbers in the different categories represent an interesting sociological reality: joining husbands, 90,786; joining wives, 6,467; joining parents, 109,669; others, 16,570. Forty-seven percent of all the new immigrants during this period were children joining their parents. These data also represent a reality about the status and/or desirability of spouses among Hong Kongers and the Chinese. For every Chinese husband joining a Hong Kong wife, 14 Chinese wives joined Hong Kong husbands.

Part of the answer to this marriage pattern is that these particular Hong Kong men are highly desirable to Chinese women. Another part is that these Hong Kong men are less desirable to Hong Kong women. Hong Kong women typically are better educated and, for traditional Hong Kong men, marrying a better-educated woman creates self-esteem problems.

In any event, for Hong Kong women, marrying beneath their educational status is a social taboo, and they tend to marry either Hong Kong men of equal or higher educational attainment, or they marry foreign husbands.

EDUCATION

A problem of major proportions is the education of the immigrant children. Education standards in China, apart from urban centers, are sadly low, especially in curriculum topics such as Chinese, foreign languages, science, civics, and world history. The self-fulfilling spiral of less educated Hong Kong men marrying even less educated Chinese women who produce children unprepared for a modern education adds to the problem of falling standards in Hong Kong education.

Hong Kongers, always quick to blame their ills on the immigrants from China, claim the falling standards in Hong Kong schools exist because of "those children." It has been our experience, however, that public confidence in the future has eroded since the signing of the Joint Declaration in 1984.

Education, more than any collective endeavor, is responsive to hopes or fears about the future. When the future is hopeful, minds soar, when it is bleak, minds stagnate.

EMIGRATION OUT OF HONG KONG
ON THE EVE OF THE HANDOVER

The data on immigration into Hong Kong are rather straightforward. They have unique characteristics, but they are simply one more wave into the entrance side of Hong Kong's revolving door. The data on emigration on the exit side toward the world, for all the reasons described above, are less transparent.

Christine Loh (1997), one of the elected representatives of the Hong Kong Legislative Council, prior to its dissolution, captured the ethos thus:

"Geographically, Hong Kong is a part of Mainland China. Legally, it is a British colony for another 100 days. Its population has been self-selected from waves of traders, refugees and immigrants, brought by ambition or to escape war, civil war and revolution." (p. 12)

Hong Kongers are a people hardened by the bitter truths of life in China. Reliable information is not given easily to anyone who might purposively or inadvertently pass it along to anyone who might use it against him or her. With these caveats, there are nonetheless some very good studies about the peripatetic Hong Kongers' plans for emigration. Especially noteworthy is the sociology-driven Hong Kong Transition Project (HKTP) and the psychology-driven Psychological Analysis of Transitional Hong Kong (PATH). Both these projects are centered in the University of Hong Kong.

HKTP Data

The majority of Hong Kongers today are second-generation immigrants or refugees from China. As with previous generations, these are the stay-behinds and the returnees from abroad who have already acquired a foreign passport. Given the general uncertainty, it is not surprising that, according to a recent poll by HKTP, "If living conditions should change for the worse following the Handover from British to Chinese rule, at least 45% of Hong Kongers would migrate" (Lo, 1997, p. 10). There is also evidence that they can migrate quickly.

Dr. Sonny Lo (1997), a University of Hong Kong sociologist, and one of HKTP's key investigators, further noted that (a) 53% have relatives living abroad with foreign right of abode, (b) 78% have relatives willing to help with immigration requirements, and (c) 25% have immediate family members abroad that will provide immediate and legitimate exit from Hong Kong.

Given that an estimated 400,000 Hong Kongers already have foreign passports, and an additional unknown number are seeking work-residency documents or passports in other countries, the specter of another mass emigration from Hong Kong looms large in the strategic plans of foreign governments and, one presumes, the chief executive designate and his advisers.

PATH Data

One of the PATH surveys involved a computer-selected randomized telephone poll of 600 Hong Kongers, every 4 months, starting January 1996. As part of a larger social identity survey, questions about immigration from Hong Kong were asked of adult Hong Kongers, male and female. For comparison purposes, only the January 1996 and January 1997 polls are cited in Table 3.1.

The PATH data revealed that in 1997, approximately 72% of Hong Kongers were Hong Kong born, 23% were China born, and 5% were born elsewhere. Not all born elsewhere are Westerners. However, it has traditionally been estimated that 5% of the international Hong Kong community were Westerners, suggesting that between 1990 and 1997, approximately 240,000 of the western community moved out of Hong Kong.

In one sense these are not profound data: they simply say there has been a demographic change in the ratio of Hong Kong– and Western–born people in Hong Kong. In another sense, however, they suggest that a by-product of the Joint Declaration was an increasing trend toward the Sinofication of Hong Kong. They also indicate, however, that the traditional demographic character of Hong Kong was changing.

Compared with the HKTP data, the PATH data also revealed much lower percentages of persons reporting having a "right of foreign abode" but similar percentages of "intent to emigrate" should the situation deteriorate after the handover.

Table 3.1
PATH Survey Data, 1996–1997

	Yes	No	Unsure	N
Do you have right of foreign abode?	110 (18.4%)	484 (81.1%)	3 (.5%)	597
Do you intend to emigrate?	120 (20.1%)	474 (79.4%)	3 (.5%)	597
	Hong Kong	China	Other	N
Respondent's birthplace	437	152	7	596

Survey Sample (N=600). Date conducted: January 11–13, 1996.

	Yes	No	Unsure	N/A	N
Do you have right of foreign abode?	128	506	3		
Do you intend to emigrate?	128 (27%)	425 (66.8%)	39 (6.1%)	128	636–128 =508
	Hong Kong	China	Other	N	
Respondent's birthplace	458 (72.2%)	146 (23%)	30 (4.7%)	634	

Survey Sample (N=638). Date conducted: January 9–11, 1997.

On the one hand, the PATH data might have suggested to the chief executive designate that he could take heart from the lower figures about right of foreign abode. He also might have been reassured by the PATH data which suggested that from January 1996 to January 1997, the percentage of those not intending to emigrate increased from 60.12% to 83.7% and that the percentage of those being uncertain increased from 30% to 39%. On the other hand, the chief executive designate likely knew that there are data and there are Hong Kong China realities.

Along with people of goodwill everywhere, we wish Hong Kong well as it takes its first steps as a part of the motherland. The path will not be easy. Which paths the new rulers will take, which paths Beijing will allow them to take, and how skillful they will be in continuing the commercial dynamism left by the British while solving the raft of social, environmental, and attitudinal problems left by the British will be a worthy challenge. Several years after the handover, they are still regular rumblings from the Hong Kong populace whenever they deem that their rights to their 50 years of "one country, two systems" have been violated. The Chinese government and the Special Administrative Region of Hong Kong are learning to adjust to each other's realities, with the latter in a more appeasing mode than the former.

Hong Kong will no doubt have to reinvent itself under vastly different historical conditions. "One country, two systems" may seem a sensible accommodation to the realities of the moment, but it has to be tested in concert with a contemporary China which has its own historical contradictions.

As psychologists and educators with years of experience in the Chinese and Hong Kong mind, we offer suggestions that might help the process: Cease the frenetic worship of Mammon (avarice is a destructive moral guide, especially for children); relegate self-aggrandizing notions of race and "foreign devils" to the ash can of history (even Confucius knew that "we are all brothers in the same sea"); *guangxi* is a healthy reminder of interpersonal obligations and mutual respect (but let it not blind leaders to the need for openness in collective endeavors). Riding off, like Lao-tse into the Western Mountains on a water buffalo is no answer. But finding your own way with dignity for everyone is.

No matter in what circumstances the Hong Kongers will find themselves, in whatever parts of the world, their pragmatic knack of being a chameleon will forever remain, through centuries of honing their adaptation skills for their survival. They have been known to overcome changes and/or calamities, whether they be familial, social, economic or political.

REFERENCES

The Basic Law of the Hong Kong Special Administrative Region of the People's Republic of China. (1990, April 4). Beijing, China: Seventh People's Congress. Beijing.

Chan, J. (1995). Hong Kong. In G. Anderson (Ed.), *Worldwide state of the family* (pp. 75–78). Seoul, South Korea: Professor's World Peace Academy.

Hsü, I. (1995). *The rise of modern China*. Oxford, England: Oxford University

Press.

Lo, S. (1997, March). Golden sunset, red sunrise: Hong Kong public attitudes in transition to PRC rule. *The Hong Kong Transition Project.*

Loh, C. (1997, March 17). Inevitable change leads to consider the environment. *South China Morning Post,* p. 12.

Hong Kong Paychological Society. (1997, March). *Hong Kongers' attitudes to new immigrants from China. Reports of the Hong Kong Psychological Society* [in Chinese]. Hong Kong: Author.

The Sino-British Joint Declaration. (1984). Hong Kong: Joint Publishers (HK).

II

The Western Hemisphere

4

Immigration to the United States: The Dream and the Reality

Florence L. Denmark, Khaya N. Eisenberg, Erica I. Heitner, and Nicola A. Holder

This chapter describes the migrant experience in the United States. Our discussion is primarily focused on immigration, as many more people move to the United States from other countries than do emigrate. For instance, data from 1990 indicate that more than 1.5 million foreigners legally immigrated to the United States. Furthermore, an estimated 275,000 to 300,000 more foreigners enter the United States annually without legal documentation. These numbers can be compared to the estimated 195,000 who return to their homelands or who emigrate elsewhere every year (Labowitz, 1996).

Although immigrants come to the United States from nearly every country, our focus is on three broad clusters of immigrants: Hispanics, Asians, and Blacks. We have chosen to address these three groups as 2000 census data indicated that migrants to the United States are increasingly and overwhelming non-European. Whereas Hispanics, Asians, and Blacks accounted for a mere 6% of the immigrant population at the beginning of the 20th century, and approximately 30% of immigrants at midcentury, they accounted for approximately 80% of immigrants documented in the United States during the later half of the 1990s (Jerding, 1997). It is expected that these percentages will continue to increase. These groups' specific countries of origin, acculturation, and social and economic consequences of immigration are enumerated and discussed.

A BRIEF HISTORY OF U.S. IMMIGRATION

The first *documented* wave of immigration to the United States, known as the "Old Immigration," took place between 1820 and 1880. The majority of this group originated in northwestern Europe, many hailing from Ireland (see Chapter 5). It is difficult to accurately assess the numbers of immigrants before 1820, because the federal government did not require that ships' passengers be counted (Shenton, 1990).

Between 1880 and 1924 almost 27 million European immigrants entered the United States. This first wave of "New Immigrants" came mostly from Russia, Austro-Hungary, and Italy, and was drawn into the economy's burgeoning manufacturing sector. At this point, debates within Congress over these immigrants' assimilation intensified, culminating in anti-immigration regulation and quotas (Shenton, 1990).

Following a lull from 1925 through 1945, legal immigration to the United States has been on the rise (Bean, Cushing, Haynes, & Van Hook, 1997). Fifteen million immigrants have legally entered the United States since 1960, approximately half during the decade of the 1980s (U.S. Department of Justice, 1991). The United States admitted 1.5 million immigrants in 1990 alone, surpassing the previous 1907 record high of approximately 1.3 million. Over the years, sources of immigrants have shifted from Europe to Latin America and Asia (Bean et al., 1997; Donato, 1994). Today, a significant number of those Europeans who migrate do so seeking economic and political refuge: for instance, the Irish, citizens of the former Soviet Union, and as of 1999, thousands from Kosovo in the Yugoslav Republic.

Since the 1960s and 1970s, illegal migrants have constituted another major flow into the country (Bean et al., 1997). Estimates hold that approximately 13% of the immigrant population reside in the United States without documentation; about 300,000 enter the United States illegally every year (The National Immigration Forum, 1994). Although the racial/ethnic distribution of illegal immigrants is not known with the same degree of certainty as that of legal immigrants, the available information indicates that, like contemporary legal migrants, the group consists mainly of Asian and Latin American natives (Warren, 1990, 1992). The vast majority of undocumented migrants originate in Mexico and enter at the U.S.-Mexico border, although many have also come from Central America in recent years (Bean, Passel, & Edmonston, 1990).

Anti-immigrant sentiments have been on the rise over the past 3 decades, especially as Americans feel increasingly threatened by the influx of workers into a tight job market (Binder, Polinard, & Wrinkle, 1997; Donato, 1994). The debate over immigration policies has intensified recently, fueled by dissatisfaction with economic decline, the failings of the welfare state, and distress about local cultural identities (Suárez-Orozco, 1996). Legislation passed in the late 1980s and 1990s attempted to check the movement of illegal immigrants into the United States and increase the number of legal, high-skilled immigrants crossing American borders (Donato, 1994). For example, Proposition 187, passed in California in November 1994, aims to exclude approximately 300,000 undocumented immigrant children from public elementary and high schools (Suárez-Orozco, 1996). Mexicans in particular appear to be targeted by these restrictions.

American attitudes toward immigrants have shifted more subtly as well. Although immigrants were originally expected to assimilate into the proverbial "melting pot," ethnic pride and multiculturalism have since influenced a model of "cultural pluralism." Miller (1998) described an assimilation crisis in which nativists argue that immigrants are incapable of assimilating and multiculturalists insist that assimilation is unnecessary. According to Miller, public policy reflects this confusion by actively inhibiting immigrants' Americanization with bilingual education and the possibility of eliminating the mandatory American history and government test as part of the naturalization process. He urged Americans to rethink these trends and provide immigrants with the opportunity to assimilate and become full-fledged Americans. However, the immigrant's internal experience may present an even greater obstacle to assimilation.

HISPANIC AMERICANS

Overview

At present, approximately 20 million Hispanics live in the United States, where they represent the fastest growing minority group (Bohon, Santos, Sanchez-Sosa, & Singer, 1994). Also called Latinos, this group accounted for 20% of the U.S. population in 1990 (U.S. Bureau of the Census, 1990). Latinos' distribution by national origin as of 1990 is as follows: 63% Mexican, 11% Puerto Rican, 5% Cuban, 14% Central and South American, and 7% "other" Hispanics (U.S. Bureau of the Census, 1991).

Demographically, Mexicans, Puerto Ricans, Central Americans, and South Americans tend to be younger (median = 24–28 years old) than Cubans (median = 39 years old) and "other" Hispanics (median = 31 years old). Cubans have the highest rate of being married (62%) and Puerto Ricans the lowest (51%). However, Puerto Ricans' rate of single female-headed families (43%) is dramatically higher than that of Cubans and Mexican (19%), other Hispanics (27%), and Central and South Americans (26%). Cuban families tend to be smaller (median = 2.81 persons) than Puerto Rican families (median = 3.37 persons), Central and South American families (median = 3.81 persons), and Mexican families (median = 4.06 persons) (Malgady, 1994).

Educationally, Cubans (61%), Central and South Americans (60%), and other Hispanics (71%) have the greatest likelihood of completing high school or above; Mexicans (44%) and Puerto Ricans (58%) are least likely to do so. All of these rates are well below the non-Hispanic rate. The unemployment rate for Mexicans and Puerto Ricans runs 4% higher than the rate for non-Hispanics, Cubans, and other Hispanics (Malgady, 1994).

In comparison with non-Hispanic males, only Cubans are as likely to be engaged in management and professional jobs. The remaining Hispanic groups tend to work as operators, fabricators, and laborers. Hispanic women, on the other hand (with the exception of Central and South American women who tend to work in service occupations), usually work in technical, sales, and administrative support positions at rates comparable to non-Hispanic women (U.S. Bureau of the Census, 1991).

For all Hispanic groups, median household income is exceeded by that of non-Hispanic households. Cuban and other Hispanic median household incomes are the highest, followed by Central and South Americans, Mexicans, and finally Puerto Ricans. The greater apparent poverty of Puerto Rican households is a likely function of their greater tendency to have single female-headed households (Malgady, 1994).

In summary, Cubans are the oldest, most educated, and best off financially; their families are smallest and least likely to be headed by a female. Puerto Ricans and Mexicans are the youngest, least educated, worst off financially, and they tend to have the largest families. Puerto Rican families are most likely to be headed by a single female (Malgady, 1994).

Acculturation is a difficult process for many Hispanic immigrants with ramifications for their first-generation American children. While Mexican immigrants struggle to integrate America into their identities, first-generation Mexican Americans appear to experience more difficulty with their Mexican heritage (Hurtado, Gurin, & Peng, 1994). Language conflicts are a problem for both U.S.-born and foreign-born Hispanic adolescents (Vega, Khoury, Zimmerman, Gil, & Warheit, 1995). U.S.-born Hispanic teenaged boys also experience acculturative strains and low family pride, culminating in low self-esteem (Gil, Vega, & Dimas, 1994). Girls acculturate more slowly than do boys but faster than their parents (Vega et al., 1995).

Difficulties with acculturation may explain, at least in part, findings that raise the question of Latin American immigrants' increased susceptibility to mental illness (Padilla, Cervantes, Maldonado, & Garcia, 1988; Rogler, Cortes, & Malgady, 1991; Salgado de Snyder, Cervantes, & Padilla, 1990). Hispanic adolescents experience many stressors that are likely to have a negative impact on their self-esteem and general mental health (Gil et al., 1994; Vega et al., 1995).

Mexican Immigrants

Mexican immigration to the United States has been divided into three waves. The first large wave took place between 1942 and 1964, when a U.S.-sponsored temporary worker program created opportunities for Mexican men seeking agricultural employment. The end of this program saw the beginning of a second wave, in which Mexicans who were now legal citizens sponsored their relatives for entry, whereas other Mexicans entered illegally. The third wave began in the late 1970s, consisting of women without children and men and women entering on a first trip without legal documents (Donato, 1994). However, some Mexicans in the United States are actually not immigrants, but were living in U.S. territory formerly in Mexican hands at the time of the U.S.-Mexican War of 1848 (Hurtado et al., 1994).

Four generations may be delineated among Mexican immigrants: the Creation Generation (1848–1900), whose cultural ties with their conationalists were severed; the Migrant Generation (1900–1942), who escaped Mexico's political turbulence and economic problems; the Mexican American Generation (1942–1966), whose participation in World War II and in the economic boom after the war increased their allegiance to the United States; and the Chicano Generation, or first-generation Americans (1966 to the present), which is the most successful group of the four, yet criticized their parents' loyalty to the United States and created their own identity, neither Mexican nor American (cited in Hurtado et al., 1994).

An increasing number of Mexican and Central American immigrants are undocumented because they arrive illegally, either with fraudulent documents or none at all (Donato, 1994). These individuals are often attempting to escape economic difficulties and political upheaval in their home countries, and may choose to stay temporarily or permanently. Many of these immigrants perceive themselves as part of the American community and intend to integrate as long-term settlers. Those who do not perceive themselves as part of the community in which they live express less desire to reside permanently in the United States (Chavez, 1994). Clearly, one's sense of belonging to (or isolation from) a group can influence important decisions as to the permanence of one's stay, a fact which may pertain to immigrants from other countries as well as Mexicans.

In Mexico, especially among the rural poor, illiteracy and minimal education remain high. The majority of Mexican immigrants to the United States have been from poorer, often rural areas. These immigrants often come to seek a better life or adventure; imbued with the work ethic, they do not rely on government programs and are law abiding (Martinez, 1993).

Many Mexican women who migrate to the United States do so as dependents in male-headed family units. This movement is involuntary, as they are frequently forced by the male head of the household to migrate. However, an increasing number of single women from Mexico migrate alone, seeking work and improvement opportunities. These women, migrating independently, are doing so voluntarily. Voluntary immigrants tend to be more receptive to the new culture, more eager to learn a new language, and have a more positive attitude in general toward the new country. Involuntary immigrants, in contrast, often resent being forced to migrate to an unfamiliar country and are homesick for their original communities (Salgado de Snyder, 1994).

Hovey (2000) found that Mexican immigrants in general experience stressors related to acculturation, social conditions (e.g., overcrowding, unemployment, discrimination, undocumented status, lack of health services, etc.). Mexican women in particular experience loneliness and health concerns, especially regarding pregnancy and childbirth. Those who are undocumented fear deportation. In addition, difficulty with the English language impedes many Mexican immigrant women from exercising their traditional gender role duties such as doing laundry, shopping, and preparing food economically. Those who are employed may experience marital conflict if they earn more than their spouses (Salgado de Snyder, 1994).

Educationally, Mexican American children tend to score lower on IQ tests given in English, which is often attributed to language barriers, impoverished educational opportunities, and/or cultural values which do not emphasize academic achievement. The mean level of education for Mexican Americans remains considerably below that of Anglos (8 vs. 12 years), and the dropout rate among school children may be as high as 40%. Bilingual education as a means of compensating for the language barrier remains a controversial issue (Martinez, 1993).

Of the largest eight contemporary immigrant groups, Mexicans (along with

Cambodians) are the most likely to become manual laborers. They have the lowest percentage of professionals and managers. People of Mexican descent dwell mostly in Texas and California (Council on Scientific Affairs, American Medical Association, 1991). Mexicans settle primarily in four cities (Los Angeles, Chicago, El Paso, and San Diego), entering areas with some of the most densely populated ethnic communities in the United States (Hurtado et al., 1994). This reflects a general trend of immigrants' choosing to settle in "binational" or "transnational" communities (Chavez, 1994).

Within the Mexican family structure, the father most often holds a position of unquestioned supremacy, whereas the mother sacrifices herself for the family. Young boys are raised to be aggressive and girls submissive. Maternal figures are idealized. These generalizations, albeit oversimplified and having many exceptions, should not be dismissed out of hand. In spite of modernization and acculturation, the tendencies described above are commonly found in recently arrived immigrant families and, if nothing else, may result in intergenerational conflict (Martinez, 1993).

Puerto Rican Immigrants

The Puerto Rican presence in the United States dates back prior to the Spanish-American War. By 1910, one third of the burgeoning Puerto Rican population had settled in New York City. During World War I and the 1920s, more Puerto Ricans entered seeking employment. Following a lull during the Great Depression and World War II, Puerto Rican migration levels reached a peak in the 1950s (Canino & Canino, 1993). Factors thought to influence Puerto Rican migration include the population increase on the island, Puerto Rico's surplus labor force, economic hardship motivating the search for better opportunities, freedom to migrate without legal or political restrictions, and the easy availability of transportation (Rodriguez, 1989).

Puerto Rican females finish an average of 9.7 years of school, the lowest educational attainment level among Hispanic subgroups. Only a little over one third of Puerto Rican males graduate from high school and only 13.3% attend college. This is in contrast with other Hispanic males, almost half of whom graduate from high school and almost a quarter of whom attend college (Canino & Canino, 1993).

Economically, Puerto Ricans have fared less well than their Hispanic counterparts. Poor representation of Puerto Ricans in the labor force is indicated by the relatively large numbers receiving public assistance receipt, almost double that of other Hispanic households (Canino & Canino, 1993). In New York City, home to a large percentage of Puerto Ricans immigrants, they have been employed in the most vulnerable segments of the manufacturing sectors: the durable goods and the garment industries. As a result of their employment vulnerability, Puerto Ricans have been severely affected by the New York City fiscal crisis, credentialism, and the federal government's reduction of social spending (Rodriguez, 1989).

Socioculturally, Puerto Ricans value several traits, including: *dignidad/*

respeto, or the dignity of an individual and respect for those deserving of it; *machismo,* or male superiority and responsibility for the welfare and honor of the family; *marianismo,* or female spiritual superiority and ability to endure suffering better than men; *verguenza* and *orgullo,* or shame and pride; *personalismo,* or the need to relate to people rather than institutions; and *fatalismo,* or fatalism (Canino & Canino, 1993; Christensen, 1979). Puerto Ricans also tend to emphasize family needs over those of the individual (Ramos-McKay, Comas-Diaz, & Rivera, 1988) and to display a tremendous love and tolerance for children (Christensen, 1979).

Puerto Rican women bear a unique burden in that the myth of the strong male authority figure often conflicts with the reality of a female provider as the only stable adult force in single-parent families. Puerto Rican women who are rigidly entrenched in traditional values and are poorly acculturated experience more conflict and maladjustment and may display symptoms such as aggression, hostility, and low self-esteem (Canino & Canino, 1993; Torres-Matrullo, 1976).

Cuban Immigrants

Historically, Cubans have tended to migrate to the United States as a result of political and economic factors. Prior to 1959 and the advent of Fidel Castro, nearly 200,000 Cubans settled in the United States. This group consisted of unskilled workers from rural areas; professionals, particularly from the health care sector; and workers, mostly from the tobacco industry. All three groups had difficulty finding employment and improving their socioeconomic condition (Ruiz, 1994).

Cuban immigration increased dramatically in the 1960s as a result of the political and economic changes wrought by Castro. The wave of Cuban migration from 1959 until the present comprised mainly (a) those who fled Cuba in the early 1960s, hoping to return quickly to the island; (b) those who left shortly after the Bay of Pigs invasion, fearing political prosecution; (c) those who migrated with the goal of improving their socioeconomic status, and (d) those who were pushed out during the "Mariel" exodus, when Castro opened the gates of the Peruvian embassy in Havana to those who were dissatisfied with the Communist regime (Ruiz, 1994).

Overall, Cuban Americans' average educational attainment levels exceed those of Mexicans, Puerto Ricans, Central Americans, and Dominicans but are exceeded by those of South Americans and the non-Hispanic population. Second-generation Cubans, however, display a greater tendency to finish high school and continue their education beyond their high school diploma than do their first-generation counterparts. This suggests a marked level of polarization between the two generations (Hill & Moreno, 1996). Economically, Cuban Americans tend to fare better than other Hispanic groups while lagging behind Anglos (Hill & Moreno, 1996).

Socioculturally, Cubans have developed a strong ethnic image. Cuban communities in Miami ("Little Havana"); Union City, New Jersey; and Washington Heights, New York, have provided supportive environments for ethnic identification, cultural reinforcement, and social integration. In addition to a strong sense of Cuban identity and ethnic awareness, Cuban migrants tend to have high levels of education, occupational skills, and motivation for success as well as good support systems within their communities and neighborhoods (Ruiz, 1994).

The Cuban family tradition is founded upon the ever-present values of love, dignity, and respect. Despite the fact that these values present a sharp contrast to Anglo cultural traditions which focus on economic success and autonomy, mutual respect and frequent contact between Cubans and Anglos have led to the successful integration of Cuban immigrants. Although a strong extended family network system frequently exists among Cuban Americans, socioeconomic improvements and assimilation have led to the emergence of the nuclear family system among Cuban Americans (Ruiz, 1994).

ASIAN IMMIGRANTS

Asians constitute the fastest growing minority group in the United States. The Asian population in the United States increased by 108% in the decade from 1980 to 1990, rising from 3.5 million to 7.3 million (Exter, 1992). The decade from 1970 to 1980 witnessed an increase of 143% in the Asian minority. High rates of immigration and above-average fertility are cited as the main reasons underlying this Asian population surge. During this decade over 2 million immigrants arrived from Asia. It is estimated that by the year 2025 the population of the United States will be 12% Asian (Cummins, 1998).

The history of Asian immigration to the United States dates back to the mid-19th century with the arrival of large numbers of Chinese men hoping to capitalize on the Gold Rush in California. This influx of Asians was the first wave of voluntary immigration. Subsequent groups of Asian immigrants were predominantly male because they were brought over as laborers while women tended to stay behind in their native countries as homemakers. Legal restrictions also precluded the immigration of females. Large numbers of Asians immigrated after the passage of the Immigration Act in 1965, more formally named the Hart-Cellar Act, which lifted quotas on those permitted entrance to the United States (Wieder, 1995).

In recent years immigrants have arrived to the United States from every Asian nation. For example, Asian immigrants come from China, Japan, Korea, India, Micronesia, Melanesia, Polynesia, the Philippines, Vietnam, and many more countries. It is impossible to discuss Asian immigration as a singular enterprise because Asians are an extremely diverse group of individuals. Patterns of immigration vary for each specific group of Asians; however, all Asians share the common bond of being subject to the same laws. Asian immigration to the United States was restricted in 1924 with the passage of the National Origins Quota system. This law, which mandated that only small numbers of people could enter the United States from each individual country, was abolished in 1965 by the new Immigration Act. This act served to lift quotas based on national origin. After 1965 there were no limits placed on immigrants entering the

United States and Asians were granted open access. Although patterns of Asian immigration have all been heavily shaped by U.S. legislation, each nation has its own unique immigration history. The scope of this chapter does not permit a thorough discussion of immigrants from each unique Asian country; however, the four Asian countries from which most immigrants to the United States originate will be considered.

Philippine Immigrants

Immigrants to the United States from the Philippines constitute the largest group of immigrants from an Asian nation and the second largest group of immigrants to the United States worldwide. In 1996 alone, 55,876 immigrants from the Philippines entered the United States.

The first wave of Filipino immigration began in 1910. At the commencement of the Spanish-American War, the Philippines became the property of the United States. However, Filipinos were not considered U.S. citizens. Filipinos were in a unique position as inhabitants of an Asian nation that was technically territory of the United States. These circumstances permitted Filipinos open entry to migrate to the United States, which other Asians did not enjoy. Filipinos initially settled in Hawaii before moving to the mainland United States where they worked primarily as farmers. Filipinos like other Asian immigrants faced racism and discrimination, as White Americans feared competition in the job market. Legally, Filipinos' access to the United States could not be restricted under the Immigration Act of 1924. To prevent the continued mass immigration of Filipinos to the United States the Philippines were granted independence under the Tydings-McDuffie Act passed in 1934. The Philippines became a commonwealth of the United States and Filipino citizens became subject to immigration quotas.

Many Filipina immigrants arrived in the United States as the wives of U.S. military men. Their assimilation process is fraught with obstacles related to their abrupt relocation and the fallout from their war-related experiences. Language barriers, culture shock, social isolation, racism, and psychological trauma including posttraumatic stress disorder affected their capacity to transition to life in the United States (Bradshaw, 1994). Second-generation Filipinos have been noted to experience conflicts arising from strong family ties of the culture (Wolf, 1997).

Indian Immigrants

According to U.S. statistics compiled by the Immigration and Naturalization Service, individuals originally born in India represent the second largest group of Asian immigrants to the United States, with 44,859 immigrants arriving in 1996 alone (U.S. Bureau of the Census, 1997).

Geographically, India is located on the continent of Asia; however, individuals born in India are not easily grouped into the same category as other Asians. Although all Asian groups differ in terms of their language, physical appearance, cultural values, and a myriad of other distinguishing attributes, Indians seem to differ the most drastically from their Asian cohorts and are frequently overlooked in discussions of Asian immigrants. Simply stated, Indians do not "resemble" the stereotypical portrait of other Asians. Indians' ethnic and phenotypic divergence from their Asian counterparts has contributed to their unique history of immigration to the United States.

Indian immigration to the United States was sparse prior to the 1960s. The first major wave of Indian immigration was instigated by the passage of the 1965 amendment to the Immigration and Naturalization Act that lifted immigration quotas and loosened restrictions. During this time Asian Indians voluntarily migrated to the U.S. seeking financial opportunities and hoping to pursue higher education. Professional and skilled workers were admitted to the United States in preference categories (Cordasco, 1990). Hence, this group of immigrants was mostly made up of educated young adults from the upper and middle socioeconomic classes. Typically, Indian immigrants had already attained postgraduate degrees in India in fields such as medicine or engineering (Jayakar, 1994). Their elite educational status may have afforded these immigrants an easier time breaking into the labor force in America; however, many immigrants battling with discrimination had no choice but to take jobs much lower than their level of training and ability dictated. In addition, Indians were often disenchanted to realize that their credentials obtained in India were not acknowledged in the United States (Mehta, 1998).

The majority of female immigrants came over to the United States as the wives and daughters of male immigrants. In India, the cultural practice of arranged marriage is very common, and highly educated women made the most desirable candidates for these unions. Thus, many of the women who migrated to the United States with their husbands were also highly educated and in a favorable position to join the U.S. labor force upon arrival. The advanced educational status of Asian Indian women has facilitated their ability to secure positions in teaching, accounting, medicine, social work, administration, and business (Jayakar, 1994).

As a result of their professional success, Asian Indians have enjoyed financial prosperity in the United States. Data from the 1980 census rank Asian Indians as being recipients of the second highest median household income among all ethnic groups (Cordasco, 1990). Asian Indians have settled in affluent suburbs located in metropolitan areas all over the country, including New York, New Jersey, California, Illinois, and Texas.

Immigrants from India are usually proficient in English skills upon arrival to the United States because the majority of academic instruction in India is conducted in English. Prior English language fluency has proven extremely beneficial in easing Indian assimilation to American culture. More specifically, English fluency has facilitated Indian immigrants' entry into the work force in the United States (Jayakar, 1994).

The mental health status of first generation Indian immigrants was investigated in a study by Mehta (1998). Results indicated that traditional demographic variables such as age of immigration, sex, and skin color, which were previously assumed to influence psychological health of immigrants, did not affect Indian immigrants' well-being. Indian immigrants' continued usage of their native Indian language at home is not associated with reduced mental health status as long as they speak English outside of the home (Mehta, 1998).

Two facets of acculturation were linked to psychological adjustment: perception of acceptance by the host culture and cultural orientation. Indian immigrants who subjectively experienced acceptance by their peers in America reported lower levels of psychological distress and acculturative stress. Simply stated, Asian Indian immigrants to the United States need to feel accepted by Americans in order to feel good about themselves. Unfortunately, one area in which Indian immigrants are apt to feel unwelcome is at the workplace. The high educational status and solid professional training of Indian immigrants can be perceived as threatening to Americans and competition for jobs fuels hostile cultural relations.

Cultural orientation refers to the manner in which immigrants strike a balance between their native culture and the customs of their host nation. Integration of the two cultures was associated with better mental health (Krishnan & Berry, 1992). Successful cultural integration entails that Indian immigrants become involved in American culture while retaining aspects of their Indian identity. The more distinct and separate the two cultures are, the worse the immigrants' psychological adjustment to living in the United States (Mehta, 1998).

This brief overview of Asian Indian immigration to the United States demonstrates the auspicious resettlement of individuals from one land to another that all immigrants strive to achieve. This does not mean that Asian Indians have not encountered racism and discrimination, for it is well documented that Indian immigrants have felt the sting of discrimination (Fisher, 1978; Gibson, 1988; Saran, 1985) and many Asian Indians have endured underemployment in the United States. Yet their struggles were mitigated by the fact that distinct attributes of Indian culture prepared them for life in America. Advanced education and English language proficiency were two key variables that paved the way for Asian Indian immigrants to settle comfortably into the United States. Although some Asian Indians migrate back to their native country, the majority remains in the United States. Immigrants who originally came to the United States in pursuit of education usually opted to become permanent residents once their studies were completed so they may reap the benefits of their expanded opportunities (Cordasco, 1990).

Vietnamese Immigrants

Vietnamese represent the fastest growing segment of the Asian population in the United States, with a population increase of 100% during the decade of 1980 to 1990. According to Immigration and Naturalization Service data, people born in Vietnam constituted the fourth largest group of immigrants to the United States in 1996, with 42,067 people. Thus, individuals from Vietnam are the third largest group of Asian immigrants to the United States.

The first major influx of Vietnamese to the United States occurred in 1975 when the government of South Vietnam collapsed following the Vietnam War.

Thousands of South Vietnamese, including government officials and military servicemen, left quickly in a state of panic and chaos as they evacuated their homeland and entered the United States as refugees. It is important to note here the legal distinction between an immigrant and a refugee; the former is someone who has chosen to leave his or her country and the latter is someone who is forced to leave his or her country due to political or religious persecution. Although the Vietnamese are certainly not the only Asian group to arrive in the United States to escape political persecution and to seek refuge from war, they are the only group to arrive in the United States as a result of a failed U.S. military attempt in their native country. The U.S. government passed the Indochina Refugee Act in 1975 to facilitate the immigration process for Vietnamese and other Southeast Asians. Under this new legislation, the usual immigration procedures were removed to accommodate swift resettlement into the United States (Nguyen-Hong-Nhiem & Halpern, 1997).

The second wave of Vietnamese in the late 1970s has been popularized in the media as the arrival of the "boat people." In contrast to the high status of the individuals who made up the first wave, this group consisted mainly of uneducated farmers, fishermen, and merchants. Some Vietnamese sailed for the United States as political refugees and others sought expanded educational and economic opportunities in the United States. The experience of these immigrants was highly tragic, as many died at sea in unsuitable vessels. Many boats were raided by pirates who raped, pillaged, and murdered their victims. Vietnamese immigrants from this wave who successfully made it to the United States were left to cope with the psychological trauma of their experiences (Nguyen-Hong-Nhiem & Halpern, 1997).

A third wave of Vietnamese immigration was driven by the passage of the Orderly Departure Program (ODP) in 1979. The ODP is a joint program between the United States and Vietnam passed by the Office of the U.N. High Commissioner for Refugees that granted clearance to Vietnamese individuals to emigrate to the United States for family reunification. In 1991, the ODP was expanded by the United States to accelerate the immigration process for Vietnamese refugees and citizens (U.S. Department of State Dispatch, 1991). This expansion effort was made to increase the safe emigration of Vietnamese into the United States and hopefully decrease the numbers of Vietnamese boat people whose resettlement journeys were fraught with tragic circumstances. Family reunification and escape from political persecution were identified as the two main tracks through which the ODP supported Vietnamese immigration (U.S. Department of State Dispatch, 1991). By 1993, over 80,000 Vietnamese had entered the United States under the auspices of the ODP (p. 927).

The majority of Vietnamese immigrants have settled in California, which is a common U.S. destination for many Asian groups. Specifically, they have settled in the southern parts of Los Angeles, near Santa Ana and Westminster, earning this area the apt nickname "Little Saigon." Other Vietnamese have settled in Houston; Dallas; Fairfax County, Virginia; and New York City. An examination of Vietnamese settlement patterns reveals that they prefer to reside in coastal areas where they can remain close to water. Vietnamese are housed in predominantly urban or suburban environments (Nguyen-Hong-Nhiem & Halpern, 1997).

Not unlike other groups of Asian immigrants, Vietnamese immigrants to the United States are a heterogeneous population. Many striking differences differentiate Vietnamese immigrants from the first, second, and third immigration waves. Oversimplified images of Vietnamese portrayed by the media mask the diversity of this group. For example, the professional and educational backgrounds of the first wave of immigrants set these individuals apart from the uneducated, unskilled refugees of the second wave. As a result, the Vietnamese community is divided and refugees feel isolated not only from mainstream American society, but from their own Vietnamese community as well (Smith & Tarallo, 1993).

Changing gender roles for men and women have stimulated many conflicts for Vietnamese immigrants. Many Vietnamese women enter the labor force for the first time when they migrate, taking on jobs out of the necessity to help maintain their family's financial stability. In contrast, many Vietnamese men are underemployed and unemployed. As they struggle to attain English language proficiency and regain the professional status they enjoyed in Vietnam, these men have been virtually stripped of their dominant status as the family breadwinner. Loss of authority outside of the home has had significant repercussions on men's power status within the home. Marital relationships and parent-child connections have been affected by the restructuring of Vietnamese households into dual-earner homes. Although Vietnamese women's self-esteem and feelings of accomplishment have been boosted by their participation in the workforce, Vietnamese men have suffered from reduced self-esteem and overwhelming frustration (Smith & Tarallo, 1993).

Emigration from the United States back to Vietnam is highly uncommon. One main reason that Vietnamese have remained in the United States is that their home country was not officially recognized by the U.S. government until 1995. Return migration has increased somewhat since the formal recognition of Vietnam, particularly among older Vietnamese who never fully adjusted to cultural life in the United States.

Chinese Immigrants

In 1996, individuals born in China accounted for the fifth largest source of immigrants to the United States. The Immigration and Naturalization Service reports that 41,728 Chinese immigrants entered the United States during that year. This dropped slightly to 41,147 in 1997 and to 36,884 in 1998. Immigrants of Chinese descent are the fourth largest category of Asian immigrants to the United States.

As stated earlier, Chinese men were among the first Asian migrants to travel to the United States. They emigrated from China in 1849 hoping to obtain fortunes in gold during the California gold rush. Not surprisingly, they settled mainly along the West coast. These Chinese immigrants, known as the first wave, were employed as laborers, farmers, and railroad workers. Chinese workers were the predominant source of cheap labor used in the construction of the transcontinental railroad spanning across the United States. The labor force of the Central Pacific Railroad was 90% Chinese. Chinese men continued to enter the United States in large numbers until the U.S. government passed several laws that impeded their entry. Specifically the Chinese Exclusion Act of 1882, the anti–Chinese Scott Act of 1888, and the Geary Act of 1892 prohibited the immigration of Chinese laborers. The principle motivation underlying these discriminatory laws was a fear of competition in the job market and racism. To cope with discrimination, Chinese immigrants often opted to enter other fields where they did not directly compete with Whites for jobs. The Chinese created their own ethnic businesses, including restaurants and laundries, and relocated to major cities across the United States. One significant outcome of this movement was the creation of areas known as Chinatowns in metropolitan areas such as New York City and San Francisco. These areas served an important role in housing and sustaining Chinese communities. In 1940, 28 Chinatowns had been established in the United States; however, as discrimination and racism diminished Chinese immigrants were able to move out into the broader community. Wong (1998) illustrated the numerous functions of Chinatowns:

Chinatown U.S.A. is a neighborhood, a work place, a social center, and a place that helps immigrants to adjust to a new land. It is an entry port for newcomers to the New World and, as such, is continually replenished with the traditional culture of the homeland. The newly arrived immigrants to the community get their first experiences with the United States and learn how to obtain employment, a social security card, open a bank account, sign up to learn English, understand their rights and obligations as members of U.S. society. America's Chinatown is an acculturation agent for the new immigrants. (pp. 160–161)

Chinese immigrants to the United States have struggled to manage the clash of their traditional cultural values with American ideals. Most notably, Chinese culture emphasizes interdependence and filial piety. It is very common for extended families to reside together in multigenerational arrangements. In contrast, autonomy and independence are revered as developmental achievements among American youths. For instance, in the United States it is customary for children to move out of their parents' house, signifying their emerging independence. The clash of cultural values is keenly experienced among the elder Chinese immigrants, who are firmly imbued with traditional Chinese values, and among Chinese adolescents, who are first entering a critical development period of identity formation.

Mental Health. Studies have shown that elderly Chinese immigrants may be vulnerable to mental health problems, particularly depression (Mui, 1996). Unfortunately, Chinese immigrants are also unlikely to seek out treatment for their depressive symptoms (Loo, Tong, & True, 1989; Snowden & Cheung, 1990). Risk factors for depression may be elevated among elderly Chinese immigrants due to the stress of immigration and acculturation. Not unlike other immigrants, they find themselves to be strangers in a strange land. Language barriers curtail their ability to form connections to others from dissimilar heritages. In addition, elderly Chinese immigrants may feel reduced family support from second- and third-generation Chinese, who may more readily embrace American cultural values and opt to split the family by leaving the home of their parents. Alterations from traditional family systems were cited as the main source of psychological distress experienced by elderly Chinese immigrants (Mui, 1996).

The process of adjusting to life in the United States is exacerbated by the developmentally appropriate need to establish an identity for Chinese adolescent immigrants. Several factors have been linked to Chinese adolescent immigrants psychosocial adjustment (Florshein, 1997). Similar to the experience of the elderly Chinese, family cohesion and conflict appear to be important elements in promoting psychological adjustment among adolescents. Adolescents who perceive their families as more cohesive and organized are inoculated against the distress caused by assimilation and acculturation. Surprisingly, immigrants who speak Chinese as opposed to English fare better in ratings of psychosocial adjustment. One possible explanation for this finding points to the adolescents' value orientation as a mediating factor. Specifically, those Chinese adolescent immigrants who continue to speak in their native tongue feel more connected to their culture, their Chinese peers and their families. Therefore, Florshein's investigation of Chinese immigrant adolescents supports earlier studies that found the maintenance of a stable ethnic identity contributes to healthy psychological adjustment (Lieber, Chin, Nihira & Mink, 2001; Rosenthal, Moore, & Taylor, 1983).

As observed with other categories of Asian immigrants, return migration to China is a rare occurrence among Chinese immigrants to the United States.

Asian Immigration Trends. The majority of Asian immigrants today hope to reunite with their families in the United States (Fawcett & Park, 1989). This trend toward family reunification highlights the link between past and future immigration. In other words, individuals who wish to migrate to the United States to join their family members must have relatives who have already emigrated before them.

The Model Minority Stereotype. The stereotype of Asian American students as high academic achievers is pervasive throughout American society. In fact, Asian Americans have been called "model minorities" because they have enjoyed academic and professional success despite their ethnic minority status. They are also portrayed as a group that is relatively free from mental illness and uninvolved in crime (Wong, Nagasawa, & Lin, 1998). Wong et al. conceptualized the model minority hypothesis as follows: "If the minority group exhibits middle-class characteristics, and if the minority group attains some measure of success on its own without special programs or welfare, then the majority group will depict the minority group as a 'model minority' and will view the group favorably" (p. 98).

The stereotype of the model minority originated in the 1960s when the African American civil rights movement was prominent in the United States. In marked contrast to African Americans who organized protests for racial equality during this time, Asian Americans were depicted by the popular media as a racial group that was successful despite past discrimination (Chun, 1995). Influential newspapers such as *The New York Times* ran feature articles highlighting the success of Asian Americans. *U.S. News and World Report* reinforced the model minority stereotype in a 1966 piece entitled "Success Story of One Minority Group" that asserted, "At a time when Americans are awash in worry over the plight of racial minorities. . . . [ ] the Nation's 30,000 Chinese Americans are moving ahead on their own—with no help from anyone else. . . . [ ] winning wealth and respect by dint of [their] own hard work" (cited in Chun, 1995). Asian Americans were portrayed as individuals who did not complain and whine over past inequality, but who worked hard to reach their goals and secure their accomplishments. They were described as model minorities because the successful status of Asian Americans provided a role model for all other minority groups to emulate.

Suzuki (1989) claimed that the model minority stereotype that emerged during the 1960s was a political tactic used to discredit the racial equality movements of African Americans and other racial minorities. Namely, Asian Americans were assigned a reputation for academic and professional success to dispel the notion that minority groups were unfairly disadvantaged and the victims of discrimination. The creation of the model minority stereotype served to contain the protests of other racial minorities, to reinforce the values of the majority group, and to showcase how racial minorities could achieve success by embracing the values of the majority group. Within the educational system, the image of Asian Americans as model minorities was crafted to demonstrate the triumph of meritocracy in the United States (Wong et al., 1998).

However, Asian Americans are a heterogeneous group and to discuss them as a homogeneous group is to make gross overgeneralizations. The minority group collectively referred to as Asian Americans comprises many different subgroups and it is important to recognize that key differences between these groups exist in the sphere of academic and professional achievement. Not only do Asian subcultures differ from one another, but intragroup differences exist within each subgroup.

All stereotypes contain distortions of reality in their attempt to neatly classify individuals into distinct categories. The model minority stereotype is riddled with problems inherent in the assumption that Asian Americans are high achievers. The danger in grouping Asian Americans under the category of model minorities is that not every Asian American conforms to the model minority stereotype. Individuals of Asian descent who do not match the portrait of the model minority are particularly vulnerable to psychological and emotional distress. Their low achievement contradicts others' expectations, including those held by parents, teachers, the public at large, and their own, bringing shame, anxiety, and embarrassment to the individual. As a result, Asian Americans who experience difficulty in school may be reluctant to seek help from teachers due to their unwillingness to admit their problems and their fear of contradicting the teachers' expectations. The Asian stereotype of the model minority undermines the recognition of individual differences and impedes the ability of Asians to forge their own identities in the United States.

BLACK IMMIGRANTS

Black migrants to the United States are in a unique position as they enter a society in which native-born Blacks as a group still exist at the lowest end of the sociopolitical and economic structures. Issues of assimilation and acculturation have different meanings and outcomes for foreign-born Blacks than they do for other ethnic groups. For many ethnic immigrants, the move and assimilation into the American culture promises economic upward mobility. However, many Black immigrants face an unpleasant reality: assimilation and acculturation into American society often correlates with a decreased sociopolitical status. That is, as assimilation and acculturation increase, status decreases. Despite these and other negative factors, Blacks continue to migrate to the United States in increasingly large numbers.

Researchers have pointed out several reasons why West Indians and Africans emigrate from their homeland, such as: pervasively insufficient resources, including limited opportunities for higher education, lack of jobs, low financial rewards, insufficient geographical space to meet the needs of the population are some of the reasons (e.g., Foner, 1986; Nwadiora, 1996; Takougang, 1995). Unlike many other ethnic groups who have moved to the United States, by and large West Indian and African migrants view migration as a temporary move, usually motivated by economic reasons. Many of these immigrants maintain strong ties to their homelands and verbalize plans to return home after improving their fortunes in the United States, educating their children, or at least when they reach retirement (Gmelch, 1992; Sutton & Makiesky-Barrow, 1987). The reality, however, is that many do not return to their native countries. The reasons are varied. One salient factor is that dwindling resources in the developing world means that they are not likely to find jobs in their countries of origin that match their acquired professional status, or that provide wages comparable to those to which they have become accustomed in the United States (Gmelch, 1992; Nwadiora, 1996; Takougang, 1995).

West Indian Immigrants

The term *Caribbean* subsumes the term *West Indian*, and when the latter is used in contemporary discourse it most often refers to British West Indians, the inhabitants of countries colonized by Britain. The British West Indies include the Bahamas, Barbados, Belize, Bermuda, Guyana, Jamaica, the Leeward Islands, the Windward Islands, and Trinidad and Tobago (Allen, 1988). These countries have English as their official language; however, various English-based Creole dialects are also spoken throughout. To date, most research has focused on the most populous nation in the West Indies: Jamaica. As such, information presented in this section is more readily applicable to the immigration population from this country and to other nations with large migrant populations such as Guyana, Trinidad and Tobago, and Barbados and to a lesser extent to the broader range of nations (see also Chapter 6).

In the 20th century, immigration to the United States from the British West

Indies has occurred in three distinct waves (Kasinitz, 1992).

The Early Migrants. The first wave of West Indian immigration began in 1890 and persisted into the early 1920s. During this time, the estimated number of legal entrants to the United States increased every year, peaking at more than 12,000 per year in 1924. A significant number of immigrants were undocumented, however, and so estimates hold that the total number of West Indians entering the United States during this period may have been double the official numbers. This first wave was curtailed by the Immigration Act of 1924, which limited the number of citizens of British colonies in the West Hemisphere allowed to legally enter the United States (Kasinitz, 1992).

A second, smaller wave of West Indian immigrants entered the United States during the period beginning in the 1930s and extending to the early 1960s. This relatively low number was influenced by a variety of factors, including the onset of the Great Depression in 1932 and the passage of the McCarren-Walter Act of 1952 (Kasinitz, 1992). For a time during the 1930s, the number of West Indians entering the United States was surpassed by those returning to their home countries (Reid, 1939).

West Indian Immigrants Today. The third wave of immigration from the West Indies began in the mid-1960s and extends to the present day. The onset of this newest surge of migration coincided with the Immigration Reform Act of 1965, which repealed the previously implemented McCarren-Walter Act (Bryce-Laporte, 1994; Gmelch, 1992). This latest wave also coincides with the 1962 Commonwealth Immigrants Act passed by the British government, which severely limited the number of citizens of Britain's former colonies allowed to move to England to work (Gmelch, 1992). At this time as well, the United States was entering the civil rights era; Americans were becoming more tolerant and less threatened by ethnic and cultural differences.

In the 10 years following the passage of the Reform Act of 1965, more West Indians migrated to the United States than had done so in the seven decades prior. This increase reached a peak in the 1980s for most countries. According to the 1990 census, nearly 600,000 legal immigrants from three of the most populous nations in the West Indies—Jamaica, Trinidad and Tobago, and Guyana—reside in the United States (U.S. Bureau of the Census, 1997). Jamaicans are the largest group of the West Indian migrant population and represent 29% of all of the documented immigrants from the Caribbean (Kalmijn, 1996). In total, 400,000 Jamaicans entered the U.S. legally in the 3 decades of the 1960s, 1970s, and 1980s (Grasmuck & Grosfoguel, 1997), more than one half of them having migrated during the 1980s. The beginning of the 1990s marked a continued increase in the number of Jamaican immigrants: More than 91,000 moved to the United States between 1991 to 1995 (U.S. Bureau of the Census, 1997). The rush to migrate has also brought large numbers of illegal immigrants from the West Indies (Kasinitz, 1992).

Approximately three quarters of West Indian immigrants are concentrated in six states in the United States: New York, Florida, New Jersey, California, Massachusetts, and Connecticut (Model, 1991). New York is by far the leading destination for most of these migrants and has been so for the last 3 decades (U.S.

Bureau of the Census, 1997). For instance, nearly half of all Jamaicans and more than two thirds of all Guyanese who moved to the United States during the 1980s settled in New York (Mueller & Howell, 1996). In New York City, the median age of the migrants from Jamaica, Guyana, and Trinidad and Tobago lies in the mid-20s, with Jamaicans being slightly younger than those from the other two countries: 24 versus 27 and 26, respectively. The largest groups of migrants from the three countries are concentrated in the "under 18" and the "25 to 44" categories (U.S. Bureau of the Census, 1997).

Economics. West Indian immigrants have been heralded as a success story by various social researchers and theorists, many of whom contend that as a group they have achieved more in the occupational, economic, and educational realms relative to African Americans (e.g., Sowell, 1978). Although these references are not new, they have taken on special significance in current times, with increasing numbers of West Indians permeating all aspects of the American workforce, academic, and community settings, and competing with Whites, African Americans, and other minority groups.

On a national level, Jamaicans have done well economically in the United States. Their annual income is $30,461, a rate that is slightly above the U.S. average and higher than their West Indian counterparts from other countries. Overall, only about 11% of Jamaicans in the United States live below the poverty line. This rate is similar to Cuban immigrants and considerably lower than other ethnic groups counted in the 1990 census (Grasmuck & Grosfoguel, 1997).

In New York, where the largest number of West Indians live, both men and women fare better in the labor market than Spanish- or French-speaking Caribbean immigrants and African Americans. For West Indian men, these advantages increase commensurate with their length of residence in the United States, with the performance of the second generation exceeding that of the first (Kalmijn, 1996).

When data for men and women are in the workforce are compared, West Indian women outearn their male counterparts and White women, whereas West Indian men earn less than their White counterparts. Differences between men and women may be related to their varying skills and subsequent employment niches. Female immigrants are more likely than their male counterparts to be concentrated in the health care industry; their numbers have grown alongside the overall growth of the industry. New immigrant women benefit from job referrals made by their compatriots in this industry (Foner, 1998). West Indian women's relatively high earnings mean that they are better able to contribute to their families' financial well-being.

Overall, West Indian immigration has also been related to economic revitalization in communities where they have invested. This phenomenon is evidenced in large number in several inner-city communities in New York City where many of these groups settle. For instance, in Brooklyn, New York, with the flight of the middle class from many communities, Jamaican, Guyanese, and Trinidadian natives have purchased homes and started business in large numbers (Kasinitz, 1992; Millman, 1996).

The question of why West Indians have apparently had such success relative to African Americans remains highly debated. Many theories have been proposed in this regard. One perspective points out that West Indian Blacks have come from countries where they were the ethnic majority, and where they were integrated at all levels of the political, economic, and social strata throughout the society. Thus, it is argued that they are more confident about their abilities than are American Blacks who have always existed in a subjugated position (Moynihan & Glazer, 1970).

Others theorists have proposed the selective migration hypothesis, which suggests that West Indian immigrants are more motivated than both their stay-at-home conationals and African Americans *because* they migrated to improve their economic conditions (e.g., Model, 1991). This hypothesis must be interpreted with caution, as very few studies have compared groups that have migrated with those who have chosen to stay at home (Kalmijn, 1996).

It is unlikely that one theory can adequately address this question, as it is likely that a number of factors interact to produce this effect. One factor that must be considered is that, as a group, West Indian immigrants migrate to the United States with many assets, all of which interrelate to produce their economic "success." For instance, Jamaican immigrants are likely to be more educated than other migrant groups from the Caribbean region. Mueller and Howell (1996) noted that 11% of Jamaican immigrants in New York City arrive with degrees from 4-year college-level institutions. That figure is significant when compared with adults from the Dominican Republic, the largest migrant group in the city, of whom 6.3% are college educated. West Indian immigrants also have high literacy rates: for instance, 98%, 94%, and 95% of Jamaicans, Guyanese, Trinidadians, respectively, are literate (Reddy, 1994). Jamaicans and Guyanese also migrate with more experience in skilled professions. When combined with English competence, overall, these groups certainly have an advantage over other Caribbean natives in the marketplace (Mueller & Howell, 1996).

Ethnicity, Culture, and Race. West Indians face many pressures to abandon their ethnic identity and identify as only Black. Whereas early immigrants downplayed their ethnic differences, today many West Indians—particularly those who are of the first generation—seek to set themselves apart from African Americans, resisting assimilation (Kasinitz, 1992). Whereas migration generally promises upward economic mobility, for West Indians, identifying as Black only is viewed as a step down (Kasinitz, 1992; Waters, 1996). Recognizing that they are judged favorably by white Americans when their ethnic different origins are known, many West Indians capitalize on this factor, although ambivalently (Brice-Baker, 1996; Foner, 1998; Kasinitz, 1992).

The issue of assimilation is even more salient for second-generation West Indians as they often lack the identifying features that have set their immigrant parents apart—most notably, a distinct accent (Waters, 1997). This factor, coupled with the larger society's desire to categorize its population along distinct racial lines, increases the pressure to assimilate. Social class, family structures, and family social networks play a crucial role in the identity chosen by second-generation West Indian immigrants (Waters, 1996).

Mental Health. The tendency toward a strong work ethic may support mental and emotional strain for immigrant families, because parents are often employed in more than one job, which means long hours away from the home. The matrifocal nature of many of these families, as supported by cultural norms, migration patterns, and the relatively higher earnings of West Indian women in the United States, may increase discord in marital and common-law relationships (Allen, 1988).

The parenting style in West Indian families, particularly those in the lower classes, is most often authoritarian, and corporal punishment may be used as one form of discipline (Allen, 1988; Brice-Baker, 1994; see also Chapter 6). Unable to confront their parents directly, children's feelings of conflict may manifest in depression, externalizing behaviors, and academic underachievement (Allen, 1988). Parents also experience stress in this regard, as they often do not understand the child protective system in the United States, and may perceive laws against corporal punishment as impingements on their parental rights (Brice-Baker, 1994). Parent-child conflict is exacerbated when serial migration is a factor (Gmelch, 1992).

West Indians in communities away from others who share their cultural and ethnic values are particularly vulnerable to culture shock and discrimination. The double minority status of being both Black and foreign exacerbates much of the above. Those immigrants who are undocumented live with the added burden of hiding their identities. Ironically, the members of this group—perhaps those most in need of emotional support—are less likely to reach out for support due to their fear of being discovered and deported (Allen, 1988).

Cultural norms do not fully support West Indians seeking counseling and psychological or psychiatric help. As such, they may turn to a mental health professional as a last resort. In times of crisis, elders in the family constellation, members of the church, and/or spiritualists who practice folk religions may be another choice. The mental health professional would do well to seek information about cultural and religious practices when treating West Indians members of this group (Allen, 1988).

Africans

The 1990 census reveals that there are more than 250,000 documented Black immigrants from Africa living in the United States, of whom more than 200,000 arrived in the 1980s. In the 1990s, the number of immigrants from this region appears to have increased. From 1991 to 1995, more than 160,000 Africans from several nations have settled in the United States. From 1996 to 1998, this number dropped slightly to about 140,000. Egyptians, Ethiopians, Nigerians, and South Africans are overrepresented in this migrant population, numbering about 50% of the group (U.S. Bureau of the Census, 1997). Significantly, many Africans living in the United States are not accounted for in the above numbers as they hold visitor or student visas, or have entered the United States illegally (Nwadiora, 1996). Perhaps the most surprising statistic is that 50% of documented immigrants from Africa are not Black: They are of European and Asian heritages, 40% and 10%, respectively (Speer, 1994). This discussion will, however, focus on Black migrants and any references to Africans from here on are meant to refer to Blacks, unless otherwise specified.

Overall, the African immigrant population has settled in large numbers in urban centers of California, Illinois, Maryland, New Jersey, New York, Texas, and Washington, DC. Africans choose these regions for three major reasons: First, the range of employment opportunities available in the large city ensures that professional and unskilled individuals alike can find work. Second, new immigrants are likely to settle in areas where family, friends, and compatriots live in large numbers. The social support provided by them serves as a buffer against potentially overwhelming culture shock. Also, new arrivals learn to negotiate the environment from those who migrated earlier. Third, new immigrants from Africa seek cities where they believe racial tolerance is high. Larger cities such as New York and Chicago have had many Blacks in visible political positions, suggesting to the migrant that he or she is less likely to be racially ostracized or discriminated against (Takougang, 1995).

Ethnicity, Culture, and Race. Africans, perhaps more so than any other immigrant group, have had to confront and surmount rigidly stereotyped negative beliefs held by Americans. These prejudiced beliefs are informed, at least in part, by Africa's history of colonialism. They are supported by images perpetuated by the American media of "primitive" and "uncivilized" native life, endemic starvation, poverty, and disease. Africans who live in communities with others who share their cultural and ethnic histories and value systems are more likely to be insulated from racism and other effects of stereotyping in American society. Africans may also hold misguided stereotyped belief systems about African Americans. For instance, Africans immigrants, lacking accurate knowledge of American history and its sociopolitical system, have questioned African Americans "acceptance" of poverty, alienation, and deprivation in the United States (Apraku, 1996; Nwadiora, 1996).

Economics. Although poor Africans represent a significant number of those migrating to the United States, recent data indicate that a significant number of Africans who move to the United States are from higher socioeconomic niches. Overall, Africans immigrants (all racial groups) are better educated than American natives, with 88% having completed 4 high school years or more, compared with 77% for their American counterparts (Speer, 1994).

An important question is raised as to why highly educated and economically equipped Africans are migrating to the United States. Migration is a costly endeavor, especially as the distance between the migrant's country of origin and the prospective destination increases. It would appear that because of the distance and the high cost of moving, only the highly motivated and those who are financially secure are likely to move to the United States (Dodoo, 1997; Speer 1994).

In reviewing the literature, several specific reasons for the immigrant patterns emerge. Many Africans attain student visas and migrate to further their education in the United States, planning to return to their native countries to work. Like their West Indian counterparts, however, members of this group discover that there is little incentive to return to countries where the chance of finding viable employment is poor. Consistent economic decline in many African nations means that the educated may be forced to seek employment in other countries. Still another reason for immigrating is that of freedom from persecution and tyranny, political and otherwise. Among this group are those refugees who seek asylum in the United States (Dodoo, 1997; Nwadiora, 1996; Takougang, 1995).

Regardless of the reasons for migrating, many Africans stay in the United States. The reasons for staying may be economic: many migrants have found that they are better able to support family left behind by working in the United States and sending money back to their native country. Others marry and start new families in the United States. For the latter group, a significant dilemma arises as they must decide whether to rear their children in the United States, where educational opportunities are available, or whether it is more important for their children to have firsthand exposure to African values and cultural traditions (Takougang, 1995). There is a dearth of research addressing the issues that first- and second-generation African youth experience in American schools and other socializing institutions (Nwadiora, 1995). However, it is safe to speculate that some of the problems experienced by first- and second-generation West Indian youth are relevant here.

An important question is raised as to whether Black Africans are subject to discrimination based on prejudiced beliefs informed by stereotypes prevalent in the media. For instance, how do Black Africans fare compared with Black Americans and other foreign-born blacks (e.g., West Indians) (Dodoo, 1997)?

One measure of the direct effect that prejudice may have on Black Africans is the fact that their wages are less likely to be commensurate with their educational attainment. When numbers for Black men are examined, 58% of African males have completed a baccalaureate degree, compared with 13.1% of African American men and 14.6% of men from the Caribbean (Dodoo, 1997). Despite these numbers indicating that African men are significantly more educated than native-born or other foreign-born Blacks in the United States, recent research indicates that they earn less than the latter two groups (Model & Lapido, 1996).

African men who earn their degrees outside of the United States earn even less than their American-educated counterparts (Dodoo, 1997). African women appear to face discrimination in the workplace as well. Dodoo (1997) suggested that the interaction of race, immigrant status, gender, and national origins may explain these women's existence near the bottom of the status hierarchy in the workforce.

African Refugees. A significant number of migrants from this region are refugees granted asylum in the United States. The country with the largest number of refugee émigrés is Ethiopia, with more than 33,500 of its citizens fleeing to the United States between 1981 and 1995. This number becomes especially significant when considering that the total number of refugees granted asylum from the continent during this period totaled slightly more than 50,000 (U.S. Bureau of the Census, 1997).

Female Refugees. A significant number of African women seeking asylum in the United States may be fleeing their native countries from a cultural and religious practice that entails genital mutilation. This practice has ties to cultural and religious history in many countries of Africa dating back some 1,000 years. It has been practiced most often by Muslims, although Africans of the Christian and Jewish faith have also supported this custom (Abusharaf, 1998).

Some women fleeing the threat of mutilation and other forms of persecution may be refused refugee status when they enter the United States. They are often confronted with discrimination and may be further traumatized by an American society not yet equipped to deal with this phenomenon. This situation is highlighted in a recently published account of an American judge telling an African refugee pleading for asylum from this type of persecution that she could very well return to her native country and accept the consequences (Rosenthal, 1996).

Some African women continue the practice of female genital mutilation in the United States. Estimates from 1990 census data suggest that more than 168,000 such operations may have already occurred or are at risk of being carried out in the United States (Abusharaf, 1998).

Mental Health. Despite varying religious customs, as determined by nationality and religious affiliations, Africans most often have in common a spiritual belief system in which a supreme being guides and protects all. The issue of differentiation or individuation versus that of the collective self is important, with many Africans subscribing to a more collective sense of self. This belief system affects all aspects of the individual's existence, and may come to the fore, especially in times of emotional or mental distress. Indeed, this sense of spirituality is positively correlated with lower stress and higher overall self-esteem and may be especially important during the resettling process (Kamya, 1997).

For women who are seeking refugee status, there are some specific and important issues that deserve attention. Whether or not a woman "consents" to female genital mutilation, significant physical and psychological ramifications have been noted. Women are likely to present with recurring depression, anxiety, and shame related to fears about infertility and painful or disrupted menstruation. The disfigurement of vaginal areas caused by scarring tissue is also a significant source of psychological distress. Most often, however, denial is the mechanism used to manage what may be distressing feelings regarding the procedure. For these women, removed from their cultures where this practice is the norm, developing an adaptive sexual self also is likely to be problematic (Toubia, 1994).

Mental health professionals who work with women who have had this procedure done would do well to provide psychoeducation for clients and their families and support systems. Otherwise, any intervention without the appropriate attention to the social context may be circumvented by important others who hold fast to their cultural belief system (Toubia, 1994). Furthermore, clinicians should also be cautious about their own potential for ethnocentrism (Nwadiora, 1996). This caution is especially relevant considering that female genital mutilation was utilized in the not too distant past to "cure" promiscuous or emotionally disturbed American women (Abusharaf, 1998).

SUMMARY

In this chapter on the migrant experience in the United States, we have presented the experiences of three broad groups, Hispanics, Asians, and Blacks. Although immigrants continue to migrate to the United States from nearly every country, and every continent on the globe, these three groups are overrepresented among the immigrant population in the latter half of the 20th century. They are also implicated in the increasingly diverse American population landscape, as we enter the new millennium.

We recognize the tremendous diversity even within these broad groups and, as such, have limited our discussion to 10 countries and/or geographic regions from which members of these groups migrate in the largest numbers. We have enumerated their countries of origin, levels of acculturation and assimilation in the United States, mental health issues, and the social and economic consequences of immigration.

Our discussion of emigration was limited because the annual immigration statistics dwarf the numbers of those emigrating from the United States. For example, in 1990 approximately seven times as many people immigrated to the United States as did emigrate. Emigration rates are particularly low among the Hispanics, Asians, and Blacks, whose experiences we have presented. Unlike European immigrants where approximately 20% have moved back to their homes (Lynch, 1999), the immigrants profiled in this chapter rarely return to their native countries permanently. Like their predecessors, and like migrants from other groups, members of these groups move to the United States seeking educational and occupational opportunities to improve the quality of their lives, and to circumvent the relatively limited pathways available in their countries of origin. When Hispanics, Asians, and Blacks do opt to return to their native countries, the decision often comes as the result of improved opportunities and/or familial obligations back home.

The process of becoming an American, of negotiating the resettling and acculturation can be a challenging one for all immigrants. Indeed, in varying degrees, Hispanic, Asian, and Black immigrants have all encountered prejudice and discrimination exacerbated by racism and xenophobia. However, despite what may seem like insurmountable conflicts and obstacles, America continues to welcome immigrants of all nationalities and ethnic origins. Immigrants from countries across every geographic region continue to flock to the American shores seeking opportunities and reaping the rewards of their efforts.

REFERENCES

Abusharaf, R. M. (1998, March–April). Unmasking tradition. *The Sciences,* 23–27.

Allen, E. A. (1988). West Indians. In L. Comas-Diaz & E. Griffith (Eds.), *Clinical guidelines in cross-cultural mental health* (pp. 303–333). New York: Wiley.

Apraku, K. K. (1996). *Outside looking in: An African perspective on American pluralistic society*. Westport, CT: Praeger.

Asian Indians. (1990). In F. Cordasco (Ed.), *Dictionary of American immigration history*. Metuchen, NJ: The Scarecrow Press.

Bean, F. D., Cushing, R. G., Haynes, C. W., & Van Hook, J. V. W. (1997). Immigration and the social contract. *Social Science Quarterly, 78*(2), 249–268.

Bean, F. D., Passel, J. S., & Edmonston, B. (1990). *Undocumented migration to the United States: IRCA and the experience of the 1980s*. Washington, DC: Urban Institute Press.

Binder, N. E., Polinard, J. L., & Wrinkle, R. D. (1997). Mexican American and Anglo attitudes toward immigration reform: A view from the border. *Social Science Quarterly, 78*(2), 324–337.

Bohon, L. M., Sanchez-Sosa, J. J., Santos, S. J., & Singer, R. J. (1994). The effects of a mental health video on the social skills knowledge and attitudes of Mexican immigrants. *Journal of Applied Social Psychology, 24*(20), 1794–1805.

Bradshaw, C. K. (1994). Asian and Asian American women: Historical and political considerations in psychotherapy. In B. Greene and L. Comas-Diaz (Eds.), *Women of color: Integrating ethnic and gender identities in psychotherapy* (pp. 72–113). New York: Guilford Press.

Brice-Baker, J. R. (1994). West Indian women of color: The Jamaican woman. In B. Greene & L. Comas-Diaz (Eds.), *Women of color: Integrating ethnic and gender identities in psychotherapy* (pp. 139–160). New York: Guilford Press.

Bryce-LaPorte, R. S. (1994). New York City and the new Caribbean immigration: A contextual statement. In C. R. Sutton & E. M. Chaney (Eds.), *Caribbean life in New York City: Sociocultural dimensions* (pp. 51–69). New York: Center for Migration Studies of New York.

Canino, I. A., & Canino, G. J. (1993). Psychiatric care of Puerto Ricans. In A. C. Gaw (Ed.), *Culture, ethnicity, and mental illness* (pp. 467–500). Washington, DC: American Psychiatric Press.

Chavez, L. (1994). The power of the imagined community: The settlement of undocumented Mexicans and Central Americans in the United States. *American Anthropologist, 96*(1), 52-73.

Christensen, E. W. (1979). Counseling Puerto Ricans: Some cultural considerations. In D. R. Atkinson, G. Morten, & D. W. Sue (Eds.), *Counseling American minorities: A cross-cultural perspective* (pp. 159–168). Dubuque, IA: Brown.

Chun, K. (1995). The myth of Asian American success and its educational ramifications. In D. T. Nakanishi & T. Y. Nishida (Eds.), *The Asian American educational experience: A source book for teachers and students* (pp. 95–112). New York: Routledge.

Cordasco, F. (Ed.). (1990). Asian Indians. *Dictionary of American immigration history*. Metuchen, NJ: The Scarecrow Press.

Council on Scientific Affairs, American Medical Association. (1991). Hispanic health in the United States. *Journal of the American Medical Association, 265,* 248–252.

Cummins, J. S. (1998). Acknowledging the extent of Asian migration. *Migration World Magazine, 26,* 24.

Donato, K. (1994). U.S. policy and Mexican migration to the United States, 1942-1992. *Social Science Quarterly, 75*(4), 705–729.

Dodoo, F. N-A. (1997). Assimilation differences among Africans in America. *Social Forces, 76*(2), 527–547.

Exter, T. G. (1992). Middle-aging Asians. *American Demographics, 14,* 67.

Fawcett, J. T., & Park, I. H. (1989). Estimating the immigration multiplier: An analysis of recent Korean and Filipino immigration to the United States. *International Migration Review, 23,* 813–839.

Fisher, M. P. (1978). Creating ethnic identity: Asian Indians in the New York City area. *Urban Anthropology, 7,* 271–285.

Florshein, P. (1997). Chinese adolescent immigrants: Factors related to psychosocial adjustment. *Journal of Youth and Adolescence, 26*(2), 143–163.

Foner, N. (1986). Sex roles and sensibilities: Jamaican women in New York and London. In R. Simon & B. Brettell (Eds.), *International migration: The female experience* (pp. 133–151). Totowa, NJ: Rowman & Allanheld.

Foner, N. (1998). West Indian identity in the diaspora: Comparative and historical perspectives. *Latin American Perspectives, 25*(3), 173–189.

Gibson, M. A. (1988). *Accommodation without assimilation: Sikh immigrants in an American high school.* Ithaca, NY: Cornell University Press.

Gil, A. G., Vega, W. A., & Dimas, J. M. (1994). Acculturative stress and personal adjustment among Hispanic adolescent boys. *Journal of Community Psychology, 22,* 43–54.

Gmelch, G. (1992). *Double passage: The lives of Caribbean migrants abroad and back home.* Ann Arbor: University of Michigan Press.

Grasmuck, S., & Grosfoguel, R. (1997). Geopolitical, economic niches, and gendered social capital among recent Caribbean immigrants in New York. *Sociological Perspectives, 40*(3), 339–364.

Hill, K. A., & Moreno, D. (1996). Second-generation Cubans. *Hispanic Journal of Behavioral Sciences, 18*(2), 175–193.

Hovey, J. D. (2000). Acculturative stress, depression, and suicidal ideation in Mexican immigrants. *Cultural Diversity & Ethnic Minority Psychology, 6*(2), 134–151.

Hurdato, A., Gurin, P., & Peng, T. (1994). Social identities—A framework for studying the adaptations of immigrants and ethnics: The adaptations of Mexicans in the United States. *Social Problems, 41*(1), 129–151.

Jayakar, K. (1994). Women of the Indian subcontinent. In B. Greene & L. Comas-Diaz (Eds.), *Women of color: Integrating ethnic and gender identities in psychotherapy* (pp. 161–181). New York: Guilford Press.

Jerding, G. (1997, February 28). Immigration is on the rise, again. *USA Today,* p. A8.

Kalmijn, M. (1996). The socioeconomic assimilation of Caribbean American blacks. *Social Forces, 74*(3), 911–931.

Kamya, H. A. (1997). African immigration in the United States: The challenge for research and practice. *Social Work, 42*(2), 154–166.

Kasinitz, P. (1992). *Caribbean New York: Black immigrants and the politics of race*. New York: Cornell University Press.

Krishnan, A., & Berry, J. W. (1992). Acculturative stress and acculturation attitudes among Asian Indian immigrants to the United States. *Psychology and Developing Societies, 4,* 187–212.

Labovitz, P. (1996, March 25). Just the facts. *The New York Times,* p. A15.

Lieber, E., Chin, D., Nihira, K., & Mink, I. T. (2001). Holding on and letting go: Identity and acculturation among Chinese immigrants. *Cultural Diversity & Ethnic Minority Psychology, 7*(3), 247–261.

Loo, C., Tong, B., & True, R. (1989). A bitter bean: Mental health status and attitudes in Chinatown. *Journal of Community Psychology, 17,* 283–296.

Lynch, D. J. (1999, March 16). Flourishing Ireland calls its children home: Tide turns as immigration sets a record. *USA Today,* p. A13.

Malgady, R. G. (1994). Hispanic diversity and the need for culturally sensitive mental health services. In R. G. Malgady & O. Rodriguez (Eds.), *Theoretical and conceptual issues in Hispanic mental health* (pp. 227–246). Malabar, FL: Krieger.

Martinez, C., Jr. (1993). Psychiatric care of Mexican Americans. In A. C. Gaw (Ed.), *Culture, ethnicity, and mental illness* (pp. 431–466). Washington, DC: American Psychiatric Press.

Mehta, S. (1998). Relationship between acculturation and mental health for Asian Indian immigrants in the United States. *Genetic, Social, and General Psychology Monographs, 124*(1), 161–179.

Miller, J. J. (1998, May 26). Becoming an American. *The New York Times,* p. A21.

Millman, J. (1996, February 12). Ghetto blasters. *Forbes, 157*(3), 76–81.

Model, S. (1991). Caribbean immigrants: A Black success story? *International Migration Review, 25*(2), 248–276.

Model, S., & Lapido, D. (1996). Context and opportunity: Minorities in London and New York. *Social Forces, 75,* 485–510.

Moynihan, D. P., & Glazer, N. (1970). *Beyond the melting pot: The Negroes, Puerto Ricans, Jews, Italians, and Irish of New York City* (2nd ed.). Cambridge, MA: MIT Press.

Mueller, E. J., & Howell, D. R. (1996). *Immigrant workers in New York City* (Immigrant New York Series: Working Paper No. 3). New York: New School for Social Research, International Center for Migration, Ethnicity, and Citizenship.

Mui, A. C. (1996). Depression among elderly Chinese immigrants: An exploratory study. *Social Work, 41*(6), 33–46.

The National Immigration Forum (1994). *Fast facts on today's newcomers.* Washington, DC: Author.

Nguyen-Hong-Nhiem, L., & Halpern, J. M. (1997). Vietnamese. In D. Levison & M. Ember (Eds.), *American immigrant cultures* (pp. 923–931). New York: Simon & Schuster Macmillan.

Nwadiora, E. (1995). Alienation and stress among Black immigrants: An exploratory study. *The Western Journal of Black Studies, 19*(1), 58–71.

Nwadiora, E. (1996). Nigerian Families. In M. McGoldrick, J. Giordano, & J. K. Pearce (Eds.), *Ethnicity and family therapy* (2nd ed., pp. 129–138). New York: Guilford Press.

Padilla, A. M., Cervantes, R. C., Maldonado, M., & Garcia, R. E. (1988). Coping responses to psychological stressors among Mexican and Central American immigrants. *Journal of Community Psychology, 16,* 418–427.

Ramos-McKay, J. M., Comas-Diaz, L., & Rivera, L. A. (1988). Puerto Ricans. In L. Comas-Diaz & E. H. Griffith (Eds.), *Clinical guidelines in cross-cultural mental health* (pp. 204–232). New York: Wiley.

Reddy, M. A. (Ed.). (1994). *Statistical abstract of the world.* New York: Gale Research.

Reid, I. (1939). *The Negro immigrant, his background characteristics, and social adjustment, 1899–1937.* New York: Columbia University Press.

Rodriguez, C. E. (1989). *Puerto Ricans born in the U.S.A.* Boston: Unwin Hyman.

Rogler, L. H., Cortes, D. E., & Malgady, R. G. (1991). Acculturation and mental health status among Hispanics. *American Psychologist, 46*(6), 585–597.

Rosenthal, A. M. (1996, April 12). Fighting female mutilation. *The New York Times,* p. A31.

Rosenthal, D. A., Moore, S. M., & Taylor, M. J. (1983). Ethnicity and adjustment: A study of self-image of Anglo-, Greek- and Italian-Australian working class adolescents. *Journal of Youth and Adolescence, 12,* 117–135.

Ruiz, P. (1994). Cuban American migration, acculturation, and mental health. In R. G. Malgady & O. Rodriguez (Eds.), *Theoretical and conceptual issues in Hispanic mental health* (pp. 69–90). Malabar, FL: Krieger.

Salgado de Snyder, V. N. (1994). Mexican women, mental health, and migration: Those who go and those who stay behind. In R. G. Malgady & O. Rodriguez (Eds.), *Theoretical and conceptual issues in Hispanic mental health* (pp. 113–142). Malabar, FL: Krieger.

Salgado de Snyder, V. N., Cervantes, R. C., & Padilla, A. M. (1990). Gender and ethnic differences in psychological stress and generalized distress among Hispanics. *Sex Roles, 22,* 441–453.

Saran, P. (1985). *The Asian Indian experience in the United States.* Cambridge, MA: Schenkmen.

Shenton, J. P. (1990). Ethnicity and immigration. In S. P. Benson, S. Brier, & R. Rosenzweig (Eds.), *The new American history.* Philadelphia: Temple University Press.

Smith, M. P., & Tarallo, B. (1993). The unsettling resettlement of Vietnamese boat people. *USA Today, 121,* 27–30.

Snowden, L. R., & Cheung, F. K. (1990). Use of inpatient mental health services by members of ethnic minority groups. *American Psychologist, 45,* 347–355.

Sowell, T. (1978). *Essays and data on American ethnic groups.* Washington, DC: Urban Institute Press.

Speer, T. (1994). The newest African Americans aren't black. *American Demographic, 16*(1), 9–11.

Suárez-Orozco, M. M. (1996). California dreaming: Proposition 187 and the cultural psychology of racial and ethnic exclusion. *Anthropology and Education Quarterly, 27*(2), 151–167.

Sutton, C. R., & Makiesky-Barrow, S. (1987). Migration and West Indian racial and ethnic consciousness. In C. R. Sutton & E. M. Chaney (Eds.), *Caribbean life in New York City*. New York: Center for Migration Studies.

Suzuki, B. H. (1989). Asian-American as the model minority. *Change November*, 13–19.

Takougang, J. (1995). Recent African immigrants to the United States: A historical perspective. *The Western Journal of Black Studies, 19*(1), 50–57.

Toubia, N. (1994). Female circumcision as a public health issue. *The New England Journal of Medicine, 331*, 712–716.

Torres-Matrullo, C. M. (1976). Acculturation and psychopathology among Puerto Rican women in the mainland United States. *American Journal of Orthopsychiatry, 46*(4), 710–719.

U.S. Bureau of the Census. (1990). *U.S. Census Summary Tape file, 3A*. Washington, DC: U.S. Government Printing Office.

U.S. Bureau of the Census. (1991). *U.S. Census Summary Tape file, 1A*. Washington, DC: U.S. Government Printing Office.

U.S. Bureau of the Census (1997). *Statistical Abstract of the United States: 1997* (117th ed.). Washington, DC: U.S. Government Printing Office.

U.S. Department of Justice (1991). *1990 statistical yearbook of the immigration and naturalization service*. Washington, DC: U.S. Government Printing Office.

U.S. Department of State Dispatch. (1991). *Fact sheet: US expands orderly departure for Vietnamese refugees, 2*(13), 225.

Vega, W. A., Khoury, E. L., Zimmerman, R. S., Gil, A. G., & Warheit, G. J. (1995). Cultural conflicts and problem behaviors of Latino adolescents in home and school environments. *Journal of Community Psychology, 23*, 167–179.

Warren, R. (1990). Annual estimates of nonimmigrant overstays in the United States: 1985-1988. In F. D. Bean, J. S. Passel, & B. Edmonston (Eds.), *Undocumented migration to the United States: IRCA and the experience of the 1980s* (pp. 77–101). Washington, DC: Urban Institute Press.

Warren, R. (1992). *Estimates of the unauthorized immigrant population residing in the United States, by country of origin and state of residence: October 1992*. Washington, DC: Immigration and Naturalization Service Statistics Division.

Waters, M. C. (1996). Ethnic and racial identities of second-generation Black immigrants in New York City. In A. Portes (Ed.), *The new second generation* (pp. 171–196). New York: Russell Sage Foundation.

Waters, M. C. (1997). Immigrant families at risk: Factors that undermine chances for success. In A. Booth, A. C. Crouter, & N. Landale (Eds.), *Immigration and the family: Research and policy on U. S. immigrants* (pp. 79–87). Mahwah, NJ: Erlbaum.

Wieder, R. (1995). Immigration. In I. Natividad (Ed.), *The Asian American almanac* (pp. 265–269). Washington DC: Gale Research.

Wolf, D. L. (1997). Family secrets: Transnational struggles among children of Filipino immigrants. *Sociological Perspectives, 40*(3), 457–483.

Wong, B. P. (1998). Chinese. In D. Levinson & M. Ember (Eds.), *American immigrant cultures* (pp. 155–168). New York: Simon & Schuster Macmillan.

Wong, P., Lai, C. F., Nagasawa, R., & Lin, T. (1998). Asian Americans as a model minority: Self-perceptions by other racial groups. *Sociological Perspectives, 41*(1), 95–118.

5

Emigration From Ireland
to the United States

T. Joseph O'Donoghue and Mary Ann O'Donoghue

An estimated 7 million men and women emigrated from Ireland to North America in the 400-year period from the beginning of the 17th century to the end of the 20th century (Drudy, 1985; Miller, 1985). Some 40 million Americans can trace all or part of their ancestry to these Irish emigrants (MacLaughlin, 1994). A related consequence is that nearly every one of the 5 million people who now live in Ireland can claim past and current relations in North America (O'Hanlon, 1998).

The first wave of Irish immigration to the United States began in the 17th century when both Ireland and what was to become the United States were colonies of the British Empire (Clark, 1991). British courts in Ireland had adopted a policy of controlling that colony's civil unrest by imposing the sentence of exile on impoverished agitators in an Ireland that served as an agriculture-providing outpost for an England in the early stages of industrialization (Botticheimer, 1971). Most of these earliest Irish emigrants to North America, estimated to number from 50,000 to 100,000 individuals over a 100-year period, arrived in the pre-Revolutionary United States or in the West Indies as indentured servants facing long terms of involuntary employment under the control of prosperous plantation owners (Coleman, 1972).

The majority of Irish immigrants to the United States during the decades immediately before and after the American Revolution of 1776 to 1783 were Protestants from Ulster, Ireland's northernmost province (Adams, 1932). Their number included Anglicans, Quakers, Methodists, and Baptists, with a preponderance of "Scotch-Irish," namely, Ulster inhabitants who traced their ancestry to Presbyterians in Scotland (Shannon, 1963). The Scotch-Irish had been forcibly moved from Scotland to northern Ireland a century earlier by British authorities intent on creating a dominant Protestant majority in the Irish province of Ulster. The British colonial policy of imposing high rents and heavy tax burdens, combined with the encouragement of Presbyterian ministers, resulted in a migratory movement of perhaps a half-million Scotch-Irish to the United States in the years immediately prior to the American Revolution (Bodnar, 1985).

This early Protestant Irish immigration pattern to the United States continued after the Revolution and into the 19th century (Fallows, 1979). The American Revolution can be regarded as the historic point at which a pattern of predominantly Catholic Irish immigration to the United States begins (O'Hanlon, 1998). In the closing years of the 19th century, Ireland's Catholics began a mass exodus primarily to the United States but also to Canada, Australia, New Zealand, and Great Britain (Clark, 1991). Slightly over 1 million Irish are believed to have migrated to the United States in the half century prior to the Great Irish Famine of 1845 to 1850 (Coleman, 1972). It is estimated that in the 150-year period from the famine to the beginning of the 21st century a total of 5.5 million Irish immigrants arrived in the United States (Hansen, 1990).

The vast majority of these immigrants began life in America at the bottom of the socioeconomic ladder because they almost universally lacked any type of work skill or economic advantage (Bodnar, 1985). They entered an American society, which in theory was pluralistic, democratic, classless, and open to immigrant labor, as an asset needed in the industrialization process about to begin (Doyle, 1991). In their daily lives, however, the newly arrived Irish Catholic immigrants tended to be regarded by their predominantly Protestant neighbors as unwelcome competition in the labor market and as undesirable aliens in civil and social affairs (Higham, 1965). Irish immigrants, in part because of this hostile reception, and in part because of a collective longing for the rural lifestyle of the Ireland they had left, initially were at a psychological as well as an economic disadvantage in the United States. They frequently regarded themselves as short-term, involuntary exiles rather than as long-term, opportunity-seeking immigrants (O'Hanlon, 1998). They were not part of a successful revolution from England in the American historical experience that was so dominant a part of the thinking of then Protestant America. Instead, the Catholic Irish often perceived themselves as defeated exiles who had been compelled to leave the Ireland which was their preference and to come to an America which was their second choice (Fallows, 1979).

The idea of immigration to the United States as a tragic exile tended to make the Irish experience very different from that of most immigrant groups where the experience was considered to be the outcome of individual decisions to seek economic improvement (Fitzpatrick, 1984). Personal advancement, of course, became as extensive a goal for Irish Americans as for other immigrant groups (Shannon, 1963). But the view of the original homeland as an unfortunate place of sorrow and unhappiness, due to its colonial status under the British as an uncaring foreign power, was to influence Irish emigrant thought and behavior patterns throughout almost the entire period of mass migration to the United States (Yans-McLaughlin, 1990).

A key component of the Irish emigrant's perception of Ireland as an unfortunate nation was the experience of the Great Irish Famine, from 1845 to 1850, which was perceived by many emigrants as linked to agricultural policies imposed on Ireland as a colony by British authorities (Hoppen, 1985). The famine had a devastating outcome on Irish society, with demographic and social consequences that continued to impact the nation well into the 20th century. In the early years of the 19th century, the agriculture-based Irish economy had experienced a moderate upswing due to its position as a regional food supplier for an England engaged in almost a century of warfare with France in Europe and in the worldwide colonial outposts of both nations (Johnson, 1967).

Napoleon's defeat at Waterloo, which brought an era of global conflict to a close, effectively ended the importance of colonial Ireland as a supplier of agricultural products to an England no longer in need of wartime food supplies. Over a 30-year period, from 1815 to 1845, the prices of Irish farm products steadily declined. Falling prices made it impossible for Irish tenants to pay the high rents imposed by English landlords in the preceding years of a war supported economy (Lyons, 1982).

Falling agricultural prices in Ireland were accompanied by an equally ruinous decline in prices for goods produced by Ireland's system of cottage industries (i.e., a pattern of household units where neighbors would assemble to produce a limited amount of finished goods) (Hoppen, 1985). British manufacturers, benefiting from the economics of scale gained by their plants in the preceding war period, flooded the Irish markets with cheap, mass-produced goods that totally destroyed the competitiveness of the small-scale Irish cottage industry system (Johnson, 1967). Large-scale production by British factories, when imported into Ireland, led to the closing of Irish linen and woolen factories that employed hundreds of Irish workers (Lyons, 1982).

Irish farmers temporarily gained a delay in a nationwide slide toward rural destitution by placing an excessive reliance on a single crop. Potato production rapidly escalated in Ireland from 1815 to 1845 when subsistence farmers desperately attempted to avoid eviction from their farms by becoming growers of a single crop that could be produced in relatively large quantities with minimal reliance on tools and supplies (Connell, 1950).

The Great Famine in Ireland, which began in 1845 and continued unbroken for 5 successive years, has been linked to the sudden appearance of a new fungus that attacked and almost totally eliminated Ireland's potato production. An estimated one million Irish died from starvation in a famine which occurred on a scale not experienced in Europe for over 100 years. During the 5 years of the famine, approximately 2.5 million Irish left Ireland, with the majority immigrating to the United States (Woodham-Smith, 1962). In a single 10-year period, from 1845 to 1855, an estimated 3 million individuals, representing one third of Ireland's famine surviving population, left the nation (Adams, 1932). The current population of Ireland, 150 years after the Great Famine, is only half of the estimated 10 million population of the prefamine Ireland of the mid-19th-century (Munck, 1993).

The Irish emigrants of the Great Famine era endured an extraordinary level of suffering in their Atlantic passage to America. The majority of famine-induced emigrants began the trip in a malnourished condition, which made them susceptible to typhus and dysentery in the overloaded ships from Ireland that became known as "coffin ships" due to high mortality rates in transit sometimes reaching 40% percent on a single vessel (Clark, 1991).

The Catholic bishops of the United States repeatedly urged emigrants from Ireland to move from their predominant ports of arrival, namely, Boston, New York, and Philadelphia, to western states where they would have the opportunity to continue their lives as farmers (Shannon, 1963). The immigrants, however, were not inclined to leave the Irish ethnic ghettoes which were quickly being established in America's major cities in favor of what appeared to them to be a disappearance into the isolation of rural America (O'Hanlon, 1998).

The twin forces of a labor shortage in industrializing America and the massive numbers of Irish immigrants, ready to start work within days of their arrival, provided Irish Americans with the first stage of a path to assimilation within the larger culture, which remained hostile to newcomers but which needed them as employees. Irish male immigrants became factory workers, construction workers, and builders of roads, canals, and railroads. Irish women found work as mill workers, entry-level personnel in shops and stores, and as household servants in middle-class America (Groneman & Norton, 1987).

The first home of the recently arrived Irish immigrants was either a shantytown on the edge of an American city, or an overcrowded tenement building in a run-down neighborhood of inner-city America. Thousands of recently arrived immigrants quickly became sick and died as the result of ghetto epidemics such as tuberculosis or as the result of excessive workloads due to economic necessity. The arrival of a major disease within an Irish immigrant family would almost universally result in the death of one or more family members because of the absence of hospital care to impoverished immigrants (Clark, 1991).

An estimated 150,000 Irish immigrants joined the Union Army during the American Civil War, from 1861 to 1865 (Fallows, 1979). For many, the army offered a small but certain income, as well as the possibility of economic advancement at the end of what many Irish recruits thought to be a short war where military service would demonstrate their patriotism. For others, however, entry into the Union Army was the result of a government policy which drafted poor immigrants into military service at a time when more fortunate and more prosperous native-born Americans were permitted to buy their way out of military service (Coleman, 1972).

In the years immediately following the end of the Civil War in 1865, the unskilled, ghetto constrained Irish immigrants did not experience the type of economic and social success which many had anticipated at the time of their arrival in the United States. Many native-born Americans took a special pride in being Protestant and thereby linked to an earlier American culture that placed a high value on British ancestry (Higham, 1965). They had succeeded economically in America; if the Irish were failing to attain the same type of advancement, it was because the Irish suffered from laziness, ignorance, immorality, and especially because of their allegiance to their superstition-based Catholic faith. American Protestantism was fragmented into a broad variety of denominations with diverse creeds and religious rituals. Most of these Protestant denominations shared an emphasis on individualism in religion with basic reliance on a self-directed interpretation of religious beliefs (Jackson, 1976). American Catholicism, in contrast, appeared to be an extremely centralized, foreign-based religious force that was inherently hostile to democratic institutions in the United States (Drudy, 1985).

The steady increase in Irish immigrants to the United States throughout the 19th century served as a constant stimulus to the prejudices of those native-born Americans who believed that in order to save American democracy the Irish should be impeded in their attempts at economic advancement. Protestant employers routinely added the words "No Irish Need Apply" to their advertisement for workers. Newspapers often depicted Irish Americans as violence prone, drunken, and crime loving individuals who threatened the American way of life (Higham, 1965).

Resistance to emigrant advancement in American society was the driving force behind the development of nativism, a mid-19th-century political movement whose major goal it was to place all economic and political power under the control of native-born Americans (Bodnar, 1985). Nativism became a nationwide political movement in the second half of the 19th century through the formation of the American Party, which won political control in several state governments, and whose members, sometimes referred to as "Know-Nothings," succeeded in passing anti-immigrant and anti-Catholic legislation. In the final decade of the 19th century, the American Protective Association, a broadly based coalition of anti-Catholic and anti-Irish organizations, asked its members to pledge that they would not associate with Irish American Catholics in any form of work or social relationship (Higham, 1965).

The tendency of most Irish immigrants to choose life in urban centers rather than the westward migration recommended by their religious leaders, eventually provided Irish Americans with political advantages in urban elections. Nineteenth-century U.S. cities developed rapidly due to massive immigration from Ireland and the nations of Western Europe (Bodnar, 1985). A century-long expansion of commerce and manufacturing occurred because of the twin forces of an ever increasing population and an ever expanding labor force available to the manufacturing sector. The political structures of most U.S. cities had been developed in an earlier era when an established elite could, through both formal and informal political mechanisms, exercise an almost total control of political, business, and social life patterns (Shannon, 1963). These older structures proved incapable of adjusting to the unprecedented infusion of impoverished immigrants who, however, quickly became voting members of the Democratic Party. Local ward leaders in the Democratic Party became extremely effective in directing recent emigrants to vote for their self-interests in terms of public employment projects and worker protection laws (MacLaughlin, 1994).

The concentration of Irish immigrants in cities such as New York, Boston, Chicago, and Kansas City, combined with the almost total commitment of Irish voters to the Democratic Party, began to provide Irish Americans with a base of political power that was to become central to their economic advancement in American society (O'Hanlon, 1998). The success of Irish candidates in local elections provided previously marginal Irish workers with a broad array of the public sector jobs formerly reserved for native Americans (Fallows, 1979). These jobs included not only the city-controlled work performed by policemen, firemen, and sanitation workers but also the much larger number of jobs in companies that were seeking business contracts from the city (Doyle, 1991). These firms were now expected to demonstrate their commitment to the hiring of Irish workers prior to gaining lucrative contracts from city governments. The U.S. political system, which from its inception in post-Revolutionary America had routinely rewarded election winners with commerce related benefits, was now regarded by the older Yankee elite as corrupt when the benefits of political dominance began to shift to a later generation of emigrants (Miller, 1985).

This type of shift in political power was not confined to cities where Irish Americans became the majority force in a dominant Democratic Party. Republican Party machines, with very limited immigrant membership, controlled the political apparatus in Philadelphia, Detroit, Minneapolis, and St. Louis, with a benefit-distribution system that rewarded native-born Americans but ignored recent immigrants who did not have the political clout linked to large voting blocs (Drudy, 1985).

The Irish immigrant experience in the 19th and early 20th centuries was unique in that there were more women than men involved in the immigration process; the preponderance of immigrants were male in the case of all other major migrating groups (Cardasco, 1985). Women in rural Ireland prior to the Great Famine had been a reliable economic asset in Irish households because of their ability to enhance otherwise subsistence levels of family income either through their occasional labor on neighboring farms or in nearby cottage industries where teams of women were involved in spinning and cloth production (Diner, 1983). The work pattern of these women became a lifelong benefit to their parents when Irish farmers adopted a pattern of confining farm inheritance to one family member in the decades immediately following the Great Famine (Harris, 1982). The famine had destroyed both the Irish cottage industry system and the availability of seasonal work in a rural Ireland, which would require almost a century to recover from a devastating reliance on a single crop (O'Malley, 1985).

Under a pattern of never dividing a farm at inheritance time, adopted as a response to a near total absence of resources in postfamine Ireland, Irish parents would will their farm intact to a single son rather than follow the prefamine pattern of subdividing their holdings to inheriting sons who would then have the opportunity to marry and raise their own families (Lyons, 1982). The actual transfer of power over the farm in postfamine Ireland was usually delayed until parents reached an advanced age. An almost universal condition was that the inheriting son delay marriage until he was middle-aged and about to take control of the farm, his aging parents, and his brothers and sisters (Higgins & Gibbons, 1980).

This no-division pattern of farm inheritance preserved the Irish farming system as an inefficient but sustainable form of subsistence agriculture. The Irish inheritance system may have been the major factor responsible for the extremely high levels of rural Irish emigration which continued for at least 50 years after the end of the Great Famine (Walsh, 1989). Noninheriting sons had the opportunity to remain as unmarried laborers in the farm household that their more fortunate brothers had inherited (Kennedy & McHugh, 1988). Most Irish males chose to take the risk of immigration to some other nation when confronted with a lifelong existence as an unmarried worker under the direction of a brother who could provide no compensation other than very limited living space (Fitzpatrick, 1984).

The life opportunities of Irish women in postfamine Ireland were even more depressed. Very few daughters of farmers were permitted to marry in late-19th-century Ireland because eligibility was confined to the small number of prosperous rural parents who could provide the required dowries of land and money to the family into which a daughter might marry (Diner, 1983). The life options available to Irish women were basically two: accept a life of total subordination, as a spinster under the inheriting brother and indirectly under the remaining noninheriting brothers, or emigrate (Cardasco, 1985).

The prospect of emigration was made more appealing to Irish women by the frequent letters that they received from women who had emigrated from their immediate area and who were reporting a high level of life satisfaction in the United States (Groneman & Norton, 1987). A large proportion of those women found domestic work in middle- and upper-class American families shortly after arriving in America (Clark, 1991). Other Irish women quickly secured positions in an expanding U.S. factory system, which preferred women employees because of their docility in the workplace and their job immobility when compared to males (Harris, 1982). The working conditions and the salary levels of these Irish women immigrants were not impressive by American standards. However, their liberated status, as reported in letters back to Ireland, stimulated an immense interest in the possibility of migration in Irish women facing almost no opportunity of advancement in rural Ireland (Coleman, 1972).

The attractiveness of emigration for Irish women was enhanced by the element of romanticism linked to immigrant life in America. Irish women domestics could send back to Ireland letters informing their sisters and friends that in America they could have a choice of suitors and that a major part of their free time was spent in social activity (Miller, 1985). Ireland's parish priests provided an unintended but highly effective encouragement to emigration by warning from their pulpit of the dangers to be encountered by women in the open society of the United States (Lyons, 1982). The letters from America and the clerical denunciations of social life in the United States helped to keep the possibility of emigration in the minds of the rural women of postfamine Ireland.

Irish women immigrants derived a special benefit from the "chain" migration pattern established by Irish male immigrants. A single Irish immigrant, arriving in the United States from a rural Ireland of extensive social networks, subsequently achieving a modest level of economic success, felt honor bound to promise temporary housing and job hunting help to the large network of friends who had remained in Ireland but who would seriously consider migration when encouraged by a successful emigrant (O'Hanlon, 1998).

Female Irish immigrants were especially effective in providing assistance in the chain network. They often provided a portion of the transportation expenses of women from their original area of residence in Ireland, and they initiated a practice of regularly sending part of their salaries back to Irish family members who could not migrate because of economic responsibilities to aging parents (Groneman & Norton, 1987). This pattern of financial support from women immigrants helped to keep intact the rural Irish family system in a difficult era, while simultaneously encouraging the emigration of Irish women who could regard life in America as both a personal advantage and as a source of assistance to the Irish family that they would leave (Diner, 1983).

The constantly expanding American economy and the slow but steady use of Irish workers in that economy throughout the second half of the 19th century radically altered the opportunity pattern available to Irish immigrants at the beginning of the 20th century. This later generation of Irish immigrants could now find an established network of contacts providing economic and social support in their transition period after arrival (Fallows, 1979). The support network had been developed in part as a response to the hostility and prejudice experienced by the Irish in earlier decades and in part due to the extensive development of the chain system of Irish immigration with its emphasis on the economic and social bonding of new arrivals to their American Irish friends who had recommended their migration to the United States (Shannon, 1963).

In many American cities, the Irish controlled Democratic Party unit was understandably eager to welcome every Irish immigrant; the new arrival represented one more automatic vote for the Democratic candidate in every district and citywide election (Fitzpatrick, 1984). An equally enthusiastic welcome was provided by the leadership of local unions intent on gaining membership power over the large urban firms with which they negotiated salaries and working conditions (Clark, 1991). The American Civil War had temporarily provided an enormous labor shortage when thousands of native-born Americans left the workforce to spend a 4-year period, from 1861 to 1865, as members of the Union Army (Coleman, 1972). Their absence from the labor force created an opportunity for previously unskilled Irish immigrants to obtain training and work experience as carpenters, ironworkers, and stonemasons. A related benefit of the new openings in the industrial expansion was the establishment of Irish workers as independent contractors and suppliers to larger firms (Shannon, 1963). The Knights of Labor, the first national labor organization in the U.S. history, included several hundred thousand skilled and unskilled Irish Americans in the closing decades of the 19th century (Doyle, 1991). In its early years the organization was led by Terrence Powderly, the son of Irish immigrants (Bodnar, 1985).

In the difficult years at the beginning of the 19th century, the Irish had encountered a widespread pattern of opposing organizations of biased native-born Americans, who collectively blocked the type of political, economic, and social advancement that might otherwise have been expected in an America that needed an upwardly mobile labor force (Higham, 1965). By the end of the 19th century, however, Irish Americans had created their own network of supportive organizations designed to provide a wide array of benefits to emigrants from a particular county or region in Ireland (Walsh, 1989). These organizations, whether political, athletic or social, served as trans-Atlantic extension of the bonding patterns established earlier by location in Ireland. Whenever needed the various organizations could easily be called on to demonstrate their collective strength at political rallies and at urban celebrations of ethnicity (O'Hanlon, 1998). For Irish Americans the key event was the St. Patrick's Day parade held in many major U.S. cities every March 17. The parade, especially in its New York City version, became an annual ritual whose planning and observance united the diverse Irish organizations, while simultaneously forcing urban political leaders, who invariably attended as reviewers, to recognize the emerging political power of Irish Americans (Drudy, 1985).

The Irish organizations provided a highly efficient bonding system between their Irish members and the leadership of the Roman Catholic Church in the United States. The Great Famine in mid-19th-century Ireland had radically altered both the belief system and the organizational focus of the Catholic Church in Ireland (Lyons, 1982). Prior to the famine the majority of rural Irish had only marginal links to the Catholic Church as a formal organization (Johnson, 1967). Most Irish peasants were sustained by devotion to religious customs that were self-directed without the assistance of clergy. Among their most important religious observances were frequent group pilgrimages to special places considered holy in a tradition stretching back to the pre-Christian era (Adams, 1932).

The practice of pilgrimages and the series of related private rituals at local shrines and holy places proved to be powerless in ending the 5-year continuation of the Great Famine (Hoppen, 1985). Irish bishops and priests, who previously had held only limited amounts of moral authority in rural Ireland, emerged from the period of the famine as leaders who had organized whatever support could be found for the dying and who had attempted to counter British newspapers when they claimed that the famine could be linked to Irish habits of laziness and immorality (Lee, 1981). Their new roles as community leaders and builders of churches proved to be a very powerful mechanism in the recruitment of priests and nuns to the religious life in Ireland. The constantly expanding number of priests and nuns served as a bonding device within American Irish communities in the United States; immigrants and second-generation Irish Americans could continue their religious practices under the direction of Irish pastors and Irish school teaching nuns who collectively had brought from Ireland a tendency to build churches and schools as a base for community power (Shannon, 1963). Irish immigrants to the United States at the end of 19th century left a parish with an imposing church building in Ireland. In the United States, the immigrant found an equally imposing church building and possibly an adjacent Catholic school. Both parishes, the Ireland version and the American version, were staffed by an extremely disciplined corps of priests and nuns intent on an almost militaristic training of young Irish American economically successful Catholics with a total allegiance to the Catholic faith (O'Hanlon, 1998).

Catholic Church membership in the United States had been minimal in the decades immediately prior to the Great Famine (Adams, 1932). Most of the Church's senior leadership was either French or British in national derivation

(Doyle, 1991). Many of these leaders did not initially encourage the vast influx of Irish immigrants as active members of their parishes and their Catholic organizations (Higham, 1965). In 1837, a Catholic convent was attacked and burned by a mob of Protestant workers in Charleston, Massachusetts (Hansen, 1961). In 1844, Philadelphia was the scene of a weeklong riot by native-born Americans who destroyed several Catholic churches and pillaged Irish neighborhoods in a series of raids conducted without any intervention by the local police force (Higham, 1965). The first St. Patrick's Cathedral in New York City, completed by prefamine Irish emigrants at the beginning of the 19th century, was built with a fortresslike wall intended as protection against mob action by Protestant neighbors (Shannon, 1963).

The massive numbers of the postfamine Irish immigrants radically altered the balance of power between Protestants and Catholics in the United States. Catholic bishops, who formerly were the leaders of small groups of city parishes, suddenly acquired the social and political muscle associated with their rock solid leadership of hundreds of thousands of urban voters (Clark, 1991). In the second half of the 19th century, the Catholic Church in the United States underwent a second radical transformation when either Irish born or first-generation Irish American bishops replaced the earlier British-French bloc of Catholic bishops due to the dominance of Irish immigrants in Catholic ranks (Shannon, 1963). Aggressively political bishops, such as the Irish-born John Hughes of New York, brought to the United States hundreds of priests and nuns from Ireland in a strategy which quickly expanded the grassroots leadership of the Catholic Church in the United States while simultaneously creating a numeric Irish advantage in determining who became the male and female leaders of a transformed American Catholicism (Bodnar, 1985). An exploding Catholic Church membership due to emigration made it possible for the bishops to develop political connections to the point where police intervention became a factor in curtailing the attacks of native-born Americans on Catholic buildings (Higham, 1965).

In mid-19th-century America, the public school system had a curriculum that placed a strong emphasis on fostering an ethical code derived from a Protestant interpretation of the Bible (Fallows, 1979). Although theoretically neutral to alternative interpretations of biblical passages, that curriculum could be used to implicitly designate the belief systems of Irish immigrant children as unacceptable in American culture. Irish American Catholic bishops, fearing a large-scale loss of faith in the first-generation Irish American children, took the unprecedented step of creating an alternative school system in which priests and sisters would be exclusively responsible for the early education of immigrant children and their offspring (Doyle, 1991). The success of the new school system was ensured when it was enthusiastically accepted as a career choice by thousands of celibate Catholic priests and sisters. Their lifelong dedication to the church as an educational institution was similar to the dedication to family made by the lifelong unmarried children of farm families in rural Ireland as cited earlier. The Catholic school system became self-perpetuating when a large number of the first-generation Irish Americans educated in Catholic schools chose to become the unmarried priests and sisters responsible for continuing the system (Shannon, 1963).

The economic and political success of the second generation of Irish Americans, at the close of the 19th century and into the early years of the 20th century, provided the resources for a steady increase of involvement by Irish Americans in the internal affairs of Ireland. Irish Americans were a major source of the funding for the Irish Home Rule Movement, a Dublin-based organization attempting to establish a political base for the eventual ending of Britain's colonial rule in Ireland (Walsh, 1989). The failure of that organization to have any impact on British policy led to a slow but steady growth in Ireland of the more radically inclined Irish Republican Army (IRA), which advocated a military rebellion within Ireland against British rule (Breen, 1990).

On April 24, 1916, almost a thousand members of the IRA took control of the General Post Office and other public buildings in Dublin. They immediately announced the formation of an independent Irish Republic. Their revolution collapsed 1 week later after the loss of over 400 lives and the destruction of most of downtown Dublin by British artillery (Kennedy & McHugh, 1988).

The rebellion in Dublin did not initially have the support of Irish Americans who tended to advocate the nonviolent political approach of the failed Home Rule Movement. A British decision to execute the surviving members of the rebellion by firing squad transformed the earlier pacifism of many Irish Americans into a financial support pattern for the new wave of Irish revolutionaries (Shannon, 1963). The "Irish cause" soon became a major concern to American Irish who began to provide substantial funding to a new Irish political party which now advocated immediate and total independence from Great Britain under the title of Sinn Fein. Members of this political party won a series of surprising victories in the British parliamentary elections of 1918. The winning Sinn Fein candidates, however, declined to take the parliamentary seats to which they had been elected. They remained in Dublin where, in January 1919, they declared themselves to be the leaders of a free Irish Republic (Fitzpatrick, 1984).

The leadership of the Irish rebellion immediately turned to Irish Americans in an effort to obtain funding for clandestine military operations to be conducted against British forces in Ireland under IRA leader Michael Collins. Eamon de Valera, the first president of the new Irish Republic, was sent to the United States in an effort to secure support from the administration of President Woodrow Wilson and from the Irish American community. Irish Americans immediately raised $10 million with the promise of additional funding as needed, thereby insuring long-term financial support for the type of guerilla warfare which was being conducted by the IRA in Ireland. President Wilson, however, declined to provide any type of political support for the Irish movement toward independence. Wilson informed British authorities that the U.S. government would not exert any diplomatic pressure to gain peace in Ireland (Shannon, 1963).

From 1919 to 1921, British forces in Ireland fought a war of attrition against a relatively small but very mobile rebel force that could rely on extensive local support in attacks on British garrisons and outposts scattered throughout Ireland.

A 1921 peace treaty negotiated between the IRA leadership and British parliamentary leaders was soon found to be unacceptable to a large number of rank and file members of the IRA who had sought a united Ireland completely liberated from British rule (Shannon, 1963). The treaty partitioned Ireland under an agreement whereby the six northernmost Irish counties, thereafter known as Northern Ireland, continued to be ruled by Britain. The remaining Irish counties gained full independence as the Republic of Ireland (Lyons, 1982). British leaders had argued that Northern Ireland, because of its Protestant majority, could not be considered as a political unit under the direction of Catholic leaders in the Republic of Ireland. The partition of Ireland was eventually accepted by a majority of the IRA leadership after a disastrous civil war in Ireland from 1922 to 1923 (Miller & Wagner, 1994).

The Catholic minority in the new Northern Ireland had the same type of extensive links to the U.S. Irish immigrant community as experienced by Catholics in the Irish Republic (O'Hanlon, 1998). Northern Ireland Catholics, however, encountered a systematic exploitation in the labor force of their native land when government and business leaders, who were almost exclusively Protestant, initiated patterns of job discrimination against Catholic employees. Thousands of Catholic workers, confronted with difficulties in the workplace in Northern Ireland, chose to use their family connections to U.S. Irish immigrants as the supporting mechanism for departure to a better life in the United States. Their emigration in ever increasing numbers indirectly intensified the amount of discrimination against Catholic workers in Northern Ireland through the annual loss of Catholic votes in a region of growing discrimination against Catholics (Miller & Wagner, 1998).

Internal warfare between Catholic militants in the IRA and independent, self-maintained Protestant military units, broke out in 1968 and continued for almost 3 decades. On one side was a Protestant majority intent on preserving an economic system that benefited Protestant workers at the expense of Catholic workers. On the other side was a Catholic minority that did not directly support the guerilla warfare techniques of the IRA but that could not find the type of government support needed to unify Northern Ireland through economic justice for all groups (Munck, 1993).

In a surprising reversal of U.S. history, 80 years later, an American president responded to the type of political pressure from Irish American voters that had failed to move President Woodrow Wilson. In 1998, President William Jefferson Clinton brokered a tentative peace agreement between warring factions in Northern Ireland through a U.S.-monitored series of discussions involving the political leadership of Northern Ireland, England, and the Republic of Ireland. The provisions of the peace treaty included a role for the government of the Republic of Ireland in the internal affairs of Northern Ireland as part of a process that could eventually reunite the Ireland partitioned into two separate units at the end of its colonial era in 1923.

The political pressure, which Irish Americans exercised in the United States in their successful effort to use American involvement to end warfare in Northern Ireland, had been slowly building throughout the 20th century. During the early 1900s, the Irish in America began to attain the type of occupational success that had been the focus of earlier generations of Irish immigrants (O'Hanlon, 1998)

By the middle of the 20th century, Irish Americans had moved ahead of the average rankings of U.S. workers in terms of compensation and social standing (MacLaughlin, 1994). Over one half of the entire Irish American workforce could be classified as skilled workers; only 15% of Irish Americans held the unskilled labor positions that their first generation of immigrant ancestors had occupied throughout their entire lives after arriving in the United States (Miller & Wagner, 1998). The Catholic school system, originally established in an effort to safeguard the faith of first-generation Irish immigrant children, can now be regarded as a remarkable vehicle in the upward mobility. The number of school years completed by Irish American immigrant children surpassed that of native-born White Americans in the early decades of the 20th century and the educational advantage experienced by Irish Americans relative to all other Americans has continued to increase in the subsequent decades of the 20th century.

This rapid rise in the educational and economic standing of Irish Americans was accompanied by a slow decline in the number of Irish immigrants to the United States throughout the 20th century. This decline was part of a century long trend in which the preponderance of immigrants to the United States shifted from northern and western Europe to southern and eastern Europe (Bodnar, 1985). A steady decrease in the number of new Irish immigrants, relative to the size of the overall Irish American community, tended to reverse the image of the Irish in America as recent arrivals. That image had been dominant throughout most of the 19th century America where cultural bias against new additions to U.S. society had served as a support base of hostility directed toward Irish Americans. In its place there emerged a less clearly defined view of the Irish American experience (O'Hanlon, 1998). First- and second-generation Irish Americans had been almost totally involved with the Democratic Party in terms of both voting patterns and ideology (Bodnar, 1985). Third-generation Irish Americans, however, began to abandon the party of their parents and their grandparents in favor of the version of Eisenhower Republicanism dominant in the American suburbs to which they had moved in the course of their economic and social upswing (Coleman, 1972). By the middle of the 20th century, most of the 40 million who then claimed some form of Irish descent appeared to be choosing a suburban life style in the recently established pattern of middle and upper-middle class Americans (Fallows, 1979).

This pattern of assimilation into middle-class America and a related disappearance of a distinctively Irish presence in American society, was abruptly reversed in the closing decades of the 20th century. An estimated half-million Irish citizens have chosen to immigrate to the United States in the period between 1980 and 1998.

The number of new Irish immigrants, reversing a century-long decline in Irish immigration to the United States, remains problematic because of two radically new characteristics of the new Irish immigrants: (a) A very large proportion of these Irish immigrants do not have documents justifying their presence in the United States and are therefore technically classified as illegal aliens, and (b) among the proportion of new Irish immigrants who initially have been granted a green card as a temporary entry permit into the United States, there is a tendency to return permanently to Ireland after what might be regarded as a career bene-fitting internship in the United States (O'Hanlon, 1998).

The recent Irish immigrants are also radically different from earlier genera-tions in terms of their advanced levels of economic and social status. A majority tend to be individuals with special skills in managerial and computer related fields of expertise. This new wave of Irish immigrants enjoy employment op-portunities that their first-generation predecessors would find difficult to be-lieve: The most recent Irish emigrants seek and obtain employment at the upper levels of American society rather than at the very bottom of the American pyra-mid as occurred earlier (Miller & Wagner, 1998). Among the new wave of Irish immigrants there is a component that can be technically classified as blue collar, namely, craftsmen and construction-related specialists who find work in the United States as either contractors or subcontractors in various industries. The major advantage held by the Irish immigrants, related to the U.S. workforce within which they compete, is that they are products of a superior early educa-tional system in Ireland with a historic emphasis on the development of writing skills and a more recent orientation toward the development of computer-based technology in all areas of study (Breathnach, 1995). The Irish educational sys-tem, which is universal in early years and merit determined in college entrance decisions, has been regarded as the basic factor responsible for Ireland's num-ber-one ranking in economic growth rates for 5 consecutive years (1993–1998) within the European Union (O'Hanlon, 1998).

Throughout most of the 20th century, the upward mobility of the U.S. de-scendants of Irish immigrants far exceeded that of the Ireland to which they traced their origin. In the 21st century, however, it appears extremely likely that the Irish homeland will mirror the economic advancements gained by Irish im-migrants to the United States. The early Irish immigrants eventually benefited from the global economic dominance being attained as a result of the U.S. posi-tion as a developer of industrial technology. Modern Ireland's status as a late developing nation, strategically located between the superindustrialized regions of Europe and North America, suggests that Ireland will hold a unique position as a provider of advanced technology across two broad regions of economic growth. Irish workers, with advanced skill levels acquired within Ireland, have the option of enhancing their work skills by short-term assignments in either Europe or the United States. Within a 150-year period the once permanent im-migration of unskilled Irish workers to America has been altered to a situation where workers with advanced skills emigrate on a temporary basis to achieve the economic and social status sought but rarely attained by the first generation of Irish immigrants to the United States.

CONCLUSION

Emigration from Ireland through the centuries is associated with all the psychological concepts usually attached to that phenomenon. The Irish emigrant sought relief from oppression and more control over individual existence than was provided by British domination, economic hegemony, and family traditions. The history of Irish emigration is inexorably linked to motivation, memory, social cognition, and learning.

Motivation to emigrate stemmed from the historical situation of land grabbing, penal laws, family hereditary restrictions, famine, poverty, and desire for a better life. Memory, both historical and personal, of the difficulties in an agrarian society, as well as the romanticized accounts of the United States, suppressed fear of the "coffin ships" and the unknown life ahead. All emigrants displayed some element of risk-taking behavior. Memory of Ireland and the family left behind played a significant part in the new immigrants' generosity and motivation to succeed.

Psychologically speaking, the Irish immigrants' social cognition initially involved some negative self-perception based on the exclusionary environment and negative stereotypes attributed to them by their U.S. neighbors. However, over time the increase of immigrants and the social structures that emerged gave a power base to self-image enhancement. With educational, economic, and political success the negative stereotypes receded and the attributions became more positive.

All of the psychological aspects of learning can be found in the history of Irish immigration to the United States. Conditioning in its operant form is associated with the repetition of behavior when that behavior is reinforced. A potential immigrant has heard only the glowing accounts of the rewards that previous immigrants to the United States have experienced. It is less likely that they have heard about the rejections that many experienced. Previous immigrants have also provided the modeling effect for more immigration. Learning in its academic sense was actively pursued by the emigrant from Ireland when the new land offered an inclusionary rather than an exclusionary system of education. Today the Irish educational system has become more comprehensive at even the postsecondary level. The Irish literary figures through history are not the only ones with a claim to international recognition. Today Irish technical experts are sought by many countries. In Ireland, the Irish provide technical expertise to foreign companies who open sites to take advantage of the many educated Irish personnel.

The history and the psychology of the Irish cannot be separated. The history of Ireland abounds with emigration. That same history demonstrates the psychology of victimization and the psychology of success.

REFERENCES

Adams, W. F. (1932). *Ireland and Irish emigration to the new world from 1815 to the famine.* New Haven, CT: Yale University Press.

Bodnar, J. (1985). *The transplanted: A history of immigrants in urban America.* Bloomington: Indiana University Press.

Botticheimer, K. (1971). *English money and Irish land.* London: Oxford University.

Breathnach, P. (1995). Uneven development and Irish peripheralism. In P. Shirlow (Ed.), *Development Ireland: Contemporary issues* (pp. 85–115). London: Pluto.

Breen, R., Hannan, D. F., Rottman, D. B., & Whelan, C. T. (1990). *Understanding contemporary Ireland.* Dublin, Ireland: Gill & Macmillan.

Cardasco, J. (1985). *The immigrant woman in North America.* Metuchen, NJ: Scarecrow.

Clark, D. (1991). *Erin's heirs.* Lexington: University Press of Kentucky.

Coleman, T. (1972). *Passage to America: A history of emigrants from Great Britain and Ireland.* London: Hutchinson.

Connell, K. (1950). *The population of Ireland 1750–1845.* London: Oxford University Press.

Diner, H. (1983). *Erin's daughters in America.* Baltimore: John Hopkins University Press.

Doyle, D. N. (1991). The Irish as urban pioneers in the United States 1850-1870. *Journal of American Ethnic History, 10,* 36–59.

Drudy, P. J. (1985). *The Irish in America: Emigration, assimilation, and impact.* Cambridge, England: Cambridge University Press.

Fallows, M. R. (1979). *Irish Americans: Identity and assimilation.* Englewood Cliffs, NJ: Prentice-Hall.

Fitzpatrick, D. (1984). *Irish emigration 1801–1921.* Dundalk, Ireland: Dundalgan.

Groneman, C., & Norton, M. B. (1987). *To toil the livelong day: America's women at work 1780–1980.* Ithaca, NY: Cornell University Press.

Hansen, M. L. (1961). *The Atlantic migration 1607–1860: A history of the continuing settlement of the United States.* New York: Harper.

Harris, A. D. (1982). *Out to work: A history of wage earning women in the United States.* New York: Oxford University Press.

Higgins, M., & Gibbons, J. (1980). Shopkeepers, grazers, and land agitation in Ireland 1895–1900. In P. J. Drudy (Ed.), *Ireland: Land, politics, and people* (pp. 25–60). Cambridge: Cambridge University Press.

Higham, J. (1965). *Strangers in the land: Patterns of American nativism, 1860–1925.* New York: Atheneum.

Hoppen, K. T. (1985). *Elections, politics and society in Ireland 1832–85.* Oxford: Oxford University Press.

Jackson, C. (1976). *American industry and the European immigrant, 1860–1885.* Cambridge, MA: Harvard University Press.

Johnson, J. H. (1967). Harvest migration from 19th century Ireland. In Institute of British Geographers (Eds.), *Transactions and raiders 1967* (pp. 84-109). London: Pluto.

Kennedy, T. G., & McHugh, D. (1988). *The economic development of Ireland in the 20th century.* London: Routledge.

Lee, J. (1981). *The modernization of Irish society 1848–1918.* Dublin, Ireland: Gill & MacMillan.

Lee, J. (1989). *Ireland 1912–1985: Politics and society.* Cambridge, England: Cambridge University Press.

Lyons, F. S. (1982). *Ireland since the famine.* London: Fontana.

MacLaughlin, J. (1994). *Ireland: The emigrant nursery and the world economy.* Cork, Ireland: Cork University Press.

Miller, K. A. (1985). *Emigrants and exiles: Ireland and the Irish exodus to North America.* New York: Oxford University Press.

Miller, K. A., & Wagner, P. (1994). *Out of Ireland: The story of Irish emigration to America.* Washington, DC: Elliot & Clark.

Munck, R. (1993). *The Irish economy: Results and prospects.* London: Pluto.

O'Hanlon, R. (1998). *The new Irish Americans.* Niwot, CO: Roberts Rinehart.

O'Malley, E. (1985). The problem of late industrialization and the experience of the Republic of Ireland. *Cambridge Journal of Economics, 9,* 246–262.

Shannon, W. V. (1963). *The American Irish.* New York: Macmillan.

Walsh, E. M. (1989). *Ireland's changing demographic structure.* Dublin, Ireland: Gill & Macmillan.

Woodham-Smith, C. (1962). *The great hunger.* London: Hamish Hamilton.

Yans-McLaughlin, V. (1990). *Immigration reconsidered: History, sociology, and politics.* Oxford: Oxford University Press.

6

Caribbean Immigrants from English-Speaking Countries: Sociohistorical Forces, Migratory Patterns, and Psychological Issues in Family Functioning

Jaipaul L. Roopnarine and Meera Shin

Traditional, monochromatic scholarly views on population movements are being assailed by postmodern theorists of cultural studies as often disregarding the complex social, economic, cultural, and linguistic transactions that are at the heart of the immigration process (Cohen, 1997; Foner, 2001a, 2001b; Schiller, Basch, & Blanc, 1995; Zhou, 1997). Today, within the context of globalization, immigration is more likely to be viewed as transnational, involving individuals who move from one country to the next for diverse reasons (e.g., seasonal farmwork, to study, for business ventures, etc.) rather than for the single purpose of settling in an area permanently. Some groups form new cultural communities within their new countries; others elect to establish cultural communities in more than one location (transmigrants; multilocal binational families) and/or move between cultural and national boundaries blurring the very notions of natal culture (culture of origin) and host nation (Cohen, 1997; Foner, 2001a; Guarnizo, 1997). Thus, to characterize any diaspora as unidirectional movement from the natal culture to a host nation, and as a process whereby immigrants typically sever all or most ties with the home country and embrace a fierce process of assimilation into a new nation and culture would be inaccurate and misleading. Population movements are affected by complex and diverse factors: colonialism/neocolonialism, class composition of the migrants, labor markets in capitalist-driven economies, economic and technical cooperation between countries, language, racism and discrimination, political oppression, foreign capital penetration into developing countries, and the legal-political aspects of immigration laws to name a few (Foner, 2001b; Grosfoguel 1997; Zhou, 1997).

In this chapter, we discuss different aspects of the social-psychological functioning of Caribbean immigrant families in North America and Europe. After providing a brief sociohistorical account of the different waves of Caribbean population movement and return migration, we focus on a few aspects of family functioning, ethnic identity, the process of reunification with children after lengthy periods of separation, and general mental health issues. Despite the fairly long history of Caribbean population movement and the exploitation and exclusionary practices that have dogged Caribbean migrants, we are only now beginning to piece together a more accurate analysis of the Caribbean diasporas. We hasten to add that the available information on the psychological functioning of Caribbean immigrants is rather sparse because most of the published work in the area has focused on economic and sociopolitical issues. Although there is a growing body of work on Cuban, Haitian, and Dominican population movement to North America (e.g., Pressar & Graham, 2001), our emphasis here is on the peoples of the Anglophone Caribbean (Guyana, Jamaica, Barbados, St. Kitts, Nevis, Trinidad and Tobago, Grenada, and the other smaller islands of the eastern Caribbean). Reference to groups from other parts of the Caribbean are for demographic comparisons only.

According to some scholars (e.g., Knight & Palmer, 1989), the Caribbean extends from the Bahamas to Trinidad and Tobago and includes the continental countries of Belize, Guyana, Surinam, and French Guyana. This definition is closely aligned with the related colonial histories of the countries in the region. The different countries were variously affected by French, Dutch, British, and/or Spanish colonization. The Caribbean has a population of over 30 million people. In the English-speaking Caribbean, Guyana has a population of around 712,000 people (83,000 square miles), Belize 239,000 (8,803 square miles), Jamaica 2,595,000 people (4,244 square miles), Barbados 257,000 people (166 square miles), Trinidad and Tobago 1,272,000 people (1,980 square miles), Grenada 95,000 people (133 square miles), and Saint Kitts and Nevis 41,000 people (104 square miles). In addition to African-Caribbean people, the English-speaking Caribbean has significant numbers of East Indians (Guyana and Trinidad and Tobago), people of mixed ethnic backgrounds (e.g., Black Caribs), and smaller numbers of Europeans, people of Middle Eastern origins, and Amerindians (Native people). Although English is the official language across the region, most people speak a patois (termed *Creole, Creolese* in a few countries), and some East Indians speak Hindi.

A BRIEF HISTORICAL OVERVIEW OF CARIBBEAN POPULATION MOVEMENTS

Population movement within and external to the Caribbean has been discussed in several articles (Foner, 2001a; Grosfoguel, 1997; Marshall, 1982; Vickerman, 2001). We present only a brief overview of the literature on Caribbean migrants as a backdrop to our current endeavor. Most readers are aware of the European conquest of the Caribbean, decimation of the indigenous population, forced importation of African slaves, and the introduction of indentured servants from Asia after slavery was abolished. Our discussion sidesteps much of that history and focuses generally on the movement of Caribbean people during the last 150 years.

According to Marshall (1982), the Caribbean population movement after emancipation can be divided into several phases. The first, occurring roughly between 1835 and 1880, was more internal and interterritorial in nature. Emancipation permitted people a greater degree of mobility both away from the plantation to pursue other forms of labor and to other territories to procure stable employment (e.g., British Guiana and Trinidad). It is estimated that there was a continuous flow of people from most of the eastern Caribbean islands, especially Barbados, to British Guiana and Trinidad. During this period, other movements occurred as well; people moved from Dominica to the goldfields of Venezuela and from Barbados to Surinam and St. Croix. These movements were influenced by several factors: a shortage of labor as sugarcane production increased in some territories, by drought on some of the islands, the limited availability of arable land, and the desire to set up free independent villages. Whereas people returned to their own islands after seasonal work, a sizable number remained in the receiving territories (Marshall, 1982).

The second phase of Caribbean population movement coincided with certain notable world events. People continued to move to other areas of the Caribbean (e.g., Cuba, Bermuda, and the Dominican Republic), but the building of the railroad across the Isthmus of Panama and the excavation of the Panama Canal encouraged movement to countries outside of the Caribbean. Between 1853 and 1914, when the Panama Canal was completed, it is estimated that in excess of 130,000 people mainly from Barbados and Jamaica may have moved to Central America (Hall, 1971). Such large-scale population movement was stimulated by high unemployment rates in the West Indian islands due to falling sugar prices, better remittances that enabled islanders to purchase land and open up small businesses, and the active recruitment of contract laborers to do the drudging, manual excavation work (Marshall, 1982). The period between 1899 and 1928 also witnessed the movement of 138,615 Caribbean people to the United States (Reid, 1939/1970).

After these two periods of active population movement, there was a relatively dormant period of out-migration. As a matter of fact, Caribbean people in Central America, in some of the other Spanish-speaking islands (e.g., Cuba), and in the United States began to return home. The Great Depression, discriminatory immigration practices, social change in labor practices, the completion of the Panama Canal, and differential wage structures for Caribbean immigrants all contributed to return migration and the virtual shutdown of out-migration (Marshall, 1982).

Finally, the period after World War II saw impressive waves of population movement from the English-speaking Caribbean to the United Kingdom, Canada, and the United States and from Surinam and Dutch Antilles to Holland. At the same time, there were significant migrations from Puerto Rico and other U.S. Caribbean islands to the United States, from Martinique, French Guiana, and Guadeloupe to France; and from Haiti, the Dominican Republic, and Cuba to the United States (Grosfoguel, 1997; Marshall, 1982). For example, in the 1950s and 1960s, between 6,000 and 8,000 workers per year left Martinique and Guadeloupe for France (Domenach & Picouet, 1990), between 1966 and 1975 about 100,000 Surinamese went to the Netherlands (Kritz, 1981), in excess of 175,000 Jamaicans moved to Great Britain between 1953 and 1962 (Patterson,

1978), and approximately 18,000 per year left for the United States between 1976 and 1985 (Vickerman, 2001).

In the 1980s and 1990s, political and economic upheavals in the Caribbean and more relaxed U.S. immigration policies since 1965 helped to speed up the rate of movement out of the Caribbean. For instance, between 1993 and 1998, 100,063 Jamaicans, 60,163 Guyanese, and 36,898 Trinidadians immigrated to the United States. By the end of the 1990s, nearly 4 million people had migrated from the Caribbean to the United States (U.S. Department of Justice, 1999). These figures exclude undocumented migrants. At the present time, the major destinations for Caribbean migrants are the United States, Great Britain, France, Canada, and the Netherlands. Cuba, Haiti, the Dominican Republic, Jamaica, Trinidad and Tobago, Guyana, and Barbados are the major sending countries. The reasons for the mass exodus are multifaceted and are explored in the next section of the chapter.

Factors that Influence Immigration

Undoubtedly, the factors that influence population movements reach far beyond economics and labor, yet these two issues dominate much of the discourse on immigration worldwide (Grasmuck & Grosfoguel, 1997). As was the case in the past, current population movement out of the Caribbean is chiefly tied to labor. Not unlike other groups of people in struggling economies, Caribbean peoples have joined the worldwide population movement toward the capitalist countries. However, although the overall picture follows this trend, there are intermediary steps in the migration process and the movement appears deliberate where people play an active role in seeking and shaping new opportunities (Duany, 1994). Staying with the economic argument for the moment, Caribbean peoples migrate in a "stair-step hierarchy"—the poorest people move to the less poor nations and people from the latter, in turn, move to the economically developed countries (Bach, 1983; Duany, 1994). In this process, some countries receive as well as send people to other countries (e.g., movement between Guyana and Surinam and between Surinam and the Netherlands). Movement between neighboring countries and within a country's territory is stimulated by wage inequalities (Duany, 1994). Most Caribbean migrants are employed in low-paying jobs (secondary job market), but smaller numbers are employed in the professional ranks with good possibilities for advancement in North America (Grasmuck & Grosfoguel, 1997; Vickerman, 2001).

Perhaps not separate from the rising desire to migrate for economic betterment is the neo-Malthusian ideology that population movement to the developed world should relieve poorer, economically strapped countries of their development woes (Campos, 1980). To this end, some Caribbean governments have encouraged outward movement with the belief that migrants will return home in the future with better skills and capital that may contribute to the development of the home country. Furthermore, the decrease in population, it is reasoned, would lead to the growth of capital (Campos, 1980). According to some scholars (e.g., Duany, 1994), this "safety valve" theory does not begin to account for the multitude of factors that are connected to migration, and with the continuous flow of people out of the Caribbean it is difficult to say whether the overall economic conditions of most countries in the region have improved much (e.g., Guyana).

Along with the economic reasons for migration is a host of interrelated factors that may govern population movements and to what countries. The post–World War II migration of people from Surinam and the Dutch Antilles to the Netherlands, from the West Indies to England, and from Martinique and Guadeloupe to France was the direct result of political ties to former colonial "mother countries" (colonial legal-political incorporation) (Grosfoguel, 1997). To some degree, these population movements were organized by the colonial governments through recruitment efforts to build the mother country after the war (e.g., London Transport), and to changes in immigration laws in the United States (e.g., the Immigration Act of 1965) and elsewhere that encouraged/permitted entire families to immigrate. Geopolitics and labor needs in the receiving countries did affect who migrated and when, whereas immigration laws assisted in sifting out professionals from unskilled people (Portes & Rambaut, 1990). Frankly, if nurses were needed in the United States, then individuals from countries with good health training programs (e.g., Trinidad) were encouraged to migrate (Phillips, 1996); if fruit pickers (men from Barbados and Jamaica) were needed to harvest crops, then they were permitted to enter North America.

A smaller but significant number of middle- and upper-class Caribbean people migrate to North America, Europe, and within the Caribbean as students and professionals to acquire skills in universities and technical schools. In one survey (Gmelch, 1987), 38% of Barbadian students went to Britain, 17% to the United States, 17% to Canada, and 10% to Jamaica. The preimmigration intention is to return after the training is complete because of contractual agreements with the home government, better job opportunities, and improved living standards or to help in the development of the home country. During the training period, most student migrants work in the host country or are supported by their relatives. No good estimates exist on how many student migrants actually return to the respective Caribbean countries.

Last but not least, political oppression and exclusionary economic policies, as evidenced in Guyana and Haiti for decades, has led to large-scale movement of people out of the Caribbean to ethnic enclaves in New York, Miami, Los Angeles, Toronto, Amsterdam, Paris, and Montreal. These large metropolitan areas have the community networks and enough internal organization to perpetuate the flow of legal and illegal immigrants to them (see Foner, 2001 and Neto & Mullet, 1998, for a discussion of the network factor in migration). There are different areas of Queens, Brooklyn, Jersey City, Newark, Miami, Los Angeles, and Toronto, among other cities, that have sizable ethnic groups from the different Caribbean islands and Guyana. Political leaders from the Caribbean countries often visit these communities recognizing their growing political influence and economic power.

The reasons why people immigrate transcend simple push-pull explanations that are so rooted in the economics of different countries. As noted above, economic conditions may be the overriding factor that fuels the population movement engine. However, political oppression, immigration laws in the receiving countries, government policies in the sending countries, labor market needs, training needs of students and professionals, and contextual and cultural factors in ethnic enclaves in the receiving societies all play a significant role in the population march from the Caribbean to North America and Europe (Grasmuck & Grosfoguel, 1997).

Factors That Influence Return Migration

Surveys of Caribbean immigrants in North America and Europe indicate that most express a desire to return to the natal culture (Rubenstein, 1983). For example, only 5% of West Indians in London reported that they wished to stay in England long term (Brookes, 1969; Foner, 1978), and among people leaving Barbados only 7% of worker and 10% of student migrants thought they were leaving the island permanently (Gmelch, 1987). However, of the Jamaicans who left for England between 1950 and 1962, only 7% returned to the island (Segal, 1969), and of the 20,000 people who left Guyana between 1970 and 1976, only 16% returned (Strachan, 1983). The fact is only a small percentage of English-speaking migrants return to settle permanently in their home country (Rubenstein, 1983), and among these quite a few emigrate again (Strachan, 1983). These figures might be lower today because of recent discouraging economic and social conditions in the Caribbean. Estimates of the contributions of return migrants to the social and economic life of the communities to which they return are at best nebulous. In this section of the chapter, we examine the characteristics of return migrants, the forces involved in their return to the Caribbean, and their impact on the economic development of their respective countries.

Researchers have classified return migrants in terms of their intentions and reasons for returning home (Gmelch, 1983, 1987). In one study (Gmelch, 1987), Barbadian migrants were classified as *worker migrants* (they venture abroad to acquire capital and skills, eventually returning home to get a good job), *student migrants* (they go abroad to study, acquire technical and other skills; most [85%] held jobs during their tenure abroad; they usually plan to stay until training is over but most stay for longer durations), and *seasonal migrant workers* (these individuals go abroad for fixed periods at a time to engage in agricultural work; may stay away for 2 to 8 months at a time and may make several trips over their lifetime; they live in enclaves with other Caribbean people).

Not all migrants return because of better economic opportunities in the home country, however. Research on Guyanese return migrants revealed that more than half (52%) of them wanted to help in the development of Guyana, 20% could not stay abroad because of visa or work permit problems, and 5% were deported for different reasons (Strachan, 1983). Similar findings regarding the desire to help develop the home country have been reported for younger, better educated Jamaican returned migrants (Taylor, 1976).

But who are the return migrants and what types of skills do they possess upon their return? Despite the overall claim that most return migrants acquired skills abroad that are essential to the development of their home countries, we should bear in mind that the skills attained may not be relevant for the current state of development of poorer nations. For example, the large-scale farming work of migrants in the North America may be of little help in small-scale farming in other parts of the world (Weist, 1979). This may also be true for highly skilled computer technologists. Nevertheless, most return migrants leave the developed capitalist countries more worldly, in some cases more educated, better off economically in the short term, and more aware of racial and economic disparities and injustices (Lowenthal, 1972).

Upon their return to Barbados, 33% of worker migrants and 54% of student migrants were in professional jobs (compared with 8% and 16%, respectively, prior to migration and to 9% in the population as a whole). Of these, 48% of worker migrants and 95% of student migrants earned a university degree. Worker migrants lived abroad on average 15.3 years and student migrants lived abroad on average 9.7 years (Gmelch, 1987). Among Guyanese returnees, 31% were in professional/managerial jobs, 22% obtained a degree and 24% a diploma, and the average stay abroad was 5.7 years (range = 1–24 years) (Strachan, 1983). From these studies, it is clear that most return migrants obtained job training or skills and were employed for different periods abroad. Although some may have been at the lower end of the economic spectrum abroad, they frequently returned to professional jobs back home (Strachan, 1983). But as laudable as the goals for returning home might be, the impact of returnees on the development of Caribbean countries runs against the tide of a steady "brain drain" to the more industrialized nations to the north. More skilled and already qualified people are attracted and in some cases recruited (as in the case of nurses from Trinidad to the United States) to the possibility of a better life in North America and Europe (Phillips, 1996).

Besides bringing educational and technical skills with them to the home country, returnees bring capital and goods that enable them to establish a better standard of living. However, most of the capital flow from migrants to the home country comes from transnationals and through remittances from relatives abroad (Rubenstein, 1983; Schiller et al., 1995). As stated earlier in this chapter, transnationals maintain social, economic, and political ties to the home country. They transfer funds to the home country with the hope of returning someday, support relatives and village wives and children, and set up joint businesses with relatives in the home country (Rubenstein, 1979). Although remittances are used for food, clothing, and shelter and to purchase property and to start up businesses, their overall impact on the economy of the different Caribbean countries has not been entirely positive. In some countries (e.g., Montserrat, St. Vincent, Nevis), agricultural production did slow down because of dependency on financial help from relatives abroad (Frucht, 1968; Rubenstein, 1979).

In sum, it is difficult to gauge how much impact return migrants have on the economic and social development of the home country. What is clear is that return migrants like migrants are not a homogeneous group and do not subscribe to set patterns of behaviors. Whereas some return to settle permanently, others move back and forth or establish ties in more than one community. And most Caribbean migrants maintain the strong belief that they will return "home" someday. Regardless of their stance, Caribbean immigrants in the United States send substantial amounts of money in remittances to the home country. (A 1981 survey of 302 Caribbean cane cutters in Florida showed that the workers remitted $19 million; Wood & McCoy, 1983.) The impact such remittances have had on the economic development of the region has been negated to some degree by the steady flow of qualified people out of the Caribbean and reduced productivity due to the expectation of financial help from relatives abroad.

Some Sociodemographic Characteristics of Select Caribbean Immigrant Groups

Because of their language skills, initial higher educational attainment, and better access networks to jobs, English-speaking Caribbean immigrants have fared relatively well in North America and Europe. To illustrate, let us examine some sociodemographic characteristics of Jamaican and Guyanese immigrants who live in the New York City area, a major destination for these groups after immigration (between 1990 and 1994, 40% of Jamaicans settled in New York City) (Vickerman, 2001). In 1990, the mean household income for Jamaicans in the United States was $45,088; 30.3% owned homes; 67.3% were high school and 14.7% (23.6% for women) were college graduates; 20.2% were in upper white-collar occupations; 9.4% were living below the poverty line; and 8.8% were unemployed (U.S. Bureau of Census, 1990). Twenty percent of Jamaicans worked for the government and the not-for-profit sectors (Grasmuck & Grosfoguel, 1997). Similarly, the labor force participation for British Afro-Caribbean people was 73%, with 53% of families living in owner occupied homes, and only 17% of workers were employed in the manufacturing industries (Grosfoguel, 1997).

An even more impressive sociodemographic profile emerges when we consider Indo-Caribbean immigrants in New York City (Queens and Bronx) and northern New Jersey (Jersey City, Newark, Bloomfield). In the households sampled for a study on the sociocultural influences on children's academic achievement, 13% of families made over $100,000, 7% made between $75,000 and $100,000, 20% made between $50,000 and $75,000, and 47% made between $25,000 and $50,000. Only 13% made below $25,000 and a remarkable 96% of the men were employed as of 1999. Most families owned homes, and 28% of the men and 22% of the women were college graduates, whereas 82% of the men and 74% of the women were high school graduates. Thirty percent of men were in professional jobs (Roopnarine, 1999).

These brief statistics do not begin to provide a complete picture of the diverse socioeconomic circumstances and experiences (e.g., racism, class) of Caribbean immigrants in North America and Europe. Nor are we suggesting that all English-speaking Caribbean immigrants are living the Horatio Alger story. Such a representation would certainly be misleading. Caribbean immigrants are still concentrated in the manufacturing industries and in service jobs (Grasmuck

& Grosfoguel, 1997) and their household income may reflect the earnings of more than two individuals. A fair number purchase homes in ethnic enclaves (e.g., East Flatbush, Brooklyn; Jamaica and Richmond Hill in Queens) that were occupied by departing White families. In the ethnic enclaves, they set up businesses, health clinics, and churches, send remittances to the home country, and disperse capital, goods, and services from North America and Europe to the Caribbean.

SOCIAL PSYCHOLOGICAL ISSUES
AND CARIBBEAN MIGRANTS

Having provided a brief historical overview of population movements within and external to the Caribbean and the reasons for why people move, we now turn to a few of the pertinent social psychological issues surrounding immigration. In particular, we focus on child-rearing practices, husband-wife relationships, separation and reunification of family members during the immigration process, the potential for family conflicts, violation of expectations about life abroad, ethnic identity, and mental health issues.

Family Relationships

Inherent in family relationships is a range of complex and interrelated factors. Our aim here is to cover specific aspects of family functioning attendant to the immigration process: parent-child practices and relationships, children's separation from and reunification with parents, and sources of family conflict/stress.

Husband-Wife/Partner Relationships. Caribbean families are diverse in their family forms with a preponderance of nonlegal unions and female-headed households. Among the various ethnic groups, marriage is more common among East Indians, Chinese Caribbean, and Amerindians than African Caribbean people (Roopnarine, 1997; Roopnarine, Clawson, Benetti, & Lewis, 2000). There is a marked pattern of gender-differentiated roles and activities among the various ethnic groups, and most men believe in and subscribe to the traditional double standard in husband-wife relationships—fidelity and subordination for women, and dominance and outside sexual liaisons for men (Roopnarine & Brown, 1997).

Both census and research data suggest that the marital patterns prevailing in the Caribbean are maintained for Indo-Caribbean immigrants in New York City (Roopnarine, 1999) and that the percentage of female-headed households for Jamaican immigrants is as high (33%) in five counties in New York City as in Jamaica (34%) (Grasmuck & Grosfoguel, 1997). By the same token, in a survey of Caribbean immigrants in New York, New Jersey, Pennsylvania, Washington, DC, and Delaware, Millette (1998) discovered that families *are* changing their views about husband-wife/partner relationships and responsibilities, but slowly. For example, the double-standard in matters of sexual exclusivity, loyalty, and obedience echoed by men in the Caribbean was clearly present in immigrant men's responses to items on the survey. By contrast, women displayed a strong intolerance for the "West Indian way of life" and expected their husbands/partners to be affectionate and provide companionship, to care for family members in growth-promoting ways, and to be a joint partner in decision making regarding family affairs (see Foner, 1994).

Information obtained from a study of two-parent predominantly married Indo-Caribbean immigrants in the New York City area indicated a largely traditional pattern of male-female roles. Men and women were far more likely to designate the provider role to fathers than to mothers. In terms of the division of household labor, women assumed major responsibility for the labor-intensive, drudging work around the home when compared to men. On a brighter note, men spent about 4.4 hours during a typical weekday and 14.4 hours on the weekend in caring for and being around children. They also spent about 7.8 hours per week in educational activities with their prekindergarten and kindergarten-aged children. Comparatively speaking, these figures indicate respectable levels of involvement on the part of Indo-Caribbean immigrant men with young children (Roopnarine, 1999).

Child-Rearing Practices. The child-rearing practices and beliefs of Caribbean and Caribbean immigrant families have been discussed in detail (Gopaul-McNicol, 1993; Roopnarine, 1999; Roopnarine & Brown, 1997). Summarily, English-speaking Caribbean parents commonly use a parenting style that embodies authoritarian/punitive control combined with indulgence and protectiveness (Leo-Rhynie, 1997). A preference for this mode of parenting has been endorsed by Caribbean immigrant parents in the United States (Roopnarine, 1999) and in Great Britain (Arnold, 1997). Accompanying this practice are the harsh discipline techniques frequently employed by immigrant parents (Deyoung & Zigler, 1994; Foner, 1997; Roopnarine, 1999) with the goal that children will be obedient and show respect to them.

As might be expected, the rigid parenting styles that the immigrant parents had experienced themselves in the Caribbean do not always serve them well abroad. As children rebel and become more disobedient, despair and depression are evidenced in mothers. Needless to say, children suffer too. Some run away, others are abandoned (Arnold, 1997; Rambally, 1995), and some parents get into trouble with social service agencies for hitting children and/or leaving them unsupervised (Baptiste, Hardy, & Lewis, 1997). Possibly, the childhood problems evidenced in children of Caribbean immigrants could be attributed, in part, to ethnic identity confusion in the new culture, problems adjusting to school, and disappointment with parents' ability to fashion a more successful life for the family in the new society (Baptiste et al., 1997).

Separation From and Reunification with Parents. During the waves of migration in the 1950s and 1960s, Caribbean parents often migrated first leaving their children behind in the care of relatives (Arnold, 1997). Today, although immediate family members migrate as a unit, there are still significant numbers of Caribbean men and women who migrate in a serial pattern leaving children for unspecified durations in the home country (Suárez-Orozco & Todorova, 2001). Within these families, the separation from and subsequent reunification with attachment figures years later may pose psychological difficulties for children. In some reports (Robertson, 1975), it was calculated that among Caribbean migrants to Great Britain the mean length of separation from children was 5.2 years. Quite often, children mourned silently for their absent parents while becoming attached to those who were charged with their care. The nature and quality of the care provided by these alternative caregivers went largely unchecked and children rarely, if ever, received any counseling for their distress.

Not surprisingly, after long periods of separation, reunification with parents was problematic for some families. After the initial delight of having their children reunited with them, some parents became disappointed with their children's lack of gratitude to be with them as children were distraught, withdrawn, and resentful (Cheetham, 1972). Problems also arose from difficulty in communicating with children and in imposing strict discipline; these problems were more common among older than younger children (Robertson, 1975; Sewell-Coker, Hamilton-Collins, & Fein, 1985). Taking our cue from a vast attachment literature (De Wolf & van IJzendoorn, 1997; Rutter, 1972), these transitional difficulties may have their origins first in the disruption of the bond to a primary attachment figure at a sensitive period in the young child's life and again later on in the termination of relationships with individuals who cared for the child during parental absence. Multiple losses to attachment figures have been linked to psychopathology (Bowlby, 1969). Furthermore, parents were attempting to reconnect with children who had spent their formative years away from them. Not knowing what had transpired in their children's lives during that time, they struggled to integrate children into the family, in a new and challenging environment. As they became more aware of the depth of transitional difficulties, mothers displayed more frustration and became less affectionate toward their children (Robertson, 1975; see also Suárez-Orozco & Todorova, 2001, for a discussion of this issue).

Ethnic/Cultural Identity. Ethnic identity has been studied in terms of bicultural existence and intergenerational conflicts (Szapocznik & Kurtines, 1993), enculturation, schooling, and social adjustment (see Gibson & Ogbu, 1991; Phinney, Lochner, & Murphy, 1990; Suárez-Orozco & Todorova, 2001), and family experiences (Greenfield & Cocking, 1994). What findings exist on children of Caribbean immigrants suggest that children rejected their "Blackness" in favor of "White" practices (Maxime, 1986), adolescent girls experienced identification conflicts with parents and had difficulties with representations of their own ethnicity (Weinrich, 1979), children experienced lower status in their peer groups (Baptiste, 1990), and some faced difficulties in school when they aligned themselves with an immigrant identity (Waters, 1999). No doubt, these setbacks can lead to confusion and uncertainty as to what might be expected of children at home and at school (Arnold, 1997). The reasons why children reject aspects of themselves and their heritage and whether this process represents a temporary phase in the ethnic identity formation of children of Caribbean immigrants need further exploration. The push toward multicultural education and the greater acceptance of diverse cultural practices in North America and Europe could attenuate some of the negative aspects of ethnic identity development reported of children in previous decades.

Potential Sources of Family Conflict/Stress. Baptiste and colleagues (1997) identified several important life circumstances and experiences that are potentially stressful and that may bring Caribbean immigrant families in for counseling. Among them are discrepancy between expectations and realities of living in the new country, changes in family relationships and parenting styles after immigration, marginality and minority status, loss of parental authority to discipline children, and the assimilation of dominant culture values by children that could replace or conflict with "Caribbean values."

As is discussed later on, immigrant families who embrace an integrationist approach to raising children in their new country have children with better mental health than those who utilize an isolationist/disenfranchised approach (Berry, 1998). In this vein, Caribbean immigrant parents who hold on to their extreme parental authority approach to childrearing and at the same time ignore the evolving selves of their children may be creating an atmosphere that is ripe for parent-child conflicts. Beliefs about the inappropriateness of physical punishment, the "lax" nature of North American society, and the right of children to question authority figures go against the grain of socialization values in the Caribbean. Sometimes, the collision in values extends beyond the family to governmental and social service agencies that may intercede to protect the rights and safety of children (Baptiste et al., 1997). Clearly, this is seen as undermining the authority of parents to raise their children as they did back home, regardless of their preparedness for parenting in post-industrialized societies.

Another potential source of family conflicts resides in the violation of expectations about life in the new country. The euphoria surrounding the trip to the "promised land" can obscure the difficulty Caribbean immigrants may encounter later on in finding employment, obtaining licenses for employment, finding housing, confronting racism, and being designated a minority group. If the benefits of immigration fall below expectations, families may experience anger, resentment, and depression. Better outcomes might be expected of families whose pre-immigration appraisals of life in North America and Europe were more realistic (Baptiste et al., 1997).

Mental Health of Immigrants

Increasingly, researchers and clinical workers are recognizing the need to develop culturally-sensitive mental health assessment tools and instruments (Dana, 2000; Lonner, 1990; Triandis, 1990) and services for immigrant families and children. In reconceptualizing mental health services for immigrants, the goal is to take into consideration the health belief systems, institutional practices, and social relationships of different ethnic groups (Berry, 1998; Sue & Sue, 1990). Unfortunately, problems continue to exist regarding the appropriate diagnosis and subsequent therapeutic treatment of Caribbean immigrants and their children (Baptiste et al., 1997; Kareem & Littlewood, 1992). Treating the social and psychological problems of Caribbean immigrants as having the same underlying causes and as being similar to nonnormative behavioral patterns manifested in the receiving countries has clouded the issue even more. A scattered literature on the mental health problems of Caribbean immigrants covers a few disparate areas: psychiatric disorders in families and children, psychological problems associated with separation and reunification, self-poisoning, the overrepresentation of families and children in the social service system, and stressors associated with the process of acculturation.

Beginning with the prevalence of psychiatric disorders, Hemsi (1967) reported that the rate of mental illness among West Indians was three times that of the British population, but Bagley (1971) found that rates of mental illnesses were similar in Caribbean immigrants in Britain and the British population. Despite very low rates of tense depression and anxiety states, Caribbean immigrants showed higher rates of schizophrenia than British-born controls. Likewise, the suicide rate through self-poisoning among West Indians in Birmingham (Merrill & Owens, 1986, 1988) was comparatively higher (56/100,000 and 180/100,000) than among residents in Trinidad and Tobago (16.3/100,000; Burke, 1974). Along the same lines, West Indian immigrant children exhibited more disturbed behaviors at school than at home (Rutter, Yule, Berger, Mortan, & Bagley, 1974), there were higher rates of mental illnesses among Black youths of Caribbean background born in Britain than in their parents (Littlewood & Lipsedge, 1988), and there exists an overrepresentation of Black youths from the Caribbean in some segments of the social service systems of Canada (Rambally, 1995). Concurrent with these tendencies are debates about the mental health interpretations of not only the etiology of psychiatric disorders but also the meaning of immigrant behaviors that are deemed pathological (see Francis, 1993, for a discussion of psychiatric racism).

More comprehensive analyses of the life circumstances of immigrant children residing in Canada (Munroe-Blum, Boyle, Offord, & Kates, 1989) revealed that they were more likely to live in crowded conditions in urban areas, to live in subsidized housing, to be from larger families, to have less educated, low-income parents, to have parents who experienced some family dysfunction, and to have families who are less likely to be on welfare. Surprisingly, in the face of these adversities, child immigrant status by itself was not a significant predictor of childhood psychiatric disorder or school failure. In related work (Pawliuk et al., 1996), it was the acculturation style of immigrant families rather than that of their children that predicted behavioral difficulties in childhood. Parental acceptance of the majority culture practices was associated with healthy psychological functioning in children.

Data specific to children of Caribbean immigrants indicate that the major sources of psychological difficulties result from conflicts with parents due to rigid and inflexible parenting practices surrounding discipline (Arnold, 1997), depression among parents that leads to ineffective parenting or a marked inability to meet children's emotional and physical needs (Gorrell-Barnes, 1975), antisocial problems in girls (Nicol, 1971), the repression of "blackness" and rejection of parents' cultural practices and status (Maxime, 1986), and abuse associated with reunification after prolonged separation from parents (daCosta, 1985). Because the problems associated with separation and reunion were discussed in the parenting section above, we turn briefly to the acculturation process as a potential source of different kinds of psychological difficulties for families who adopt different coping strategies (Berry, 1998).

In a recent paper on acculturation and health, Berry (1998) cogently argued that immigration in and of itself does not automatically lead to social and psychological problems. Basically, Berry (1998) suggested that some families adjust well during the postimmigration period by learning the skills necessary to function successfully in the new culture while simultaneously discarding behavioral tendencies that may not be as functional for life in the new society. As the process is not uniform across ethnic groups and individuals, some immigrants experience "acculturative stress," whereas others are so overwhelmed by the demands for change required of the new environment that they become psychologically debilitated. The view at this time is that those families who utilize an integrationist (value and combine aspects of heritage and new culture), as opposed to a marginalization approach to acculturation experience better mental health (Berry & Sabatier, 1996; see also Chapter 2). Undoubtedly, understanding variations in acculturation strategy makes better sense than other propotions (e.g., Sluzki, 1979) that focus on fixed pattern stage sequences or linear assimilation. After all, immigrants enter the postindustrialized societies with different levels of professional and linguistic skills, education, and economic resources. These different "entry points" coupled with gender and ethnicity are bound to affect the adjustment patterns and destinies of Caribbean immigrant families and those of their children (Foner, 1997; Waters, 1999; Zhou, 1997).

CONCLUSION

In this chapter, we provided a brief synopsis of Caribbean population movements and return migration. Individuals from the English-speaking Caribbean migrate for diverse reasons, though economics may be the major impetus. Thus far, several analyses suggest that the impact of migration on the social and economic life of people in the sending countries has not been favorable. The constant brain drain of highly qualified people out of the Caribbean, and the increased likelihood that those who acquire skills abroad and return home look to migrate again, can only conspire against economic growth throughout the region.

With respect to social and psychological issues, overall families who use an integrationist approach to parenting by incorporating both natal and new culture practices have been shown to have better mental health (Berry, 1998). Most new Caribbean immigrants, however, tend to stick to parenting practices that are predominantly aligned with those in the home country. Their punitive/authoritarian parenting styles can lead to parent-child conflicts. Equally troublesome are problems that may stem from discrepancies in beliefs about husband-wife roles and responsibilities, perceived loss of parental control over children, prolonged separation of children from and reunification with parents, violation of expectations about life in the new country, fusing an identity using natal and new culture values and practices, racism and minority status, and finding suitable employment. Judging from the employment patterns, levels of school achievement, home ownership figures, and remittances sent home, Caribbean immigrants of the last 2 decades have done remarkably well in North America and Europe.

NOTE

This chapter was written while the authors were supported by funds from the Faculty Development Fund in the College for Human Development at Syracuse University. We extend our sincere gratitude to Lomarsh Roopnarine who provided valuable insights into the immigration process and extensive comments on the paper. The chapter matured quite a bit as a result of his feedback.

REFERENCES

Arnold, E. (1997). Issues in re-unification of migrant West Indian children in the United Kingdom. In J. L. Roopnarine & J. Brown (Eds.), *Caribbean families: Diversity among ethnic groups* (pp. 243–258). Norwood, NJ: Ablex.

Bach, R. L. (1983). Emigration from the Spanish-speaking Caribbean. In M. M. Kritz (Ed.), *U.S. immigration and refugee policy: Global and domestic issues* (pp. 133–153). Lexington, MA: Heath.

Bagley, C. (1971). Mental illness in immigrant minorities in London. *Journal of Biosocial Science, 3,* 449–459.

Baptiste, D. (1990). The treatment of adolescent immigrants and their families in cultural transition: Issues and recommendations. *Contemporary Family Therapy, 12,* 3–22.

Baptiste, D. A., Hardy, K. V., & Lewis, L. (1997). Clinical practice with Caribbean immigrant families in the United States: The intersection of emigration, immigration, culture, and race. In J. L. Roopnarine & J. Brown (Eds.), *Caribbean families: Diversity among ethnic groups* (pp. 275–303). Norwood, NJ: Ablex.

Berry, J. W. (1998). Acculturation and health: Theory and research. In S. S. Kazarian & D. R. Evans (Eds.), *Cultural clinical psychology: Theory, research, and practice* (pp. 39–57). New York: Oxford University Press.

Berry, J. W., & Sabatier, C. (1996, August). *Acculturation and adaptation of second generation youth in Montreal.* Paper presented at the meeting of the International Association for Cross-Cultural Psychology, Montreal, Quebec, Canada.

Bowlby, J. (1969). *Attachment and loss.* London: Hogarth Press.

Brookes, D. (1969). Who will go back. *Race Today, 1*(5), 131–134.

Burke, A. W. (1974). Clinical aspects of attempted suicide among women in Trinidad and Tobago. *British Journal of Psychiatry, 116,* 489–491.

Campos, R. (1980). Poblacion y migracion: Perspectivas Teoricas en su estudio [Population and migration: Theoretical perspectives in their investigation]. In R. L. Rameriz & W. S. Deliz (Eds.), *Crisis y critica de las ciencias sociales* [Crisis and a criticism of the social sciences] (pp. 215–230). Rio

Piedras, Puerto Rico: Center for Social Investigations, University of Puerto Rico.

Cheetham, J. (1972). *Social work with immigrants*. London: Routledge & Kegan Paul.

Cohen, R. (1997). *Global diasporas: An introduction*. Seattle: University of Washington Press.

daCosta, E. (1985). *Reunion after long-term disruption of the parent-child bond in older children: Clinical features and psychodynamic issues*. Toronto, Ontario, Canada: Clark Institute of Psychiatry.

Dana, R. H. (2000). Multicultural assessment of child and adolescent personality and psychopathology. In A. L. Comunian & U. P. Gielen (Eds.), *International perspectives on human development* (pp. 233–258). Lengerich, Germany: Pabst.

De Wolf, M., & van IJzendoorn, M. (1997). Sensitivity and attachment: A meta-analysis on parental antecedents of infant security. *Child Development, 68*, 571–591.

Deyoung, Y., & Zigler, E. F. (1994). Machismo in two cultures: Relation to punitive child-rearing practices. *American Journal of Orthopsychiatry, 64*, 386–395.

Domenach, H., & Picouet, M. (1990). French West Indies. In W. Serow, C. N. Nam, D. F. Sly, & R. H. Weller (Eds.), *Handbook on international migration* (pp. 69–89). Westport, CT: Greenwood.

Duany, J. (1994). Beyond the safety valve: Recent trends in Caribbean migration. *Social and Economic Studies, 43*, 95–122.

Foner, N. (1978). *Jamaican farewell: Jamaican migrants in London*. Berkeley: University of California Press.

Foner, N. (1994). *Ideology and social practice in the Jamaican diaspora* (Working Paper No. 65). New York: Russell Sage Foundation.

Foner, N. (1997). The immigrant family: Cultural legacies and cultural changes. *International Migration Review, 31*, 961–974.

Foner, N. (2001a). Introduction: New migrants in New York. In N. Foner (Ed.), *New immigrants in New York* (pp. 1–31). New York: Columbia University Press.

Foner, N. (Ed.). (2001b). *Islands in the city: West Indian migration to New York*. Berkeley: University of California Press.

Francis, E. (1993). Psychiatric racism and social police: Black people and the psychiatric services. In W. James & C. Harris (Eds.), *Inside Babylon* (pp. 179–205). London: Verso.

Frucht, R. (1968). Emigration, remittances and social change: Aspects of the social field of Nevis, West Indies. *Anthropologicia, 10*, 193–208.

Gibson, J., & Ogbu, J. (Eds.). (1991). *Minority status and schooling: A comparative study of immigrant and involuntary minorities*. New York: Garland.

Gmelch, G. (1983). Who returns and why: Return migration behavior in two North Atlantic societies. *Human Organization, 42*, 46–54.

Gmelch, G. (1987). Work, innovation, and investment: The impact of return migration in Barbados. *Human Organization, 46*, 131–140.

Gopaul-McNicol, S. (1993). *Working with West Indian families*. New York: Guilford Press.

Gorell-Barnes, G. (1975). Seen but not heard. *Social Work Today, 5*, 646–648.

Grasmuck, S., & Grosfoguel, R. (1997). Geopolitics, economic niches, and gendered social capital among recent Caribbean immigrants in New York City. *Sociological Perspectives, 40*, 339–363.

Greenfield, P., & Cocking, R. (Eds.). (1994). *Cross-cultural roots of minority child development*. Hillsdale, NJ: Erlbaum.

Grosfoguel, R. (1997). Colonial Caribbean migrations to France, the Netherlands, Great Britain and the United States. *Ethnic and Racial Studies, 20*, 594–612.

Guarnizo, L. E. (1997). Going home: Class, gender and household transformation among Dominican immigrants. In P. Pressar (Ed.), *Caribbean circuits* (pp. 13–60). New York: Center for Migration Studies.

Hall, D. (1971). *Five of the Leewards, 1834–1870: The major problems of the post-emancipation period in Antigua, Barbuda, Montserrat, Nevis, and St. Kitts*. Bridgetown, Barbados: Caribbean Universities Press.

Hemsi, L. (1967). Psychiatric morbidity of West Indian immigrants. *Social Psychiatry, 2*, 95.

Kareem, J., & Littlewood, R. (Eds.). (1992). *Intercultural therapy: Themes, interpretations and practices*. Oxford, England: Blackwell.

Knight, F. W., & Palmer, C. A. (1989). The Caribbean: A regional overview. In F. W. Knight & C. A. Palmer (Eds.), *The modern Caribbean* (pp. 1–19). Chapel Hill: University of North Carolina Press.

Kritz, M. M. (1981). International migration patterns in the Caribbean basin: An overview. In M. Kritz, C. B. Keely, & S. M. Tomasi (Eds.), *Global trends in migration: Theory and research on international population movements* (pp. 209–233). Staten Island, NY: Center for Migration Studies.

Leo-Rhynie, E. (1997). Class, race, and gender issues in child rearing in the Caribbean. In J. L. Roopnarine & J. Brown (Eds.), *Caribbean families: Diversity among ethnic groups* (pp. 25–55). Norwood, NJ: Ablex.

Littlewood, R., & Lipsedge, M. (1988). Psychiatric illness among British Afro-Caribbeans [Editorial]. *British Medical Journal, 296*, 950–951.

Lonner, W. (1990). An overview of cross-cultural testing and assessment. In R. W. Brislin (Ed.), *Applied cross-cultural psychology* (pp. 56–76). Beverly Hills, CA: Sage.

Lowenthal, D. (1972). *West Indian societies*. Oxford: Oxford University Press.

Marshall, D. I. (1982). Migration as an agent of change in the Caribbean Island ecosystem. *International Social Science Journal, 34*, 451–467.

Maxime, J. (1986). Some psychological models of Black concepts. In S. Ahmed, J. Cheetham, & J. Small (Eds.), *Social work with Black children and their families* (pp. 100–116). London: Batsford Press.

Merrill, J., & Owens, J. (1986). Ethnic differences in self-poisoning: A comparison of Asian and White groups. *British Journal of Psychiatry, 148*, 708–712.

Merrill, J., & Owens, J. (1988). Self-poisoning among four immigrant groups. *Acta Psychiatrica Scandinavica, 77*, 77–80.

Millette, R. (1998). West Indian families in the United States. In R. Taylor (Ed.), *Minority families in the United States: A multicultural perspective* (2nd ed., pp. 46–59). Upper Saddle River, NJ: Prentice-Hall.

Munroe-Blum, H., Boyle, M. H., Offord, D., R., & Kates, N. (1989). Immigrant children: Psychiatric disorder, school performance, and service utilization. *American Journal of Orthopsychiatry, 59*, 510–519.

Neto, F., & Mullet, E. (1998). Decision-making as regards migration: Wage differential, job opportunity, and the network effect. *Acta Psychologia, 98*, 57–66.

Nicol, A. R. (1971, January 12). Psychiatric disorder in West Indian school children. *Race Today*, pp. 14–15.

Patterson, O. (1978). Migration in Caribbean societies: Socioeconomic and symbolic resources. In W. H. McNeill & R. S. Adams (Eds.), *Human migration: Patterns and policies* (pp. 106–145). Bloomington: Indiana University Press.

Pawliuk, N., Grizenko, N., Chan-Yip, A., Gantous, P., Matthew, J., & Nguyen, D. (1996). Acculturation style and psychological functioning in children of immigrants. *American Journal of Orthopsychiatry, 66*, 111–121.

Phillips, D. (1996). The internationalization of labor: The migration of nurses from Trinidad and Tobago (A case study). *International Sociology, 11*, 109–127.

Phinney, J., Lochner, B., & Murphy, R. (1990). Ethnic identity development and psychological adjustment in adolescence. In A. Stiffman & L. Davis (Eds.), *Ethnic issues in adolescent mental health* (pp. 53–72). Newbury Park, CA: Sage.

Portes, A., & Rumbaut, R. G. (1990). *Immigrant America: A portrait.* Berkeley: University of California Press.

Pressar, P. R., & Graham, P. M. (2001). Dominicans: Transnational identities and local politics. In N. Foner (Ed.), *New immigrants in New York* (pp. 251–273). New York: Columbia University Press.

Rambally, R. T. (1995). The overrepresentation of Black youth in the Quebec social service system. *Canadian Social Work Review, 12*, 85–97.

Reid, I. (1970). *The Negro immigrant: His background, characteristics and social adjustment, 1899–1937.* New York: AMS Press. (Original work published 1939)

Robertson, E. (1975). *Out of sight—Not out of mind. A study of West Indian mothers living in England, separated for a long period from their children through leaving them behind when migrating and subsequently reunited.* Unpublished master's thesis, Sussex University, Sussex, England.

Roopnarine, J. L. (1997). Fathers in the English-speaking Caribbean: Not so marginal. *World Psychology, 3*, 191–210.

Roopnarine, J. L. (1999, April). *Father involvement and parental styles in Caribbean immigrant families.* Paper presented at the American Educational Research Association Conference, Montreal, Canada.

Roopnarine, J. L., & Brown, J. (Eds.). (1997). *Caribbean families: Diversity among ethnic groups.* Norwood, NJ: Ablex.

Roopnarine, J. L., Clawson, M. A., Benetti, S., & Lewis, T. Y. (2000). Family structure, parent-child socialization, and involvement among Caribbean families. In A. L. Comunian & U. P. Gielen (Eds.), *International perspectives on human development* (pp. 309–329). Lengerich, Germany: Pabst.

Rubenstein, H. (1979). The return ideology in West Indian migration. *Papers in Anthropology, 20,* 330–337.

Rubenstein, H. (1983). Remittances and rural underdevelopment in the English-speaking Caribbean. *Human Organization, 42,* 295–306.

Rutter, M. (1972). *Maternal deprivation reassessed.* Hammondsworth, England: Penguin.

Rutter, M., Yule, W., Berger, M., Morton, J., & Bagley, C. (1974). Children of West Indian immigrants: 1. Rates of behavioral deviance and psychiatric disorder. *Journal of Child Psychiatry, 15,* 241–262.

Schiller, N. G., Basch, L., & Blanc, C. S. (1995). From immigrant to transmigrant: Theorizing transnational migration. *Anthropological Quarterly, 68,* 48–63.

Segal, A., with Earnhardt, K. C. (1969). *Politics and population in the Caribbean* (Special Study No. 7). Rio Piedras: University of Puerto Rico, Institute of Caribbean Studies.

Sewell-Coker, B., Hamilton-Collins, J., & Fein, E. (1985). West Indian immigrants. *Social Casework, 60,* 563–568.

Sluzki, C. E. (1979). Migration and family conflict. *Family Process, 18,* 379–390.

Strachan, A. J. (1983). Return migration to Guyana. *Social and Economic Studies, 32,* 121–141.

Suárez-Orozco, C., & Todorova, I. (2001). *The transnationalization of families: Immigrant separations and reunifications.* Paper presented at the American Family Therapy Academy. Miami, FL.

Sue, D. W., & Sue, D. (1990). *Counseling the culturally different* (2nd ed.). New York: Wiley.

Szapocznik, J., & Kurtines, W. (1993). Family psychology and cultural diversity: Opportunities for theory, research, and application. *American Psychologist, 48,* 400–407.

Taylor, E. (1976). The social adjustment of returned migrants to Jamaica. In F. Henry (Ed.), *Ethnicity in the Americas* (pp. 213–229). The Hague, Netherlands: Mouton.

Triandis, H. (1990). Theoretical concepts that are applicable to the analysis of ethnocentrism. In R. W. Brislin (Ed.), *Applied cross-cultural psychology* (Vol. 14, pp. 34–55). Beverly Hills, CA: Sage.

U.S. Bureau of Census (1990). *Population of the United States.* Washington, DC: Government Printing Office.

U.S. Department of Justice, Immigration and Naturalization Service. 1998. *Statistical Yearbook of the Immigration and Naturalization Service.* Washington, DC: U.S. Government Printing Office.

Vickerman, M. (2001). Jamaicans: Balancing race and ethnicity. In N. Foner (Ed.), *New immigrants in New York* (pp. 201–228). New York: Columbia

University Press.

Waters, M. (1999). *Black identities: West Indian immigrant dreams and American realities.* Cambridge, MA: Harvard University Press.

Weinrich, P. (1979). Ethnicity and adolescent conflicts. In V. S. Kahn (Ed.), *Minority families in Britain* (pp. 99–107). London: Macmillan.

Weist, R. (1979). Anthropological perspectives on return migration: A critical commentary. *Papers in Anthropology, 20,* 167–187.

Wood, C. H., & McCoy, T. L. (1983). Migration, remittances and development: A study of Caribbean canecutters in Florida. *International Migration Review, 19,* 251–277.

Zhou, M. (1997). Segmented assimilation: Issues, controversies, and recent research on the second generation. *International Migration Review, 31,* 975–1008.

7

Enduring Separation: The Psychological Consequences of Mexican Migration to the United States

V. Nelly Salgado de Snyder and Rogelio Díaz-Guerrero

Human migration has two major components: those who go and those who stay behind. When addressing issues related to migration, however, it is a common error to speak only from the perspective of the migrant and ignore those who are left behind. This is reflected in the great number of studies that have been conducted with immigrants in the host countries, and the very little knowledge that exists about the immigrants' family members, friends, and acquaintances that remain in the country of origin. This chapter, based on recent research findings, focuses on the psychosocial impact of Mexican migration to the United States on the lives of the immigrants and on the spouses, children, and significant others they left behind. It should be noted that this chapter addresses these issues mostly in the context of male labor migration, because the majority of Mexicans who go north are males and heads of households who are seeking jobs and opportunities to improve their and their families' living conditions.

Mexican-origin people represent the majority of the Latino population in the United States. Recent estimates indicate that there are over 7 million Mexican immigrants in that country and that this is the youngest of all immigrant groups (Secretaría de Relaciones Exteriores, 1997). The geographic mobility of Mexicans to the United States is a social and economic process that has transformed the lives of Mexicans and Americans alike. It is interesting to note that in spite of its long tradition, the presence of Mexicans in the United States continues to be a current theme in the social, political, and economic spheres in both countries.

The migratory movements of Mexicans to the United States result from a mixture of historical, geographical, economic, and social factors. These include Texas and the southwestern states of the United States, which belonged to Mexico until 1848; the first migratory movements go back to the 19th century; the two countries share a common border of over 2,000 miles most of which is not guarded; and the historical, social, and structural conditions in both countries act as "push-pull" forces. However, researchers have consistently found that the most important factor for a Mexican to migrate north is financial need (i.e., Portes & Rumbaut, 1997; Zenteno & Massey, 1999). Personal motivations, such as pursuing a better quality of life for himself and his family are also deeply ingrained in his decision to migrate (Salgado de Snyder, Díaz-Pérez, Acevedo, & Natera, 1996).

The presence of Mexicans in the United States is a consequence of the volume, permanency, and continuity of the migratory movements especially of young men. Several large-scale research projects that had the purpose of evaluating the volume and characteristics of the migratory flow of Mexicans between the two countries suggest that Mexican immigrants have the following characteristics: They are mostly males, heads of households, from rural areas, who held a job in Mexico (mostly in agriculture), with a mean age of 24 and an education of 7.4 years (EMIF, 1994–1995; ETIDEU, 1986), 1.4 grades above the national average. In a more recent analysis of data, other factors emerged that appear to determine migration. These include a lack of property in Mexico, residing in villages with a migratory tradition to the United States, having children under age 12, previous migratory experience, being part of a social network that extends from the community of origin to the final destination place, parents or relatives who were or are migrants in the United States, and being in possession of legal documents that allow one to cross the border (Zenteno & Massey, 1999).

Men who go north usually do so alone regardless of their marital status. Most of them go only temporarily for periods of time that vary depending on the kind of agriculture they will be involved in, the need for laborers in the United States, and their commitments and financial obligations in Mexico. Most immigrants originate from western Mexico, specifically from the states of Jalisco, Guanajuato, Michoacán, and Zacatecas. These states are located in a Mexican region characterized by a significant migratory tradition to the United States that goes back to the early 1900s when the United States established labor recruitment centers in those states. Thus, it is not surprising that migration among the inhabitants of this region has become an institutionalized process (Durand, 1994; Massey, Alarcón, Durand, & González, 1991). In the United States, Mexican immigrants are concentrated in the states of California, Texas, Colorado, Arizona, and Illinois (Secretaría de Relaciones Exteriores, 1997) where the presence of Mexicans is so prevalent that it has changed not only the demographic characteristics of the inhabitants but has also transformed the sociocultural nature of those states.

Mexican labor migrants participate in a transnational circuit that is keeping the door open between the United States and Mexico. It is through this revolving door that a constant exchange of communication takes place regarding culture, language, values, customs, and lifestyles (Rousse, 1989). This exchange has had an impact on the lifestyles of both Mexicans and Americans, and it has been studied extensively from different perspectives: demographic (Winnie, 1984); financial (Cockroft, 1988); political (Bustamante, 1995); sociological (Massey et al., 1991); labor (Morales, 1989); historical (Durand, 1991; Fonseca & Moreno, 1984); anthropological (Trigueros & Rodríguez, 1988); and psychological (Salgado de Snyder, 1993, 1994, 1996; Salgado de Snyder & Maldonado, 1992, 1993). In the United States, the magnitude of the exchange has been analyzed mostly for the state of California, where Mexican immigrants are concentrated (e.g., Acuña, 1981; Castillo & Rios Bustamante, 1989; Gutierrez, 1998).

The international migration process had its origin in various structural changes occurring in both the host and the sending societies. The "push" factors in the sending communities include among others the lack of jobs, low wages, lack of opportunities for self-development, limited access to basic services, and so on. On the other hand, the "pull" factors in the receiving country are mostly related to the possibility of finding a job that pays well so that immigrants can send money back home and improve the living conditions of their families. Thus, migration, once a unique phenomenon, has become for many a continuous process related to the survival strategies of the family. For others, one trip tends to provoke another trip, and as the aspirations of the migrant change because of his migratory experience, the structural causes that had been responsible for the initial migratory movement become less important. Thus, the experiences of the last trip (besides the economic needs of the family) appear to determine the probability of making later trips.

Most Mexicans migrate to the United States with the purpose of working hard and earning an income that will allow them to provide their families with a better quality of life. This is indicated in the following excerpt from an interview that forms part of a study aimed at assessing the well-being of families headed by Mexican immigrants (Salgado de Snyder, 1996): "My family wants me to go north because they have a better life here if I work in the United States. My family is happier now, we have fewer economic problems, and our finances have improved" (p. 3).

In this regard, it has been proposed by Bustamante (1996) that the migratory behavior of Mexicans has two dimensions: subjective and objective. The subjective dimension refers to the motivation of the individual to leave his home country and to seek out new opportunities to improve the quality of his life and that of his family. The objective dimension is the migrant's actual physical movement from one country to another. The latter is an observable and frequently hazardous behavior that is conceived by the migrant as the means to achieve his final purpose.

Many Mexican male immigrants cross the border without legal papers; thus, attaining one's goals often involves risking one's life. They face other stressors associated with a prevailing "double standard" (hero in Mexico vs. criminal in the United States) that places them in a highly vulnerable position for the development of mental health problems. Bustamante (1996) suggested that in their hometowns, undocumented immigrants are regarded as courageous and brave first for risking their life when crossing the border and then for living and working under conditions that involve being the target of aggression and persecution because of their undocumented status. They endure this hardship, but we still know little about the long-term psychological consequences of this double standard. Evidently, this is an area that remains to be studied.

SOURCES OF POTENTIAL STRESS AMONG THOSE WHO GO

The direct and continuous contact between individuals from two or more different cultures is a source of stress, and such contact is often determined by international migration. Consequently, research has shown that there is a clear connection between geographic movement and change in psychological well-being (Furnham & Bochner, 1986). The uprooting from the immigrants' original culture requires a great deal of adaptation on their part because major differences exist between their home country and the host society.

Although all culturally different groups in an unfamiliar environment are prone to the experience of stress, immigrants are a particularly vulnerable group because the experiences of uprooting and resettlement are important sources of psychological tension (Nann, 1982b). Studies have consistently shown that newly arrived Mexican immigrants in the United States are faced with unknown and often hostile situations that generate stress and anxiety until they become acquainted with the culture, the norms, and the lifestyle of the host society (Ainslie, 1998; Salgado de Snyder, 1996).

Either voluntarily or involuntarily, immigrants are physically removed from their customary environment and relocated in a new unfamiliar milieu where their original language, customs, values, and traditions no longer apply (Berry, 1997). Many Mexican immigrants perceive migration as a positive challenge that involves the possibility of enhancing their life opportunities (Salgado de Snyder et al., 1996). This very challenge, however, may turn into a source of unbearable conflict that hinders the immigrant's coping abilities. The outcome of the conflict will depend on whether the process of immigration is perceived by the individual as a wanted or an unwanted experience and on the personal and social resources available to the individual to cope with change (Berry & Kim, 1988; Cervantes & Castro, 1985; Cervantes, Padilla, & Salgado de Snyder, 1991; Rogler, 1994).

Voluntary Mexican immigrants tend to adapt more easily to the host society and feel more satisfied with their life condition in the United States than their involuntary counterparts. In contrast, the involuntary immigrants, most of whom are women and youngsters, felt pressured by others to leave their home country, and are neither interested nor motivated to learn and to adapt to the new culture. Such pressures from the past work in the present as an additional source of stress in their lives, and such stresses manifest themselves in conflicting feelings and emotions (Salgado de Snyder, 1986).

For Mexican immigrants, there are important physical and psychological hardships associated with the journey to the United States. For instance, undocumented immigrants cross the border with falsified papers or without papers, and during their journey, they encounter many risky situations that endanger their physical and psychological integrity (Salgado de Snyder, Díaz-Perez, Acevedo, et al., 1996). The experience of crossing the border may leave an important imprint in the immigrants' psyche, particularly those of women, who more often than men are the subjects of victimization during the crossing (Gaselum Gaxiola, 1991; Morales, 1989).

Once in the United States, immigrants are faced with the necessity to change their lifestyle in order to adapt to their new life. Much has been written about the adaptation to a new, unfamiliar environment and the many challenges that immigrants face once they arrive in the host society (e.g., Berry, 1997; Furnham & Bochner, 1986). Psychological stress among immigrants usually develops during the process of acculturation, when the immigrant experiences as negative and unwanted the behavioral changes demanded from the new environment. The deleterious consequences of acculturation are not inevitable, but they do represent a major problem for the newcomers (Berry & Kim, 1988).

Furthermore, once in the United States, Mexican immigrants are exposed to a variety of stressors related to their living conditions, which are typically characterized by poverty and lack of access to societal goods. Such conditions exacerbate the impact of acculturation-related stressors, thus placing the immigrants at risk for the development of psychological and mental health problems (Cervantes & Castro, 1985). For instance, many recent Mexican immigrants in the United States are surrounded by chronic insalubrious living conditions. Overcrowding, unemployment and underemployment, low levels of education and income, lack of access to many societal goods and resources, and discrimination are only some of the situations they must face on a daily basis (Cervantes et al., 1991).

It is common for immigrants to exert pressure on themselves to learn as much as they can about the host society (i.e., language, traditions, norms, social cues, lifestyles, and the social, health, and political systems). Learning a new language and particularly the ability to express one's feelings is important because immigrants are otherwise unable to discuss many personal matters that oftentimes afflict them. In spite of their efforts, immigrants may not fully succeed in learning all they want to and need to, something that is particularly true of those who have only a limited command of the English language (Padilla, Cervantes, Maldonado, & Garcia, 1988). For some, having an accent in their speech is considered a source of stress (Salgado de Snyder, 1986). Furthermore, it has been proposed that because of an apparent lack of a clear connection between the behavior one is trying out and its expected results, immigrants may develop learned helplessness. This problem subsides when the immigrant is finally able to influence the behavior of culturally different persons (Triandis, 1976). Learned helplessness can provoke depressive symptomatology as well as conflictive feelings of alienation.

An additional and very important source of stress in a host society is discrimination. A recent report suggests that Mexican immigrants along with other Latin American groups rank among the least favored in the public opinion of the United States (Espenshade & Belanger, 1998). Discrimination and prejudice against Mexicans seem to be based on a phenotype that identifies them as members of a minority group. Individuals with a darker skin and a more Indian appearance experienced these characteristics as sources of stress leading to depression (Codina & Montalvo, 1994). Additionally, the ignorance about Mexican culture that prevails in the host society encourages negative stereotyping (Smart & Smart, 1995). This is illustrated in the following interview quote: "Americans believe they are better than us because they think of themselves as Europeans, but they don't know that we also have European blood. They call us [Mexicans] "wetbacks" but I did not cross the ocean, they did. We [Mexicans] just walked through the border" (Salgado de Snyder, 1996, p. 34).

Discrimination affects immigrants on two levels: the personal level, which is the result of an action from one person or from a small group, and the institutional level, involving actions taken by and approved of as part of the normal operation of an institution (Feagin & Feagin, 1978). Both have insidious and devastating effects on many immigrants' lives. Furthermore, when discrimination is experienced as a continuing part of one's daily existence, it is likely to have an even more devastating impact (Willie, Kramer, & Bertram, 1973). It appears, however, that these steep hurdles may not lead to even more devastating effects because Mexicans have been found to be flexible, adaptable, and *aguantadores* (highly withstanding) (Avendaño-Sandoval & Díaz-Guerrero, 1990; Melgoza-Henriquez & Díaz-Guerrero, 1990).

Social support and social networks have been identified as sources of strength to successfully deal with stress and its psychological consequences. By definition, immigration involves an important reduction of social support networks; thus, immigrants are deprived of important social network qualities such as intimacy and warmth. These have been found to serve as important buffers against depression (Vega & Kolody, 1985). Many ethnic communities in the United States have developed networks that re-create familiar environments and have important functions for the immigrants, such as maintaining cultural and ethnic loyalty and helping each other with informational, emotional, and practical issues (Gutierrez, 1998; Nann, 1982a).

With the passage of time, Mexican immigrants—especially those who work in agriculture—often see their productive capacity worn out at an early stage of their lives due to the intensity of their work. They begin complaining about health problems and eventually are unable to work as much as they would desire. Their perceived as well as their actual limited physical capacity to work provokes feelings of deterioration, dissatisfaction, and inability to find meaning in their life (Salgado de Snyder, 1996).

Leaving family members behind in the country of origin provokes in the immigrant guilt feelings and concern about the well-being of his wife and his children. It has been documented that most male immigrants are married but that they travel to the United States alone. The anxiety derived from separation and guilt for having left one's family behind is an important source of stress (Cervantes et al., 1991). Furthermore, it has been proposed that many Mexican immigrants go through a mourning process whose intensity depends on the length of stay in the United States. Such mourning is related to the loss of relationships with people and places with whom the immigrant had strong bonds (Ainslie, 1998). The desire to return to one's homeland is always present in the immigrant's mind in the form of "return fantasies" that help him to cope with what he perceives as a temporary situation.

THE SOCIOCULTURAL CONTEXT IN MEXICO

At the individual level, the life conditions and the sociocultural context that surround Mexican immigrants to the United States have been analyzed intensively in that country possibly because the migrant is considered the main actor in the migratory process. This position wrongly implies that immigration affects only those who migrate. It is important to acknowledge that the remaining wives, children, and extended family members receive the impact of the departure with the same intensity as the migrant because of their close bonds and mutual commitments. Those left behind constitute the often invisible human component that is generally ignored in the migratory process.

The first author of this chapter has dedicated the last 10 years of her research efforts to a better understanding of the psychosocial dynamics that take place among those left behind when one family member decides to migrate to the United States. The information reported in this and the next section of this chapter is based on the results of several studies that were conducted using both qualitative and quantitative methods and that have been published elsewhere. The following is a summary of relevant findings that has the purpose of giving voice to the most ignored individuals who participate in the process of migration.

To fully understand the findings that are about to be presented, it becomes necessary to provide a general context of the social and cultural spheres of the rural inhabitants of Mexico, particularly those who live in communities with an extensive migratory tradition to the United States. It is important to first address some issues related to the extremely traditional gender roles assigned to men and women in rural Mexico. Passivity, dependence, submissiveness, and self-sacrifice characterize the assigned role for women (Tuirán, 1995). Furthermore, gender bias has fostered an ideology that magnifies women's role in childbearing as the central aspect of female identity (Amuchástegui, 1996; Del Rio-Zolezzi, Liguori, Magis-Rodríguez, Valdespino, García, & Sepúlveda, 1995). As a consequence, research and health care services for women in rural Mexico have been addressed primarily insofar as they affect reproduction, reflecting a one-dimensional view of women's roles and needs (Tuirán, 1995).

In these communities the family structure is patriarchal. A man's role revolves around his earning power and his capacity to demonstrate his authority, strength, and power usually through fathering many children, which is considered a proof of masculinity and transcendence (Amuchástegui, 1996; Rivas-Zivy, 1996). Men continue to enjoy considerable power and control over their own lives, the lives of the other members of their family, and the family's resources. Overall, men are the providers and the holders of unquestionable authority (Trigueros & Rodriguez, 1988). The second author, who has extensively probed the psychology of the Mexican (Díaz-Guerrero, 1975, 1994, 1995; Díaz-Guerrero & Pacheco, 1994; Díaz-Guerrero & Szalay, 1991) has speculated that for historical reasons, the Mexican culture has endowed women for making decisions in matters of love and men for making decisions in matters of power. This, of course, has been changing in the last decades.

As for their lifestyle, many inhabitants of these regions have no other option but to go north, for without this alternative the survival of the family members could be precarious indeed. In some households, children, especially boys, work to help their families. In a previous contribution (Salgado de Snyder, Díaz-Pérez, Acevedo, & Natera, 1996), it was reported that in several villages children work in what is locally known as "fertilizer factories," that is, cattle ranches where children fill up sacs with cows' droppings (which are later used as fertilizer). Children get paid about $ .15 (in U.S. currency) for each sac.

Compared with the rest of the country, "sending" communities in Mexico tend to have limited access to goods and services, and many of its members are poor and live in marginal conditions. Paradoxically, however, in these apparently traditional and poor communities, the lifestyles of the villagers have come under the sway of modernization. For instance, antennas can be seen on the roofs of the small adobe houses. The inhabitants display a variety of electronic home appliances in the household, such as television receivers, videocassette players, washing machines, and so on, many of which are not used but are proudly shown in the living room. Most of the cars and trucks in these villages carry license plates from American states such as California, Texas, or Illinois. In these communities, it is common to find at least one small store that sells imported goods, such as canned foods, toiletries, and home appliances. During the local religious celebrations it is common to see displays of the American flag alongside the Mexican flag and the Virgin of Guadalupe. Especially conspicuous is the absence of young men together with the presence of large numbers of women, children, and elderly men.

Due to the poverty in which many people live, migration to the United States is highly valued by many villagers because it represents an alternative to improving their lives. The positive impact of migration on their lives is reflected in the commonly used expression *Dios y el Norte*, meaning "God and the North," which is commonly used by the villagers to acknowledge the survival function of migrating to the United States. Finally, in the context of survival strategies, it is important to mention that the poorer people cannot migrate. The cost of migration, which refers to the money a person stops earning from the time he makes the decision to go north to the time he earns his first salary in the United States, acts as a barrier to attaining their goal. The decision to migrate, however, is not a decision that depends exclusively on the potential migrant's willingness to migrate, because it involves many other factors such as the acceptance of his decision by the women and the immediate family.

STRESS AMONG THOSE LEFT BEHIND

In the rural communities of Mexico where male migration is the norm, the departure of the head of the household and its consequences are perceived as stressful events that appear to have a negative impact on the mental health of the wives left behind. For instance, our data suggest that their husband's migration is usually accompanied by many undesirable changes in the family's lifestyle and dynamics (Salgado de Snyder, 1993; Salgado de Snyder & Maldonado,

1993). Our respondents reported increased levels of stress reflecting the commitment, obligations, and responsibilities that the women are forced to assume because of the absence of their husbands. They resent the fact that they now have to face alone the various problems associated with their children, including problems related to their health, education, discipline, and survival. Also, they are directly responsible for maintaining the unity of the household. This may be seen in the following interview quotes:

I have to be both father and mother; this is hard because I am a woman and sometimes the children don't mind me. A man is always necessary in the family. I am sad when he is not here, I miss him because I feel I cannot solve all the problems by myself. (Salgado de Snyder, 1996, p. 41)

Women are expected to solve all the problems, but they frequently feel—especially those whose husbands migrate for the first time—that they are unready or ill prepared for assuming such responsibilities, because they are lacking the necessary experience. The responsibilities include the management of money, the care of animals and land, harvesting, and disciplining the children.

The women frequently experience feelings of loneliness mostly due to the lack of emotional support from the absent husband. For many, the departure of their husbands means not knowing when they will see him next, especially because some of the men going north do not come back. The sadness surrounding a husband's first migration is reflected in the following excerpt of an interview with a pregnant woman whose husband had gone to the United States for the first time 8 months prior to the interview. He had not communicated with her since his departure nor did he know his wife was pregnant. She said: "Yesterday I was thinking that a year ago we were here, still together, and now I am all alone with this big belly. I felt very sad, my mother found me crying, but I told her that nothing was the matter, that I just felt like crying" (Salgado de Snyder, 1996, p. 36).

Statements such as these reflect how distant many women feel from the new life chosen by their spouses. The women's stressors reflect the existence of an increasing geographical, emotional, and cultural distance between them and their spouses. They worry that their husbands may forget their customs and traditions, and many fear that their husbands might start a new family in the United States and abandon them. The perceived changes associated with the threat of family disintegration are experienced as very stressful, including increasing problems with their children and the perceived inability to discipline and control them (Salgado de Snyder, 1996).

They report a great deal of preoccupation regarding the welfare of their spouses, such as not having sufficient money to eat or to pay for a doctor's visit in case they become ill. They worry about their spouses' lifestyle because many women ignore the living arrangements of their husbands; many do not even have an address where they can send a letter. Women also fear that their husbands might get involved in heavy drinking and drug abuse, or that they might be taken to jail and then deported.

In spite of all of these stress-producing situations related to their husbands' departure, for many women the return of their spouses is not experienced with joy and positive expectations but rather with fear and anxiety. This is true mostly for two reasons: the possibility of an unwanted pregnancy and the difficulty they have in including their husbands in their daily life routines (Salgado de Snyder, 1996). In relation to the first factor, women's pregnancies coincide with the visits of their husbands, because they usually have sexual contact but do not use contraception. The possibility of an unwanted pregnancy is an important source of stress among these women, because they know they will be left with the responsibility of caring for one more child in an already large family (Salgado de Snyder, Acevedo, Díaz-Pérez, & Saldivar, 2000; Salgado de Snyder, Díaz-Pérez, & Maldonado, 1996). As one of the women indicated: "No, I do not want to have more children; life is hard as it is, but my husband loves it when I am pregnant" (Salgado de Snyder, 1996, p. 38). It should be noted that pregnancy, for many immigrant men, is a way to ensure the fidelity of their wives while the men are in the United States.

Many women agree against their wishes to have sexual intercourse with their husbands with no protection whatsoever. This places them at risk for contracting sexually transmitted diseases and HIV/AIDS. The women interviewed considered that one of their important obligations was to please their husbands. They believe that their husbands are entitled to this because they work very hard and relinquish many things so that the family would survive. It is interesting to note that most women consider giving sexual pleasure to their husbands as a minor sacrifice, and they justify it by saying that their husbands come to visit them for a short of period of time once a year (Salgado de Snyder et al., 2000).

As for the women's apparent inability to integrate their husbands into their daily life, our data suggest that little by little most migrants lose their place in the household for their children and wife, but they do not lose their power. The following excerpts illustrate this point:

What I see is that we are not used to being together anymore. We are both used to surviving without each other. With the children it is the same; when he is here they look at him as a burden. They do not like it when he scolds them because they are not used to having a father anymore; they fight all the time and I am the one who mediates between them. (Salgado de Snyder, 1996, p. 39)

The children always ask, Where is my daddy? Why doesn't he live with us? Why does he get drunk? All I tell them is that he has to go north to work in order to give us what we need and that he drinks because he likes to drink, but that he is a good person. Well, when he drinks too much he hits me. (Salgado de Snyder, 1996, p. 40)

Women make ends meet by informally working mostly in the rapidly developing textile industry in that region. They do detailed embroidery and receive a minimal amount of money for this time-consuming job. For instance, women embroider by hand complicated designs on sweaters and other feminine apparel, which are then exported mostly to the United States. They only get paid about $ .15 (in U.S. currency) for every flower they embroider on a sweater, even though making each flower can take up to 30 minutes. The villagers, however, do not condone the work of the women in these communities, especially if they are married to men working in the United States.

He does not like me to work because he says that when women work they find another man. This is true: When a woman works and makes her own money she can do what she wants, it is like having wings. (Salgado de Snyder, 1996, p. 38)

I don't let my wife work because a decent woman must stay home and wait for her man to come home. Women who go to the United States are looking for adventures, not for a job, like men. (Salgado de Snyder, 1996, p. 31)

In spite of those statements, women tend to agree with the traditional gender role conceptions. Even in these communities where the influence of American culture and American lifestyles is evident, traditional values, customs, and morals remain dominant. The role of Catholicism continues to be important in maintaining traditional views and lifestyles in many of these rural communities.

In summary, migration to the United States constitutes a family strategy for improving the living conditions of many Mexicans who without this option would have to continue living in an impoverished environment. As one woman commented: "There is nothing in this little town. If it wasn't for God, first, and then my husband who is working in the North, I think we would have starved to death" (Salgado de Snyder, 1996, p. 30).

CONCLUSIONS

This chapter reinforces the conceptions on which this book is based: Only the accumulation of systematic impartial information can support the development of humane programs to deal with the many issues and challenges involved in international migration. We have documented how those who migrate do so not only for economic but also for powerful psychological reasons. The families that stay behind improve financially but must also face separation and at times breakdown and disintegration. We invite the reader to reflect on the implications of the findings reviewed in our contribution. Because Mexican people have a well-documented ability to endure suffering and the flexibility to adapt, migration to the United States cannot be stopped easily as long as there are major differences in job opportunities and income between the two countries.

REFERENCES

Acuña, R. (1981). *Occupied America: A history of Chicanos*. New York: Free Press.
Ainslie, R. (1998). Cultural mourning, immigration, and engagement: Vignettes from the Mexican experience. In M. Suárez-Orozco (Ed.), *Crossings: Mexican immigration in international perspective* (pp. 283–300). Cambridge, MA: Harvard University, David Rockefeller Center for Latin American Studies.

Amuchástegui, A. (1996). El significado de la virginidad y la iniciación sexual. Un relato de investigación [The meaning of virginity and sexual initiation: An account of a study]. In I. Szasz & S. Lerner (Eds.), *Para comprender la subjetividad. Investigación cualitativa en salud reproductiva y sexualidad* (pp. 137–172). Mexico: El Colegio de México.

Avendaño-Saldoval, R., & Díaz-Guerrero, R. (1990). El desarrollo de una escala de abnegación para los mexicanos [Development of a scale of abnegation for Mexicans]. In AMEPSO (Ed.), *La psicología social en Mexico* (Vol. 3, pp. 9–14). Mexico City: Mexican Association of Social Psychology.

Berry, J. W. (1997). Immigration, acculturation and adaptation. *Applied Psychology: An International Review, 4,* 5–68.

Berry, J. W., & Kim, U. (1988). Acculturation and mental health In P. R. Dasen, J. W. Berry, & N. Sartorious (Eds.), *Health and cross-cultural psychology: Towards applications* (pp. 207–238). Newbury Park, CA: Sage.

Bustamante, J. A. (1995). Migración de México a Estados Unidos; un enfoque sociológico [Migration from Mexico to the United States: A sociological perspective]. In Secretaría de Relaciones Exteriores (Ed.), *La migración laboral mexicana a Estados Unidos de America: Una perspectiva bilateral desde México* (pp. 25–76). Mexico: Instituto Matías Romero de Estudios Diplomáticos.

Bustamante, J. A. (1996). *El marco teórico-metodológico de la circularidad migratoria: Su validación empírica* [A theoretical and methodological framework for the study of the circular character of migration: Its empirical validation]. Unpublished manuscript.

Castillo, P. G., & Ríos Bustamante, A. (1989). *México en Los Angeles* [Mexico in Los Angeles]. Mexico: Alianza Editorial.

Cervantes, R. C., & Castro, F. (1985). Stress, coping and mental health: A systematic review. *Hispanic Journal of Behavioral Sciences, 7,* 1–73.

Cervantes, R. C., Padilla, A. M., & Salgado de Snyder, V. N. (1991). The Hispanic Stress Inventory: A culturally relevant approach to psychosocial assessment. *Psychological Assessment, 3,* 438–447.

Cockroft, J. (1988). Migración mexicana, crisis e internacionalización de la lucha laboral [Mexican migration, crisis, and internationalization of labor]. In G. López-Castro & S. Pardo-Galván (Eds.), *Migración en el occidente de México* (pp. 41–64). Zamora de Hildago, Mexico: El Colegio de Michoacán.

Codina, G., & Montalvo, E. F. (1994). Chicano phenotype and depression. *Hispanic Journal of Behavioral Sciences, 3,* 296–306.

Del Río-Zolezzi, A., Liguori, A. L., Magis-Rodríguez, C., Valdespino, J. L., García, M. L., & Sepúlveda, J. (1995). La epidemia de VIH/SIDA y la mujer en México [The HIV/AIDS epidemic and women in Mexico]. *Salud Pública de México, 37,* 581–591.

Díaz-Guerrero, R. (1975). *Psychology of the Mexican: Culture and personality.* Austin: University of Texas Press.

Díaz-Guerrero, R. (1994). *Psicología del mexicano, descubrimiento de la etnopsicología.* [Psychology of the Mexican: Discovering ethnopsychology]. Mexico City: Trillas.

Díaz-Guerrero, R. (1995). Una aproximación científica a la etnopsicología [A scientific aproach to ethnopsychology]. *Revista Latinoamericana de Psicología, 27,* 359–389.

Díaz-Guerrero, R., & Pacheco, A. M. (1994). *Etnopsicología: Scientia Nova.* [Ethnopsychology: A new science]. San Juan, PR: Servicios Profesionales y Científicos.

Díaz-Guerrero, R., & Szalay, L. B. (1991). *Understanding Mexicans and Americans: Cultural perspectives in conflict.* New York and London: Plenum.

Durand, J. (1991). *Migración México—Estados Unidos. Años veinte* [Migration between Mexico and the United States: The Twenties]. Mexico City: CONACULTA.

Durand, J. (1994). *Mas alla de la linea, patrones migratorios entre Mexico y Estados Unidos* [Beyond the border: Migratory patterns between Mexico and the United States]. Mexico City: CONACULTA.

EMIF. (1994-1995). *Encuesta sobre migración en la frontera norte de México FASE II., diciembre de 1994 a diciembre de 1995* [Migration survey taken at the northern border of Mexico: Phase 2: December 1994–December 1995]. Mexico City: COLEF, CONAPO, Secretaría de Trabajo y Previsión Social.

Espenshade, T. J., & Belanger, M. (1998). Immigration and public opinion. In M. M. Suárez-Orozco (Ed.), *Crossings: Mexican immigration in international perspectives* (pp. 363–403). Cambridge, MA: Harvard University, David Rockefeller Center for Latin American Studies.

ETIDEU. (1986). *Encuesta de la frontera norte a trabajadores devueltos por las autoridades de los Estados Unidos: Resultados estadisticos* [Survey among workers returned by the United States authorities at the Mexican northern border: Results and statistics]. Mexico City: CONAPO.

Feagin, J. R., & Feagin, C. B. (1978). *Discrimination American style: Institutional racism and sexism.* Englewood Cliffs, NJ: Prentice-Hall.

Fonseca, O., & Moreno, L. (1984). *Jaripo, pueblo de migrantes* [Jaripo, town of immigrants]. Jiquilpan, Mexico: Centro de Estudios de la Revolución Mexicana "Lázaro Cárdenas" A.C.

Furnham, A., & Bochner, S. (1986). *Culture shock: Psychological reactions to unfamiliar environments.* London: Methuen.

Gaselum Gaxiola, M. A. (1991). *Migración de trabajadores indocumentados a los Estados Unidos* [Migration of undocumented workers to the United States]. Mexico City: National Autonomous University of Mexico, Faculty of Law.

Gutierrez, D. G. (1998). Ethnic Mexicans and transformations of "American" social space: Reflections and recent history. In M. M. Suárez-Orozco (Ed.), *Crossings: Mexican immigration in international perspectives* (pp. 307–335). Cambridge, MA: Harvard University, David Rockefeller Center for Latin American Studies.

Massey, D., Alarcón, R., Durand, J., & González, H. (1991). *Los ausentes: el proceso social de la migración internacional en el occidente de México* [The absentees: The social process of international migration]. Mexico City: Alianza Editorial.

Melgoza-Henriquez, E., & Díaz-Guerrero, R. (1990). El desarrollo de una escala de flexibilidad en sujetos mexicanos [Development of a scale of flexibility for Mexicans]. In AMEPSO (Eds.), *La psicología social en México* (Vol. 3, pp. 20–24). Mexico City: Mexican Association of Social Psychology.

Morales, P. (1989). *Indocumentados Mexicanos: Causas y razones de la migración laboral* [Undocumented Mexicans: Causes and reasons of labor migration]. Mexico City: Grijalbo.

Nann, R. C. (1982a). Settlement programs for immigrant women and families. In R. C. Nann (Ed.), *Uprooting and surviving: Adaptation and resettlement of migrant families and children* (pp. 85–94). London: Reidel.

Nann, R. C. (1982b). Preface. In R. C. Nann (Ed.), *Uprooting and surviving: Adaptation and resettlement of migrant families and children* (pp. xi–xv). London: Reidel.

Padilla, A. M., Cervantes, R. C., Maldonado, M., & Garcia, R. (1988). Coping responses to psychosocial stress among Mexican and Central American immigrants. *Journal of Community Psychology, 16,* 418–427.

Portes, A., & Rumbaut, R. (1997). *Immigrant America.* Berkeley: University of California Press.

Rivas-Zivy, M. (1996). Cambios y permanencias en los significados de la sexualidad femenina. Una visión trigeneracional [Changes and permanence in the meanings of feminine sexuality: A three-generation perspective]. *Salud Reproductiva y Sociedad, 2,* 7–12.

Rogler, L. (1994). International migrations. A framework for directing research. *American Psychologist, 49,* 701–708.

Rousse, R. (1989). *Mexican migration to the United States: Family relations in the development of a transnational migrant circuit.* Unpublished doctoral dissertation, Stanford University, Stanford, CA.

Salgado de Snyder, V. N. (1986). *Mexican immigrant women: The relationship of ethnic loyalty, self-esteem, social support and satisfaction to acculturative stress and depressive symptomatology.* Doctoral dissertation, University of California, Los Angeles. (UMI No. 8621129)

Salgado de Snyder, V. N. (1993). Family life across the border: Mexican wives left behind. *Hispanic Journal of Behavioral Sciences, 15,* 391–401.

Salgado de Snyder, V. N. (1994). Mexican women, mental health and migration: Those who go and those who stay behind. In R. G. Malgady & O. Rodríguez (Eds.), *Theoretical and conceptual issues in Hispanic mental health* (pp. 113–139). Malabar, FL: Krieger.

Salgado de Snyder, V. N. (1996). *Psychosocial well-being of Mexican immigrants and their families: A longitudinal study.* Final research report presented to United States-Mexico Commission for Educational and Cultural Exchange. Mexico City: Fulbright-Garcia Robles Program.

Salgado de Snyder, V. N., Díaz-Pérez, M. J., Acevedo, A., & Natera, L. (1996). Dios y el Norte: The perceptions of wives of documented and undocumented Mexican immigrants to the United States. *Hispanic Journal of Behavioral Sciences, 3,* 283–296.

Salgado de Snyder, V. N., Díaz-Pérez, M. J., & Maldonado, M. (1996). AIDS: Risk behaviors among rural Mexican women married to migrants. *AIDS, Education and Prevention, 8,* 134–142.

Salgado de Snyder, V. N., & Maldonado, M. (1992). Respuestas de enfrentamiento e indicadores de salud mental en esposas de emigrantes a los Estados Unidos. [Coping responses and mental health indicators among wives of immigrants to the United States]. *Salud Mental, 15,* 28–35.

Salgado de Snyder, V. N., & Maldonado, M. (1993). Funcionamiento psicosocial en esposas de migrantes mexicanos a los Estados Unidos. [Psychosocial functioning among wives of Mexican immigrants to the United States]. *Revista Latinoamericana de Psicología, 25,* 167–180.

Salgado de Snyder, V. N., Acevedo, A., Díaz-Pérez, M. J., & Saldivar-Garduño, A. (2000). Understanding the sexuality of Mexican-origin women and their risk for HIV/AIDS. *Psychology of Women Quarterly, 24,* 100–109.

Secretaría de Relaciones Exteriores. (1997). *Estudio binacional Mexico-Estados Unidos sobre migracion.* [Binational study on Mexico-United States migration]. Mexico City: Editorial y Litografia Regina de Los Angeles.

Smart, J., & Smart, D. W. (1995). Acculturative stress of Hispanics: Loss and challenge. *Journal of Counseling and Development, 4,* 390–396.

Triandis, H. (1976). *Interpersonal behavior.* Monterey, CA: Brooks Cole.

Trigueros, P., & Rodríguez, J. (1988). Migración y vida familiar en Michoacán: Un estudio de caso [Migration and family life in Michoacan: A case study]. In G. López-Castro (Ed.), *Migración en el Occidente de México* (pp. 201–232). Zamora de Hilgado, Mexico: El Colegio de Michoacán.

Tuirán, R. (1995). Familia y valores: Cambios y arraigos tradicionales [Family and values: Changes and traditional roots]. *Demos, 8,* 30–31.

Vega, W. A., & Kolody, B. (1985). The meaning of social support and the mediation of stress across cultures. In W. A. Vega & M. Miranda (Eds.), *Stress and Hispanic mental health* (pp. 48–75). Rockville, MD: U.S. Department of Health and Human Services.

Willie, C. B., Kramer, B. M., & Bertram, S. (1973). *Racism and mental health.* Pittsburgh: University of Pittsburgh Press.

Winnie, W. (1984). *La movilidad demográfica y su incidencia en una región de fuerte migración* [Geographical mobility and its incidence in a region of high levels of migration]. Guadalajara, Mexico: Universidad de Guadalajara.

Zenteno, R., & Massey, D. (1999). Especificidad vs. representatividad: Enfoque metodológicos en el estudio de la migración mexicana hacia Estados Unidos [Specificity vs. representation: Methodological approaches in the study of Mexico-United States migration]. *Estudios Demográficos y Urbanos, 14,* 75–116.

8

Migrations in Colombia

Wilson Lopez-Lopez

All around the world migrations are characteristic of many human populations. Most of these movements are not sudden or inexplicable but are instead shaped by multiple and changing variables related to ecology, economy, politics, religion, technological innovations, various types of violence, and various ethnic and sociocultural issues. Understanding the complex interactions between variables and explaining migrations in a particular context is not only a conceptual challenge but also represents a basic need for those nations like Colombia that must endure several severe consequences in their economic and social progress.

MIGRATION IN THE 20TH CENTURY: CHARACTERISTICS AND CONSEQUENCES

At the beginning of the 20th century Colombia had a very precarious economy, due to its multiple civil wars, low industrial development, poor infrastructure, and lack of exportations. However, between 1904 and 1930 the Colombian economy showed great improvement, mainly linked to the exportation of coffee, bananas, and petroleum, the incipient growth of the textile industry, and an increasing focus on economic development (Ardila, 1992; Bushnell, 1966; Gutierrez, 1975; Lievano, 1963). This development defined the beginning of a slow but steady increase of the urbanization process. The growth of the cities in different regions of the country was related to the population movements; these movements were in turn tied to new variables in addition to laws governing the possession of land, geographic factors, the ecology and the environment, and the country's climate. The new factors included a series of complex elements associated with the entrance of Colombia into the "modern world."

Cardona and Simmons (1977), in a book that summarized an innovative approach to the study of migrations in Colombia, identified a series of factors causing the migrations in Latin America. Their model failed, however, to include some of the fundamental variables shaping migration during recent years. Nevertheless, it did outline an assortment of causes responsible for the population movements in Colombia.

The authors discussed first a series of hypotheses derived from the Ravenstein (1885) theory about the migrations in the 19th century. According to this theory, migrations frequently followed changes in technological development. The hope for a better standard of living was also a basic cause for migration. Most immigrants came from places near their final destinations, but those immigrants who traveled long distances generally settled in thriving, industrially developed places. Whereas immigrants from rural regions frequently settled in small towns, the immigrants from small towns preferred to move to the larger cities. In other words, those people who enjoyed few economic opportunities generally moved to places where industrial jobs were available.

A series of studies has supported and expanded on the Ravenstein (1885) propositions, for instance by providing empirical evidence related to the migrants' age and sex. In Latin America, there was a disproportionate number of young adults, and depending on the place where the migrants would settle there tended to be more men than women. In the same way, other studies identified various relationships between migration and certain educational and occupational backgrounds, as well as the migrants' expectations and goals. In addition, the relationships between difficult migration conditions and various stages in the familiar cycle of immigrants' social and psychological adjustment had to be considered.

Cardona and Simmons (1977) reported on the immigration and emigration rates of different states within Colombia. They found that the Colombian population as a whole had a high rate of mobility: Half the people who moved crossed the boundaries of their towns or states. The migrants pursued the available opportunities that were signaled by a region's economic and developmental level. The major attractive areas during this time were Atlantico, Magdalena, and Valle del Cauca, which showed high levels of immigration and low levels of emigration. These places and cities appeared to offer attractive lifestyles to the incoming people, whereas generally the local population stayed and did not leave.

Several states including Antioquia, Santander, Narino, and Bolivar showed little movement of people by following cultural traditions tied to stability. For instance, in the case of Antioquia, there existed links to agricultural reforms; Santander was known for the existence of large and poor farms; and Bolivar experienced low economic development but contained large farms. Finally, there were states with many people both immigrating and emigrating, like Huila and Cauca, and these experienced economic progress. The migrants moved to be near the states that offered more employment opportunities, and better remuneration, education, and health services. This process can be understood as having been a part of the economic development in Colombia during this period.

This tendency remained stable until the 1970s. A change only occurred in the 1980s and 1990s when new internal movements arose that were mainly tied to different forms of violence. Consequently, forced mobility became a special characteristic of migration within Colombia.

MIGRATION IN THE RECENT YEARS: FORCED MIGRATION PROBLEMS

During the last 18 years, internal mobility has frequently been linked to acts of violence. Most migrations occurred in the rural districts and can be labeled "forced."

The Episcopal Conference of Colombia conducted a study about displaced people in which it was shown that during the last 10 years the number of displaced persons for reasons of violence was between 544,801 and 627,720; this represented 2% of the total Colombian population (Conferencia Episcopal Colombiana, 1995, p. 43). Of the displaced persons, 58% were females and 72% were not more than 25 years old. Sixty-seven percent moved with their family, and 39,316 had lost a family member because of violent acts prior to their migration. Their destinations were generally the big cities such as Bogotá, Medellín, Cali, Barranquilla, and Barrancabermeja. Of the migrating populations or displaced persons, some had moved only once (20.08%), others moved twice (56.32%), and still others three or more times (23.6%). This phenomenon was explained by the fact that most displaced or migrating people faced many problems during their relocation, and consequently they were often forced to move again to other places.

The forced migrations led to many adaptation problems among the migrants reflecting the impact of new and unknown rules, regulations, laws, and rights on them in their new environments. Because the displaced persons had been risking their own lives, they preferred to accept the new conditions for which, however, they were neither socially nor technologically prepared. In addition, the local residents were not prepared either (Bejarano, 1997; Giraldo, Abad, & Perez, 1997; Osorio, 1993; Rojas, 1993).

The migration problem in Colombia displayed several characteristics throughout recent history. First of all, the problem reflected ecological conditions in nature; second came environmental factors intertwined with variables reflecting a specific cultural tradition concerning ownership of land and property; and third, Colombia became a semi-industrialized country that generated new riches and wealth due to the manufacturing of industrial goods, the development of new means of communication, and the formation and expansion of cities. These in turn became economically attractive areas of development. Finally, the economic progress occurred together with much political and economic violence, creating a new kind of migration accompanied by aversive consequences for both the immigrants and the local populations. This new kind of migration is known as forced migration.

Forced migration requires the formulation of policies and designs for directives as well as functional, active strategies in order to establish manageable conditions. Provisions for help, guidance, and pertinent information for both the immigrants and the local residents are needed. In this way they can adapt more successfully to the new environmental conditions and to the new economic, political, technical, and cultural exigencies associated with them.

NOTE

The author thanks Maria Constanza Aguilar, his wife, for the suggestions and corrections she made to this chapter, and John J. Sanabria for his work on the translation.

REFERENCES

Ardila, R. (1992). *La psicologia del hombre colombiano* [The psychology of the Colombian man]. Bogotá, Colombia: Plantea.

Bejarano, J. (1997). *Colombia: inseguridad, violencia y desempeno economico en las areas rurales* [Colombia: Insecurity, violence and economic performance in rural areas]. Bogotá, Colombia: Universidad Externado de Colombia, Fonade.

Bushnell, D. (1996). *Colombia una nacion a pesar de si misma: de los tempos precolombinos a nuestros dias* [Colombia its own nation: From the pre-Colombian times to our days]. Bogotá, Colombia: Planeta.

Cardona, R., & Simmons, A. (1977). *Destino de la metropoli: un modelo general de las migraciones internas en America Latina* [Destiny and metropoly: A general model of the internal migration in Latin America]. Bogotá, Colombia: Corporacion Centro Regional de Poblacion.

Conferencia Episcopal Colombiana. (1995). *Derechos humanos y desplazamieto interno en Colombia* [Human rights and internal displacement in Colombia]. Bogotá, Colombia: Conferencia Espicopal de Colombia.

Giraldo, C., Abad, C., & Perez, D. (1997). *Relatos e imagenes: el desplazamiento en Colombia* [Stories and images: Displacement in Colombia]. Bogotá, Colombia: Cinep.

Gutierrez, V. (1975). *Familia y cultura en Colombia: tipologias, funciones y dinamica de la familia. Manifestaciones multiples a traves del mosaico cultural y sus estructuras sociales* [Culture and family in Colombia: Typologies and dynamics of the family. Multiple manifestations through the cultural mosaic and its social structures]. Medellín, Colombia: Universidad de Antioquia.

Lievano, I. (1963). *Los grandes conflictos sociales y economicos en nuestra historia* [The great social and economic conflicts in our history]. Bogotá, Colombia: Tercermundo.

Osorio, F. (1993). *La violencia del silencio, desplazados del campo a la ciudad* [The violence of silent displacement from the country to the city]. Bogotá, Colombia: Codhes.

Ravenstein, E. G. (1885). On the laws of migration. *Journal of the Royal Statistical Society, 48*, 167-235.

Rojas, J. (1993). *Desplazamiento, derechos humanos y conflicto armado* [Displacement, human rights, and armed conflicts]. Bogotá, Colombia: Codhes.

III

Europe

9

Migrant Families in Germany

Leonie Herwartz-Emden

MIGRATION AND POPULATION STRUCTURE

Aspects of Present Immigration Into Germany: Migration Movements and Consequences

Since the first recruitment agreements with littoral states of the Mediterranean were concluded 40 years ago[1], nearly 7 million foreigners have taken up permanent residence in Germany. Nearly every fifth foreign national comes from a member state of the European Union, or EU. At the end of 1999, there were 7,340,000 foreigners living in Germany, which amounts to 8.9% of the overall population.

In 1999, the largest group of foreigners was represented by Turks, with 2.05 million people (28%), followed by the group of migrants from the former Yugoslavia (Serbia and Montenegro) with 737,200 people (10.0%), Italians with 615,900 (8.4%), Greeks with 364,400 (5%), Bosnians with 167,700 (2.3%), Polish migrants with 291,700 (4.0%), Croatians with 214,000 (2.9%), and Austrians with 186,100 (2.5%) (Statistisches Bundesamt, 2000, p. 16*ff*)[2]. After the extension of the European Union on January 1, 1995, EU citizens comprised 25.5% of all foreigners residing in the Federal Republic of Germany. They included Italians (32.5%), Greeks (19.7%), Austrians (10.1%), Spaniards (7.2%), Portuguese (7.1%), British (6.3%), Dutch (6.2%), and others.

Although the majority of foreigners living in Germany have taken up permanent residence here for a relatively long period, there is a steady flux of immigrants who leave the country again as well as new migrants entering the country. In 1994, there was an increase of approximately 100,000 immigrants, a large part of whom fled from the civil war in former Yugoslavia. In addition to the war refugees, about 10,000 recognized asylum seekers registered in the same year. Between the years 1988 and 1992, the balance of migrancy showed a positive development with an upward trend, although there were significant differences among the various groups of migrants.

In 1997, it became apparent that for the first time in 12 years there were more foreigners returning to their country of origin than those newly entering the country. Still, the number of foreign residents in Germany increased from 7,314,000 to 7,366,000 in the period from 1996 to 1997, due to the high birth rate of foreign residents.

During recent years, divergent trends have been observed in migrant movements making it difficult to observe the exact development of immigration and emigration processes. For instance, it is hard to draw clear distinctions between immigrants, working migrants, and other migrants who enter the country such as asylum seekers and illegal immigrants. Floating populations, which had been noted in Europe's Early Modern Age and in the Middle Ages (Bade, 1996), are again becoming a normal feature of the continent.

An important aspect of the present migration movements is the increase in German-origin immigrants from the former Soviet Union (*Aussiedler*). From the end of 1951 until the end of 1988, as many as 1.6 million *Aussiedler* passed the "border-transition camps" (*Grenzdurchgangslager*) of West Germany without much public attention. Since 1987, after the fall of the Iron Curtain, the number of *Aussiedler* has increased sharply; they exceeded the previous record of 200,000 per year and reached a figure of 377,055 persons by the end of 1989. During the following year, figures increased only slightly to 397,073 and in 1991 they decreased to 221,995 immigrants although numerous applications were submitted for immigration permits. This development led to a phase of consolidated immigration at a high level (1992: 230,565; 1993: 218,888; 1994: 222,591; 1995: 217,898; 1999: 104,916).

With *Aussiedler* immigration growing into a mass movement, the problem of how best to integrate these *Aussiedler* turned into a distinct social challenge. Prior to the dramatic increase of immigration figures, integration seemed to work quite well thanks to strong financial support granted by the government and the communities. With an increasing number of *Aussiedler* entering the country, these integration measures were reduced as a result of financial pressures. As large cuts were made in language courses and in professional integrative measures for retraining and for further educational qualifications, there were only a few opportunities for *Aussiedler* to enter the employment market. This holds especially true for women. After receiving unemployment benefits for half a year, many of them will then have to depend on welfare. With this in mind, more and more communities began to protest against further unlimited immigration of *Aussiedler*, and the problem has become part of the public debate involving all political parties (e.g., Social Democrats) who advocate limited admission of *Aussiedler* into the country.

Aussiedler are immigrants according to social, cultural, and psychological criteria (Bade & Oltmer, 1999) although *not* according to legal criteria. In contrast to foreign immigrants, *Aussiedler* have a legal status that corresponds to that of German citizens. This implies that in their daily existence, *Aussiedler* do not have to deal with the insecurities that derive from various specific legal policies for foreigners (e.g., the right to stay, etc.). However, the process of integration of *Aussiedler* is very similar to that of other immigrant groups. It involves the same difficulties, despite all the integrative measures provided for *Aussiedler* over long periods of time and their more advantageous status. All groups of immigrants coming to Germany enter a Western free-market society, a society defined by consumption and by efficiency, with an economic and sociocultural structure mainly unknown to them. Their adjustment process is characterized by many disruptions that can be detected in areas such as knowledge acquisition, values, and patterns of communication. Furthermore, they are sometimes confronted with an atmosphere of xenophobia and experiences of exclusion and discrimination.

Immigration into Germany is based on a vital need of this country: Because the population pyramid of the German society reflects declining tendencies, the country depends on immigrants in order to secure a satisfactory functioning of the labor market. Employment of foreigners guarantees the efficiency of national labor market policies and of the welfare system because it leads to general increases in both income levels and private expenditures. These in turn lead to an increase in tax payments and in contributions to the social security system. In the long run, the immigration of labor forces also stabilizes the country's work potential, especially in times of a local labor shortage. Only if these factors come into play, will it be possible to maintain the present level of social security payments for future generations (Körner, 1996).

The employment situation of women is affected by immigration in the following way: Just as in other European societies and in the United States, the higher professional qualifications of native German women and their employment possibilities depend both qualitatively and quantitatively on the employment of migrant women in private households (Rerrich, 1993). An estimated 2.4 million women work in private households in Germany in employment positions that are not officially registered. It may be safely assumed, however, that foreign women form a large part of this group (Rerrich, 1993, p. 271).

Demographic Features of the Present Migrant Population in the Federal Republic of Germany: Age Structure of Foreign Citizens

During the 1960s, the migrant population in Germany was characterized by a large percentage of 20- to 40-year-old men who lived alone in this country and who came to Germany on the basis of recruitment contracts. However, one must not forget the important role of female migrants that is neglected in many studies. An estimated 10% of the foreign married women living in Germany in 1979 originally came into the country as pioneer migrants without their husband or their family in order to find employment (Borris, 1973, and the representative study conducted by the "Bundesanstalt für Arbeit" in 1985).

In the meantime, the number of foreign families has increased. According to estimates of the German Commissioner for Safeguarding the Interests of Foreigners, 83% of all foreigners in 1993 lived in families (Beauftragter der Bundesregierung für die Belange der Ausländer, 1997, p. 53). At the end of 1990 the percentage of foreigners amounted to 8.2% when compared with the total population of West Germany and to 8.5% in the old *Bundesländer* (Federal German regional states). This percentage corresponds to approximately 6.6 million foreigners with a very uneven distribution in the different *Länder*. In comparison with the total population, the percentage of foreigners in the new *Bundesländer* (the former German Democratic Republic) amounts to 1.15%, or about 212,000 persons. (This implies that about 97% of all foreigners live in the old and only 3% in the new *Bundesländer*.) A considerable number of German *Aussiedler* women and other migrant women from Eastern European countries should be added to this figure.

During the 1980s, many first-generation foreigners reached retirement age. A great number of them live in families together with the next generation (i.e., women, men, and children who came to Germany under the provisions of the German government program for family reunion). Many of them have grand-children, that is, third-generation immigrants born in Germany whose grandparents once entered the county as working migrants. Considering the long duration of their stay, a large majority of foreigners living in Germany have in fact immi-grated to this country. In 1999, about 32% of the migrant population had lived in Germany for at least 20 years.

Since 1970, between 10% to 15% of all newborns in Germany have foreign parents; and in 1992, over 50% of them were of Turkish nationality (Beauftragte der Bundesregierung für die Belange der Ausländer 1994, p. 57). In 1991, there were about 2.48 million children and young people under the age of 25 who lived in the Federal Republic of Germany with a foreign passport (Geißler, 1992, pp. 155, 161). This corresponds to 9.4% of all German residents of the same age group.

The change in age structure mentioned above is reflected in a decrease in employment figures: In 1960 the percentage of men in the active working population was 70%, in 1990 it was only 63%, in 1997 it was 59%. In the same period the percentage of women in the group of the active working population grew from 31% to 45% and fell to 37.5% in 1997 (Bundesministerium für Familie, Senioren, Frauen und Jugend, 2000, p. 144).

In the 1990s, the number of children, young adults, and old people increased disproportionately. At present, the population of foreigners does not only consist of working migrants but also includes all age groups ranging from children to pensioners (Nauck, 1988)[3]. Comparing the age structure of the foreign popu-lation with that of the local German population, the following differences may be noted: Although there exists an increasing number of immigrants from the first generation who are reaching retirement age, the economically active second generation as well as children and young people from the third generation pre-dominated in 1997. Contrary to this development, the age structure of the local population is characterized by a growing percentage of elderly people and a smaller percentage of children and young adults. These trends are caused by a continuous decrease in birth figures (Bundesministerium für Familie, Senioren, Frauen und Jugend, 2000, p. 69).

Duration of Stay (in Years)

The composition of the foreign population did not remain constant, because most foreigners preferred to return to their country of origin. From 1961 to 1987 there were about 15 million foreigners living in Germany, but about 11 million of them left the country again. During the course of the 1980s, a notable change in many migrants' motivation occurred: Only a small percentage of foreigners (1989: 11%) made definite plans to return (Geißler, 1992, pp. 155, 161). Between 1980 and 1987, the percentage of foreigners with a minimum stay in Germany of 10 years rose from 30% to 60%, and by the end of 1988, 43% of all foreigners had been living in the Federal Republic of Germany for over 15 years (1999: 40%). By the end of 1995, as many as 66% of all foreign children and young adults had been born in this country; and in 1997, 87.5% of the under 6-year-old foreign children and 53.9% of the 6- to 18-year-olds (Beauftragte der Bundesregierung für Ausländerfragen, 2000, p. 234).

Geographic Distribution of the Foreign Population

The distribution of foreign persons varies strongly within the territory of the Federal Republic of Germany, with strong concentrations in the big cities and centers of industry (rural-urban divide). Furthermore, almost 75% of all immigrants live in the federal states of Baden-Würtemberg, Bavaria, Hesse, and Northrhine-Westfalia (Beauftragte der Bundesregierung für die Belange der Ausländer, 1997, p. 22).

In addition, there exists a distinct west-east divide, which may reflect the formerly different migration policies in the eastern and western parts of Germany (Isoplan, 1995, p. 15). Most migrants are concentrated in the old federal states, with 97% (6,666,000) living in the territory of the former Federal Republic of Germany and Berlin and only 3% (212,000) residing in the new federal states.

Comparisons between the old and new federal states also show differences in the national composition of the foreign population. Those foreigners still residing in the new federal states originally entered the German Democratic Republic on the basis of bilateral agreements as so-called contractual workers. They came from Vietnam, Mozambique, Angola, Poland, and Romania, and right from the beginning of their stay they had temporary employment contracts and only a temporary right to residence. Correspondingly, no efforts were made to facilitate their integration into the society of the former German Democratic Republic and there were few contacts with the German population. In general, only a few foreigners living in the new federal states have a secure right to reside there, and this also implies that they have no right to receive retraining or financial support paid by Germany's employment office (Isoplan, 1995, p. 15).

The integration policies within the newly united German state basically assume that xenophobic tendencies are much stronger in the new *Bundesländer* than in the old *Länder*. This inevitably leads to the development of different approaches in the new and old *Länder* and a concentration on different fields of work. Whereas the west concentrates on social, professional, and economic "integration," the east places more emphasis on attempting to reduce information gaps throughout the German population, particularly among teachers (Beauftragte der Bundesregierung für die Belange der Ausländer, 1995, p. 2).

The distribution of foreigners into the different *Bundesländer* occurs according to a scheme agreed on by all regions (Law on Allocation of Residence, or *Wohnortezuweisungsgesetz*). This law states that all *Bundesländer* are obliged to receive a certain number of foreigners, with a corresponding distribution of all expenditures and related tasks according to region. In 1995, this law was extended for 5 more years in order to prevent the possible concentrations of foreigners in certain regions of the country.

MIGRANT FAMILIES AND GERMAN FAMILIES: SIMILARITIES AND DIFFERENCES

Education and Rates of Employment

In general, working migrants' qualifications reflect lower educational levels than those of other migrant groups or of Germans, and in most cases they do not exceed the level of lower secondary-school-level qualification (*Hauptschulabschluß*). Compared with working migrants, a much larger percentage of *Aussiedler* are qualified at a higher secondary school-level (*Realschule*) or the *Abitur* (entry qualification for university studies corresponding to English A-level examinations). The same differences become apparent when comparing the professional training of both groups. Although both refugees and *Aussiedler* achieved a relatively high level of professional qualifications, only 20.7% of working migrants were trained in a qualified occupation (Hauser & Kinstler, 1994, pp. 8*ff*)[4], compared with nearly 70% of all *Aussiedler*. A high overall rate of unemployment in Germany is the major reason why working migrants cannot find work: Unemployment affects German and migrant workers in distinctively different ways.

Differences in Income Level: Housing and Housing Costs

Germans (both men and women) earn more than foreigners (Diekmann, Engelhardt, & Hartmann, 1993, p. 389)[5], irrespective of the fact that men in general and regardless of their nationality earn more than women. However, the difference in income level between foreign men and women is less drastic than that between German men and women.

On the whole, immigrants live in poor housing conditions (Hauser & Kinstler, 1994, p. 11). For example, only one third of the *Aussiedler* live in apartments equipped with bathrooms/toilets and central heating. The majority of working migrants live under similarly poor conditions. Furthermore, over 40% of working migrants and *Aussiedler* live in apartments that do not offer sufficient living space. Nevertheless, the proof of sufficient living quarters (Hauser & Kinstler, 1994, pp. 10-11) is a legal requirement for working migrants in order to secure the right to stay.

The CARITAS study on poverty (Hauser & Kinstler, 1994) estimated the highest acceptable limit of expenditure for rent at a maximum of 28% of the net family income. According to these calculations, nearly 25% of working migrants must pay a rent amounting between 28% and 40% of their income or higher. For *Aussiedler*, these figures are even higher because 40% of all them have to pay such a high rent. Clearly, many *Aussiedler* must shoulder severe financial burdens because of their rent.

Unemployment

In 1999, 19% or 493,005 of all migrants in the West Germany were unemployed. This figure is nearly twice as high as the unemployment rate (11%) for the general population during the same period (Beauftragte der Bundesregierung für Ausländerfragen, 2000, p. 142).

Between October 1992 and March 1994, the unemployment figure of foreign workers had risen by 1% (from 15.9% to 16.9%) (Isoplan, 1995, p. 2; Regionale Arbeitsstellen zur Förderung ausländischer Kinder und Jugendlicher (RAA) Essen, 1993, p. 5), with a very different distribution among the various national groups. The following foreign nationals were especially affected by unemployment: Turks (20.9%), Italians (18.4%), and Greeks (17.5%).

In addition, data contained in the Zwischenbericht der Enquete-Kommission (1994) on unemployment and reemployment show a higher rate of reemployment of German nationals when compared with foreign nationals. Analyses by gender demonstrate that the unemployment periods of foreign women are significantly longer than those of male foreigners. In contrast, the reemployment periods of German men and women differ only slightly, although the periods of women's reemployment are lower than those of men (cf. Zwischenbericht der Enquete-Kommission, 1994, p. 199, Table 45).

In view of increasing mass unemployment, unemployment is a major risk factor for poverty. This is particularly alarming for foreigners, because the labor market has its own rank order reflecting nationality-specific criteria (Germans are ranked highest, followed by foreigners from EU member states, next come foreigners from non-EU member states, and finally the *Aussiedler*).

Structural Characteristics

As stated above, the local German population and the foreign population have quite different age distributions. As a result of an extremely low birthrate, which, according to the estimates of the demographer Birg (1996), since the 1970s has been among the lowest in the world, the local German population is steadily declining. At present, the average birthrate in Germany is 1.26 children per woman. This figure also includes the newborn children of the foreign population. (For the long-term stability of a population, it would be necessary that each woman give birth to 2.1 children). The local German population is an aging population (Birg, 1996), whereas the foreign population group and the *Aus-*

siedler group are both young populations characterized by a "normal" age structure.

In 1998, 100,100 children born in Germany had foreign parents. The family size of the foreign population varies considerably among the different national groups, but it is generally not characterized by a large number of children, contrary to what most people assume. On the average, Turkish families have 2.2 children, whereas the average number of children in Spanish and Yugoslavian families is 1.8. Although little is known about children of migrant families who remained in the countries of origin, there are apparently only very few children younger than 9 years who live in their parents' home country. Most children who live there are at least 16 years old. In addition, most children living in their country of origin are of Turkish nationality, irrespective of the age factor (Beauftragte der Bundesregierung für Ausländerfragen, 2000, p. 18).

It can be observed that over time the foreign population group tends to adopt many German forms of social and family behavior such as increasing age of marriage, decreasing number of children, living in improved housing conditions, and increased levels of education. The latter, however, are still far below that of the local German children and young adults.

Central demographic features of private households in Germany have undergone drastic changes, and all indicators for Germany show that modern forms of private life can take on very diverse and different forms. However, the general public still clings to the image of the "typical family," although this idea is indeed quite unrealistic for the following reasons:

• Only about one-third of all households can be classified as traditional family households, meaning a unit which consists of parents and children. Furthermore, households are increasingly shrinking in size.

• The number of married couples without children is constantly increasing. Over 50% of all marriages lead only to one child or no children at all, a trend that has already persisted for 100 years.

• The percentage of different forms of partner relations based on nonmarital status has been increasing, although for statistical purposes these forms are difficult to categorize. Within the age group of 18- to 35-year-olds, the number of partner relations based on nonmarital status has increased eightfold during the period from 1972 to 1995. About 1 million partnerships in Germany are now of a nonmarital nature.

• Divorce figures are increasing; at present one marriage out of three to four ends in divorce.

• The number of single-parent families is increasing, and in most cases these families include mothers. At present, every eighth child in Germany is brought up in a single-parent family. There is also a growing number of stepfamilies.

• The number of married women and mothers who work outside their homes is growing constantly. From 1950 to 1980, the number of employed mothers nearly doubled (Rerrich, 1993, p. 120).

Summing up all these facts leads to the conclusion that although the traditional family structure is still a very common form of life in Germany, there are many other forms of living together which many German families prefer. Today, the term *family* may take on diverse meanings: For example, both parents may be employed; one parent may bring up one or more children alone; children may live together with adults who are not their biological parents; or people from different cultural origins may live together with their children in a foreign country or even live separated from their family for much of the year (Rerrich, 1993, pp. 112–132).

Orientations

It is difficult to say for certain whether the structural changes in partner relations, marriage, and family coincide with a corresponding change in individual attitudes and conceptions. Unlike demographic trends, personal meanings are not easily accessible and they are difficult to measure. Changes in social conditions do not automatically result in changes of personal attitudes about specific life concepts (Rerrich, 1993, p. 121).

The processes of individualization and modernization within the German society and the different forms of life that go along with them apparently did not lead to any basic changes in those attitudes that endorse the model "family" as a desirable form of life. There remains a strong tendency to include children as well as a partner/husband or wife as part of one's major life objectives. No evidence exists for the common assumption that modernity inevitably leads to the destruction of the family unit. What can be confirmed, however, is that individuals continue to be willing to establish stable social bonds, even if their ways of life take on different forms and follow new models. However, many persons now hold very strong expectations regarding their partner and how they should relate to him or her (Burkart, 1995). Two major trends in the development of personal life can be regarded as indicators for a partial change of individual attitudes toward partner relations, marriage, and family: the liberalization of social norms referring to sexuality and cohabitation and the various forms of living together without being legally married. Within a very brief period of time, the latter became generally accepted and they have been turned into a normal, unspectacular biographical phase which, for some social groups, constitutes a viable alternative to marriage (Rerrich, 1993, p. 124).

CONDITIONS FOR SOCIALIZATION AND EDUCATION IN MIGRANT FAMILIES

Comparing German families with foreign families, one might start with the assumption that to lead a good family life remains a major objective of most individuals for whom the family continues to play a central role in their value system. In the case of migration, the family is usually the focus of emigration, the reason for seeking employment in a foreign country, and a crucial motivation for emigration in general. To secure the survival of one's children and to guarantee them a better future are the main motives that lie behind nearly all migration movements.

For immigrants, the family offers survival, security, and a structure to solve the organizational problems of daily life. Furthermore, the family offers protection and a social space for both ethnic identification and anchoring of one's identity in an environment that is often hostile. It is the family that takes care of children day after day, and most processes of socialization and education are focused here. In Germany, the main conditions for everyday life with children and the education of children are just as important for foreign families as for German families with children, but these conditions are changing.

First, the social conditions of childhood have changed. The mothers, in particular, are those responsible for taking their children to nursery or primary schools where they can establish contacts with other children. In Germany, it is becoming increasingly dangerous to have children playing outside unattended—a completely new situation for most foreign families, including *Aussiedler* families. Also, many parents are quite used to having their children take part in their own leisure activities.

Second, in addition, the way in which children are taken care of has changed from mere care to a focus on an intensified relationship and communication with the child. The strong attention that all sections of the German population pay to childhood and its educational and psychological aspects—a process that is reinforced by the higher education standards now prevailing for women—has resulted in the fact that the daily amount of time and effort needed for proper child care has not been reduced although childcare assumes now different forms (Rerrich, 1993, p. 130). The stronger emphasis placed on supporting the child's individual needs implies for the parents, in particular for mothers, that they must cope with a heavier workload in everyday life. This greater daily workload also holds true for institutionalized child care (e.g., self-organized nurseries/"non-authoritarian" children's shops, or *Kinderläden*, parents' reunions at schools during evening hours). However, in spite of all these changes, something "remained the same in a contra-factual manner" (Rerrich, 1993): The time intervals and rhythms in nurseries and schools still follow the same traditional family patterns as before (e.g., father is expected to work in a full-time job, whereas mother is expected to be always available at home). Consequently, institutions typically assume that "naturally" there is always somebody at home to be contacted, a condition that is difficult to meet for foreign families. As a rule, the women in this group hold regular jobs much more frequently than do comparable German women, and it is unrealistic to assume that most of them "merely" fulfill the tasks of a housewife. In the past, many migrant families had to cope with this break in traditions; now the *Aussiedler* are learning to deal with it. In their countries of origin, child care was usually organized by the state on a nationwide basis. Additionally, the older generation readily provided help with this task. In Germany, however, families are expected to take care of their children individually and personally and to always be at their disposal as "quality parents."

Opportunities for Education and Professional Qualification as a Precondition for Integration

First of all, it should be noted that foreign families are considerably less likely to enroll their children in nursery schools than are German families. Compared with 74.2% of all German children aged 3–8 years who attend nursery schools, only 57.7% of all children with a foreign passport visit the same institution (see Beauftragte der Bundesregierung für die Belange der Ausländer, 1994, p. 61*ff*). Nevertheless, migrants generally appreciate the availability of nursery schools.

In Germany, there are about 1.8 million children and young adults with foreign parents (within the age group of 0 to 20 years). Within the age group of 14- to 25-year-olds, 1.5 million children and young adults have foreign parents, and there exists a continuous increase of those already born in Germany.

Due to different social origins, nationality, and legal position, this group of young migrants is a very heterogeneous one, including second- and third-generation immigrants from both EU member and nonmember states, *Aussiedler*, and refugees. However, all these immigrants have one thing in common: During the process of professional orientation and qualification, they do not enjoy equal opportunities with their German peers (Brunken, 1995, pp. 109–115).

On the whole, migrant families place a strong emphasis on the importance of education. As explained before, their major motivation for immigration was the objective of securing their children's future. Because they frequently could (or can) not return to their countries of origin, such families tend to consider their children's success in the receiving society as a visible sign of a successful migration process; as a reward for all the hardship and deprivations they had to endure. However, a very limiting factor for successful immigration of foreign families is the fact that foreign children still have only a limited chance of achieving within the German educational system.

Participation of Migrant Children and Young People in Education

The following statistics illustrate the different educational achievements between German and migrant families:

- Within the age group of 6 to 15 years, the participation rate in education is 95%, which corresponds to an equivalent rate for German children and young adults.

- Within the age group of 15 to 20 years, the participation rate reaches a level of 60%, a much lower rate than that of German young adults (90%).

- Thirty-six percent of young female migrants achieve the level of *Realschule* (Secondary School II level) or the German *Abitur* (the German entry requirement for university study).

- Foreign pupils remain underrepresented at the higher educational levels. It is evident that despite their improved situation, the differences between the foreign and German pupils have so far not been leveled out.

- With regard to professional training, foreign young persons concentrate on a few

occupations. Although young adult males are mainly trained in skilled trades or la-
bor-technical jobs, the professional training of young adult females is mainly focused
on the service sector. In addition, an overproportional rate of young adult foreigners
continue to drop out of their training program before finishing it. In 1988 to 1989, for
example, a total of 24% of young adult foreigners broke off their professional training.

A second barrier is the search for work: Young adult foreigners looking for
jobs run an unemployment risk about twice as high as that of their German
counterparts. This is partly due to their specific fields of training, which frequently are in areas offering only limited employment chances.

Young female migrants are more likely to be trained at schools than being
enrolled in company training programs (such as serving as an apprentice). These
forms of professional training at schools are often sought out as alternative solutions when there are no training possibilities at companies. Furthermore, studies
on young foreign women's professional preferences point to the gender-specific
segmentation of the labor market: within a spectrum of over 200 qualified jobs,
they concentrate mostly on 10 to 15 occupations such as becoming a hairdresser,
medical assistant, shop assistant, and so on. Many of these predominantly female occupations do not guarantee permanent employment. In contrast, German
young women tend to select a broader spectrum of careers.

Studies of the integration processes of young migrants indicate that the integration of the second and third generations of foreigners does not happen automatically in a quasi-natural way but instead depends predominantly on their
professional situation. Apart from granting equal political rights to foreigners, a
demand whose fulfillment has long been overdue, it is an absolute must to improve qualified job training facilities for young adults so that young migrants
may fully participate in the social and cultural life of a country that is and will
be the center of their lives (Brunken, 1995, p. 113).

INTEGRATION INTO SOCIETY AS A FAMILY TASK

Potential Conflicts in Migrant Families and Tasks of Integration

During the course of immigration, there occur many different kinds of conflicts that vary both in their intensity and their persistence. Katharina Ley's
(1979) publication, based on empirical and theoretical studies of immigrant
situations experienced by Italian working migrants in Switzerland in the 1970s,
and Mirjana Morokvasic's (1987) project, which focused on the integration of
Yugoslav female immigrants in various European countries, have shown that
migrant women change both their ideas and their behavior during the different
stages of their integration into the new society. A recent comparative study carried out by the research project FAFRA on the lives of migrant women, their
families, and individual family members pointed to similar conclusions for two
quite different groups: *Aussiedler* from the former Soviet Union and migrants
from Turkey (Herwartz-Emden, 2000).

Research has shown that conflicts in families arise primarily from the fact that migration is always linked to separation—a situation that is full of emotional stress. A typical and well-known example is provided by children who are separated from their parents, develop disturbances in their relationships with others, encounter difficulties at school and consequently fail, and find it impossible to adapt to the local context and to develop feelings of psychosocial well-being.

The entire psychosocial situation of immigrant families is of a special character: The problems of separation and subsequent family reunion are not solved immediately when the core family is reunited in Germany. Although it might appear as if the migration processes had ended at this moment, situations of separation and family reunion are in actuality problems that each generation will have to cope with permanently. Migration within the country, commuting, remigration, and a possible new emigration require consistent reorganization of the whole family. Experiences of grief go together with great emotional strain that involves not only grief but conflicts of loyalty as well. This is particularly true in cases of divorce and whenever feelings of guilt are created. Many of these emotional challenges for migrants have so far been studied only in an insufficient manner. The few publications available restrict themselves to the analysis of the emotional and psychosocial aspects of integration and immigration processes (e.g., Hettlage-Varjas & Hettlage, 1989, pp. 26–48), or they analyze these processes according to gender and generation (e.g., Kürsat-Ahlers, 1995, p. 157*ff*). It may be assumed that female immigrants are particularly exposed to emotional stresses and strains because they assume major roles in the areas of social and health care within their family. Typically these reflect their gender-specific responsibilities. If the families' old parents or small children have to be left behind in their country of origin, it is in particular the women who feel all the pain deriving from such events together with the guilt feelings that go along with it. Here it becomes evident that women and especially mothers play a decisive role during the integration process of the family in the receiving country. The psychosocial family situation depends largely on their ability to cope with a variety of contradictory expectations as well as conveying these in the right way to the individual family members.

A further strain for migrant families is the different way in which all individual family members are integrated into the receiving society. At present many *Aussiedler* families have to cope with the problem that one of the married partners—whether it be the husband or the wife—has no employment prospects whatsoever. Consequently, the chances of this partner being integrated into the German society are reduced to a large extent. He or she will fail to have the same social and emotional experiences as those experienced by his or her partner—a situation that may easily create conflicts in their relationship. Many young adults unable to find an opportunity for professional training are faced with a similar difficult situation, one that frequently leads to personal crises.

As mentioned before, the changing roles making up the gender relations prevailing in the wider German society represent a major challenge for migrant families. Day by day migrants are confronted with a society that presents different images of women and men, different gender-specific role attributions, a changing division of labor, and new definitions of "psychosocial movement spaces" available for men and for women. All of this causes confusion and irritation. However, any attempts to interpret these kinds of conflicts merely by means of the simple formula "tradition versus emancipation" would certainly be wrong. For instance, recent studies have shown that the self-concepts and female images of migrant women from less industrialized societies and more traditional contexts are actually less characterized by female dependency on men than those of modern western women. Furthermore, it would be misleading to characterize either their self-concept or their image of what it means to be a female on the basis of recent western concepts of polarization. In addition, there exists no evidence that male migrants are generally more authority-minded or that they assume the role of a patriarch more easily than modern western men (Herwartz-Emden, 2000).

Female and Male Migrants Achieve
Excellent Progress in Integration Processes

In his studies on the personal careers of migrant women, the sociologist and family researcher Nauck (1988) demonstrated that the local society influences their biographies and their family lives in a radical way. Migrant women adapted to local conditions in a minimum period of time, a phenomenon that was reflected both in their birth rates and in the new forms of their marriage relation (Herwartz-Emden, 1995). In situations of decision making and in the allocation of daily tasks according to gender-specific roles, the power hierarchy between men and women undergoes radical changes. Women are as responsible for the financial plans of the family as their husbands, and men as fathers are as responsible for the education and school careers of their children as their wives.

The question of gender-typical role attributions and task allocation as part of the partnership, and the way the married partners look at their relation to each other constitute sources of conflict for migrants. In 1992, over 80% of all those foreign women working on the basis of employment contracts subject to compulsory insurance were employed in full-time jobs. These women spent just as much time on work outside their home as their husbands did. Still, they had to cope with all the extra work involved in housekeeping and taking care of children, seemingly without much notice being paid to it. In 1990, 32.6% of all foreign women worked in a job outside their home (Beauftragte der Bundesregierung für die Belange der Ausländer, 1994, p. 58). In addition, it may be assumed that the real percentage is much higher because many foreign women work in jobs that are not subject to compulsory insurance (i.e., they work in insecure and unprotected employment situations). According to estimates, about 2.4 million German women work in private households in unregistered employment conditions, and a large part of these women are presumably foreigners (Rerrich & Jurczyk, 1992, p. 333).

The latest international studies have shown that migration typically entails both gains and losses for the participants; for example, women frequently gain personal freedom but also lose important resources because of the loss of their female networks (e.g., Zlotnik, 1990, pp. 372, 381). The simple idea that women automatically gain more freedom when they work in a paid job should therefore be abandoned. The migration situation is a challenge for all persons involved, and it requires from them a change in many of the ideas they hold together with a mutual search for new solutions to many problems. In general, migration constitutes a mutual task for both men and women who will have to adapt their marriage or partner relationship to the new conditions. Recent empirical studies in Germany have shown that both Turkish and *Aussiedler* immigrants tend to arrive at mutual agreements between married partners on how to share the work involved in child care, what the parents' respective tasks are, and on how to solve various corresponding practical problems (Herwartz-Emden, 1995, 2000).

NOTES

1. From 1955 to 1973, foreign workers came to Germany for work on the basis of binational recruitment agreements with the following countries: Italy, Spain, Greece, Turkey, Poland, former Yugoslavia, Morocco, and Tunisia.

2. Information on migration fluxes, emigration, and immigration of the different migrant groups may also be found in the regularly published report *Mitteilungen des Beauftragten der Bundesregierung für die Belange der Ausländer* [Reports of the German Government Commissioner for Ensuring the Interests of Foreigners], e.g., March 1994, December 1995, December 1997.

3. The following three initiatives taken by the German receiving society had considerable influence on the demographic structure of foreign residents in Germany. At the same time, they mark in a characteristic form the 10-year intervals of sociostructural changes:

1. intensified recruitment of foreign workers at the beginning of the 1960s;
2. recruitment prohibition pronounced in 1973;
3. induce foreign workers to return to their country through financial initiatives and through legal barriers against prolonged residence (Nauck, 1988, p. 281).

4. All figures indicated refer to clients interviewed in the CARITAS study on poverty (Hauser & Kinstler, 1994, pp. 8*ff*).

5. These figures are taken from an econometric investigation on the unequal distribution of and discrimination against foreign women and *Aussiedler* women on the German labor market. Based on a microcensus in 1985, income-related functions were estimated according to theoretical human-capital principles. This investigation focuses on the problem of whether and to which extent gender- and/or nationality-specific differences in income can be traced to different individual resources of human capital and to which extent they stem from discrimination.

REFERENCES

Bade, K. (1996). Einleitung: Grenzerfahrungen—die multikulturelle Herausforderung [Introduction. The experience of borders: The multicultural challenge]. In K. Bade (Ed.), *Menschen über Grenzen—Grenzen über Menschen, die multikulturelle Herausforderung* (pp. 8–19). Munich, Germany:

Verlag C. H. Beck.

Bade, K., & Oltmer, J. (1999). Einführung: Aussiedlerzuwanderung und Aus-
siedlerintegration [Introduction: Immigration and integration of *Aussiedler*].
In K. Bade & J. Oltmer (Eds.), *Aussiedler, deutsche Einwanderer aus Ost-
europa.* Schriften des IMIS der Universität Osnabrück (Vol. 8, pp. 9-51).
Osnabrück, Germany: Rasch-Verlag.

Beauftragte der Bundesregierung für die Belange der Ausländer. (1994). *Bericht
der Beauftragten der Bundesregierung für die Belange der Ausländer über
die Lage der Ausländer in der Bundesrepublik Deutschland, März 1994* [Re-
port of the Deputies of the Federal Government for the Affairs of Foreigners
About the Situation of Foreigners in the Federal Republic of Germany,
March 1994], Bonn, Germany.

Beauftragte der Bundesregierung für die Belange der Ausländer. (1995). *Bericht
der Beauftragten der Bundesregierung für die Belange der Ausländer über
die Lage der Ausländer in der Bundesrepublik Deutschland, Dezember 1995*
[Report of the Deputies of the Federal Government for the Affairs of Foreigners About the Situation of Foreigners in the Federal Republic of Germany, December 1995], Bonn, Germany.

Beauftragte der Bundesregierung für die Belange der Ausländer. (1997). *Bericht
der Beauftragten der Bundesregierung für Ausländerfragen über die Lage
der Ausländer in der Bundesrepublik Deutschland, Dezember 1997* [Report
of the Deputies of the Federal Government for the Affairs of Foreigners
About the Situation of Foreigners in the Federal Republic of Germany, December 1997], Bonn, Germany.

Beauftragte der Bundesregierung für Ausländerfragen (2000). *Bericht der
Beauftragten der Bundesregierung für Ausländerfragen über die Lage der
Ausländer in der Bundesrepublik Deutschland, Februar 2000* [Report of the
Deputies of the Federal Government for the Affairs of Foreigners About the
Situation of Foreigners in the Federal Republic of Germany], Berlin, Bonn,
Germany.

Birg, H. (1996, February). *Bevölkerungsentwicklung in Deutschland und Ein-
wanderungen* [The development of the population in Germany and immi-
gration]. Paper presented as part of the "IMIS-Tagung," Einwanderungsland
Bundesrepublik in der Europäischen Union–Gestaltungsauftrag und Regelungsmöglichkeiten, Osnabrück, Germany.

Borris, M. (1973). *Ausländische Arbeiter in einer Großstadt* [Foreign workers in
a big city]. Frankfurt/Main, Germany: Europäische Verlagsanstalt.

Brunken, U. (1995). Jugendliche MigrantInnen beim Übergang von der Schule
in das Erwerbsleben [Youthful migrants at the transition from school to being an employed person]. *Zeitschrift für Jugendsozialarbeit, 46*(2/3), 109–
115.

Bundesministerium für Familie, Senioren, Frauen und Jugend (2000). *Sechster
Familienbericht, Familien ausländischer Herkunft in Deutschland* [Sixth
family report: Families of foreign origin in Germany]. Berlin, Germany.

Burkart, G. (1995). Zum Strukturwandel der Familie [About the structural
change of the family]. *Aus Politik und Zeitgeschichte, Beilage zur Wochen-*

zeitung Das Parlament, B52–B53.

Diekmann, A., Engelhardt, H., & Hartmann, P. (1993). Einkommensgleichheit in der Bundesrepublik Deutschland, Diskriminierung von Frauen und Ausländern? [Equality of income in the Federal Republic of Germany: Discirmination of women and foreigners?]. In K. M. Bolte & F. Buttler (Eds.), *Mitteilungen aus der Arbeitsmarkt- und Berufsforschung, 26,* 386–398.

Geißler, R. (1992). *Die Sozialstruktur Deutschlands. Ein Studienbuch zur sozialstrukturellen Entwicklung im geteilten und vereinten Deutschland* [The social structure of Germany: A study book about the social-structural development in the divided and the united Germany]. Opladen, Germany: Westdeutscher Verlag.

Hauser, R., & Kinstler, H.-J. (1994). Zuwanderer unter den Caritas-Klienten. Sonderauswertung der Caritas-Armutsuntersuchung [Immigrants among the clients of Caritas: Special analysis of the Caritas poverty investigation]. *Zeitschrift für Caritasarbeit und Caritaswissenschaft, 95*(1), 4–20.

Herwartz-Emden, L. (1995). *Mutterschaft und weibliches Selbstkonzept, Eine interkulturell vergleichende Untersuchung* [Motherhood and female self-concept: An intercultural comparative investigation]. Munich, Germany: Juventa-Verlag.

Herwartz-Emden, L. (Ed.). (2000). *Einwandererfamilien: Geschlechterverhältnisse, Erziehung und Akkulturation* [Immigrant families: Relationships between the sexes, socialization, and acculturation]. Schriften des IMIS der Universität Osnabrück (Vol. 9). Osnabrück, Germany: Universitätsverlag Rasch.

Hettlage-Varjas, A., & Hettlage, R. (1989). Auf der Suche nach der verlorenen Identität. Kulturelle Zwischenwelten—eine soziopsychoanalytische Deutung des Wandels bei Fremdarbeitern [On the search for lost identity. Cultural inbetween lands: A sociopsychoanalytic interpretation of change among foreign workers]. *Journal, Psychoanalytisches Seminar Zürich, 20,* 26–48.

Institut für Politikwissenschaft der Westfälischen Wilhelms-Universität Münster. (1994). *Landessozialbericht. Ausländerinnen und Ausländer in Nordrhein-Westfalen, Die Lebenslage der Menschen aus den ehemaligen Anwerbeländern und die Handlungsmöglichkeiten der Politik* [Social report of the state: Foreigners in North Rhine-Westphalia. The life situation of persons from the former recruitment countries and the possibilities of political action] (Vol. 6, pp. 50–55). Neuss, Germany: Ministerium für Arbeit, Gesundheit und Soziales des Landes Nordrhein-Westfalen.

Isoplan, Institut für Entwicklungsforschung, Wirtschafts- und Sozialplanung GmbH. (1995). *Ausländer in Deutschland/AID (1995). Informationsdienst zu aktuellen Fragen der Ausländerarbeit* [Foreigners in Germany/AID (1995). Information Service concerning actual questions about the work situation of foreigners]. Saarbrücken, Germany: Isoplan.

Körner, H. (1996, February). *Arbeitsmarkt und Immigration* [The employment market and immigration]. Paper presented at the "IMIS–Tagung," Einwanderungsland Bundesrepublik in der Europäischen Union—Gestaltungsauftrag und Regelungsmöglichkeiten. Osnabrück, Germany.

Ley, K. (1979). *Frauen in der Emigration. Eine soziologische Untersuchung der Lebens- und Arbeitssituation italienischer Frauen in der Schweiz* [Women in emigration. A sociological investigation of the life and employment situation of Italian women in Switzerland]. Frauenfeld/Stuttgart, Germany: Huber.

Morokvasic, M. (1987). *Jugoslawische Frauen. Die Emigration—und danach* [Yugoslav women: Emigration—and what comes afterwards]. Frankfurt/Main, Germany: Verlag Stroemfeld/Roter Stern.

Nauck, B. (1988). Zwanzig Jahre Migrantenfamilien in der Bundesrepublik. Familiärer Wandel zwischen Situationsanpassung, Akkulturation und Segregation [Twenty years of migrant families in the Federal Republic. Family change in-between situational adaptation, acculturation, and segregation]. In R. Nave-Herz (Ed.), *Wandel und Kontinuität der Familie in der Bundesrepublik Deutschland* (pp. 279–299). Stuttgart, Germany: Enke-Verlag.

Regionale Arbeitsstellen zur Förderung ausländischer Kinder und Jugendlicher (RAA) Essen (Eds.). (1993). Informationen aus Gemeinsam. Ausländer und Deutsche in Schule, Nachbarschaft und Arbeitswelt [Information from "Together:"Foreigners and Germans in school, neighborhood, and the world of work]. *Monatlicher Informationsdienst, 1*, 5.

Rerrich, M. (1993). Familie heute, Kontinuität oder Veränderung [Today's family: Continuity or change?]. In K. Jurczyk & M. Rerrich (Eds.), *Die Arbeit des Alltags—Beiträge zu einer Soziologie der alltäglichen Lebensführung* (pp. 112–132). Freiburg/Breisgau, Germany: Lambertus-Verlag.

Rerrich, M., & Jurczyk, K. (1993). Lebensführung, soziale Einbindung und die Strukturkategorie "Geschlecht" [Conduct of life, social integration, and the structural category "sex"]. In K. Jurczyk & M. Rerrich (Eds.), *Die Arbeit des Alltags—Beiträge zu einer Soziologie der alltäglichen Lebensführung* (pp. 262–278). Freiburg/Breisgau, Germany: Lambertus-Verlag.

Statistisches Bundesamt (2000). *Datenreport 1999* [Data report 1999]. Bonn, Germany: Bundeszentrale für politische Bildung.

Zlotnik, H. (1990). International migration policies and the status of female migrants [Conference Report]. *International Migration Review, 24*(2), 372–381.

Zwischenbericht der Enquete-Kommission (1994). *Demographischer Wandel—Herausforderung unserer älter werdenden Gesellschaft an den Einzelnen und die Politik* [Demographic change: The challenge of an aging society for the individual and for politics]. Bonn, Germany: Deutscher Bundestag, Reuferat Öffentlichkeitsarbeit.

10

Migration Processes in Poland

Halina Grzymala-Moszczynska

HISTORICAL OVERVIEW

Migratory flows vary at different historical periods. As far as Poland is concerned, at distinct historical periods the country was predominantly a sending or receiving country. Until the second half of the 18th century, Poland mostly hosted immigrants who sought personal and religious freedom, higher educational opportunities, freedom of expression in fine arts and architecture, and opportunities for developing networks for the trading of corn and wood. Many of these people settled permanently in Poland and became prominent figures in Polish history and architecture, although their numbers were probably rather small. Reliable statistics in this area are not available.

Major factors contributing to the changes in migratory flows in Poland were the partitions of Poland between 1772 and 1792. At that time Poland was divided among three neighboring states: Austria, Prussia, and Russia, and Poland itself ceased to exist until 1918. The partitions led to several unsuccessful uprisings targeted against the partitioners. Numerous participants in the uprisings were sentenced to long periods of imprisonment, exiled to Siberia, or received death sentences. To avoid these persecutions, many who had taken part in the uprisings emigrated to Western Europe (mainly France and England), but in some cases they settled further afield in North America and South America, and Australia. Due to a lack of reliable statistics, the number of people who migrated from Poland is unknown, but the process became significant in Polish culture because the majority of those who emigrated or were exiled from Poland were intellectuals, writers, poets, or musicians, who vividly described their experiences of exile and migration.

A massive outflow of people began only in the second half of the 19th century. According to a contemporary analysis:

Poland experienced rapid, albeit belated, modernization relative to western Europe following social reforms (including the final abolition of serfdom and limited enfranchisement of the peasants) and industrialization. A huge overmanning in agriculture was quickly revealed which could hardly be coped with by demand for labour generated by the local industrial sector which was still in its infancy. To make things worse, this period also saw an unprecedented acceleration in population growth between 1860 and 1890, and a massive outflow of people, mostly inhabitants of the overpopulated regions of central Eastern and South Eastern Poland began. It is estimated that within around 50 years more than 3.5 million persons emigrated, the majority of them to overseas destinations. They were followed by over 2 million migrants or displaced persons who left Polish lands during the First World War and nearly 2 million who emigrated in the period 1918-1939. (Okólski, 1997, p. 4)

The majority of migrants, mostly impoverished or landless peasants, headed for the United States, Germany, and Latin America.

A second outflow of people began in 1939 after the occupation by the Soviet Union of the eastern half of the Polish Republic. The area contained 13 million people, and the imposition of Soviet rule triggered involuntary population movement on a large scale. Soviet authorities decided to remove whole classes of Polish citizens. They were transported to the Soviet interior, and in many cases they joined descendants of Poles exiled by the Czars after their involvement in uprisings in the 18th and 19th centuries. In addition, the Soviets ejected many Poles from their houses, apartments, and towns, turning them into an internal displaced people.

Between January 1940 and June 1941, a large number of Polish citizens were transferred to Soviet territory. Sword (1996) provided the following insight into the whole process:

The following people were included in categories considered "socially undesirable" and "Anti-Soviet:" University professors, teachers, engineers, the whole of the forestry service, wealthier peasants and small-holders, and certain categories of workers. Families of military personnel outside Poland (e.g., in the West) were included, as were refugees from Western Poland and small merchants and craftsmen. The adopted policy was aiming not just to punish an individual but to uproot the whole family network in which he had been raised and had lived. So, the army officer, mayor or policeman was not alone in his "guilt"; equally culpable or at least equally threatening to the Communist social and political order—were his parents, his wife and children, and his siblings—especially if they were sharing accommodation. Hence a large number of women and children were caught up in the deportation. (pp. 14–15)

Official statistics concerning this movement are not available, mainly because the Moscow archives have still not released documentary evidence relating to those events. Existing estimates range between 1,250,000 and 1,600,000 people (Gross, 1988). The Polish deportee population later became a rich source of new waves of recent immigrants coming to Poland, the so-called Poles from Kazakhstan. This phenomenon is analyzed in greater detail later in this chapter.

Altogether during World War II, more than 5 million Polish citizens or every sixth inhabitant of Poland's territory (as of 1938), left the state frontiers. Large groups of people left Poland to join the Polish Army, which had been reconstructed in France and Britain after the German invasion. Also, large numbers were incarcerated in Germany in concentration and labor camps, or sent to compulsory work camps on German farms (Piesowicz, 1988). Migration related to displacement during World War II significantly contributed to the creation of the Polish diaspora, which currently consists of 12 million people.

In the period after World War II (1950-1979), Poles rarely emigrated, and there were also very few immigrants into Poland. The only exception to emigration was created by the anti-Jewish hysteria of 1968 after which approximately 50,000 people of Jewish origin were pressed to leave Poland, and they settled in Western Europe, the United States, and Israel.

THE CONTEMPORARY SITUATION

The next period of significant migratory outflow from Poland was connected to the political upheavals of 1980 and 1981, which were influenced by both "pull" and "push" factors. The lack of perceived economic and political prospects in Poland was definitely a push factor; at the same time, the very lenient policy of the Federal Republic of Germany toward Poles applying for *Aussiedler* status and preferential treatment for Polish asylum seekers in the West constituted pull factors.

Okolski (1997) pointed to the following aspects of the situation:

It might be argued that a large share of people who participated in those two types of politically and ethnically motivated flows, were in fact economically motivated migrants, and that the two flows to a large degree concealed a major objective of migrants which in reality was a search for a better quality of life in the relatively little known but acclaimed "western paradise." An estimate of gross long-term emigration (i.e., related to at least a one year long stay in a foreign country) in 1980–1989 suggests a number between 1.1 and 1.3 million persons, of whom only around 20 percent returned to Poland by the end of 1989. One might mention that in the 1980s, Poland ranked as the top net emigration country in Europe, in both relative and absolute terms. (p. 6)

The psychological characteristic of these migrants can best be illustrated by the fact that the majority of them were ready to burn all bridges behind them and begin a new life. Only 15% of long-term migrants entered the host country legally; the rest came as visitors who overstayed their tourist visas. According to administrative regulations during that time, every person who failed to return within the time stated on the exit visa was subject to punishment. This meant that the authorities could confiscate a person's passport for many years or even permanently. In addition, most family members of illegal residents were deprived of their passports for a number of years. Consequently, people who emigrated at that time had to consider seriously the likelihood that they would never again see their homeland and that they could not predict if or when their families would be able to visit them. The visit abroad and the decision to prolong a stay was psychologically speaking a one-way trip because no return ticket was available; it meant a total uprooting from both country and the family network.

Another group of Poles who decided to embark on this journey consisted of people living in the psychological state of "inner exile" or "psychological emigration." This state involved rejection, as much as possible, of participation in public life. Such emigrants restricted their real social involvements to a private world consisting of friends and family. Their involvement in public life was restricted to work or to school and was accompanied by a clear awareness of the existence of two different value systems guiding the private and official spheres of life.

The right to keep one's passport at home and consequently the right to leave Poland at any time was proclaimed and implemented in 1988 by the then Communist government. For Poles, the chance to go abroad became an everyday reality, and Poland very quickly became both a sending and a receiving country. According to the *Rocznik Statystyczny* [Statistical yearbook] (Polish Statistical Office, 1996), the second trend quickly predominated over the first trend. Between 1988 and 1995, the number of foreign citizens crossing the border into Poland increased from 6 million to 82 million and the number of exits by Poles from 10 million to 36 million. The dramatic increase in the number of arrivals illustrates a new trend—short visits undertaken by petty traders and small peddlers who were entering Poland for only a few hours and traveling to the nearest marketplace. Along the German border, the majority of short-term entries into Poland took place during the weekends. German shoppers usually visited shops and markets within a 20-kilometer strip from the border. A dramatic increase of legitimate border crossings on the western boundary has made journeys into Poland very easy. The southern borders (with the Czech Republic and the Slovak Republic) and the eastern borders (with Lithuania, Russia, Belorussia, and Ukraine) have experienced less of an increase in terms of absolute numbers of border crossings, but they too experienced a highly dynamic movement of arrivals from those countries. The flow across the southern border has become rather similar to that of the German border in terms of a major weekend influx of people. The eastern border has become not only a permeable boundary through which organized groups of shoppers as well as individual traders travel daily to the adjacent cities, but visitors are now traveling to Warsaw, the capital of Poland, which has become the biggest marketplace in Central and Eastern Europe.

Poland's eastern border is also crossed by workers coming from post-Soviet (CIS) countries who are searching for short-term jobs such as bricklaying and carpentry, though the majority are unskilled workers. In addition, Poland has become a market for highly skilled and legally employable workers in international companies. CIS immigrant workers who assume jobs in Poland receive higher salaries and better prospects for professional promotion than in their home countries. About 10,000 such specialists were given official work permits in Poland in 1997. Another 10,000 work permits have been issued to unskilled or semiskilled workers employed for seasonal work in the building industry and in farming.

The sharp increase in the number of Poles traveling outside the country consists chiefly of people engaged in trade, but others are involved in business or tourism. An important factor facilitating travel undertaken by Poles has been the so-called Schengen agreement, which led to the mutual abolition of visa requirements between Poland and almost all the countries of Western Europe. Free travel to these countries has resulted in the amelioration of some of the negative effects of massive layoffs in Polish heavy industry as well as helping people from overpopulated farms find new employment in Western European countries. Field research conducted in Austria among Polish guest workers has found that in terms of legal employment, Poles were the third largest national group employed in Austria (after people from the former Yugoslavia and Turkey). A majority of Polish workers were residing in Austria illegally, but even with the obvious economic disadvantage resulting from their illegal status, they were still able to earn as much as six times more in Austria than for the same work in Poland (Mydel & Fassmann, 1997). The same situation pertains to Polish immigrants to Germany, another traditional destination of Polish clandestine workers.

A NEW CATEGORY OF IMMIGRANTS

The incoming flow of people also includes asylum seekers. They are led by the perception of Poland as a country that offers personal safety and a better standard of living than their own country. According to the available statistics, there exists a steady increase of people applying for refugee status. In the past, the Polish authorities granted asylum to groups of foreigners according to the political principles of communist brotherhood. Between 1948 and 1956, almost 15,000 political refugees from Greece and Macedonia settled in Poland. The majority of them had returned home by the late 1970s. Also in the 1970s, nearly 1,000 Chilean political refugees settled in Poland. All these groups were granted asylum, although Poland did not sign the Geneva Convention on Refugee Status until 1991. The first group of applicants for refugee status appeared in Poland in 1990 after the Swedish authorities had deported a group of 600 people from Asia and Africa. Almost half of the group—385 people—were granted refugee status. In 1991, the Polish Ministry of the Interior received approximately 2,500 applications. War in the former Yugoslavia brought 900 children and adults from Bosnia to Poland in the autumn of 1992, all of whom received refugee status. The number of applicants continues to grow steadily, and in 1997, 3,200 applications were received. Each year, only 10–12% of all applicants are granted refugee status. In 1997, the largest number of applications was received from Sri Lanka (879), Afghanistan (634), Armenia (514), and Pakistan (366). Approximately 300 applications have been received from other republics formerly belonging to the Soviet Union (Russia, Belorussia, Azerbaijan, Georgia, Moldova, Lithuania, Latvia, Tadzhikistan, and Uzbekistan).

There is justifiable expectation that Poland may become a primary target for an increased flow of refugees in the very near future, due to increasing restrictions for accepting refugees by Western countries. At this point the majority of migrants who apply for refugee status are passing through Poland as transitory migrants only, hoping to acquire refugee status in the West. A confusing situation is caused by the fact that the conceptual category of "refugee" remains relatively obscure and very inclusive for a majority of Poles. All kinds of economic migrants, illegal workers, small traders, and Gypsies who beg on the streets are called "refugees" in popular discourse. Lacking is a consistent definition of what constitutes a refugee (Nowicka & Nawrocki, 1996). In part, because of this inconsistency, Poles generally perceive refugees unfavorably. A comparison of survey research results (Central Office for Opinion Research, 1992, 1997) from 1992 (first refugees coming to Poland) and 1997 showed a steady increase in the proportion of people who believed that refugees should be returned to their countries of origin (12% in 1992, and 31% in 1997). At the same time, there was a sharp decrease in the number of people agreeing to permanent settlement of refugees in Poland (55% in 1992, and 29% in 1997). The better educated and economically more stable Poles generally expressed more positive attitudes toward refugees. A general concern among Poles was the bringing to Poland of new customs (e.g., new religious traditions, new patterns of family life) that might collide with Polish tradition. Respondents who were more accepting of external differences between Poles and immigrants nevertheless proposed that the latter should remain as a separate closed group and should not try to integrate. In general, the level of acceptance of foreigners within the Polish community is strictly governed by the degree to which they are able to adapt themselves to Polish habits and Poles' expectations of them.

The image of refugees is to a great extent created by newspapers and magazines. A very detailed analysis conducted in 1996 (Mrozowski, 1997) showed that approximately 150–200 Polish articles pertaining to various immigrant groups were published monthly in magazines and newspapers. The majority of the articles (almost 75% of the analyzed sample) appeared in local newspapers, 20% in national newspapers, and another 20% in various weekly and monthly publications. Most articles consisted of brief narratives on local events involving migrants, and there was relatively little analysis or more general commentary.

The image of immigrants in the media was frequently threatening. In 35% of all publications, immigrants were perceived as a threat to the Polish state. The articles discussed immigrants who cross the Polish borders illegally or prolong their stay illegally. Therefore, it was suggested that they expose the inadequacy of the safety measures undertaken by Poland to protect its borders. Less numerous publications (28%) portrayed immigrants as violators of Polish law. Immigrants are accused of stealing cars, organizing prostitution, importing drugs, and also killing easily for very little money. More than 30% of all publications contained articles relating to the various economic activities of immigrants. Immigrants were portrayed as wholesalers as well as small shop owners, but mainly as illegal workers employed in the building industry who willingly work for a fraction of the salaries demanded by Polish workers.

Fewer than 14% of all publications pertained to the everyday life of immigrants who were generally presented as people living on the margins of Polish society. Highly skilled immigrants who work in Poland and are business owners were described as living a life that is distant from that of the average Polish citizen; they were said to be secluded in their own luxurious offices, residential communities, and golf clubs. Less privileged immigrants were presented as unassimilated refugees who are incapable of taking care of themselves, being held in refugee reception centers in Poland or in the new country. Sometimes they (mainly Vietnamese or Chinese immigrants) were also presented as living in close-knit communities totally inaccessible to Poles.

Generally, immigrants coming to Poland from the east and south are presented as a very large, diverse, and quite anonymous population. Press publications are more concerned about the ways they chose to enter Poland and about their numbers than about them as specific individuals. Brief remarks about the reasons that compelled them to leave their countries and all the trials and difficulties they overcame before entering Poland largely replaced any more insightful analysis of individual cases. This leaves ample space for popular thinking about immigrants on the basis of widely held ethnic stereotypes.

A STUDY OF POLISH-ORIGIN IMMIGRANTS
TO POLAND FROM KAZAKHSTAN

Poles from Kazakhstan are a group of immigrants who, although not very numerous at this point in time, might grow in number in the near future and have a pronounced influence on the cultural diversity of Polish society.

The contemporary immigration to Poland of Poles from Kazakhstan is the result of several factors, two of which predominate. Far-reaching changes in Soviet policy took place in 1985, when perestroika and glasnost were announced and in 1989, Poland regained its independence. One immediate effect of perestroika was the relative liberalization of borders and the waiving of restrictions on emigration—a term not officially recognized by the Soviet regime, given the direct implications it bore for issues of defection.

After 1989, the situation of Polish exiles in Kazakhstan was almost immediately perceived as one of the most neglected issues by Polish politics and requiring immediate attention. To allow the exiles to remigrate was treated as almost a symbolic obligation by the new Parliament and government. Nevertheless, the consequences of such an immigration were also perceived as being likely to lead to a marked shift from a distinctly homogenous to a distinctly heterogeneous society—and such a shift was not necessarily welcomed by all members of the Polish Parliament. The new conception had changed from Poland as a country sending emigrants worldwide to one of Poland receiving immigrants from around the world.

Until 1996, the situation of arrivals from Kazakhstan was chaotic. Most families and individuals coming on tourist vouchers or by individual invitation received only a residence permit, and only in very rare cases and under very special circumstances were they granted Polish citizenship. The first wave of arrivals brought about 1,500 people. In 1996, new legal regulations became effective. Repatriation to Poland was now allowed if a specific commune (*gmina*) issued an invitation and guaranteed accommodation, employment, and some financial support for the initial period. Approximately 2,000 people arrived at that time. On January 1, 1998, a new act on aliens became effective. Poles from abroad may now be invited to return to Poland by any company or association, and they need not wait for an official invitation by a commune. A heated parliamentary discussion about the proposal to limit repatriation because of economic conditions in Poland led to the dismissal of this argument as being invalid. The general tenor of the debate was colored by the fact that in 1957, Poland had successfully accepted 270,000 repatriates from the Soviet Union. Acknowledging this, it was argued that even accepting a large number of Poles from Kazakhstan who might wish to resettle (up to 50,000 people, according to estimates given by the Polish embassy in Kazakhstan) would not be an impossible task.

According to the new law, after receiving a repatriation visa in the Polish consulate in Kazakhstan, these persons automatically acquire Polish citizenship upon crossing the Polish border. The criterion for issuing such a visa (an invitation from any type of institution or individual) is proof by the applicant of his or her Polish origin, which needs to be documented on the basis of one's nationality in one's passport, or by family and personal documents such as birth certificates, documents of exile from former Polish regions of Ukraine or Byelorussia, or baptism certificates. Before issuing the visa the Polish Ministry of the Interior might acquire information from the *voivodship* [district authority] on whose territory the person is planning to live, and determine the possibility that the organization or person inviting him or her to Poland is able to provide applicants with housing, employment, and financial support. The Ministry of the Interior also needs to ensure that the prospective immigrant does not constitute a danger to national security. Under this rubric the following aspects of the person's life history are checked: inclusion in the KGB or NKWD (Narodnyj Komissariat wnutriennich dieł) membership and criminal records (e.g., ex-membership in the Ukrainian Mafia or committing offenses during past visits to Poland). In 1997, 1,400 persons had initiated the process of acquiring a repatriation visa to Poland. The new, less restrictive regulations promise to increase this number in the future.

During the 1996–1998 period, I conducted research with a group of 220 immigrant Poles from Kazakhstan. The group comprised entire families as well as individual university students and young people who were high school graduates and who had participated in a preparatory course before entering university. Interviews have also been conducted with 30 administrative officers in various regions of the country who were, or are, responsible for making legal and sometimes practical arrangements for the immigrants.

Several methods of obtaining research data were used. The most important one was a semistructured interview conducted with all participants. The interviews were collected at the current homes of Poles from Kazakhstan, at student dormitories, and in administrative offices. The social image of Poles from Kazakhstan was investigated by collecting press information from newspapers and magazines. In several cases, participant observation was possible. The observations were particularly interesting in the case of interactions between the Poles from Kazakhstan and administrative officers, and also with their new neighbors.

Initially the students participating in the research planned to develop separate theoretical approaches pertaining to the refugees discussed earlier and to Polish emigrants from Kazakhstan. Refugees were considered involuntary and Poles from Kazakhstan voluntary migrants. In the course of the research it became much less certain whether such a clear-cut differentiation was realistic. Actually, these groups turned out to be quite similar to each other because they had shared many experiences prior to and during the process of migration. Accordingly, we applied Berry, Kim, Minde, and Mok's (1987) well-known model to analyze the particular stages by which a person becomes a refugee. At least some stages of this model appeared suitable for an analysis of the experience people undergo when passing through the repatriation process. The following stages constitute the model: (a) preemigration period, (b) flight, (c) arrival to the country of the first asylum, (d) settlement in the new country, and (e) return to the home country.

This model stresses that becoming a refugee implies moving between two potentially very different cultures. It also points to the fact that this difference demands ongoing processes of cultural adaptation.

The first stage of the model pertains to the reality prevailing in the original home country. At some point, the overall situation in this country will contain factors that create stress and fear among those persons who eventually decide to leave. The situations, which oftentimes stimulate discomfort, include various kinds of social unrest, ethnic cleansing, economic crises, or war.

In the case of people arriving from Kazakhstan, several factors combined to act together. After becoming an independent country, there began in Kazakhstan a battle for the regaining of its national identity. The task was immense because people of Kazakh ethnicity accounted for less than 30% of the entire population, which otherwise consisted of more than 100 different nationalities. In contrast, "Whites"—that is, Russians, Ukrainians, Poles, and Germans had been the most privileged and best-educated group of people. Hardly any of them spoke the Kazakh language. In 1992, as a formal step to elevate the importance of Kazakh ethnicity, Kazakh became the official language of the Armed Forces and of the administrative, educational, agricultural institutions and industrial companies. The result was that almost all non-Kazakh people in high-level positions lost their posts. For example, former medical doctors were now only allowed to serve in the role of supporting staff such as being nurses or cleaning personnel in the hospitals. A further difficulty arose because even many educated Kazakh people do not speak the Kazakh language, which contains little professional terminology and is spoken as a form of dialect primarily by poor and uneducated farmers and shepherds. Until 1992, among the Kazakh, fluency in Russian was considered a status symbol and a source of individual pride. Thus, the elevation of the Kazakh language to the status of lingua franca created immediate difficulties such as finding individuals who could teach it and who could publish teaching materials. Furthermore, only a few specialists from the Institute of Kazakh Philology taught the language courses that were created in 1992. Although in all offices and factories courses in the Kazakh language were organized for senior staff members, these courses soon lost their importance because it became obvious that language was at best only of secondary importance for appointment to senior posts, which typically were given to citizens of Kazakh origins.

Additional language courses were organized in Islamic schools connected to mosques. In this context, it is of interest to note that the Kazakh language belongs to the Turkish group of languages (which also includes Tartar, Kyrgyz,

Turkmenian, Azer, Tajik, and of course Turkish) and does not bear any similarity to the Russian language. During the Russian regime the Kazakh language was written with Cyrillic characters. It is still undecided if the country will adopt Latin characters (as Turkey has) or Arabic characters (as Saudi Arabia tries to encourage).

Parallel to the changing status of the Kazakh language, another cultural change took place pertaining to the status of Kazakh music and art. For a short time the only music allowed in public concert halls was Kazakh national folk music, and the only accepted style in art was Kazakh folk art. All other forms of music and art were eradicated and its performers became unemployed. Religion was the third area in which the crucial importance of the Kazakh national tradition was emphasized. Although a majority of Kazakhs during the Soviet regime were officially atheists, Islam became the national religion after Kazakhstan regained independence. Representatives of all other religions, although not completely deprived of their rights, were clearly treated as people of lesser value.

An additional factor contributing to the strengthening of the Kazakh aspects of national identity was the creation of a more favorable demographic structure by encouraging the repatriation of people of Kazakh origin from Mongolia. They brought with them an even more traditional form of national identity based to a considerable degree on a very fundamentalist vision of Islam. However, after a short time the authorities perceived this version of Islam as posing a threat rather than supporting the process of building the new Kazakh state.

The process of introducing the supreme value of Kazakh national identity was coupled with the process of eliminating numerous elements of "alien" culture. As mentioned earlier, people who did not speak Kazakh began to face the reality of losing their jobs or at least of being demoted to the lower ranks in their professions. In some places the reaction toward "alien elements" was more militant. Physical attacks by "unknown elements" against "Whites" (especially after dark) resulted in restricting the freedom of the latter to move and filled them with the fear that even at home one might be attacked, robbed, or killed. The main response of most non-Kazakhs was the attempt to emigrate from Kazakhstan back to their "homelands." This led to four major streams of emigration from Kazakhstan involving, respectively, Poles, Germans, Greeks, and Russians.

A person's decision to leave Kazakhstan was influenced by a number of factors: the rapid emigration of many "White" neighbors (mainly Germans); the economic crisis resulting in unpaid salaries to employees for several months; the likelihood of young men being drafted into the army (who then, with no proper training, might be sent to fight in one of the local wars); and a fear that one's non-Kazakh female kin might be kidnapped by a Kazakh man and eventually forced into marriage. Our respondents reported all these concerns as creating strong pressures and stresses and as influencing their decision to leave Kazakhstan. For people who came to Poland, this decision was often strengthened by Polish officials as well as representatives of various Polish nongovernmental organizations (NGOs) who visited Polish centers in Kazakhstan and suggested that Poland would receive Poles from Kazakhstan with open arms as "returned brothers" or "long lost children."

Again, both push and pull factors were influencing people to leave the country, including fears stimulated by the political changes and economic crises in Kazakhstan and the welcoming invitation to reside in Poland. However, at the same time the decision to leave was not a very easy one to make. Quite often the first question to be answered by the future emigrant was which country (countries) ought to be considered as a possible settlement place for the family. Because Polish, German, Russian, and Ukrainian groups were living quite close to each other and kept many contacts, numerous interethnic marriages existed. In the case of many families, a choice existed about which country should be considered for possible emigration. Among those people who had finally taken up residence in Poland, quite a number had previously investigated other options by traveling to Ukraine, Russia, and Germany. This process of examining the options for permanent residence outside Kazakhstan is functionally similar to the process of searching for the country of first asylum in Berry et al.'s (1987) model. Only after determining that these countries did not offer them a real chance to start a new life did people decide to settle in Poland.

The decision to leave Kazakhstan was frequently accompanied by a high level of personal stress and even by feelings of guilt. In many instances, elderly parents were left behind, families had to part, and many important personal belongings were sold or abandoned. The selling price for houses and apartments was determined by the state and was typically very low compared with their market value. Sometimes even such a price did not attract buyers and then the home or apartment was simply abandoned. Officials needed to be bribed in order for them to issue the necessary documents to permit official departure. In some cases emigrants also sold all their belongings for a very low price, trying to accumulate as much cash as possible to begin their new life abroad. In contrast, other emigrants purposely did not attempt to sell their house because they preferred to keep their preparations for leaving secret, to protect themselves against robberies. People pretended that they were just going for a "visit" to the nearby city and then left the country secretly. This kind of preparation was especially true of the early arrivals between 1992 and 1995. Later on those people experienced difficulties because they lacked a valid passport, which prevented them from receiving an extension of their residence permit in Poland. As it turned out during our interviews, separation from the family was for many individuals among the most difficult situations to which they had to adapt during their residence in Poland. Quite a common reaction originating from that was a sense of mission and felt obligation to help as many members of their families as possible to get out of Kazakhstan.

Psychologically speaking, the many technical difficulties experienced by the emigrants during their departure from the country tended to have an influence on their later psychological competence in their efforts to function in the new environment. The distress diminished their coping resources needed to adapt to the new culture.

The third stage of Berry et al.'s (1987) model pertains to the actual departure from the country. For the reasons just described (secrecy, fear of attack), the journey to Poland is sometimes reminiscent of the kind of flight specified in the model. On the borders—especially on the Byelorussian border—customs officers were charging emigrants in transit from Kazakhstan with high and unlawful customs fees before they would allow them to cross the Polish border. High taxes were levied on the personal belongings people were carrying with them.

The fourth stage of Berry et al.'s (1987) model, which needs to be considered, refers to the immigrants' arrival in Poland and the beginning of a new life. Two major versions of this stage could be identified. Some of the immigrants were coming on the invitation of a specific commune, city council, or county board. As it turned out during interviews, people responsible for selecting prospective immigrants were often less than adequately informed as to the type of people who might succeed in the new environment. No description of helpful criteria was available. The groups who had invited the immigrants were frequently quite idealistic, expressing the view that all Poles in exile should return to Poland. The people responsible for the selection were using the Polish names of the candidates and their declared professions as the basis for their selection. With a few exceptions, they lacked a developed rationale explaining how a particular family might succeed in the new environment.

Administrative officers or NGOs were also contacting Polish organizations in Kazakhstan and taking the names of prospective candidates from their lists. Unfortunately, these lists were often created in a very nonobjective manner, and many of these "Polish associations" were created only to facilitate departure to Poland. People of Polish origin had been living in Kazakhstan in dispersed communities at great distances from each other, and many of them had never had a chance to put their names on any list of prospective immigrants invited by communes. During our interviews, it was also discovered that some Poles traveling from Poland to Kazakhstan were selling invitations to enter Poland at a very high price.

In the case of families coming to Poland on the invitation of a specific commune, at least basic preparations had been made for them. Usually preparations for accommodation had not been finalized, and depending on the commune an apartment or house was furnished more or less completely. An initial job offer was also prepared and money for financial support allocated. However, even then the possibility of conflicting expectations between guests and hosts was great. Communes often selected prospective "guests" on the basis of declared professional competencies and the commune's needs. Because many ethnic Poles in Kazakhstan were employed on collective farms (*kolhoz*), they unanimously declared competence in farming. Polish communes, which had empty farms in their territories, expected people from *kolhoz* to be able to handle farming in Poland. By inviting them, the communes wanted to achieve both the fulfillment of a patriotic obligation toward "exiled brothers" and to prevent these farms from being sold to Germans who might like to settle in Poland. (In spite of the very low number of such cases, the fear of these occurrences remains immense.) Unfortunately, many of the newcomers were only able to do very specific jobs, such as operating one particular type of truck they used to drive in the *kolhoz* or attending one specific operation on the chicken farm. Therefore, they lacked the skills and experience necessary for handling the multifaceted reality of a farm in Poland. Such a mismatch resulted in mutual disillusion and a great deal of disappointment. When the selection of prospective immigrants was more subtle, the new immigrants were able to enter into a requalification process, to begin to learn the language, and to eventually fulfill their own expectations as well as those of the inviting communes.

Among the important conditions for successful adaptation to life in Poland were the presence and the characteristics of the person who guided the newcomers through the first period of their stay in Poland. Such a person has the role of mediator between guest and host population, serves as a "culture broker," and acts literally as a culture and language translator. This role was usually performed by one of two categories of people: city/commune/county officers who were ordered to help newcomers settle in or volunteers from the community who promoted the arrival of the immigrants to Poland. Typically these people lacked specific training for this task. In the case of officers, this function was perceived as both difficult and time-consuming, and they lacked adequate training and any additional financial incentive. In the case of volunteers, no training was available, but a great deal of empathy and sense of mission led individuals to complete the task more successfully. Characteristically, those officers who were disillusioned by the lack of success in their work with newcomers emphasized in the interviews that in the future they would not support any new attempts to invite additional immigrants from Kazakhstan into Poland.

Another typical pattern of arrival to Poland was through an invitation issued by a member of the family who resided in Poland or by some other private individual. These people were usually trying to help newcomers acquire support from the commune and adapt. Many invitations were generated with the help of children who were sent to study in Poland. For the last 5 years, the Polish Ministry of Education has offered 100 yearly grants for students from Kazakhstan of Polish origin who want to study in Poland. Students can choose the discipline and the school where they want to study. A special commission from the Ministry of Education travels each year to Kazakhstan in order to select candidates. Commissioners check students' language skills and competence in the areas covered in the entrance exam for admittance to colleges or universities. Once accepted, students move to Poland for a 1-year course during which they receive language training as well as training in some subjects in which they will require proficiency when they enter the university, such as mathematics, Polish history, and literature. For many families, preparation for the selection exam in Kazakhstan, and later on receiving support for their children while they are studying in Poland, constitutes their strategy for getting to Poland. Consequently, for many students one of the major goals upon their arrival in Poland is to find a way to help their families join them in Poland. Much more difficult is the situation of those people who bought fake invitations at exorbitant prices and on their arrival in Poland were left unaided in trying to acquire support from various social agencies. They depended completely on the friendship of strangers and volunteers for help.

Even in the best scenario, people arriving from Kazakhstan are likely to encounter rather mixed reactions from established residents in the community. The
chief reason for this is created by the fact that they do not fit the prevailing
stereotypical image of what it means to be a Pole. A "Pole from Kazakhstan"
seemingly implies a Pole who due to a political decision by the Soviet regime
was forced to live in Kazakhstan. But other than that it is assumed that the Poles
from Kazakhstan are more or less like ordinary Poles living in Poland. A very
strange gap exists in the national collective memory about the fate of these people. Despite Poles' having been exiled to Kazakhstan in 1936—over a half century ago—the Poles who remained in Poland somehow expected the Kazakhstan
Poles to retain their Polishness—to speak Polish, to be knowledgeable about
Polish history and the contemporary political and social situation, and to be
grateful and happy for the chance offered to them to return to Poland. Furthermore, it is expected that the Kazakh Poles should welcome any type of job as
well as any kind of accommodation. In addition, Kazakh Poles are expected to
hate Russia and all aspects of Russian culture including Russian language, music, and art.

However, within interpersonal encounters it unfolded that almost all newcomers failed to fulfill these expectations. First of all, the majority of them are
third generation descendants of the original Polish immigrants to Kazakhstan.
This means that they very rarely know enough Polish to be able to communicate
adequately. Even if they do, then most likely they will speak with a heavy Russian accent that immediately earns them the derogatory label "Russki." Second,
they speak Russian at home, and they use it as their mother tongue because in
Kazakhstan dozens of different minorities were living together and Russian was
the only language that bound people together. To the dismay of their Polish
neighbors, the Kazakh Poles also listen to Russian songs and usually refer to
Kazakhstan as "our country." Many of them openly express their disillusionment about the conditions they have met in Poland. They did not have adequate
information about what to expect after arrival in Poland, and they found that
Poland did not match their image of the "heaven on earth" they expected to find.
To their dismay, they also found that most Poles are not particularly concerned
about their needs and their future. Instead, they are expected to find their own
way and to use their own initiative to create a new life. Having to make their
own way is particularly demanding because it requires the overcoming of a
"learned helplessness" syndrome, which was cultivated in all communist societies.

On the Polish side, a major source of disappointment with the guests comes
from the fact that in many cases the newcomers are considered to have a "Russian work ethic" (i.e., they do not express appreciation of the opportunity and
are assumed by Poles to be working in the least efficient way, not taking care of
the tools, and trying to cheat on the time spent on work).

In spite of all the mutual disappointments, overcoming the initial social distance usually occurs in a short time. Neighbors are willing to help in many ways.
Especially in the rural areas people are helping the newcomers understand how
to use unfamiliar machines and providing them with support when they

encounter everyday problems. In the schools, teachers take extra time to help children learn the Polish language. In most cases, the children succeed at school and are well liked by their schoolmates.

What predictions can be made about the future of this group in Poland? Specifically, what kind of adaptive strategy will they choose—melt into the Polish culture or remain isolated from Polish culture and society to form a kind of ghetto? To answer this question, Berry (1990) developed a two-dimensional model of acculturation, which has four different options that result from two questions being answered either positively or negatively: (a) Is it desirable to remain in one's heritage culture, and (b) is it desirable to maintain positive contact with other groups in the new society? When both of these questions are asked, a combination of four possible varieties of acculturation strategies may be delineated: (a) The *assimilation* strategy implies that the individual rejects his or her original culture and seeks to become a member of the new culture; (b) *integration* represents an option in which the individual wants to both maintain the original culture and also learn about the new culture; (c) *separation* means that the individual wants to maintain his/her original culture and avoid the new culture; (d) *marginalization* implies that the individual rejects both the original and the new culture.

One may expect that for the population of immigrants from Kazakhstan an assimilation strategy is a particularly suitable one. They came to Poland because they accepted the identity of Poles returning to the homeland. Discarding a Russian identity provides a guarantee of succeeding in the new society, at least socially, and it is also a strategy of gaining acceptance in order for them to benefit from the help provided by Poland. However, assimilation for this particular group also means rejecting myths about Poland, which originally had influenced their decision to move to Poland, thereby coming to terms with the real Poland and the real Polish people. For some it may also imply a complete denial of the past—(e.g., coming to believe that living in Kazakhstan was worthless), and consequently all their experiences and memories need to be questioned and abandoned. Total denial, if even possible, is a very costly process on the individual level and makes a person very vulnerable, stripping him or her of any resources from the past for coping with the present reality.

The second strategy, integration, seems an almost unrealistic goal, which would involve retaining one's emotional attachment to the traditions of Kazakhstan while learning to accept the realities in Poland. This strategy is also socially risky, because the new arrivals can be accused of unlawfully appealing for Polish resources that would restrict the help that could be given to "real Poles." It might also result in a separation between the newcomers and Poles that is instigated by the host population. Finally, marginalization may occur, in which the individual cannot find her/his place in Poland but also does not feel attached and connected to Kazakh society. Young people coming to study in Poland and experiencing identity conflicts stemming from cultural clashes are most susceptible to this process. Separation is likely to occur only in some extreme cases, as, for example, when a group of families forms a kind of ghetto and is unwilling to establish contact with the established residents in the larger community. Fortunately, due to organizational restrictions, the settlement of Poles from Kazakhstan in one particular location is quite unlikely.

Psychological research points to the fact that an integration strategy is most beneficial in terms of the health and well-being of immigrants (Sam & Berry, 1995; Schmitz, this volume). However, this specific coping strategy seems to be very difficult to achieve. The individual risks being ostracized by the local community if too much adherence to the past life is shown. In addition, in many cases so many negative experiences are associated with life in Kazakhstan that individuals do not want to retain previous commitments. In many cases a cultural gap between the past and present realities creates the feeling that there is a need for radical change because no possibility is perceived to exist for building bridges that could connect both periods of life. A painful statement made by one of the interviewees expresses this experience: "I came to church in Poland because I thought I would discover something similar to what I used to feel in Kazakhstan, but even God is alien here." She also complained that even in the church community she feels quite marginalized and not accepted because of her perceived Russian identity.

Individual characteristics existing prior to migration, such as age, gender, and education, and group factors, such as cultural orientation and work ethic, may have a profound influence on the degree of adaptation to the new society. Each of these factors is likely to moderate or affect the acculturation process. For children and young adults this process is likely to be smoother than for relatively older persons. Elementary school–aged children (7–15 years old) in the researched population typically succeeded in entering their social group. They received ample help and support from their classmates and teachers. In many families they quickly began to act as interpreters of the language and social mores for the rest of the family. Slightly older individuals (gymnasium-aged from 16 to 19 years old) encountered more problems with social acceptance but experienced no problem with language acquisition. For students, especially those migrating alone, their time in Poland was a difficult one. They often felt ostracized by their peer group, and if several of them lived together separation was a pretty common outcome of this process. Even within the dormitories, students lived quite a solitary life without much contact with their next-door neighbors. They struggled very hard with identity issues, and the people they met during their preparatory year before entering university did not make the struggle any easier. In many cases, they described this year as "time lost" in terms of their acculturation to Polish life and culture. They were also deprived of any psychological support during this period; colleges and universities did not provide an adviser who could give special attention to this group to help them adapt to the new environment.

Among the adult population, people having higher education, specialized professions (teachers, doctors), and better language skills appeared to achieve a more positive adaptation. They were able to assimilate relatively easily into their profession and were also more skillful in making choices and selecting elements from both cultures, which they found helpful for successful functioning in Poland. A common experience for returnees is a combination of status loss and limited status mobility. One's "entry status" in the host society is almost always lower than one's "departure status" in one's society of origin. In the case of people with technical professions, such as engineers, low professional status was likely to continue only for a limited period until the language skills improved, whereupon the person would regain the higher status he or she had held before migration. In the case of doctors, a more complicated procedure needed to be fulfilled; language skills were only part of the problem. Stricter professional exams needed to be passed before a permit to operate a medical practice was issued. In other professions, skills brought from Kazakhstan were obsolete. A lawyer specializing in Russian law and lacking knowledge of the Polish legal system is unable to continue in the profession unless a full course of further studies is undertaken. Similarly, professionals in the agricultural field found that their skills were totally useless in the new context.

Looking to the future, the procedures for selecting ethnic Poles who want to return to Poland need closer scrutiny, and there should be more preparatory work before issuing invitations to enter Poland. It would be more cost effective to send examiners and language teachers to Kazakhstan who could help to determine the level of language skills of the prospective candidates. In addition, much more factual information must be given to people in Kazakhstan about life conditions and work in Poland. During the preparatory year for prospective students, more emphasis should be placed on cultural education and guidance which are a necessary addition to language skills training if the students are to enter successfully into the peer group at the university. In terms of accommodation arrangements for returnees and in particular communes or cities, it is necessary to designate a person as "cultural mediator" who then can attempt to bridge the gap between the newcomers and the local population. The tasks of this job should not be given to someone who is overburdened with a permanent job with the expectation that he or she will perform extra work without receiving extra pay. The ideal candidate would have the necessary skills and cross-cultural competence. Finally, because the process of return migration from Kazakhstan is going to continue, a good investment at the national level would be to introduce into the curriculum at social-work schools and pedagogical colleges basic information about how immigrants adapt to a new culture and the ways teachers and social workers can assist them in this process.

To sum up this analysis of migratory processes in contemporary Poland, it can be said that there are important factors to be considered in the transition from a very closed society to a more open society. Poland has in many ways become similar to countries in Western Europe. People wishing to emigrate from Poland do not face the alternative "stay or leave permanently." People wishing to immigrate can do so as well, and those willing to remain permanently have to go through a similar legal procedure to that of their Western counterparts. Many people immigrate to Poland because the West is increasingly closing its doors to non–Western European migrants but also because Poland presents an economic and political climate offering better options for starting a new life than the home countries of the immigrants (mainly people from the former Soviet Union and refugees from Asia and Africa). At the same time, growing diversity causes many Poles to experience culture shock (DeMarinis & Grzy-mala-Moszczynska, 1995) and the fear of becoming a minority in their own country. They then are tempted to make immigrants the scapegoats for all social problems prevailing in Poland, such as unemployment, low salaries, and ineffi-cient policing.

INTEGRATION OF IMMIGRANTS INTO POLISH SOCIETY: THEORETICAL AND EMPIRICAL CONSIDERATIONS

The state's policy currently aims at the integration of both refugees and Poles from Kazakhstan into the host society. Although integration of immigrants and refugees in the new society is certainly a desirable goal, it is one that is difficult to reach and is generally achieved only by those who have acculturated most successfully.

The process of acculturation of guests involves changes in the host commu-nity as well. This fact, self-evident as it is, has gone largely unnoticed during several decades of research on guests' adaptation process. One of the first re-searchers who did justice to this aspect of immigrants' acculturation process was Taft (1953) who pointed to the fact that the host culture changes because of the presence of culturally distinctive immigrants. The importance of the input of the changing host culture to the acculturation process resurfaced again in the 1980s. Studies (Baboo & Singh, 1985; Berry, Kim, & Boski, 1988) have begun to ex-plore the importance of structural and cultural acculturation for host communi-ties and refugees, as well as the important differences played by dominant cul-tural characteristics in different host cultures. Similarly, the Canadian scholars Sayegh and Lasry (1993) emphasized the fact that it is difficult "to imagine a host society which would not be transformed after immigrants have been ac-cepted as full participants into the social and institutional networks of that soci-ety" (p. 99).

Meaningful analyses of the mutual changes in both guests' and hosts' popu-lations during the acculturation process require a broader framework—one that takes into account the reality of the state in which double acculturation takes place. An important aspect of this reality is the way it creates the religious iden-tity of both parties. Recently, Bourhis, Moise, Perreault, and Senecal (1997) presented an inclusive model providing this broader context for the study of ac-culturation processes. The list of key elements in this model consists of general guidelines found in the state's immigration policy, followed by the state integra-tion policy, which influences both the dominant host contact with migrant groups and the acculturation processes of immigrants and refugees. These in turn bring about different kinds of outcomes resulting from the relations be-tween newcomers and hosts.

The state immigration policy is based on the recognition of two kinds of boundaries: physical boundaries, resulting from international treaties, and psy-chological boundaries, resulting from shared beliefs about who has the right to membership in a particular group living in a specific territory.

According to Hammar (1985), the state determines when and to whom to open or close its frontiers, how many immigrants of various kinds can be accepted, and when and how to change the rules for admission of newcomers. Admission of newcomers takes place on several grounds. The only one that is usually unchallenged (at least in the short term) is the economic and social self-interest of the state. In the Polish case, admission of Poles from Kazakhstan who were expected to settle on empty farms reflects this criterion. The remaining reasons include humanitarian considerations, historical relations with the countries of emigration, and the state's inefficiency in controlling its own borders. All these noneconomic and nonsocial reasons are sources of concern for the host population and may sometimes stimulate negative attitudes toward the newcomers. Particularly challenging for the host population is being confronted with the fact that the state falls short of controlling immigrants. The media are usually very instrumental in bringing such developments to the awareness of the general public (Nowak, 1998) and often in a quite exaggerated fashion. As mentioned before, the Polish media frequently present refugees and immigrants as individuals crossing into Polish borders and creating various difficulties within Poland (Mrozowski, 1997). Religion also becomes a factor in public disputes for two other reasons. This became clear from research conducted in those local Polish communities, which due to humanitarian reasons, hosted children from Bosnia during the Yugoslavian war (Grzymala-Moszczynska & Nowicka, 1998). Some of the respondents expressed their doubts concerning the fact that Poland chose to help Muslims who are of a religious persuasion considered to be hostile to Roman Catholicism. Others feared the proverbial cruelty of adherents of Islam feeling they might bring harm to their local communities. Similarity or diversity on religious grounds has a differentiating effect on the admission of people from countries with which historical relations have already existed for some time.

A far more problematic factor than religious dissimilarity concerns internal boundaries. According to Breton (1988), internal boundaries are related to the relational problems posed by the role of the immigrant vis-à-vis native members of the host society. Issues of economic, social, and legal equality relate to that problem, as well as the general desirability of the presence of immigrants and refugees in the territory of the host society. Hosts may believe that the newcomers are only temporary, marginal residents in their country. Hence, there is an unwillingness to invest in the integration process that in turn results in a lack of provision in the host country for successful integration of refugees and immigrants. If the religion professed by the host population differs from that of the latter, this may be perceived as a threat to the moral unity of the country. This is an issue for contention in those religiously homogeneous host societies that are dominated by a central religious institution. This is especially true when the social network of the religious culture in the host society is itself in the process of cross-cultural transition, evoking a reaction of culture shock on the societal level (DeMarinis & Grzymala-Moszczynska, 1995).

An important challenge created by guests to the host culture lies in the fact that local participants in the culture have to reexamine their own identity. The result of this reexamination might be to justify the exclusion of newcomers from the host society on the basis of ethnic, religious, or cultural differences. These differences are more likely to be used as a justification in homogenous than in heterogeneous societies. Each society also creates its own set of priorities among these differences that in turn determine what the necessary characteristics are to be presented by those guests willing to be recognized as rightful members of the host society. Policymakers should establish such priorities before entering into broader action aimed at helping refugees and immigrants to acculturate success-fully into the new society. Again, in the Polish case an obvious mistake on the part of policymakers was not to take into account that Poles and Kazakh Poles differ significantly in language skills and general work attitudes from the host population. Paradoxically, even refugees coming from very distant cultures are accepted more easily because they are not expected to become fully assimilated into Polish society.

The state plans not only a general *immigration policy* but also an *integration policy* for refugees and immigrants. The immigration policy can be shaped by four different ideologies, which can be situated on a continuum ranging from the "pluralism ideology" through the "civic ideology" and the "assimilation ideol-ogy" to the "ethnist ideology" (Bourhis et al., 1997). All these ideologies expect that the immigrant will adopt the public values of the state expressed in basic legal documents like the constitution or the civil and the criminal codes. They differ, however, in their attitude toward the private values of immigrants. Only a pluralist ideology sees it as valuable for the host community that the guests re-tain their cultural distinctiveness. Other ideologies either provide no support for preserving ethnocultural features (civic ideology) or, with differing degrees of pressure, insist that the immigrants give up or even actively deny their previous culture, language, and values (assimilation and ethnist ideologies). Ethnist ide-ology, however, does not present a coherent pattern in that respect because it may not put any pressure on the guests to give up their private values since there is no expectation that they will ever be fully accepted into the host society. The ethnist ideology is the one most likely to create boundaries for those immigrants and refugees who differ religiously from the local community. Because the identity issue is deeply woven into a state's integration policy, it is not uncom-mon for integration ideology to be used instrumentally for achieving political goals by different segments of society. What may be created is a situation in which apart from the officially promoted ideology, various political parties ac-tively endorse several others, as, for example, during political campaigns before an election. The issue of the religious identity of the newcomers is then very easily used in political battles launched on behalf of the "best interests of the nation." In Poland, assimilation ideology gets promoted de facto whereas civic ideology is often officially promoted.

Both kinds of ideologies—those officially recognized by the state and those acting semiofficially in the different segments of the society—have an immedi-ate effect on the outcome of the acculturation process of both hosts and guests. Both ideologies need to answer a similar set of questions. For the immigrants the crucial questions pertain to the retention of their own identity and their willing-ness to make contact with the host society. For the host society the questions relate to its willingness to recognize that the guests will adopt the host society's identity while also maintaining their own cultural identity. Analysis based on the interactive acculturation model (Bourhis et al., 1997) shows that both the host society and the immigrants can present concordant or discordant patterns of expectation toward the acculturation process. Bourhis et al. stated that only three out of 25 possible theoretical combinations of the strategies favored in relation to acculturation by hosts and guests have the possibility of providing fully positive relationships between host and guest communities, and only one of those three may actually lead to integration in the full psychological sense. This means that only a very unique combination of factors can lead not just to the acceptance of newcomers into the new society but will also allow them to draw on their cultural heritage while coping with the problems of the new culture. All the other 24 combinations imply various levels of disagreement between the hosts and the guest society as far as the value of the cultures and the identities of the two groups are concerned. Depending on the level of conflict, the remaining combinations can be clustered into "problematic" or "conflictive" in relational outcomes of the encounter between hosts and guests. Poland currently faces a high ratio of conflictive and problematic to nonconflictive results as an outcome of the acculturation process of immigrants.

An interesting psychological question can be asked about this encounter: What does it really mean for the host community to change as a result of a new type of religion being practiced in the society? Bouma (1997) rightly points out that

it involves much more than the assimilation of individuals and families. . . . [It] involves making room for a diversity of orientations, understandings, ways of seeing the world, ways of shaping priorities. . . . [It] involves tolerance, a willingness to try to understand before judging, a willingness to be one among others rather than the determinative way of seeing and doing things. . . . [It] includes settling religious cultures. (pp. 55–56)

As the previous analysis pointed out, it is almost impossible to achieve successful acculturation resulting in the integration of newcomers into the local society without helping both parties to shape their priorities toward the acculturation process. It is impossible to provide a quick fix promising automatic success in this enterprise. However, it should be obvious that a careful assessment of the context of the integration process, in both the host population and in the immigrant and refugee communities, is truly necessary.

REFERENCES

Baboo, B., & Singh, S. (1985). A sociological study of refugees in Rohtak town Guru Nanak. *Journal of Sociology, 6*(2), 107–117.

Berry, J. W. (1990). Psychology of acculturation: Understanding individuals moving between cultures. In R. W. Brislin (Ed.), *Applied cross-cultural psychology* (pp. 232-253). Newbury Park, CA: Sage.

Berry, J. W., Kim, U., & Boski, P. (1988). Psychological acculturation of immigrants. In Y. Y. Kim & W. B. Gudykunst (Eds.), *Cross-cultural adaptation: Current approaches: Vol. 11. International and intercultural communication annual* (pp. 62–89). Newbury Park, CA: Sage.

Berry, J. W., Kim, U., Minde, T., & Mok, D. (1987). Comparative studies in acculturative stress. *International Migration Review, 21*(3), 491–511.

Bouma, D. G. (1997). Religion and the migration process. In G. D. Bouma (Ed.), *Many religions all Australian: Religious settlement, identity and cultural diversity* (pp. 53–68). Kew, Australia: The Christian Research Association.

Bourhis, R. Y., Moise, L. C., Perreault, S., & Senecal, S. (1997). Towards an interactive acculturation model: A social psychological approach. *International Journal of Psychology, 32*(6), 369–386.

Breton, R. (1988). From ethnic to civic nationalism: English Canada and Quebec. *Ethnic and Racial Studies, 11*(85), 85–102.

DeMarinis, V., & Grzymala-Moszczynska, H. (1995). The nature and role of religion and religious experience in psychological cross-cultural adjustment: Ongoing research in the clinical psychology of religion. *Social Compass, 42*(1), 121–135.

Gross, J. T. (1988). Wywózki [Deportations]. *Aneks* (London), *51, 52.*

Grzymala-Moszczynska, H., & Nowicka, E. (1998). *Goscie i gospodarze: Problem adaptacji kulturowej w obozach dla uchodzców oraz otaczajacych je społecznosciach lokalnych.* [Guests and hosts: Problems of cultural adaptation in the refugee centers and local communities]. Cracow, Poland: Zakład Wydawniczy Nomos.

Hammar, T. (1985). *European immigration policy: A comparative study.* Cambridge, England: Cambridge University Press.

Mrozowski, M. (1997). *Obraz imigranta na łamach prasy polskiej.* [The Polish media image of immigrants]. Warsaw, Poland: Instytut Studiów spoeczn ych UW.

Mydel, R., & Fassmann, H. (1997). *Nielegalni robotnicy cudzoziemscy i czarny rynek pracy: Polscy nielegalni pracownicy w wiedniu.* [Foreign illegal workers and the job black market: Polish illegal workers in Vienna]. Cracow, Poland: Instytut Geografii Uniwersytetu Jagiellońskiego.

Nowak, W. (1998). Przejdziem Nyse, przejdziem Odre [We'll pass all rivers on the Polish frontiers]. *Gazeta Wyborcza, 45*(296), 9–16.

Nowicka, E., & Nawrocki, J. (Eds.). (1996). *Inny-Obcy-Wróg* [Different-alien-enemy]. Warsaw, Poland: Oficyna Nakowa.

Okólski, M. (1997). *Recent migration in Poland: Trends and causes.* Warsaw, Poland: Instytut Studiów Społecznych UW.

Piesowicz, K. (1988). Wielkie ruchy migracyjne w latach 1945–1950, czesc 1 [Great migratory movements between 1945–1950, Part 1]. *Studia Demograficzne, 4.*

Polish Statistical Office. (1996). *Rocznik Statystyczny* [Statistical yearbook].

Sam, D. L., & Berry, J. W. (1995). Acculturative stress among young immigrants in Norway. *Scandinavian Journal of Psychology, 35*, 10–24.

Sayegh, L., & Lasry, J. C. (1993). Immigrants' adaptation in Canada: Assimilation, acculturation, and orthogonal cultural identification. *Canadian Psychology, 34*, 98–109.

Schmitz, P. (1992). Acculturation styles and health. In S. Iwasaki, Y. Kashima, & K. Leung (Eds.), *Innovations in cross-cultural psychology* (pp. 84–96). Amsterdam: Swets & Zeitlinger.

Sword, K. (1996). *Deportation and exile: Poles in the Soviet Union, 1939–48.* London: Macmillan.

Taft, R. (1953). A shared frame of reference concept applied to the assimilation of immigrants. *Human Relations, 6*(45), 45–55.

11

Psychosocial Adjustment and Migration in Norway

Deborah A. Stiles and Thomas Hylland Eriksen

LOCATION, CLIMATE, AND
NATURAL RESOURCES OF NORWAY

"Talk of home—snow and spruce woods are home," begins a poem by Norwegian poet Vesaas (1998, p. 13). Norway, the way to the North, extends 1,100 miles from south to north with beautiful landscapes of snow-covered mountains, deep green forests, dramatic fjords, fertile valleys, rich pastures, and seacoasts. Norway is situated at the top of Europe and shares borders with Sweden, Finland, and Russia and faces the Norwegian Sea and the Atlantic Ocean to the west. Half of Norway lies north of the Arctic Circle, and Norway is known as the land of the midnight sun. Norway's climate is temperate on the west coast but colder inland. Norway is a largely glacial country of which large parts are uninhabitable.

Consequently, Norway is a sparsely populated country with a population of about 4.4 million; there are only 13 Norwegians for every square kilometer. Only a small percentage of Norwegians live in the circumpolar north region and about half of Norway's population is concentrated (within 2 hours traveling time) in or around the capital city, Oslo. Still, the quintessential national symbol remains the taciturn mountain farmer in the "gray quiet day" who can "set potatoes, rake leaves, carry brushwood" (Hauge, 1990, p. 43). Photo 11.1 shows snow-covered trees in Oslo.

Norway is rich in natural resources. It is one of the major suppliers of crude oil, natural gas, and hydroelectric power to Europe. A combination of hydropower and extensive forests has created thriving paper and lumber industries. Fishing has always been important; Norway exports fish and fish products, and the annual catch is the fifth largest in the world. Norway is a leading producer of aluminum, magnesium, iron, and chemicals.

POLITICAL AND ECONOMIC ENVIRONMENT IN NORWAY

Politically, Norway is a constitutional monarchy with full parliamentary democracy. Most of the executive power is vested in the prime minister.

Equality is a basic value in Norway, and all Norwegians can depend on their government to provide the basic necessities of life. The modern welfare system is based on these concepts. Families with children receive financial support, free education in state schools and universities, and free treatment in public hospitals. The system attempts to give people equal access to places to live and work. Norway's legislation is designed to support a society based on equal rights. There are equal rights for individual citizens and equal rights for men and women.

In the 19th century, Norway was a poor and underdeveloped country, but today Norway is one of the most prosperous countries in the world due to its enormous energy resources and highly skilled labor force.

Photo 11.1
Snow-Covered Trees, Oslo, Norway

Photo courtesy of the author

CULTURAL AND EDUCATIONAL ENVIRONMENT IN NORWAY

About 88% of the population are members of the Evangelical Lutheran Church, the state church of the country. Norwegian is the official language; two forms (Bokmal and Nynorsk) are spoken. The Sami language, which is unrelated to Norwegian, is the official language in parts of northernmost Norway and is spoken by many Sami people.

Three aims of Norwegian schools are to promote freedom of thought, to prepare students to be responsible democratic citizens, and to teach tolerance. In spite of these goals, the majority of Norwegians are not knowledgeable about the culture and lifestyles of immigrants groups such as the Vietnamese, the Chileans, the Turks, and the Moroccans. "Information about the background and situation of the immigrants ought to become a more extensive part of the curriculum in Norwegian schools" (Jenssen & Engesbak, 1994, p. 48).

Leisure plays an essential role in Norwegian life and the recreational use of nature is especially popular. *Ski* is a Norwegian word and Norway is a leading nation in winter sports.

HISTORY OF MIGRATION IN NORWAY

Most Norwegians live near the coast, and this has been the case since the first settlers arrived some 10,000 years ago. Many years ago the Vikings crossed the sea on their expedition to foreign shores. Over the years, close to a million Norwegians have immigrated to the United States.

Most of the population of Norway is homogenous in appearance; Norwegians are stereotypically tall in stature, fair-skinned, and fair-haired. There are, of course, many exceptions to the stereotype. The more than 20,000 Samis within Norway, an indigenous, traditionally nomadic people who have lived in Samiland for at least 2,000 years, represent a minority group. The Sami Act of 1987 provided the legislative base for the Sami Parliament.

Beginning in the 1960s, people from Pakistan, northern Africa, southern Europe, and Turkey migrated to Norway for economic reasons. The largest group of labor immigrants was of Pakistani origin. In 1975, the Norwegian government passed an immigration law called *Innvandringstopp*, which limited new immigrants to family members of immigrants already in Norway, refugees, asylum seekers, immigrants from other Scandinavian countries, and specialists needed for important Norwegian industries in the oil business, medicine, research, and so on. From 1975 to 1990, 6,633 Southeast Asian refugees moved to Norway; Vietnamese people are the largest refugee group in Norway. Other refugees have included those from war-torn or politically repressive countries such as Somalia, Iran, Sri Lanka, and Bosnia-Herzegovina. In January of 2000, the immigrant population totaled 282,487 or more than 6% of the population, and immigrants accounted for half of Norway's population growth. In the late 1990s the largest group of first-generation immigrants, 23,240, has been from Sweden (Statistics Norway, 2001). When both first- and second-generation immigrants are accounted for, the second largest group is from Pakistan

(22,831), Denmark is third (18,863), Yugoslavia is forth (15,466), followed by Vietnam (15,390) (Statistics Norway, 2001). Second-generation immigrants include 3,236 from Turkey, 2,698 from Sri Lanka, 1,957 from India, 2,064 from Yugoslavia, 1,710 from Morocco, 1,874 from Somalia, and 1,104 from Chile. Migration within Norway has tended to be from the rural to the urban areas.

MIGRATING GROUPS IN NORWAY

Migration Within Norway

Since 1945 the major migration paths within Norway have been from the north and the west to the east and the greater Oslo area; the pattern of movement has been from the less populated rural areas to the more populated urban areas. A study of Norwegian men found that long-distance migration within Norway provided greater benefits in income and occupational prestige than short-distance migration; the greatest gains came from long-distance, urban to urban migration (Ringdal, 1993). In northern Norway, there are fewer young women than men (Dahlstrom, 1996; Hamilton & Otterstad, 1998). The rural areas of northern Norway provide the greatest economic opportunities for fishing, farming, forestry, manufacturing, and construction work. The modern young women in rural Norway tend to have higher educational and vocational aspirations than their male peers and are not likely to aspire to becoming fishermen's or farmers' wives. There is a shortage of women in the 20- to 39-year-old age groups in northern Norway because women in this age group have migrated to urban areas seeking educational training and jobs in the public and service sectors.

Swedish Immigrants

Swedish immigrants now are the largest group migrating to Norway, and in 1997 net migration from Sweden was 4,100. Swedish migration to Norway is voluntary. Such immigrants are unlikely to experience discrimination in the labor and housing markets. There is a joint labor market agreement in the Nordic countries, enabling Swedes to work in Norway without applying for a work permit. Swedes are not even included in the colloquial term *innvandrer* (immigrant). In general, Swedish immigrants to Norway have not experienced problems in psychosocial adjustment. Consequently, there are no special therapies or interventions for Swedish immigrants.

Norwegians are also migrating to Sweden. Sweden and Norway are culturally and linguistically similar Scandinavian countries. Foreign stereotypes of Scandinavians are that they are affluent, educated, progressive, tolerant, and egalitarian (Eriksen, 1997b; Knudsen, 1997). The stereotypical Swedish identity of the 20th century has been that of a modern, sophisticated, and industrial country, and the Norwegian national identity has drawn more on a rural tradition. More recently, Norway has enjoyed greater economic success due to rich natural resources than its more industrialized Swedish neighbor.

Sweden and Norway have had different attitudes toward immigrants to their respective countries. Compared with Swedes, Norwegians are more chauvinistic, believe more in the legitimacy of their government, and are more xenophobic (Knudsen, 1997). In both Sweden and Norway, however, the people who are the least fearful of foreigners are likely to be women, young people, and the well educated.

Studies in the 1960s found that when Swedes and Norwegians were compared, Swedes were more likely to migrate for work-related reasons and Norwegians for educational reasons (Ringdal, 1993).

Samis

The largest of the nonimmigrant minority groups in Norway is the Sami people. Historically, the Sami were seminomadic reindeer herders, hunters, and fisherman in the circumpolar north. The Samis have inhabited northernmost Norway, Sweden, Finland, and the Kola Peninsula of Russia for at least 2,000 years, and today, between 60,000 to 70,000 Samis live in the region. Today, the majority of the Sami who reside in Norway are not migrating with their reindeer herds; only 2,500 to 3,000 Samis draw their income from reindeer herding (Aikio, 1983; Hovland, 1995). Currently, snowmobiles and helicopters are available to assist the reindeer herders. Reindeer herding is most important because of its symbolism; within Samiland, reindeer herding represents cultural hegemony whereas outside Samiland it represents the "real" Sami (A. Hovland, personal communication, December 4, 1998).

"From the nineteenth century, Norway started an overt policy to eradicate Sami language and culture" (Kvernmo & Heyerdahl, 1996, p. 455). The Sami poet Guttorm (1982, p. 156) wrote "Saame speech, golden speech—O, why did you joyless sleep? Die not, mother tongue of ours." For many years the Sami people were discriminated against and their language was forbidden in schools. Until the 1960s the official policy of the Norwegian government was one of assimilation. An intense ethnopolitical struggle led up to Sami hunger strikes in 1979 and 1980 outside the Norwegian Parliament building. In 1987, the Norwegian government proclaimed the Sami Act, which enabled a cultural revival of the Sami people and provided a legislative base for the Sami Parliament. Today, approximately 7,500 Sami people are registered to vote in the Sami Parliament. In Norway, there are more than 20,000 people who could be called Samis, but many of them choose instead to think of themselves as Norwegian.

Samis living on the coast of Norway and those inhabiting the interior highlands lead different lives from each other. Because they were a minority group and there was a stigma attached to the Sami identity, Samis residing in the coastal areas tended to reject their indigenous heritage and teach only Norwegian to their children. In the 1990s, only 10% of the adults on the coast spoke Sami. "Through processes of migration, intermarriage, linguistic change, changing economy and official policy, to mention but a few aspects, a large number of individuals in these societies have had their ethnic identity redefined. They are no longer considered and do not consider themselves Sami" (Hovland, 1995, p. 1). Most recently, there has been a Sami cultural revival among the youth; in the coastal region some young people in their late teens and early 20s have joined together to form organizations to promote the Sami identity. "The current movement should be considered as but one of several periodic and localized intensifications of ethnic identity" (A. Hovald, personal communication, December 4, 1998).

In the interior highlands, 80–90% of the population are Samis and speak the Sami language. "In the highland the traditional life of the semi-nomadic reindeer herders in people's minds represents the 'real Sami culture'" (Kvernmo & Heyerdahl, 1996, p. 460). With the majority of people speaking Sami and the establishment of Sami educational and research institutions in this area, the ethnic revitalization process has been stronger among the adults.

Kvernmo and Heyerdahl (1996, 1998) have studied ethnic identity and behavioral problems among the adolescents living in both these areas. Due to the stigma associated with being a Sami, many young people do not describe themselves as Sami. For this reason, the researchers asked the participants about the languages spoken by their parents and grandparents in order to classify their ethnic identities. They found that among the adolescents who had two Sami parents (monoethnic), ethnic self-identification was strongly Sami in the highlands and mostly bicultural and Norwegian at the coast. Monoethnic Sami adolescents living along the coast reported more behavioral problems than monoethnic Norwegian adolescents and Sami adolescents living in the highlands. Among those adolescents living in the coastal region, multiethnic Sami adolescents reported fewer problems than monoethnic Samis, but more than monoethnic Norwegians. In all groups, girls reported more emotional problems than boys. In their conclusion, Kvernmo and Heyerdahl (1998, p. 750) called for "public policy supporting integration, avoiding cultural shedding, preventing discrimination and prejudice, and thereby reducing acculturative stress."

Adjustment to Norway by Third World Immigrants and Refugees

Berry and Sam (1997) have identified five specific factors that affect the process of psychological and sociocultural adjustment of immigrants. These factors include the societies of settlement, the immigrants' societies of origin, group acculturation, moderating factors prior to acculturation, and moderating factors during acculturation.

In the society of settlement, the majority of Norwegians are tolerant, hospitable, and nonracist. "The majority of Norwegians accept immigrants' right to equal privileges with Norwegians" (Jenssen & Engesbak, 1994, p. 47). In 1997, a government report on attitudes toward immigration and immigration policy found that 67% believed that Norway should continue to admit refugee and asylum seekers, and 86% thought that immigrants should have the same work opportunities as Norwegians. The Norwegians who are most favorably disposed toward immigration and immigrants are persons with postsecondary education, and those who are young, middle aged, and females (Statistics Norway, 1996, 1998a, 1998b).

Currently the largest group migrating to Norway is from Sweden, a predominantly Lutheran, economically successful, egalitarian democracy. Third World immigrants to Norway come from societies with very different languages, religions, values, political systems, and economic conditions. The majority of immigrants to Norway from Pakistan, Iran, Bosnia, Morocco, Turkey, Somalia, and Eritrea are Muslims, and the majority of immigrants from Vietnam, Sri Lanka, and India are Buddhists and Hindus. These societies of origin tend to endorse traditional gender-role expectations, authoritarian parenting, and hierarchical work relationships. Norwegians tend to be religiously tolerant and committed to gender-role equality. Conflicts arise at schools about curricular issues such as sex education and religious education and behavioral issues such as school attendance, nonauthoritarian teachings, and appropriate school dress.

For instance, conflicts can develop in gymnastics classes. Norwegian schools want girls to have equal opportunities for participation in sports. Muslim parents may want their daughters to be modestly clothed and fully covered. During the acculturation process, Muslim girls adopt a variety of strategies to maintain their ethnic and religious identity and to adopt the expectations of Norwegian schools. Muslim girls may cover their hair and wear long clothes during gym. One creative solution is for a girl to wear a gym suit on top of a sari, thus pleasing the family and the school (Stiles, 1995; Stiles, Gibbons, Lie, Sand, & Krull, 1998; Stiles, Sand, Gibbons, & de Silva, 1994). Photo 11.2 shows seven adolescent girls: a girl from Morocco, four Norwegian born girls, a girl from Kurdistan, and a girl from Pakistan.

"In many Third World societies, males are permitted greater social freedom, independence, and educational opportunities, but restraints are placed on female behavior" (Sam, 1995, p. 240). Stiles (1995) noted that girls are consistently more likely to be in favor of gender-role equality than boys. Adolescent boys from Spain and Mexico expressed traditional views toward the rights and roles of women, but Third World immigrant boys living in Norway were as nontraditional in their views as American boys and endorsed gender role equality almost as strongly as Norwegian boys. More than 90% of Third World immigrant boys living in Norway agreed that boys and girls should have the same freedoms.

During acculturation, immigrants may adopt strategies of assimilation, separation, marginalization or integration (Berry & Sam, 1997). In his studies of young immigrants in Norway, Sam (1995, 1998a) found that their preferred and most successful strategy was integration, maintaining the cultural heritages of their societies of origin combined with strong identifications with Norwegian cultural values and norms. Separation was the second most preferred strategy for all groups except for the Vietnamese. Marginalization, low identification with both ethnic heritage and the host country, was associated with negative psychological adaptation outcomes (Sam, 1998a).

A recent study demonstrated that young immigrants had a more positive adaptation to Norwegian society (Sam, 1998c), whereas an earlier study reported more problems in psychosocial adjustment (Sam, 1994). Stiles (1995; Stiles et al., 1994; Stiles et al., 1998), who also studied young adolescent immigrants to Norway, found that immigrant students expressed more positive attitudes about school and themselves than did their Norwegian peers. Discrepancies in the

Photo 11.2
Seven Friends

Photo courtesy of the author.

findings most probably arise from the characteristics of sample selection. In Sam's (1994) study, Pakistani immigrants were underrepresented, and the Norwegian comparison data were collected at a different time. A selection bias in Stiles's studies was that most of the immigrant students participated because the teachers who taught Norwegian as a second language had a vested interest in the project.

Stiles (1995; Stiles et al., 1994; Stiles et al., 1998) interviewed young adolescents and collected additional data from them in the form of questionnaires and drawings. Stiles also found some evidence that young adolescent immigrants to Norway preferred an integration mode of adaptation. An example of a young adolescent's adopting an integration mode of acculturation may be inferred by the drawing by a 16-year-old adolescent from Eritrea (Figure 11.1). This boy drew a picture of himself engaged in hiking, which seems very Norwegian, but there are aspects of the drawing that also seem very African in appearance. He described himself as happy and stated that he never wishes to be someone else. He explained that he is someone who is kind and makes friends easily. He described himself as hardworking and good at reading and mathematics.

Pakistani Immigrants

Most Pakistanis came to Norway as unskilled laborers beginning in the late 1960s. The Pakistani community has grown in size to more than 20,000.

There are ethnic, religious, and social-class differences within the Pakistani community of Norway. A center for fundamentalist Pakistani in Norway is the Islamic Cultural Center in Oslo; the members are urban and Urdu speaking. Many of the Pakistani immigrants, who have come from the rural Punjab region, speak Punjabi and practice a more "popular" Islamic religion.

Whereas in Norway there is a privatization of religion, the Islamic tradition is more inclusive. Conflicts have arisen over such issues as religious education and burial customs. In Norway, gender equality is emphasized, but in the orthodox Muslim tradition women's place is in the home. In addition, some conflicts have arisen over the Pakistani custom of arranged marriages.

Many Pakistanis have assimilated, adopting Norwegian citizenship and language. Although there is not organized hostility toward persons of Pakistani origin, Pakistanis experience discrimination, especially in the workplace. When the Pakistanis first immigrated to Norway they immediately found employment, but today many second-generation Pakistanis find it difficult to gain employment. When Pakistanis lose their jobs, they are significantly less likely to find employment within a year than persons of Nordic descent (Statistics Norway, 1996).

Sam (1998b) studied the adjustment of Third World adolescent immigrants to Norway from Pakistan, Turkey, Chile, and Vietnam. He found that compared with boys, girls adjusted better to school and that among the four immigrant groups the Pakistani adolescents adjusted the best.

Figure 11.1
Drawing of the Ideal Man by a 16-Year-Old Boy From Eritrea

The largest group of young adolescent Third World immigrants studied by the first author were Pakistani (38%) (Stiles, 1995; Stiles et al., 1994; Stiles et al., 1998). No statistically significant differences were found among ethnic groups, but the sample sizes were small; the total number of Third World immigrants was 199. Third World immigrants reported more positive views of school and their teachers than their Norwegian peers. Figure 11.2 shows the self-portrait of a Pakistani boy who drew himself at work on a computer. The same boy drew the ideal man as a teacher and described himself as someone who likes reading, working with computers, doing homework, and playing soccer and basketball.

Aambo (1997) described a solution-focused group therapy program with 11 Pakistani women living in Norway. The group met once a week beginning in 1994. The content of the program was developed in cooperation with the women. Topics for discussion included grief, health, child rearing, and adjustment to Norway. To raise money for baby-sitters, the participants developed a Pakistani cooking course for Norwegians. In the preparation of the cooking course, the group leaders posed questions about Pakistani-Norwegian relations. Throughout the program the participants were encouraged to identify their own problems and solutions.

Another type of "ethnically sensitive preventative intervention" with Pakistani immigrants was sponsored by the Levanger College of Education (Schlüter, 1986). Trainee teachers learned about the geography, history, religions, and social conditions of Pakistan and India. The Immigrant Project included school visits, press conferences, cultural arrangements, curriculum development, and discussions about dealing with racism.

Figure 11.2
Self-Portrait by a 14-Year-Old Boy From Pakistan

Vietnamese Refugees

From 1975 to 1990, 6,633 Southeast Asian refugees migrated to Norway and the Vietnamese constitute the largest refugee group in Norway. A high proportion of the Vietnamese boat refugees has been exposed to catastrophic life events including war and flight traumatization (Ellingsen & Hauff, 1988; Hauff & Vaglum, 1993, 1994a, 1994b). About one tenth of Vietnamese refugees have posttraumatic stress disorder and about one fourth had some symptoms of traumatic stress when they arrived in Norway (Hauff & Vaglum, 1993, 1994b). Two studies by Hauff and Vaglum (1993, 1997) found that 3 years after arriving in Norway, the majority of Vietnamese boat refugees had established good intra-ethnic social contact (contact with other Vietnamese) but very limited interethnic contact and integration into the Norwegian labor market.

Vietnamese adolescents generally adjusted well to Norway, although they tend to be less satisfied with life than Pakistani and Chilean immigrants (Sam, 1998c). Figure 11.3 shows the self-portrait of a 16-year-old girl from Vietnam. She described herself as "not beautiful" and "a little fat" with long hair that she puts into a ponytail on top of her head. She sometimes likes and sometimes dislikes the way she looks. She is similar to other immigrant girls living in Norway in that she is dissatisfied with her appearance and concerned about her weight (Stiles, 1995; Stiles et al., 1994; Stiles et al., 1998; Wichstrom, Skogen, & Oia, 1994).

Another difficulty for Vietnamese adolescent immigrant girls can be differing gender-role expectations at home and at school (Sand, 1992). A Vietnamese girl who lived in Norway for 9 years explained in an interview that parents believe that "girls are supposed to be at home and help and cook everything.

Figure 11.3
Self-Portrait by a 16-Year-Old Girl From Vietnam

You have to be polite, sit like a girl, and do what they say. In Norway, girls and guys are equal. At school, you can be yourself and be with your friends" (C. Le Vu, personal communication, December 9, 1998).

CONCLUSION

In an article titled "Immigration Theory for a New Century: Some Problems and Opportunities," Portes (1997) described gender as a "master dimension of social structure" (p. 816) and called on social scientists to carefully consider the role of gender in migration studies. In Norway, males and females differed in their attitudes and psychosocial adjustment to migration. Immigrant adolescent girls showed better school adjustment and held more nontraditional views toward gender roles than immigrant boys. Sami adolescent girls report more emotional problems than Sami boys, and immigrant girls had more problems with body image than immigrant boys. Adult women had different reasons than men for migrating within Norway. Adult women had more favorable attitudes toward immigration and immigration policy than adult men.

The migration-morbidity hypothesis states that in comparison with the general population, immigrants are at greater risk for developing psychological problems (Klimidis, Stuart, Minas, & Ata, 1994). The Vietnamese refugees in Norway were exposed to catastrophic events and about 10% have suffered from posttraumatic stress disorder. This statistic is higher than in the general population. Vietnamese adolescents appear to be less satisfied with life than Pakistani and Chilean adolescents. In Norway, state policies are not racist, but they are culturalist, favoring Norwegian culture (Eriksen, 1997b). Most Norwegians are not conversant about the culture and lifestyles of Third World immigrant groups. Immigrant groups learn Norwegian, but Norwegians almost never learn Tamil, Urdu, or Vietnamese. "When a culturally homogeneous society pursues a policy of assimilation for its ethnic minorities and immigrants, there may be a tendency on the part of that society to belittle the traditional culture of the minority groups" (Sam, 1995, p. 252). In Norway, among the Sami and Third World adolescents, the acculturation strategies of weak ethnic identification (marginalization and assimilation) are associated with less successful psychosocial adjustment than strong ethnic identification (integration and separation). Ethnically sensitive preventative and educational interventions may assist Third World immigrants and minority groups in the acculturation process.

In summary, there are some differences in psychosocial adjustment based on gender and ethnic group affiliation. There are many psychological and sociocultural risks for immigrants and refugees, but overall migration in Norway is associated with positive adaptation among children, adolescents, and adults.

NOTE

This research was supported in part by two grants to the first author—a Fulbright Award and a Webster University Faculty Research Grant.

REFERENCES

Aambo, A. (1997). Tasteful solutions: Solution-focused work with groups of immigrants. *Contemporary Family Therapy: An International Journal, 19*(1), 63–79.

Aikio, P. (1983, February). Culture in a cold climate: The reindeer herdsmen of Lapland. *UNESCO Courier*, pp. 30–34.

Berry, J. W., & Sam D. L. (1997). Acculturation and adaptation. In J. W. Berry, M. H. Segall, & Ç. Kagitçibasi (Eds.), *Handbook of cross-cultural psychology: Social behavior and applications* (2nd ed., pp. 291–236). Boston: Allyn & Bacon.

Dahlstrom, M. (1996). Young women in a male periphery: Experiences from the Scandinavian North. *Journal of Rural Studies, 12*(3), 259–271.

Eriksen, T. H. (1997a). *Images of the neighbor: Reciprocal national stereotypes in Scandinavia* [Online]. Available: www.uio.no/~geirthe/Scandinavian _images.html

Eriksen, T. H. (1997b). *The Pakistani Norwegians* [Online]. Available: www.uio.no/~geirthe/Forthight.html

Ellingsen, I. L., & Hauff, E. (1998). Psychosocial rehabilitation of refugees in Norway. *International Journal of Mental Health, 17*(3), 38–45.

Guttorm, A. (1982). Saame speech. In M. Allwood (Ed.), *Modern Scandinavian poetry: The panorama of poetry 1900-1975*. New York: New Directions.

Hauff, E., & Vaglum, P. (1993). Integration of Vietnamese refugees into the Norwegian labor market: The impact of war trauma. *International Migration Review, 27*(2), 388–406.

Hauff, E., & Vaglum, P. (1994a). Chronic posttraumatic stress disorder in Vietnamese refugees: A prospective community of prevalence, course, psychopathology, and stressors. *Journal of Nervous and Mental Disease, 182*(2), 85–90.

Hauff, E., & Vaglum, P. (1994b). Vietnamese boat refugees: The influence of war and flight traumatization on mental health on arrival in the country of resettlement: A community cohort of Vietnamese refugees in Norway. *Acta Psychiatrica Scandinavica, 88*(3), 162–168.

Hauff, E., & Vaglum, P. (1997). Establishing social contact in exile: A prospective community cohort study of Vietnamese refugees in Norway. *Social Psychiatry and Psychiatry Epidemiology, 32*(7), 408–415.

Hamilton, L. C., & Otterstad, O. (1998). Sex ratio and community size: Notes from the northern Atlantic. *Population and Environment, 20*(1), 11–23.

Hauge, O. (1990). *Selected poems*. Fredonia, New York: White Pine Press.

Hovland, A. (1995, June). *Literal identity? On the textual reconstruction and manifestation of ethnic identity among young Sami*. Paper presented at the Symposium, Ethnic Identity: Psychological and Anthropological Perspectives, Karasjok, Norway.

Hovland, A. (1996, August). *On the politics of Sami identity management: An anthropological study of youth in northern Norway*. Keynote address presented at the meeting of Nordic Youth Research Information Symposia

(NYRIS), Tonsberg, Norway.

Jenssen, A. T., & Engesbak, H. (1994). The many faces of education: Why are people with lower education more hostile towards immigrants than people with higher education? *Scandinavian Journal of Educational Research, 38*(1), 33–50.

Klimidis, S., Stuart, G., Minas, I. H., & Ata, A. W. (1994). Immigrant status and gender effects on psychopathology and self-concept in adolescents: A test of the migration-morbidity hypothesis. *Comprehensive Psychiatry, 35*(5), 393–404.

Knudsen, K. (1997). Scandinavian neighbors with different character? Attitudes toward immigrants and national identity in Norway and Sweden. *Acta Sociologica, 40*(3), 223.

Kvernmo, S., & Heyerdahl, S. (1996). Ethnic identity in aboriginal Sami adolescents: The impact of the family and the ethnic community context. *Journal of Adolescence, 19*(5), 453–464.

Kvernmo, S., & Heyerdahl, S. (1998). Influence of ethnic factors on behavior problems in indigenous Sami and majority Norwegian adolescents. *Journal of American Academy of Child and Adolescent Psychiatry, 37*(7), 743–751.

Ringdal, K. (1993). Migration and status attainment among Norwegian men. *Acta Sociologica, 36*(4), 327–343.

Portes, A. (1997). Immigration theory for a new century: Some problems and opportunities. *International Migration Review, 31*(4), 799–825.

Sam, D. L. (1994). The psychological adjustment of young immigrants in Norway. *Scandinavian Journal of Psychology, 35*(3), 240–253.

Sam, D. L. (1995). Acculturation attitudes among young immigrants as a function of perceived parental attitudes toward cultural change. *Journal of Early Adolescence, 15*(2), 238–258.

Sam, D. L. (1998a, August). *Acculturation strategies of adolescents with immigrant background: Preferences and predictors*. Paper presented at the 24th International Congress of the International Association for Cross-Cultural Psychology, Bellingham, WA.

Sam, D. L. (1998b, August). *School adjustment of ethnocultural adolescents in Norway: Similarities and differences among five ethnic groups*. Paper presented at the 24th International Congress of the International Association of Applied Psychology, San Francisco, CA.

Sam, D. L. (1998c). Predicting life satisfaction among adolescents from immigrants families in Norway. *Ethnicity and Health, 3*(1-2), 5–18.

Sand, T. (1992, March). *Living with two cultures: Flight and resettlement seen as sociocultural change*. Paper presented at the 20th Nordic Congress on Educational Research, Oslo, Norway.

Schlüter, R. (1986). The immigration project 1980-1981. *European Journal of Teacher Education, 9*(2), 153–168.

Statistics Norway. (1996). Decline in unemployment among immigrants. *Weekly Bulletin, 50* [Online]. Available: www.ssb.no/english/wekly-bulletin/editions/9650/1.html

Statistics Norway. (1998a). Population statistics. Migration, 1997: Large immigration surplus from other countries. *Weekly Bulletin, 34* [Online]. Available: www.ssb.no/english/weekly-bulletin/editions/9834.1.shtml

Statistics Norway. (1998b). Well-educated young women from Oslo most immigrant-friendly. *Weekly Bulletin, 38* [Online]. Available: www.ssb.no/englishweekly_bulletin/editions/9838/2.shtml

Statistics Norway. (2001). Immigration and immigrants 2001–updated numbers of immigrants [Online]. Available: www.ssb.no/english/subjects/02/sa_innvand_en/main.html

Stiles, D. A. (1995, February). *Gender role expectations of Norwegian adolescents.* Paper presented at the meeting of the Society for Cross-Cultural Research, Savannah, GA.

Stiles, D. A., Gibbons, J. L., Lie, S., Sand, T., & Krull, J. (1998). Now I am living in Norway: Immigrant girls describe themselves. *Cross-Cultural Research, 32,* 279–298.

Stiles, D. A., Sand, T., Gibbons, J. L., & de Silva, S. S. (1994, February). *Gender role conflicts in children of immigrants in Norway.* Paper presented at the annual meeting of the Society for Cross-Cultural Research, Sante Fe, NM.

Vesaas, T. (1988). *Selected poems.* London: Barnett.

Wichstrom, L., Skogen, K., & Oia, T. (1994). Social and cultural factors related to eating problems among adolescents in Norway. *Journal of Adolescence, 17*(5), 471–483.

IV

Asia and Australia

12

Armenian Migration and a Diaspora: A Way of Life

Meliné Karakashian and Gevorg Poghosyan

This chapter is a study of the migration of the Armenian people in the past 100 years. Although studies exist of Armenian migration and settlements in specific countries, such as the United States (Hagopian, 1988; Kulhanjian, 1975; Mirak, 1983), there is a need for a global study of Armenian migration with an understanding of its antecedents, consequences, and implications. The chapter attempts to address this need within space limitations.

In the span of the past 100 years, numerous routes existed for Armenian emigrants which necessitates the adoption of a criterion for including them in the chapter. To avoid oversimplification, examples are presented from five types of migration respectively based on: (a) political determinants, (b) ecological determinants, (c) repatriation, (d) economic and educational determinants, and (e) transient migration. The study looks at migration flows starting from 1894, because significant changes in migration habits occurred after that date and these are relevant to a better understanding of Armenian migration in the 20th century. The sources of this information can be found in the Republic of Armenia's State Library archives, the Genocide Museum library in Yerevan, historical and contemporary research studies, eyewitness accounts, interviews, and news releases. Because narration offers information on the human experience aspects of migration, case examples are cited.

The chapter provides information on the fate of a people who lived on the biblical lands where Noah's ark is believed to have landed (Mount Ararat is in historic Armenia), who were the first nation to adopt Christianity as a state religion in A.D. 301, and who embarked on a worldwide celebration of their 1,700th anniversary in the year 2001. Table 12.1 presents the latest statistics of Armenians in the world.

Table 12.1
Armenian Population in the World

Formerly Soviet States		Europe		Africa and Asia		The Americas and Australia	
Russia	1,800,000	England	17,000	United Emirates	5,000	United States	1,000,000
Ukraine	50,000	Austria	4,000	Turkey	65,000	Argentina	100,000
Kazakhstan	20,000	Belgium	4,000	Israel	3,000	Brazil	20,000
Byelorussia	5,000	Bulgaria	30,000	Iran	180,000	Canada	70,000
Uzbekistan	60,000	Germany	15,000	Iraq	22,000	Uruguay	15,000
Georgia	430,000	Denmark	4,000	Cyprus	4,000	Venezuela	4,000
Tajikistan	6,000	Italy	3,000	Lebanon	120,000	Chile	1,500
Moldova	3,000	Poland	10,000	Jordan	4,000	Other countries	2,000
Latvia	3,000	Holland	3,000	Syria	130,000	Australia	30,000
Lithuania	2,000	Greece	15,000	Kuwait	10,000		
Estonia	4,000	Hungary	8,000	Hindustan	1,000		
Karabagh	160,000	Sweden	4,000	Asian countries	10,000		
Turkmenistan	60,000	Switzerland	5,000	Egypt	10,000		
Kyrghyzstan	5,000	Rumania	6,000	Republic of South Africa	3,000		
		France	400,000	Sudan	1,000		
		Other	3,000	Other African countries	2,000		
Total	2,608,000	Total	531,000	Total	570,000	Total	1,242,500

Note: Table prepared in 1995 by Armenag M. Voskanian, Curator/
Historian of the Genocide Museum at Dzidzernagaperd Monument in Yerevan, Armenia.

HISTORICAL OVERVIEW

The Republic of Armenia is situated in the Near East, specifically, south of Georgia and Russia, east of Turkey, west of Azerbaijan, and north of Iran. David Marshall Lang (1970) called it the "cradle of civilization." Armenians from ancient times were described as migratory merchants and wealthy entrepreneurs (Walker, 1980). Walker stated that the location of Armenia and people's perception that Armenians were wealthy contributed to its fate in history, which has included invasions, deportations of its inhabitants, and attempts at their extermination.

Historically, Armenian merchants migrated along the "Silk Route" from Europe to China, and established settlements in distant countries. In the 1st century b.c., the Armenian king Dikran created an empire extending from sea to sea (meaning from the Mediterranean to the Caspian). Not only did Armenians settle in these lands, but King Dikran brought artisans from Jerusalem to his capital, including 10,000 Jews whose descendants are part of the Jewish community in Armenia.

In the Middle Ages, Armenian feudal princes settled in Cilicia, presently south central Anatolia, Turkey and established the Cilician kingdom. Cilician Armenia played host to the Crusaders and participated in their marches to the Holy Land. Many settled in Jerusalem and their descendants form the core of the Armenian residents of Jerusalem.

Armenia was at the crossroads of invasions by the Mongols, Tatars, Seljuks, and Ottoman Turks who contributed to the dissolution of the Armenian kingdom in the 14th century. The population lived under the Ottoman Turkish rule for several centuries thereafter. At the turn of the 20th century, the majority of Armenians lived in central Anatolia in Turkey, the historical Lesser Armenia, in Iran, and in Russian held territories, east of Turkey, the historical Greater Armenia.

In religion, Armenians followed the Apostolic or Eastern Orthodox, Catholic, and Protestant doctrines. The seats of the heads of the Armenian Apostolic church, the Catholicosi were in Etchmiadzin, Greater Armenia and in Sis, Cilician Armenia. At one time in history four Catholicosates concurrently existed due to the prevailing political situation. The Armenian Apostolic church has had Patriarchates in Constantinople (Istanbul), Turkey and in the Holy City. Other significant religious institutions included the Catholic Mekhitarist brothers' seminaries on the San Lazzaro island in Venice, Italy (established in 1711) and in Vienna, Austria (established in 1817). These two centers that were the bastions of Armenian spiritual and intellectual life continue to serve the religious needs of Armenian Catholics and the educational needs of all Armenians. The Armenian Missionary Association of America is located in Paramus, New Jersey. It serves the spiritual needs of Armenian Protestants and the educational and charitable needs of all Armenians.

A review of the archives at the National Library in Yerevan, Armenia, reveals that by 1914, 202 migratory settlements (*kaghtojakhner,* or "migration homes") existed ranging from Madras, India, to Australia; Argentina; Ethiopia;

North America; and various European, Middle Eastern, and Russian cities. Indeed, the first Armenian paper was published in Madras in 1794, suggesting that a substantial Armenian community lived in India at that time.

There is evidence (Hagopian, 1988; Kulhanjian, 1975; Mirak, 1983) that a slow rate of emigration from Turkey to the United States and Europe existed prior to 1895. The emigrants mostly pursued commerce and education. Hagopian (1988) attributed expatriation from Turkey to the United States in the second half of the 19th century to the efforts of American missionaries. The American Missionary Society established schools for Armenian youths and children in Turkey, who upon graduation looked toward the United States to pursue their higher education in medicine or theology. Some of these youth returned to Turkey, whereas others sought permanent residence in the United States.

CATEGORIES OF MIGRATION IN THE 20TH CENTURY

Political Determinants

Political determinants include forced emigration; emigration due to adverse political conditions, including human rights violations and civic restrictions; and emigration due to internal instability and war. It is our hypothesis that not only the location of the country and the wealth of the merchants, as Walker (1980) stated, but also the personality characteristics of the Armenian people contributed to victimization. The majority of the Armenian population were agrarian; a minority were artisans and merchants. Religion played an important role in the moral, spiritual, and intellectual life of the people. In the Bagratid city of Ani, currently in ruins in eastern Turkey, there were 1,001 churches. Ruins of numerous seminaries and churches exist in the Republic of Armenia, Azerbaijan, Georgia, Anatolia, Turkey and Nagorno Karabagh. Seminaries were spiritual and intellectual centers where literature was created. Armenians traditionally loved peace and strived to maintain the integrity of the beautiful land they lived on. In fact, their folklore and music is filled with themes of love for their country and its mountains and rivers. Mount Ararat, where Noah's ark is said to have landed in the Great Flood and which is situated in historic Armenia, symbolizes resilience, protection, hope, and pride. Nature takes on sensual characteristics for romantic poets and writers. A flowering cherry tree is likened to a beautiful bride, a mountain to a proud man, and wheat fields to oceans. Its peace-loving nature, religiosity, and also its serf mentality (acquired through centuries of domination by the Ottoman Turks) prevented the people from asserting their human and civic rights as Turkish citizens. Toward the end of the 19th century, however, Armenian young adults having obtained higher education at European universities and exposed to political thoughts, founded political and civic organizations that lobbied for civil rights for Armenian citizens of Turkey. The events that followed were efforts to crush this spirit once and for all.

Emigration From Turkey

Major changes occurred in the life of Armenians in Turkey from 1894 to 1914 and from 1915 to 1922 resulting in significant migratory flows. The consequences of these changes are observed currently in the diaspora at the close of the 20th century.

From 1894 to 1915. In 1894, the people of two villages in Sassoon, eastern Turkey, refused to pay taxes, claiming the burden of double taxation by the government and the local Kurdish feudal lords (Dadrian, 1995). Armenians as Christians were considered to be of lower class and had few or no civil rights. The refusal resulted in the government's order to massacre the residents of 25 villages. Subsequent to the massacres, 4,000 Armenians held peaceful protest demonstrations in Constantinople, which ended with their massacre. The following year, an uprising took place in Zeitoon, which ended with the massacre of the population of Zeitoon and the environs. In addition, organized massacres continued in the southeastern town of Adana in 1909.

It is estimated that 200,000 Armenians (Dadrian, 1995) perished from 1894 to 1896, which set the stage for the organized attempt of the Ottoman government to annihilate the Christian Armenians or *giavours* (infidels) in 1915 and to end the "Armenian question" once and for all. Between 1894 and 1896, some 100,000 Armenians found refuge in other countries (Dadrian, 1995), and between 1895 and 1899, an estimated 70,982 Armenians entered the United States (Tashjian, 1947, p. 18).

In his memoirs, H. Jamgotchian (1998) cited his mother's report that the Turks in the village of Gurun axed his grandfather in 1895. He called his three sons to his deathbed and advised them to leave Turkey. After the massacres, numerous Armenian men left their towns and villages for the United States to find work, to support their families back home and to pave their way to freedom.

The emigration out of Turkey continued into the early 20th century. Hagopian (1988) observed that from 1899 (when the nationality of immigrants was recorded rather than the country of origin) to 1907, 14,583 Armenians migrated to the United States, and between 1908 and 1910, 11,915 did so. Of these people, 10,441 came from central Turkey and approximately 2,000 from the Shirak district in Russian-held territories. Between 1899 and 1910, the remaining went to the following countries: Austria-Hungary, 12; Belgium, 10; Bulgaria, 95; Germany, 20; European Turkey, 1,267; Spain, 5; Italy, 24; Greece, 109; Great Britain, 411; Sweden, 1; Switzerland, 10; Portugal, 1; Rumania, 69; Russia, 663; France, 160; other European countries, 1. From 1911 to 1917, 4,922 more arrived in the United States, including Armenians from Norway and Holland. Hagopian (1988) summarized that between 1899 and 1910, 26,498 Armenians left for the United States and between 1911 and 1917, 28,559 did so. Between 1899 and 1917, then, the number of Armenian immigrants totaled 55,057. Of the emigrants, 39% were skilled craftsmen (e.g., blacksmiths, cobblers, tailors, carpenters), 23% were farmers, 17% were factory workers, 17% had other jobs (e.g., tradesman, agents, servants), and 2% were intellectuals (e.g., teachers, lawyers, editors, musicians, artists). Twenty-four percent of the immigrants were literate. Hagopian noted that 80% of the emigrants between 1908 and 1910 paid their own way, and 84% stayed with a relative upon arrival. About 5% had previously been in the United States. In fact, during that period, 1,316 Armenians emigrated from the USA. It is probable that a considerable percentage of them migrated back to Turkey to join their families.

The Genocide. The Genocide and forced deportation of Armenian residents of Anatolia, Turkey, starting in 1915, which was ordered and carried out by the Young Turk Ottoman government, resulted in the dispersion of survivors in various parts of the world. To a great extent, the Armenian diaspora of today is a consequence of the genocide.

Recent research places the genocide in the context of large schemes developed by world powers. Historically, Great Britain and France financially supported the Turkish sultan to wage war against eastern Armenian feudal princes in an effort to halt the czarist expansion toward Iran. Armenians who handled Anatolian commerce as entrepreneurs, also stood in the way of the German government's economic expansion interests to the Caspian Sea (Walker, 1980). Colluding with the Ottoman Turkish government, the German government supported the latter's efforts to eliminate the Armenians from the corridor leading to the Caspian Sea, then a Russian stronghold (Dadrian, 1995; Walker, 1980). Although the major commerce was in the hands of the Armenians, Walker (1980) estimated that 70% of the Armenian population were peasants. These peasants felt the brunt of the Turkish sword during the genocide and were the victims of the major deportations.

On April 24, 1915, the Turkish government ordered the imprisonment of key intellectuals and leaders. In the weeks to follow, Armenian men were imprisoned in towns and villages and taken away in chains with the excuse that they were to serve in the Turkish Army. Later reports indicated that these men were shot, or forced to work in labor camps and then buried alive. The remaining women, children, and elderly were forcefully deported. There are different estimates of the number of Armenians who perished as a result of the genocide, deportations, and death marches.

Taking the report of the Armenian patriarchate of 1878 and adding a conservative estimate of the normal growth statistics for Armenians, Khatanassian (1965) estimated the Armenian population in Ottoman Turkey in 1915 to have been 2,623,000. Khatanassian's estimate of the number of Armenians massacred and perished is a minimum of 1.5 million. These calculations leave the number of survivors of the genocide from Turkey at 1 million. The first column in Table 12.2 presents the number of Armenians living outside of Turkey until 1914, and the second column the number of genocide survivors that found refuge in the countries noted above until 1922 (Khatanassian, 1965).

The refugees—mainly women, children, and the elderly—walked for months through the hot and dry mountain chains to southern Kurdish villages and towns seeking shelter (Dadourian, 1995; H. Jamgotchian, 1998; Papazian, 2000). Many died from exposure, starvation, and attacks. Large numbers were sent to Deir el Zhor in the deserts of Syria and perished. Others went along with a conversion-to-Islam ceremony to avoid being sent to Deir el Zhor. They were taken

Table 12.2
Armenian Settlements Before and After 1915

Number of Armenians Living Outside of Turkey until 1914		Migration Sites of Genocide Survivors 1915-22	
US and Canada	75,000	USA and Canada	22,000
Iran	60,000	Iran	35,000
Syria, Lebanon and Palestine	60,000	Syria and Lebanon	85,000
Egypt, Sudan, and Ethiopia	12,000	Egypt, Sudan, and Ethiopia	15,000
Bulgaria	8,000	Bulgaria	20,000
Romania	5,000	Romania	15,000
Greece	1,000	Greece	35,000
India, Java and other Asian countries	15,000	Iraq	15,000
Mesopotamia, Bagdad, Musul, Basra	1,000	Cyprus	7,000
Europe	10,000	South America	10,000
		Constantinople	55,000
		Turkey	50,000
Total	247,000	Total	402,000

Note: From Khatanassian (1965).

231

in by Kurds as domestics and thus survived. In the city of Ayntab, Near East Relief founded orphanages where the children were fed, cleaned, and cared for. After the armistice, Near East Relief transported the refugees and orphans to Aleppo and then to Lebanon where orphanages were founded and where the children received elementary education and vocational training (H. Jamgotchian, 1998; Zaroukian, 1985).

There are individual reports that a small proportion of Armenian refugees returned to their homes in south-central Turkey, such as in the city of Ayntab from Aleppo, Syria where they had found refuge in 1915. Some of them left Turkey again in 1922 when civil laws changed. At this time, Turkish citizens were given permission to take over the abandoned homes of deported Armenians. For instance, in the town of Gurun, St. Mary's Armenian Apostolic Church appears to have been made into a mosque. The dome of the church still appears next to a minaret. An inscription on the mosque states the date of its founding as 1922. The shape of the windows on the first floor carries the Islamic design while the windows on the dome have the rounded tops of the Armenian churches, suggesting that a quick face-lift had converted the church into a mosque. Currently, residents refer to it as the formerly Armenian church (M. Karakashian, 1997). The alteration of historical monuments continues to date (Markarian, 1999).

There is evidence that localized massacres in eastern Turkey continued to 1922. On May 18, 1918, a battle in Sardarapad (outskirts of Yerevan, capital of present-day Armenia) contributed to the creation of an independent state on a small portion of the historic land. The independence was recognized by major nations, including the United States. The independence lasted for 2 years. In 1921, the Bolshevik expansion to the south of Russia resulted in the takeover of the Republic of Armenia and the eventual formation of the Soviet Armenian state. The leadership of the independent republic escaped to safety in Iran. Later, Stalin, drawing the boundaries of Soviet states, annexed the Karabagh (historic Artzakh) and Nakhichevan regions of Armenia to Azerbaijan, in his effort to create a union of interdependent states.

From 1922 to 1953. Another wave of forced emigration took place in 1922, when organized fires swept the Armenian and Greek quarters of the coastal city of Izmir, then called Smyrna in Turkey (Housepian, 1966/1972). The fire was an attempt to force the Christians to leave the city and the environs. Currently, Turkish tour guides refer to it as "the population exchange program when Armenians, Greeks, and Jews were exchanged with Turkish citizens from the respective countries." In fact, no such exchange of Turks took place with Soviet Armenia. K. Karakashian (1990) reported that her family in Odemis was forced to board the train to Smyrna. The train was attacked in the night and passengers hid behind bushes. When daylight arrived and she reboarded the train, she could not find her mother. She lamented the loss of her mother until her own death in 1997. Upon arrival in Izmir, she jumped into the waters of the Aegean and swam a long distance to reach the large boat because the shuttle boats were full. Boats took the refugees to Salonica, the island of Paros, and Pireus in Greece (E. Arpiarian, personal communication, October 5, 1962, New York City; K. Karakashian, 1990).

A number of survivors migrated from Greece to Lebanon and Syria (A. Khashkhashian, personal communication September 1, 1962, Beirut, Lebanon), some to Jordan (K. Karakashian, 1990), Australia (W. Hairabedian, personal communication, October 10, 1998, Vienna, Austria), France (G. Bedrosian personal communication, August 5, 1997, Paris, France), the United States (E. Arpiarian, personal communication, October 5, 1962, New York City), Argentina (Karakashian, 1990), and to other countries. The remaining survivors form the core of the Armenian population in present-day Greece.

Emigration from European Countries

An American program for displaced people was initiated after World War II. A large number of Armenians lived on territories occupied by Nazi Germany. Many Armenian prisoners from the Soviet Army were held hostage by Germany. They were spared from the Holocaust through negotiations held by Armenian representatives who presented proof that Armenians were from the Indo-European family of peoples. An organization headed by the late San Francisco restaurateur, George Mardikian appropriated congressional funding for the transportation and establishment of displaced Armenians in the United States.

Later, it conducted a similar service for the Armenians of Bulgaria and Romania. Armenians had been established in these countries since medieval times. Having survived the Communist regime, a substantial proportion of them left their homes in order to offer their children safety as well as educational, social, and economic opportunities in the United States.

Emigration From Middle Eastern Countries

From Jordan. A wave of Armenian migration occurred concurrent to the 1947 takeover of the Palestinian section of Jerusalem by the new Israeli state. A demilitarized buffer zone was created. Armenians who lived in the demilitarized zone migrated to the Jordanian section of Jerusalem. Many sought shelter in the cabins of the Armenian patriarchate complex where centuries earlier the Crusaders had lived. Others settled in Amman, the capital of Jordan. In the 1950s, a United Nations initiative sponsored their resettlement in the United States as Palestinian refugees (N. Karakashian, personal communication, August 5, 1999, Morganville, New Jersey).

From Lebanon. Another wave of migration occurred in the 1970s during the Arab-Israeli war. Thousands of Armenians sought the safety of countries in Europe, Australia, United States, and Canada. The once 250,000 strong Armenian community of Lebanon was reduced to less than 120,000 in the span of 2 decades. These immigrants brought their own subcultures and traditions and changed the profile of established communities. A considerable number of them live now in California together with Armenian immigrants from Iran, Jordan, Syria, Armenia, and native Armenian Americans.

From Egypt. In the 1950s, the ascension of Gamal Abdul Nasser to power saw a wave of Egyptian nationalism and the nationalization of businesses. Armenians, many of whom were business owners, feared the loss of their enterprises and consequently emigrated from Egypt to other Middle Eastern countries, Canada, and the United States.

Emigration Within and From Communist Countries

From Soviet Armenia to Siberia. In the 1920s and 1930s, Stalin's policy in Soviet Armenia resulted in the forced exile of thousands of nationalistic residents—many with connections to the former government of the independent republic. They were exiled to Siberian labor camps where few survived, and their descendants can still be found in Siberia (Tjeknavorian, 1998). The suffering of these exiles has not been studied yet, nor fully documented. A recently released documentary film, *Enemy of the People* (Tjeknavorian, 1998), described the mass hysteria that the Armenians endured under Stalin's regime.

From Azerbaijan. Waves of forced emigration of Armenians took place in Azerbaijan from 1988 to 1992. In February of 1988, the Azerbaijani government conducted pogroms against the Armenian residents of Baku that were reportedly witnessed by Russian soldiers (Mosesova & Hovnanyan, 1992). Massacres in Sumgait and Kirovabad followed (Shahmuratian, 1990). Hundreds of thousands of survivors of these massacres found refuge in Armenia, Russia, and also the United States. For instance, a Pentecostal church sponsored the way of some of these refugees to the United States and helped them to become established in Pentecostal communities located in Cleveland, Ohio, and in Washington state. The majority, who remained in Armenia presented "management challenges" for the Armenian government due to the language barrier.

In the wake of the post-Soviet transitional period, Russian is less frequently spoken and taught in Armenia because a new national awakening there has focused on the promotion of the Armenian language. The Armenian refugees from Baku, Sumkait, and Kirovabad knew Azerbaijani and Russian only, and they had to learn Armenian. In addition, their professional expertise was appropriate to large industries and could not be utilized in a country that experienced an energy crisis. Armenia faced a crisis due to Azerbaijan's economic blockade and the devastations caused by the earthquake. With the help of international humanitarian programs, the Armenian government adopted programs for the refugees' adaptation and integration into the society because a return to their homes would not guarantee their safety.

In 1992, during the Armenian-Azerbaijani war, the residents of the Shahumian and Martagerd districts of Azerbaijan (neighboring the Karabagh enclave) were forced to emigrate. These refugees reported that Russian armored tanks invaded their villages together with the Azeri military, and that the population was asked to leave their homes. The refugees expressed the belief that their homes and lands were used as pawns by the "leadership" (M. Karakashian & Tavosian, 1992).

The number of Armenian refugees that migrated to Armenia from Azerbaijan between 1988 and 1992 is estimated to be 375,000. However, the United Nations High Commissioner for Refugees (UNHCR) journal, *Refugees* reports the number in 1994 to be as high as 500,000. In addition, 6,000 settled in Armenia coming from Abkhazia and about 78,000 citizens were internally dispersed from border villages due to constant shelling.

Many refugees from Karabagh and Azerbaijan encountered different lifestyles and customs in Armenia from those prevailing in their homeland. They found city life in Yerevan very different from their agrarian life in Karabagh (M. Karakashian, 1993). For example, they complained that the price of bread and meat in Yerevan had skyrocketed and that the residents of Armenia were not actively resisting this. They pointed out that if the price of meat rose in Karabagh, residents boycotted the item, thereby bringing about price cuts.

Ecological Determinants

The catastrophic earthquake of 1988 in Soviet Armenia produced a wave of internally and externally dispersed refugees. In the days immediately following the disaster, an evacuation was organized that brought the survivors to shelters in the capital, Yerevan. Numerous injured people were flown to other countries for medical treatment. According to government statistics, about 130,000 people were displaced to the countries of the Soviet Union and 70,000 left for other countries, 25% of whom have remained in their host countries (Poghosyan, 1990).

Repatriation

There were two major waves of repatriation after the Sovietization of Armenia. The first had its origins in some Middle Eastern countries in 1946 and the second one originated all over the world in the early 1990s after the dissolution of the Soviet Union. Table 12.3 presents Khatanassian's (1965) figures of migration to Soviet Armenia from 1925 to 1965. Considering that the major repatriation took place in 1946, Khatanassian's figures probably represent realistic estimates of this repatriation.

To Soviet Armenia

In 1946, the Soviet Armenian government extended invitations to the Armenians living in the diaspora to migrate to Armenia. The invitation was well received by many people. For instance, V. Jamgotchian (personal communication, August 5, 1999, Nazlet, New Jersey) reported witnessing trains of repatriates going from Aleppo to Beirut (the seaport capital of Lebanon) and passing through the village of Bhamdoon. There she heard repatriates sing as the trains moved: *"Hey garavan, jan garavan, kushir ko jampan; garodel em hairenikis koones chi danir"* [Oh, caravan, oh caravan, drive along your route; I miss my homeland, I have lost sleep]. Similarly, N. Karakashian (personal communica-

Table 12.3
Number of Migrants to Soviet Armenia from 1925 to 1965

Iran	50,000
Iraq	5,000
Lebanon, Syria	55,000
Egypt	5,000
Cyprus & Palestine	5,000
Greece	35,000
France	10,000
Bulgaria	5,000
Romania	5,000
The Americas	3,000
Total	178,000

Note: From Khatanassian (1965).

tion, August 5, 1999, Morganville, New Jersey) recalled the song repatriates sang while they boarded the boat *Pobeda* in the Mediterranean port of Jaffa. *Pobeda* transported them through the Bosphorus to Odessa in the Black Sea, from where they traveled by land to Soviet Armenia. Here are the lyrics: *"Ov too Pobeda shdabeh shoodov tebi baghestin; menk hay zavagner achkernis haradz michergraganin; kez yenk sbasoom poorn garodov hayoo trakhdin."* [Oh, *Pobeda*, hurry fast to Palestine; we are children of Armenians gazing with our eyes at the Mediterranean; we wait for you with longing for the Armenian heaven.] Although Soviet, eastern Armenia was nevertheless regarded by genocide survivors and their families as the motherland.

H. Jamgotchian (1998) reported that the Soviet Armenian government advised the leadership in the diaspora to encourage only the working class to migrate. Soviet Armenia had lost tens of thousands of men during World War II in addition to the loss of the exiled men and women in Siberia, and the country needed working hands. As a result of this directive, tens of thousands people from all walks of life in the Middle Eastern countries of Lebanon, Syria, Palestine, Egypt, and Greece sold their possessions and embarked on boats. Ultimately, these migrants encountered numerous difficulties, especially because the Soviet government confiscated their possessions. They had to live in dire conditions in the cold mountainous country just like the other citizens. N. Karakashian (personal communication, August 5, 1999) recalled that repatriot relatives of his family agreed to send abroad information about their well-being in coded messages. A standing position in the photographs signified well-being, a sitting position signified poor conditions. The photos that arrived from Soviet Armenia showed relatives lying on the floor! Disillusioned the repatriots began to leave Armenia in the 1970s when their relatives petitioned for their migration to the United States. Their migration to the United States and to European countries continues to this date.

To Armenia

The second large wave of repatriots came to Soviet Armenia following the catastrophic earthquake in 1988. They came in connection with national and international projects, including disaster relief. After achieving independence in 1992, the newly created republican state opened the doors to more projects in the fields of health and education, social reforms, and the establishment of businesses, and Armenians from the diaspora bought homes and established residences in Armenia in an effort to quench their longing for the motherland and to help rebuild it.

Economic and Educational Determinants

Migration due to economic and educational determinants continued in the 20th century. The major migration routes were from the Middle Eastern countries, Turkey, and Armenia to Western countries, such as some of the former Soviet states, Australia, and North and South America.

From Turkey

Following World War II, Armenian survivors of the genocide who still lived in central and eastern Anatolia migrated to Constantinople (Istanbul) to obtain higher education and better jobs (Khatanassian, 1965). This flow has continued to recent times. As late as 1997, for instance, residents of Gurun, Turkey, reported to the first author that a handful of Catholic Armenians who had lived in Gurun until 25 years ago, had sold their properties, closed the church, and left for Constantinople.

Armenian residents of Constantinople immigrated to Europe and North America starting in the 1950s to avoid civic restrictions, obtain higher education, and pursue economic goals. The immigrants have formed organizations and held cultural programs to fund educational and charitable programs and preserve their subculture in the host countries. Currently, it is estimated that there are still about 50,000 Armenians living in Constantinople and its surrounding areas.

From Syria and Lebanon

In the 1960s, a wave of migration to the West took place. A brief civil war and instability in Lebanon in 1958, the gradual leaning of the Syrian government toward the left, fear of nationalization of businesses, perceived limitations in business and professional fields, and the attraction of American and European cultures prompted the college age generation (i.e., children of survivors of the genocide) to migrate to countries in Europe, such as France, Germany, and the United States in order to obtain higher education and establish themselves in these countries. They formed cultural and charitable organizations similar to the ones in Syria and Lebanon and founded Armenian language schools. Examples are the Hamazkain Cultural and Educational Association, and the Tekeyan Cultural Association.

From the Independent Republic of Armenia

The dissolution of the Soviet Union, the opening of the Iron Curtain in the early 1990s, and economic hardships led to a new wave of emigration from Armenia to Russia, Europe, and the United States. The winters of 1992 and 1993 were particularly harsh. Apartments had no gas, and electricity was restricted to daily periods of 1 to 2 hours. Industrial fuel was unavailable and the factories were idle. More than 80% of the industry and public transportation did not function. Motor fuel was scarce and expensive. Hundreds of thousands left Armenia. In the course of the past decade, close to 700,000 individuals have emigrated, some with their families (Poghosyan, 1997a). They established themselves mostly in former Soviet states, in particular Russia, and 15–20% of them left for Europe and the United States. Many left the country temporarily, preserving their citizenship and apartments. In fact, they frequently live illegally in Russia where they engage in commerce. In the early 1990s, the majority of emigrants to the Commonwealth of Independent States (CIS) countries, Russia, and Europe were men between the ages of 20 and 45 who supported their families left behind (Human Development Report, 1996). Others took their families with them.

These economic migrants provide assistance to a considerable proportion of the population of the republic; they support the social conditions of the state and attract outside funds for economic development. Although these migrants contribute to the population's survival, their absence hurts the economy of the republic. It depletes the country of enterprising citizens for the free-market economy and retards the establishment of a middle class. There are also moral consequences. For instance, very often, simple conflicts occur in Russia between local Russians and newcomer Armenians, Georgians, and Azeris that contribute to a negative attitude of Russians toward persons of "Caucasian nationality." The anti-Caucasian attitude has intensified in the central region of Russia where there are established Armenian communities, such as in Krasnodarsk and Stavropol. With the process of privatization of land, these attitudes may lead to future conflicts and consequently some of the migrants may return to Armenia.

The Armenian government announced in 1998 that it is ready to accept back Armenian migrants from Europe, in particular from Germany, Belgium, and Greece. The German government has already adopted a decision for the gradual return of 7,000 Armenians who had found temporary shelters (Poghosyan, 1997b). The return of tens of thousand migrants from Western Europe is expected in the near future. In addition, families are migrating back to Armenia from Central and Middle Asia, in particular from Turkmenistan and Russia.

Transient Migration

Transient migrants are people who find temporary residence in a country prior to settlement in a country of choice. In the 1950s, Armenians from the former Palestine found temporary residence in Lebanon prior to boarding the boats that brought them to the United States on behalf of the United Nations initiative. Similarly, Armenians from Rumania and Bulgaria found temporary residence in Lebanon in the 1950s and 1960s prior to obtaining their visas for the United States.

In recent years, the Republic of Armenia has seen transient migrants such as Kurdish refugees who illegally crossed the Armenian-Turkish border, reached the capital, and were detained at Zvartnots International Airport while they tried to leave for Amsterdam. Currently, Armenia seems to be used as a buffer state from where transient migrants attempt to leave for Western Europe.

IMPLICATIONS OF MIGRATION

Migration and acculturation are known to be difficult adjustment processes for most ethnic groups. Acculturation is generally facilitated by established ethnic communities where elements of the ethnic culture are preserved while adaptation to the host country begins.

Armenian immigrants to the United States, Canada, and Australia, for example, joined already established institutions and organizations or founded their own, thus creating unique subcultures. This was based on the traditions of the country of origin and the cultural demands of the host countries. The subculture changed in a dynamic manner as children of immigrants assimilated in the host culture. For instance, Peter Balakian's (1998) *Black Dog of Fate* describes the subculture of Armenian Americans in New Jersey in the early 1960s, which differs from today's subculture in New Jersey.

Migration may cause problems to the country of origin and the host country as well. For example, emigration from Armenia reduces the number of working hands in Armenia while causing housing and management problems in the host country. The second author proposes a three-step process to settle the refugee problem in the post-Soviet era: (a) Establish a system that can predict varying types of migration long before they occur, (b) assist the states of the region in establishing their own migration services for taking accurate account of displaced persons, and (c) regulate the process of labor migration in the region by creating state services and programs through interstate agreements. These three steps should prove useful for regulating the migration processes and for addressing problems of security to some extent.

CONCLUSION

We attempted to present an overview of the migration of Armenian people in the past 100 years. Our study has led to interesting information and human interest stories, the collection of which could fill a book. There is a need for additional literature and texts on this subject.

A look at the past 100 years indicates that like some other ethnic groups, Armenians have migrated for reasons of genocide, deportation, political and religious oppression, war, economic disadvantage, education, crises, and natural disasters. The reasons for migration have not been very different from those prevailing in past centuries with the exception of the genocide.

In the 20th century, the genocide and the en masse dispersion of survivors contributed to the establishment of close-knit Armenian communities throughout the world. These communities support the motherland financially and spiritually in its transition to democracy. It is noteworthy that a small nation numbering fewer than 10 million has been able to survive under adverse conditions and perpetuate its culture. Its resilience in overcoming adversities is a testament to the psychological strength of individuals, the family, various institutions, and the specific culture.

The Armenian case represents only a small sample of the human condition and behavior. The global perspective on migration represented by this book indicates that populations move throughout our world in times of peace and in times of upheaval. Although some persons are forced to leave and adjust to host countries, adapt and acculturate, others migrate in order to better their existence and to avail themselves of economic opportunities and achieve personal growth. When one takes a global look at world migration, one wonders whether there are actual boundaries in the world among people, whether the existing state boundaries are merely an artificial means of having one group's interests prevail over those of others, and whether human beings as residents of this planet will ever enjoy equal rights and equal access to the resources and wonders of this world.

REFERENCES

Balakian, P. (1997). *Black dog of fate: An Armenian son uncovers his Armenian past.* New York: Basic Books.
Dadourian, S. (1995). *Oral history interview* [Videotape]. Available from M. Karakashian, P O Box 6, Morganville, NJ 07751.
Dadrian, V. (1988). The circumstances surrounding the 1909 Adana Holocaust. *Armenian Review, 41,* 1–16.
Dadrian, V. (1995). *The history of the Armenian genocide: Ethnic conflict from the Balkans to Anatolia to the Caucasus.* Providence, RI: Belghahn.
Jamgotchian, H. (1998). *My memoirs* [in Armenian]. Available from H. Jamgotchian, 57 Fieldcrest Way, Hazlet, NJ 07730.
Hagopian, G. (1988). The immigration of Armenians to the United States. *The Armenian Review, 41,* (2/162), 67–76.
Housepian, M. (1966–1972). *Smyrna 1922: The destruction of a city.* London: Faber & Faber.
Karakashian, K. (1990). *Oral history interview* [Videotape] conducted by Fr. Haigazoun Najarian, 9/3/90. Available from V. Karakashian, 2 Marvin Rd., Middletown, NJ 07748.
Karakashian, M. (1993). *Clinical notes in group treatment of refugee children,* March 7, 1993–June 6, 1993. Physics-Mathematics Institute, Yerevan, Armenia.
Karakashian, M. (1997, August 27). [Interviews with residents]. Gurun, Tukey.

Karakashian, M. & Tavosian, A. (1992). *Interviews with refugees from Shahu-mian and Mardagerd districts of Nagorni-Karabagh* [Videotape]. Available from M. Karakashian, PO Box 6, Morganville, NJ 07751.

Khatanassian, Y. (1965). *The number of the Armenians* (Hayots Tivuh). Boston: Committee for the Commemoration of the 50th Anniversary of the Genocide. (In Armenian)

Kulhanjian, G. A. (1975). *An abstract of the historical and sociological aspects of Armenian immigration to the United States, 1890–1930.* San Francisco: R & E Research Associates.

Lang, D. M. (1970). *Armenia: The cradle of civilization.* London: George Allen & Unwin.

Markarian, H. (1999, April 18). *Western Armenia: History, stones and dreams.* Lecture presented at the Armenian remembrance observance, Brookdale Community College Holocaust Center, Lincroft, NJ.

Mirak, R. (1983). *Torn between two lands: Armenians in America 1890 to World War I.* Cambridge, MA: Harvard University Press.

Mosesova, I., & Hovnanyan, A. (1992). *The massacres of Baku.* Yerevan, Armenia: Naregatzi.

Papazian, S. (2000). *Verabroghi meh votisaganeh* [The odyssey of a survivor]. Yerevan, Armenia: Amaras.

Poghosyan, G. (1990). The man in the calamity zone. In *The industry, building and architecture of Armenia* (No. 1–2). Yerevan, Armenia: Academy of Sciences (pamphlet in Armenian and Russian).

Poghosyan, G. (1997a). *Armenian returnees from Germany.* Yerevan, Armenia.

Poghosyan, G. (1997b). *Human development report.* Yerevan, Armenia: UNDP.

Shahmuratian, S. (Ed.). (1990). *The Sumgait tragedy: Vol. 1. Eyewitness accounts, Pogroms against Armenians in Soviet Azerbaijan.* Cambridge, England: Zoryan Institute.

Tashjian, J. H. (1947). *The Armenians of the United States and Canada.* Boston: Hairenik Press.

Tjecknavorian, Z. (1999). Interview with author, January 24, 1999, Armenian Radio Hour, Seton Hall University, South Orange, NJ.

Tjeknavorian, Z. (1998). *Enemy of the people* [Film]. New York: The Armenian General Benevolent Union.

Walker, C. (1980). *Armenia: The survival of a nation.* New York: St. Martin's Press.

Zaroukian, A. (1985). *Men without childhood* (Trans. E. Bayizian & M. Margossian). New York: Ashod Press.

13

Migration From and To Japan

Seisoh Sukemune

Japan, located on the Pacific Rim of the Far East, is a country made up of a great number of islands. Their combined shape resembles the form of a seahorse swimming around in the Sea of Japan. Its head is at a latitude above the 40th-degree parallel, where one can find the snow-clad mountainous island of Hokkaido. Situated in the main torso is the most densely populated island of Honshu, where Tokyo, Osaka, Kyoto, and other major cities are located. The southern base begins with the islands of Kyushyu and Shikoku; and the seahorse's tail tapers off at the subtropical Ryukyu Islands, that is, Okinawa.

The origins of the first inhabitants of Japan are largely unknown. Waves of human settlers began immigrating to Japan from the adjacent Asian continent. They came from Korea, China, and Southeast Asia. Over the centuries, later settlers gradually absorbed these people and their ancient cultures. The Japanese people of today are descendants from these early immigrants. According to two ancient chroniclers from the 8th century, Kojiki and Nihonshoki, the legendary first emperor Jinmu began his reign in 660 B.C.E. The date given for his ascension to the throne is February 11, now set aside as the National Foundation Day holiday.

JAPAN'S MODERNIZATION AND MIGRATION:
THE MEIJI RESTORATION AND JAPAN'S OPENING
TO THE WORLD

Prior to the Meiji Restoration period, feudal Japan had been cut off from the rest of the world for more than 200 years in self-imposed isolation. The transition to modern Japan began with Commodore Matthew C. Perry's arrival with a U.S.-American squadron of ships in 1853. Soon thereafter, in 1858, U.S. Consul General Townsend Harris was able to sign a treaty for friendship and commerce with Japan. This stimulated the desire among many Japanese to replace the ruling Tokugawa shogunate with a new government that would adopt Western ideas and programs.

A historical decision was made, which drew from the wisdom of both the forces aligned with and against the shogunate. When the shogun ended his rule and returned his power to the emperor, the Meiji Restoration began in 1867. It led to the establishment of prefectures (states or provinces) to replace the feudal ownership in the Tokugawa shogunate. The most urgent policy change for Japan was to catch up and be equal to the Western industrialized countries. The organization of the Meiji emperor's imperial regime was to be strengthened by the availability and applicability of knowledge throughout the world.

MIGRATION OF THE JAPENESE PEOPLE

During the early Meiji era, the Japanese government encouraged people to immigrate to Guam, Hawaii, and Mexico as agricultural migrants. Among the many countries to which Japanese people immigrated prior to World War I were mainly those in Latin America, such as Brazil, Bolivia, Peru, Argentina, and others. In addition, North American countries such as the United States and Canada became further destinations for migrants. However, not all immigrants were permanent migrants. Some worked hard to save enough money in order to return home to Japan with large sums of money. Unfortunately, local workers in these host countries persecuted a great number of Japanese sojourners and, consequently, the Japanese government began to select other receiving countries. For example, the designated new country for permanent emigrants was Brazil. As a result, 791 Japanese people left Kobe Port for Santos Port in Brazil.

During the following Taisho era, the circumstances in Brazil changed. The coffee industry experienced a labor shortage in 1850, due to the end of the slave trade and the traditional importation of Negro slaves. The first Japanese immigrants to Brazil received low incomes, ran up heavy debts, and suffered from a lack of food, which was exactly the opposite outcome of their initial dreams. Nevertheless, the Japanese government continued to encourage many people to immigrate to Brazil, especially after World War I and the ensuing world depression, because of the poverty in rural farm villages. Table 13.1 depicts the number of emigrants that left Japan after World War II (as of December 1989) and the estimated number of emigrants and their descendants currently living abroad by country (as of November 1989).

At present, the descendants of the early Japanese emigrants work in a variety of different professions in Brazil. Recently, however, many Japanese Brazilians have returned to Japan. Although these so-called U-turn workers now work for a higher income, they also bring back with them a diffused Japanese culture. This in turn, may make their readaptation to Japanese society more difficult.

The single major event of the 20th century to change the destiny of Japan was the unexpected military attack by the Imperial Navy on Pearl Harbor, Hawaii, on December 7, 1941. The Pacific War between Japan and the United States was most unfortunate and a nightmare to both the Japanese and the American people. A great number of Japanese Americans, who were living in

Table 13.1
Number of Japanese Immigrants After World War II by Receiving Country
(as of December, 1989)

Country	
Brazil	71,372
Peru	2,615
Argentina	12,066
Mexico	671
Paraguay	9,612
Bolivia	6,357
Chile	NA
Colombia	NA
Venezuela	NA
Cuba	NA
Dominican	1,390
Uruguay	NA
U.S.A.	134,842
Canada	11,226
Australia	1,525
Others	10,402
Total	252,078

Estimated Number of Japanese Immigrants and Their Descendants
Currently Living Abroad by Country
(as of November, 1989)

Brazil	1,300,000
Peru	80,000
Argentina	32,000
Mexico	12,000
Paraguay	7,700
Bolivia	6,700
Chile	1,600
Colombia	1,200
Venezuela	800
Cuba	800
Dominican	800
Uruguay	500
U.S.A.	1,000,000
Canada	NA(55,000)
Australia	NA(11,000)
Others	NA
Total	2,500,000

Note: NA= Not available. Table adapted from Ministry of Foreign Affairs, Japan
(1996).

Hawaii and on the West Coast of the United States also suffered. They were taken into custody on the mainland by presidential order, to prevent possible espionage and sabotage. Regardless of age, gender, American citizenship, and U.S. birthplace, all Japanese Americans were regarded as Japanese sympathizers and were retained in internment camps until the end of the war. In September 1951, the San Francisco Peace Treaty as well as the Japan-American Treaty of Mutual Cooperation and Security were enacted. In August 1988, President Ronald Reagan signed the Compensation Law for the Japanese Americans, who were interned during the war. Complying with this law, all Japanese American internees received compensation after September 1990.

Postwar Development of the Japanese Economy, Politics, and Education

Great changes occurred not only in politics but also in economics after World War II. Among the many underlying factors the following are some of the most remarkable ones. The Japanese people have an intense commitment to their work ethics accompanied by achievement of high levels of education and technical skills. Prosperity was thought to be achievable by becoming the major trading partner of the United States through the export of Japanese goods. As far as politics were concerned, there occurred a great change from a constitutional monarchy to a people's democracy.

Another historic change took place in the Japanese educational system, because the new Western system was introduced by the U.S. occupation forces. Mandatory school education in the new Japanese system included 6 years of elementary school and eventually 4 years of college. The Fulbright Exchange Program played a great role in furthering the mutual understanding between Japan and the United States. Not only did many Japanese graduate students in the program depart for the United States to study in every possible field and discipline, but many Americans were also visiting Japan to work and gain much knowledge and information about Japan and the Japanese culture. During the postwar years, an extensive exchange of cultural, economic, and industrial personnel was initiated between Japan and the countries around the world, especially between the United States and Japan. However, most of them did not stay permanently. Still, a great number of Japanese people immigrated to the United States to settle there, and vice versa.

SIGNIFICANT TOPICS IN CONTEMPOARY JAPAN

At the beginning of the new millennium, the Japanese economy, industry, and finance that had prospered for years on the basis of top technology, high productivity, and a well-functioning political bureaucracy were now on the verge of collapse. Countless failing companies and enterprises were closing their doors to college students. The rate of unemployment for male adults has reached over 5% and is still rising. However, there is also an increasing number of people from neighboring economically depressed countries who are entering Japan illegally; though in most cases they receive only low wages. Table 13.2 depicts the number of immigrants in Japan in the years 1992, 1994, and 1997, respectively, and Table 13.3 depicts the number of registered aliens for 1980, 1990, and 1996, respectively.

One of the most important areas of attention has centered on early childhood education and care, because numerous emigrant children are arriving from Latin America, Southeast Asia, and other areas around the globe. Some of the younger children are going to kindergarten and day-care centers. Their teachers are working diligently in various ways. For example, college professors have been conducting research on a variety of current topics that are pertinent to these

Table 13.2
Number of Immigrant Workers in Japan by Professional Areas

Legal immigrants in Japan	1990	1994	1997
Professor	1,824	3,757	5,086
Arts and music	560	220	276
Religion	5,476	5,631	5,061
Press	382	419	420
Investment & management	7,334	4,548	5,055
Law & accounting	76	72	58
Medical services	365	177	131
Research	975	1,697	2,462
Technology	7,569	6,752	7,769
International business	3,398	10,119	12,874
Transfer in business	14,426	24,774	29,941
Transfer in enterprises	1,488	5,841	6,372
Show business	21,138	34,819	22,185
Technical skills	2,972	6,790	608
Total	67,983	105,616	107,298
Specific jobs (working holidays, etc.)	3,260	6,418	12,144
Part-time jobs (international students, etc.)	10.935	33,499	32,486
Immigrants (permanent residents)	71,803	181,480	234,126
Illegal residents	106,497	288,092	276,810
Total	260,478	615,105	662,864

Note: Table adapted from Ministry of Labor, Japan (1997).

Table 13.3
Number of Registered Aliens by Geographical Areas

Continent	1980	1990	1996
Asia	734,476	924,560	1,060,081
North America	24,743	44,643	54,668
South America	2,719	71,495	248,780
Europe	15,897	25,563	35,136
Africa	795	2,140	5,609
Oceania	1,561	5,440	8,753
Stateless	2,719	1,476	2,109
Total	782,910	1,075,317	1,415,136

Note: Table adapted from Ministry of Justice, Japan (1996).

young Japanese immigrants and their education and care. Three especially important areas of concern are (a) socialization (i.e., social interaction and play), (b) classroom routines and preparation for entering elementary school, and (c) study habits to succeed in school. At the same time the keyword for immigrants of all ages is acculturation.

SUMMARY

During the early Meiji era (1867–1912), the Japanese government encouraged people to emigrate to Guam, Hawaii, and Mexico as agricultural migrants. Afterward great numbers of Japanese people emigrated to mainly Latin American countries such as Brazil, Bolivia, Peru, and Argentina. However, the United States and Canada were also popular destinations for migrants. Japan became one of the world's great economic powerhouses reflecting its high levels of education and technical skills. In this context, it should be noted that a great number of descendants of Japanese migrants to Latin America and others are entering Japan to work there these days. These descendants, however, must cope with many physical and psychological demands that they are not always able to meet successfully. In addition, more pertinent psychosocial research is needed to help the immigrant children adapt better to the kindergartens and day-care centers they are attending.

NOTE

Many thanks are due to Dr. Chok C. Hiew, Professor of Psychology at the University of New Brunswick, Fredericton, New Brunswick, Canada, for his kind editing of an earlier draft, especially with regard to English language usage. The author also thanks Drs. Leonore L. Adler and Uwe P. Gielen for their constructive editing of this chapter.

REFERENCES

Ministry of Foreign Affairs, Japan. (1996). *Kaigai zairyu houjinsu tokei* [Statistical report of Japanese residents abroad]. Tokyo, Japan: The Ministry of Foreign Affairs.
Ministry of Justice, Japan. (1996). *Shutsunyukoku kanri tokei nenpo* [Statistical annual report of immigration bureau]. Tokyo, Japan: The Ministry of Justice.
Ministry of Labor, Japan. (1997). *Gaimusho ryoken hakkyu tokei* [Statistical report of passport issue]. Tokyo, Japan: Japan.

14

Filipino International Migration: A Continuing Saga

Elena L. Samonte

The Philippines is an archipelago located in Southeast Asia. Although it comprises 7,107 islands, there are three main islands: Luzon, Visayas, and Mindanao. A tropical country, its weather is warm and humid.

The 72 million Filipinos belong to more than 100 ethnological groups, 90% of whom are speakers of eight major languages. Many Filipinos speak at least two official languages, Filipino and English. After having been a colony of Spain for almost 400 years, it was governed by the Americans for 50 years. During World War II, it was under Japanese occupation. Apart from the cultural influences from these countries, other influences on the Filipinos are those stemming from India, China, Borneo, and some Muslim countries. Although its neighboring countries are either Buddhist or Muslim, it is predominantly a Catholic country.

The Philippines is known to be a source country for both immigrants and migrant workers (Cariño, 1998). Filipino migrant workers can be found in some 130 countries. Some of them are permanent migrants (immigrants), others are temporary migrants (overseas Filipino workers [OFWs]), and still others are temporary migrants who eventually become permanent. Statistics from the Commission on Filipinos Overseas (CFO, 1997) show that there are, at present, some 6.97 million Filipinos abroad, 2.94 million of whom are OFWs, 2.15 million are immigrants, and 1.88 million are undocumented.[1]

This chapter reviews the Filipino migration literature (Perez & Patacsil, 1998; Yukawa, 1996) through three phases of the migration cycle: the predeparture, the sojourn, and the return phases. It poses questions addressed to various sectors involved in the migration process such as political-economic planners, community officials, nongovernmental organizations (NGOs), families, and the migrants themselves. Finally, the chapter explores areas where psychologists can play a significant role.

HISTORICAL BACKGROUND

Philippine out migration is not a recent phenomenon. Such movement across state boundaries has been documented in "waves." As early as 1565, Filipino seafarers manned the ships that plied the Manila-Acapulco trade route. This was followed in the 1800s by the second wave of Filipinos who went to Europe to escape political persecution from the Spanish colonial authorities. In Europe, they not only produced excellent literary and artistic pieces but also worked for political and social reforms (Samonte, Maceda, Cabilao, del Castillo, & Zulueta, 1995). Then in the early 1900s, mostly male Filipinos were recruited as agricultural workers in Hawaii, the West Coast, and even Alaska. Between 1906 and 1930, some 120,000 Filipinos worked in Hawaiian plantations (Abella, 1984). In the late 1950s, Filipinos worked in British North Borneo as barbers, musicians, and contract personnel (Lazo, Teodosio, & Sto. Tomas, 1982, as cited in Institute of Labor and Manpower Studies, 1984). This was followed after 1965 by groups of professionals such as doctors and nurses, domestic helpers, and sailors who went to the United States, Thailand, Malaysia, Indonesia, and Europe to seek greener pastures (de Guzman, 1993; Perez & Asis, 1993; Salazar, 1987; Samonte et al., 1995).

The next wave in the 1970s was a result of the overseas employment program launched in 1974. This was a step taken by the Philippine government to "ease the country's high unemployment and foreign exchange problems" (Department of Labor and Employment [DOLE], 1995). There was an exodus of both skilled and unskilled workers to the Middle East, mainly to Saudi Arabia in connection with infrastructure and development projects. These Middle East countries reaped the benefits of the increased oil prices. In the 1970s, blue-collar workers were in demand; by 1983, the demand was for professional, technical, and service workers. By this time, there was also an increased demand for seamen that was filled by Filipino seafarers.

Another wave of Filipinos were the Filipinas who married foreigners through the "mail-order bride" business (Paganoni, 1986). This started in the early 1970s and began to flourish with the help of travel bureaus, pen pal clubs, and individual homes that were used as fronts to entice Filipinas to avail themselves of the matchmaking services (Samonte & Carlota, 1989). In addition, there were Filipinos whose marriages to foreigners were "brokered" by Filipinos already established in the host countries (Brown, 1996) or by municipal officials in both the host and sending countries (Ishii, 1996; Samonte, 1996).

Data from the CFO show that from 1989 to 1997, there were 147,815 who registered with them as fiancées or spouses of foreign nationals. Of this number, the majority were bound for either the United States (41.0%) or Japan (30.2%). Other countries included Australia (8.9%), Germany (4.1%), Canada (3.7%), and the United Kingdom (1.6%).

The next decade saw more and more women leaving the country to go to East Asian (Japan, Korea, Hong Kong, Taiwan) and Southeast Asian (Singapore, Malaysia) countries, the Middle East (Saudi Arabia, United Arab Emirates, Kuwait, Quatar), and Europe (Italy, Spain) to work as entertainers, domestic helpers, or factory workers (Cheng; 1996; Go, 1998; Osteria, 1996; Tigno, 1993; Wong, 1996).

Starting out as a male-dominant phenomenon, international migration has become feminized, partly as a consequence of the changing gender roles and gender liberation of women in receiving countries as well as in the Philippines. Filipino women are now attracted to the labor market in the leisure and entertainment industries as well as the service sectors, particularly domestic work (Tigno, 1993). In 1994, domestic helpers made up 13.6% and entertainers made up 10.2% of the total land-based workers. New hirees saw even a greater proportion of those entering vulnerable occupations with 26.3% domestic helpers and 18.2% entertainers (DOLE, 1995, p. 7).

Four centuries after the first Filipinos were recorded to have worked on foreign ships, the Filipino diaspora continues.

OVERSEAS SITUATIONS

The major destinations of OFWs during 1985 to 1993, in descending order, are Saudi Arabia (49.2%), Hong Kong (9.5%), Japan (9.3%), United Arab Emirates (5.5%), Kuwait (3.7%), Singapore (2.4%), Qatar (1.7%), Bahrain (1.7%), Brunei (1.6%), Oman (1.5%), all other countries, 13.9%. Women migrant workers outnumber men. The median age for women is 29 whereas that for men is 36 years. Some 5.5% of the women are in the 15–19-year-old age group (DOLE, 1995, p. 1). On average, OFWs stay abroad for 3 years.

The profile of emigrants who registered with the CFO (CFO Statistics) show that for the 1981–2000 period, an average of 53,702 Filipinos migrated to various countries in the world each year. The majority (71.5%) of the 1,074,023 who were registered with the CFO still travel to the United States. Other major countries of destination included: Canada (13.2%), Australia (7.4%), and Japan (4.7%). By occupational grouping, before they left the Philippines, these emigrants included students (24.2%), housewives (21.4%), and professionals (10.4%). They were generally well educated, with one fourth (24.9%) having graduated from college and 15.7% having attended some college. The migrants were young; the majority (64.9%) were under 35 years old, with one fifth (19.8%) being 14 years old and under. A good proportion came from the major island of Luzon including the National Capital Region (40.2%), Central Luzon (17.5%), Ilocos Region (11.5%), and Southern Luzon (13.4%). The sex ratio of males to females was 67:100.

Remittances of OFWs have been as high as U.S. $6 billion per year (Romero, 1998, p. 1). These "remittances peak twice a year, in June when schools open and during the holiday season" (Romero, 1998, p. 6). This money is the country's biggest source of foreign exchange, which has helped the Philippines to survive the financial crises that the country has undergone repeatedly. From 1975 to 1994, these OFWs sent home a total of U.S. $18.20 billion.

Many of the Filipinos working abroad are employed in vulnerable occupations: as housemaids, entertainers, and construction workers. In 1998, from January to September, more than 500 overseas Filipino workers died. Figures from 1997 show that 576 Filipino workers died, 156 of them being women. Most of the deaths are due to accidents, crimes, and health problems (Associated Press, 1998).

There are also 936 overseas Filipinos being held in jails, mostly in the Pacific Rim countries (359), the Middle East and Africa (356), Central and South America (172), and Europe (49) (Associated Press, 1998).

THE MIGRATION CYCLE

Predeparture: Motivation

The exodus of Filipinos underscores their basic motivation, which is to better their lives by improving their economic lot. The push factors for labor migration have been mainly economic in nature: high unemployment rate; low wages and per capita/gross national product income; and deteriorating economic conditions as seen in the mass poverty, high inflation rate, huge foreign debts (Osteria, 1996). The unemployment rate in the Philippines increased steadily from 5.2% in 1976 to 11.2% in 1988 (Amante, 1990). Every year, an average of 680,000 workers join the labor force (Osteria, 1996). Underemployment figures were even higher, ranging from 20.9% to 30% in 1990 (Osteria, 1996). Moreover, a comparison of monthly salaries in manufacturing companies in various countries showed the Philippines to have the lowest salaries in all categories (Samonte, 1991). Even salaries of technical, professional, and managerial personnel show gross differences between the Philippines and its Asian neighbors (Samonte, 1990). The aggressive labor policy promoted by the Philippine government also created channels for the labor force to try their luck abroad (Cheng, 1996).

Social-psychological factors also affect the desire to migrate. These include values, particularly those stressing the welfare of one's family members; a sense of adventure; the status of having gone or lived abroad; and general curiosity (Jocano, 1992; Paganoni, 1986; Samonte, 1998b). The main driving force, however, is concern for the welfare of one's family (Cruz & Paganoni, 1989; Samonte, 1999; Tacoli, 1996). This is followed by an emphasis on self-development through one's exposure to a different kind of environment and culture, to different kinds of people, and to new knowledge. One can also travel.

For those who marry foreigners, other than for love and personal attributes of the partner, the reasons given by Filipinas who decide to marry and live abroad include (a) enhancement of one's status, (b) saving one from economic marginalization, (c) gaining the means to help one's family financially, (d) the belief that those children who are fair skinned with light-colored hair and eyes are beautiful, (e) the desire to petition for their family, (f) the pressure to get married, and (g) disappointment with a Filipino boyfriend (Cabigon, 1995; Samonte, 1994b, 1994c).

Pull factors such as a strong foreign currency, a great demand for certain skills or human power, facilitation of travel by syndicates, brokers, promoters, operators and fixers, geographical proximity (for Asian countries), and success stories continue to exert a strong influence on the decision-making process to work or live abroad (International Catholic Migration Commission [ICMC], 1998).

Whether they are push or pull factors that motivate the Filipino to go abroad, the move is seen as instrumental for attaining one's goals and is considered worth the risk (Beltran, Samonte, & Walker, 1996; Samonte, 1997b). The advantages are seen to outweigh the disadvantages (Samonte, 1998b). The main advantage is the financial reward and its instrumental value; because one is paid a higher salary, one can save for the future and provide for the education, shelter, and security of family members. The individual wishes to build a house, provide for her or his children's education, help the family financially, save for some big purchase, and secure the future (Añonuevo 1994; Ballescas & Guerrero, 1994; de Guzman, 1993; Salazar, 1987; Samonte, 1991). In the final analysis, there is a net gain.

Sojourning Abroad: Adjustment and Adaptation

Many difficulties face the Filipinos when they live and work abroad. These include sociocultural and financial problems, the physical environment, differences in family life, legality of one's stay, work opportunities and working conditions, personal and emotional problems, the perceived expectations of the family one left behind in the Philippines, and distrust (Arenas-Yap, 1997; Paganoni, 1986; Samonte, 1991, 1992a, 1992b, 1992c, 1994a, 1994b, 1994d). In some countries like Saudi Arabia, strict Islamic rules and practices such as the prohibition of alcoholic drinks, movie houses, and non-Muslim organizations, and the covering of women from head to toe are such difficult realities for Filipinos that they view the country as a "prison without bars" (de Guzman, 1993).

For Filipinos working in a country whose climate and food differ considerably from that of the Philippines, adjustment to extremely cold temperatures and different types of food may take a considerable toll (de Jesus, 1982; Jocano, 1992; Samonte, 1998b). Another major hurdle for these workers is loneliness. They miss their home and loved ones, find difficulty in adjusting to a seemingly unfriendly and alien culture, and worry about their family (ICMC, 1998). This is one of the main problems leading overseas Filipino workers to break their contract (Licuanan, 1982, p. 267).

On the home front, there are social costs, particularly households in which both spouses are migrant workers: Their children are left in the care of grandmothers or aunts and may become increasingly spoiled or more demanding of material things (Pertierra, 1992).

For those in vulnerable occupations such as entertainers and domestic helpers, they must face problems such as (a) rape, suicide, mental illness; (b) mysterious deaths; (c) drug use and addictions; (d) physical illness; (e) violence; and (f) unwanted pregnancies/becoming an unwed mother (Abrera-Mangahas, 1998; Amante, 1990; Arenas-Yap, 1997; Ballescas, 1992; Cheng, 1996; Cox, 1997; de Guzman, 1993; Shah & Menon, 1997; Stasiulis & Bakan, 1997).

Adjustment to a different culture is not easy, but Filipinas, having been socialized to be patient, persevering, and understanding (National Commission on the Role of Filipino Women, 1984) are frequently expected to be tolerant, ready to sacrifice, and to trust in God. This is a lesson they have learned through their religious training. Such endurance, however, is sometimes stretched to the limits, to the point where these workers suffer abuse and torture while others have even come home in a coffin (Abrera-Mangahas, 1998; Associated Press, 1998; Javate-de Dios, 1992; Jocano, 1992; Samonte, 1998b).

Central to the lives of Filipinos is their religion. Filipinos will always gather in church on Sundays. Sunday is a day of leisure for Filipinos, during which they often go to the malls to shop or window-shop. Filipinos, particularly those in Singapore, Hong Kong, and Japan, are well known for the places and areas they frequent. There they spend the afternoon trading stories, selling home-cooked Filipino food, clothes, and objects and generally enjoy their free time.

Filipinos transplant the Filipino culture to foreign shores, including their propensity to organize themselves. In Hong Kong alone, where there are said to be some 132,000 to 190,000 Filipino migrant workers (Samonte, 1997b), there are more than 200 Filipino associations/groups based on various religious, ethnic, and professional affiliations. They celebrate Philippine festivals and holidays (e.g., Santacruzan, which is celebrated in May) by serving typical Filipino dishes and having a program showcasing Filipino songs and dances (Filipino Community of Thailand, 1998). They set up Filipino restaurants and video rental stores, and they tune into the Filipino channel or read Filipino newspapers (Vergara, 1996). In a manner of speaking, they re-create their lives in the host country such that there is still that thread of continuity in the lives that they led in the Philippines.

Sources of social support include spouses (for those who are married to non-Filipinos), parents, and siblings, and the Filipino community. For a minority, additional sources of support include non-Filipinos, the government of the host country and other governmental agencies, church, and religious figures such as priests and nuns (Cahill, 1990).

Their social network is such that it is usual for these Filipinos to have not only a relative in the same foreign city where they are working but persons from their hometown as well. Through the *"kuha* system,"[2] friends and relatives work out the papers for their family members or friends and neighbors, vouching for the trustworthiness of these people (Samonte, 1995a). In so doing, they maintain their links to the hometown and the family back home.

Apart from adjusting to the new environment, permanent migrants, such as spouses of foreign nationals, must deal with individual and cultural differences. Studies have shown substantial differences between Filipinas and their foreigner fiancés or spouses (Brown, 1996; Cahill, 1990; Samonte, 1992c, 1994a; Samonte & Carlota, 1989). The Filipina is usually much younger than her spouse, better educated, Catholic, not previously married, from a large family, and frequently (46%) unemployed. The most common ways by which these couples met are through personal introduction (40%), at one's place of work (25%), or as a pen pal referred by a relative (25%). Other means are through a pen pal club (4%), becoming pen pals through ads/columns (3%), and through a marriage bureau (2%). On average, the couples have known each other for 15 months. A small percentage (2%) have known each other for a month or less (Samonte, 1994c). When asked about their plans, the most frequent response is to send financial support to one's family of origin, a practice that many a foreigner husband finds difficult to accept (Cahill, 1990; Samonte, 1992c, 1994c).

Marriages to foreign nationals are generally perceived as successful (Cabigon, 1995; Samonte, 1997a). The factors that contribute to successful marriages point to a twofold adjustment: to the marriage and marriage partner and to a new country and its sociocultural context (Cahill, 1990; Samonte, 1992c, 1994a, 1996). There are prejudices and biases that Filipinos must deal with. In countries where there are large numbers of Filipinas working as entertainers or domestic helpers, all Filipinas tend to be considered as such. Moreover, there are new cultural norms and practices to be learned. For example, in Japan, Filipina brides have had to deal with the following: problems with the Japanese language, limited socialization with co-Filipinos, being unable to practice one's religion, lack of support from the husband in raising children, differences in communication style, management of finances, expectations of in-laws regarding the wife's role, conflicts between Filipino and Japanese customs/values (Ishii, 1996; Kasuga, 1991; Samonte, 1994a, 1996). The two types of adjustment mentioned above are intertwined. Over time, acquiring greater facility with the new language and increased familiarity with the new environment contribute to better adjustment. Individual strength of character, confidence, realistic expectations, willingness to learn, patience, and flexibility are strategies reportedly utilized in their adjustment. Respondents also pointed to increased participation in the new environment, adopting the ways and practices of the host culture, and forgetting one's parents and Filipino ways (Cahill, 1990).

Return of Migrant Workers:
Reintegration, Impact, and Consequences

The word *Balikbayan* is used to describe returning Filipinos. The *Balikbayan* program was started by former President Ferdinand Marcos to induce overseas Filipinos to come home to the Philippines for the holidays. The program has continued to include overseas contract workers, that is, Filipino citizens who have been continuously out of the Philippines for a period of at least 1 year from the date of last departure, and former Filipino citizens and their families who had been naturalized in a foreign country. *Balikbayans* are entitled to privileges, travel tax exemptions, and visa-free entry into the country for 1 year (Blanc, 1996).

But are the migrant workers returning? There are very few studies to document this part of the migration cycle and to answer questions regarding their intentions to return, what skills they bring back with them, or whether they remain productive workers upon their return (Asis, 1995; Cariño, 1994b). In preparation for the possible return of Filipinos who were working in Hong Kong prior to the handover of Hong Kong to China, a study of these workers' plans and an inventory of their skills was conducted. Results showed that their most common skills were service oriented. As far as plans to return were concerned, half intended to stay in Hong Kong and only 14.3% planned to return to the Philippines after the handover. Logistic regression analysis showed the following variables to be significant in the worker's decision to stay in Hong Kong: number of family members employed in the Philippines, plans to buy a house and lot, and self-development (learning new skills, gaining confidence, and developing new interests). Thus, if they had more than two employed family members, had plans of buying property, and plans to develop themselves, in all likelihood these workers would stay in Hong Kong (Samonte, 1997b).

Given the out-migration of a large proportion of the labor force of the Philippines, one would think that this brain-and-brawn drain would create a considerable impact on the Philippines. However, despite the fact that the Philippines has had one of the world's highest rates of labor emigration in recent decades "and one of the world's most regulated recruitment systems, the three migration R's—recruitment, remittances, and returns—have had few noticeable effects on the structure of the Philippine economy and labor market" (Martin, 1993, p. 60). Pernia (1976, as cited in Cariño, 1994b) argued that the brain drain problem manifests the "basic inability of [the Philippine] economy to absorb the growing supply of certain high level skills" (p. 778).

Moreover, the returning migrants tend to be poorly integrated in their village of origin (Pertierra, 1992). They experience feelings of dislocation and restlessness such that they and their families may look forward to the time when the returning spouse becomes a migrant worker again (Samonte, 1998b). Most of them do not find a job on their return and either are unable to find jobs or consider the remuneration too low (Ballescas & Guerrero, 1994).

In general, lifestyles have changed for migrant families. There are changes in consumption patterns, with a marked increase in the consumption of essential over nonessential items. They also spend their earnings on consumer durables while also being able to put more children to school. Many of them become house owners or have their houses improved. Although a few invest their remittances in productive assets, more invest in the education of their children. Those who having been cheated by illegal recruiters find themselves "on the brink of subsistence as a result of loss of land and other assets due to the debts incurred through usurious loan agreements" (Ballescas & Guerrero, 1994, p. 725)

However, one may also note positive consequences of the migration experience. Financial advantages are primary. Earning more money enables migrants to meet their financial obligations and to purchase a lot of things that they could not afford otherwise. As far as personal growth and development are concerned, migrants frequently gain confidence; become self-reliant; learn new skills (e.g., cooking foreign cuisine); improve their financial skills (budgeting, managing a business, investment); broaden their perspectives (Cruz & Paganoni, 1989; Pertierra, 1992; Samonte, 1998b); gain prestige in their local community (Licuanan, 1982), and develop and enhance such positive traits as flexibility, independence, discipline, patience, industry, and thriftiness. Many show an enhanced awareness and appreciation for work and global events (Ballescas & Guerrero, 1994). They also get to know themselves better and learn to relate better to different kinds of people (Samonte, 1998b).

For the permanent migrants, such as the Filipina wives of Japanese men, studies have shown that they quickly learn the Japanese language, customs and practices; display role-appropriate behavior, particularly within the Japanese context; and learn to cope with racial discrimination (Samonte, 1994a, 1996). There are mixed findings regarding their level of marital satisfaction. On the one hand, in comparison to wives of other foreign nationals, these Filipinas were shown to have expressed a significant level of dissatisfaction (Cahill, 1990). On the other hand, in comparison to Japanese wives, the Filipinas married to Japanese showed significantly higher levels of marital satisfaction in the areas of management of family finances, discussion of wife's problems, and discussion of wife's ambitions (Samonte, 1997a).

For those in the United States, a study of 200 Filipino migrants and 100 Caucasian controls in the San Francisco Bay area showed that assimilation processes can be detected in Filipinos over a 12-year period (Card, 1984). However, their cultural assimilation occurred faster than their socioeconomic assimilation. Moreover, although socioeconomic and structural assimilation were moderately related to migrant adaptation, cultural assimilation was not. This moderate comingling with host nationals is also reported in other studies (Pertierra, 1992; Samonte, 1991, 1992b, 1992c), and it underscores the preference of Filipino permanent migrants to turn to conationals for friendship.

Immigrants are faced with differences in values, especially with respect to raising children. Used to having relatives take care of their young children, it is difficult for couples to leave their children in day-care centers. They also learn to deal with a different approach to the disciplining of children such as "talking to them" instead of spanking them (Heinonen, 1996).

Some negative effects of international migration include increased consumerism, infidelity, separation, breakup of the family, conflict, negative behavior of children left behind, faulty development of self-concept among adolescent children, and deskilling (Aganon, 1995; Javate de-Dios, 1992; Ballescas & Guerrero, 1994; Pertierra, 1992; Samonte, 1997b, 1998b; Santamaria, 1992). Although there are those who are able to save and invest their hard-earned money, others splurge their money or fail to invest their earnings productively.

A growing area of concern is the problem of children of cross-cultural marriages, particularly those Filipino-Japanese children who have been abandoned or whose fathers refuse to recognize them (Samonte, 1998a, 1998c).[3] These legal problems (i.e., the failure to register the child within the prescribed period and the refusal of the Japanese father to recognize the child) lead to economic problems such as lack of financial support for the child and even questions regarding the legitimacy of the mother's stay in Japan. Consequently, the mother, who is often an entertainer in Japan, loses the opportunity to earn her living in Japan. She is then repatriated and is unable to adequately support her Japanese-Filipino child(ren) in the Philippines.

These children must face also social psychological problems: The social stigma attached to being a child of a *Japayuki*;[4] the negative identity brought about by having a Japanese name and facial features which earns him/her the derogatory term *Hapon* ("Japanese," referring to World War II), being an illegitimate and often poor child; not having a father; and having to suffer from stereotypes attached to being both Filipino and Japanese (Samonte, 1998c).

The feminization of migration has led to a shift in the role of women, from the reproductive to the productive, consequently leading to more self-determination, autonomy, and transcendence, i.e. developing oneself through pleasurable and significant work (Cruz & Paganoni, 1989). Migration is a learning experience and may have a liberating impact for the women involved (Yun, 1996). However, the whole process is wrought with social-psychological costs that have neither been systematically studied nor measured.

A study on the reintegration needs of returning overseas workers (ICMC, 1998) shows that they need the following: (a) Information on various aspects of life, (b) financial advice and assistance, (c) local job placement, (d) self-employment opportunities or advice about how to open a business venture, (e) legal services for those who experienced abuse or exploitation, and (f) equitable opportunities for women so as not to marginalize them by relegating them to low-earning jobs and/or stereotypical roles. Although there are various reintegration programs offered by the Philippine government and by NGOs, there is not much awareness regarding these options. Moreover, there exists a significant lack of funds, human resources, and expertise among service providers.

Successful reintegration has been characterized by the economic viability of the returnee's business venture and by his or her self-efficacy. Factors that contribute to such perceptions include:

1) The returnees' ability to continue providing for their families; 2) involvement in an income-generating activity; 3) closer family relationship; 4) increased risk-taking behavior of women migrant returnees; 5) application of skills and learning acquired abroad; 6) emotional maturity and growth, positive sense of self-worth, increased self-confidence. (ICMC, 1998, p. 5)

QUO VADIS

The pressing question is, Where to from here? There are manifold issues that must be addressed. The first issue concerns the stand of government and policymakers. Despite the many bills filed in the House of Representatives and the Senate addressing the various aspects of overseas labor (welfare and protection, migrants' rights, recruitment, remittances, administrative procedures), policymakers still seem to be sending mixed messages about the real policy of government (Asis, 1992; Battistella, 1998; Samonte, 1995a; Samonte et al., 1995). Even the passage of the Migrant Workers and Overseas Filipinos Act of 1995 (Republic Act No. 8042)[5] was done in haste and as a reaction to the Flor Contemplacion case in Singapore.[6] Government, despite its protestations that overseas employment is not a government policy, has in fact admitted through this law that it has a deliberate labor-export policy. It uses the present level of unemployment and underemployment as the excuse for making this reality inevitable. Although it promises to protect the Filipino migrant workers, it also favors deregulation and the full-disclosure policy.[7] It assumes that the recruitment agencies will supply the information that the workers need to decide what is in their best interest. In other words, it is the migrant workers' responsibility and should anything go wrong, they only have themselves to blame (Battistella, 1998, pp. 104–105). However, this 1995 act exempts domestic workers and performing artists from the full-disclosure policy because these are vulnerable occupations. It remains to be seen what the implementing guidelines for the recruitment process in these two occupations will be.

A second fundamental question concerns the type of protection provided by the Philippine government. Clearly, the response systems of the various government agencies need to be integrated. The primary agencies mandated to take care of Filipino nationals overseas are the Department of Foreign Affairs and DOLE, but they cannot manage it alone. Many other branches of government and institutions need to be involved in the various stages of the migration cycle. Moreover, these interventions need to be coordinated with other NGOs that seek to protect the rights and welfare of migrant workers (Fajardo, 1992; ICMC, 1998; Samonte, 1997b; Samonte et al., 1995).

Although considerable research has been undertaken on what needs to be done and what types of interventions are appropriate, the findings and recommendations from all these studies still need to be incorporated in the plans and programs of the authorities and organizations concerned.

There are other issues that must be addressed on the national level. One example concerns the bilateral agreements to protect Filipino workers. To date, the Philippines has signed labor agreements only with Jordan, Iraq, and Quatar. There have been proposed agreements with various countries in Asia, the Middle East, and Europe, and the U.S. Trust Territories. However, these remain to be signed (Samonte et al., 1995). Much could also be said about the slow justice system that should mete out the proper punishment to illegal recruiters and to those who are exploiting migrant workers. Unfortunately, very few, if any, are prosecuted.

On the local level, municipal governments and NGOs need to adopt a more active role in providing the much needed support for these migrant workers and their families—for example, by providing them with accurate information about migration, devising investment opportunity schemes and livelihood programs to encourage them to stay, and providing the psychosocial support for the families of the migrant workers (ICMC, 1998; Samonte, 1994b).

Because migration is basically a family decision, families would do well to discuss seriously the various available options to solve economic and social/family problems and to put into question certain long-held values. Are family expectations putting too much pressure on women to take on the role of breadwinner? Are the values upheld by the family worth the risks and psychosocial costs that migrant workers must take and endure? With respect to the migrant workers or immigrants, do they ask themselves whether they have the strength and flexibility to weather the acculturative stresses and changes that come with migration? Are they willing to confront their own value systems and patterns of behavior and perhaps learn new ones?

Another important consideration is the role of psychologists in this whole process. First and foremost, psychologists need to take an active part in sharing knowledge in their various fields of specialization—cross-cultural, assessment, social, clinical, cognitive, developmental, educational, and industrial/organizational—to enable all concerned, be these the caregivers, policy makers, employers, or the migrant workers themselves and their families, to deal differently with the decision-making points, experiences, and challenges that come their way. Psychologists could contribute much more to policy formulation, human resource planning, research, and direct intervention in the various programs to assist migrant workers and their families (Samonte, 1993, 1998b).

Their inputs are critical in the various stages of the migration cycle, be this at the very start (as part of the preemployment orientation seminars that are important venues for disseminating information needed for decision making) or during the sojourn (by helping these sojourners in developing the skills needed on site) to the final reentry stage (to help them realign roles, rework family-community relationships, and reassess values and plans) (Samonte, 1992b; Santamaria, 1992).

The economic impact of migration has been well discussed by various Filipino economists as well as the World Bank (Amjad, 1996). They have pointed to both positive and negative effects. Migration has helped reduce unemployment by almost 40%. Moreover, the remittances have certainly helped the Philippine economy. However, migration has also led to negative consequences, such as the loss of professionals and highly skilled workers and the creation of skills shortages (Amjad, 1996).

However, there is a need for more systematic studies on the social psychological impact of international migration on the individuals concerned as well as on various institutions such as the family, community, and eventually, on the nation as a whole. The findings of such studies must be introduced into the agenda of both policymakers and the implementers of the overseas employment program. This is where the research agenda could use some much needed support (Samonte, 1993). Data gathered can help all concerned make better informed decisions and they can guide behavior. In addition, more longitudinal studies are needed to assess the impact of this phenomenon on individuals and their families and communities.

The saga continues. However, given what we know, we need not repeat history. The time to act is now.

NOTES

1. These are Filipinos who usually leave the country as tourists but stay on in a particular country in the hope of finding a job.

2. In the vernacular, *kuha* means "to get." This is a system whereby Filipinos get their relatives or friends to join them abroad by finding work for them or by petitioning for them or otherwise certifying means of support, to facilitate their entry into the foreign country.

3. The Japanese Nationality Law stipulates that a child shall be a Japanese national in any of the following cases:

1. When, at the time of its birth, the father or the mother is a Japanese national;

2. When the father who died prior to the birth of the child was a Japanese national at the time of his death;

3. When both parents are unknown or have no nationality in cases where the child is born in Japan (Civil Affairs Bureau, Ministry of Justice, http://www.moj.go.jp/ ENG-LISH/CIAB/ciab-04.html)

The condition "the father is a Japanese national at the time of birth" means "a child has the legitimacy of the Japanese father," or "a child is recognized legally by the father during the time the child is a fetus" (Kobayashi, 1997, p. 169). For this "recognition of the fetus" (*taiji-ninchi*), the father has to submit a copy of the family register. The mother, on the other hand, has to submit a copy of her passport or certificate of birth (which identifies her) and file the "Recognition Blank" which can be obtained at the local municipality office (Kobayashi, 1997, p. 171).

4. *Japayuki* is the term used to describe Filipinas and other Asian women entertainers working in Japan. It has a pejorative connotation, as it is patterned after the term *kara-yuki* (literally meaning "going to China"), which is used to refer to Japanese prostitutes bound for China to service the sexual needs of Japanese soldiers prior to and during the Second World War.

5. Republic Act No. 8042 was meant to institute policies of overseas employment and to establish a higher standard of protection and promotion of the welfare of migrant workers, their families and overseas Filipinos in distress. As stated in Section 2, "the State shall afford full protection to labor, local and overseas, organized and unorganized, and promote full employment and equality of employment opportunities for all. Towards this end, the State shall provide adequate and timely social, economic and legal services to Filipino migrant workers." It further states that "the State does not promote overseas employment as a means to sustain economic growth and achieve national development. The existence of the overseas employment program rests solely on the assurance that the dignity and fundamental human rights and freedoms of the Filipino citizen shall not, at any time, be compromised or violated. The State, therefore, shall continuously create local employment opportunities and promote the equitable distribution of wealth and the benefits of development" (Republic Act No. 8042) (Migrant Workers and Overseas Filipinos Act of 1995).

6. A Filipina domestic helper in Singapore, Flor Contemplacion was convicted and hanged by the Singaporean government for the murder of her friend and fellow domestic helper, Maga, whom she allegedly strangled to death for reasons unknown. This triggered a nationwide protest that compelled authorities to order an investigation of the case (*The Sunday Chronicle,* July 30, 1995, pp. 1–2, 7).

7. Full disclosure is "a mechanism whereby all parties to a contract declare the real terms and conditions of all aspects of the worker's employment" (Battistella, 1998, p. 99).

REFERENCES

Abella, M. I. (1984). Export of Filipino manpower. As cited in *Working abroad.* Manila: Institute of Labor and Manpower Studies.

Abrera-Mangahas, M. A. (1998). Violence against women migrant workers: The Philippine experience. In B. V. Cariño (Ed.), *Filipino workers on the move: Trends, dilemmas and policy options* (pp. 45–80). Quezon City, Philippines: Philippine Migration Research Network.

Aganon, M. E. (1995). Migrant labor and the Filipino family. In A. E. Perez (Ed.), *The Filipino family: A spectrum of views and issues* (pp. 79–96). Diliman, Quezon City, Philippines: University of the Philippines Office of Research Coordination.

Amante, M. S. V. (1990, October). *The "Filipino Dekasegi Rodosha" in Japan.* Paper presented to the Faculty of Business and Commerce, Keio University, Tokyo, Japan.

Amjad, R. (1996). Philippines and Indonesia: On the way to a migration transition. *Asian and Pacific Migration Journal, 5*(2–3), 327–346.

Añonuevo, C. (1994). Towards an understanding of international migration of women from the third world: The Philippine case. In A. N. Herrin (Ed.), *Population, human resources and development* (Vol. 2, pp. 989–1042). Quezon City, Philippines: University of the Philippines Press and the Center for Integrative and Development Studies.

Arenas-Yap, G. (1997). *A psychosocial study on mental distress among Filipino women migrants from Japan.* Unpublished masters thesis, Asian Social Institute, Department of Social Work. Manila, Philippines.

Asis, M. M. B. (1992). The overseas employment program policy. In G. Battistella & A. Paganoni (Eds.), *Philippine labor and migration. Impact and policy* (pp. 68–97). Quezon City, Philippines: Scalabrini Migration Center.

Asis, M. M. B. (1995). Overseas employment and social transformation in source communities: Findings from the Philippines. *Asian and Pacific Migration Journal, 4*(2–3), 327–346.

Associated Press. (1998, December 2). More than 500 OFWs die abroad. *The Philippine Star,* p. 6.

Ballescas, M. R. (1992). *Filipina entertainers in Japan: An introduction.* Manila, Philippines: Foundation for Nationalist Studies.

Ballescas, M. R., & Guerrero, S. H. (1994). Population processes and Philippine social institutions: The impact of fertility and migration on the family, the political institution and the church. In A. N. Herrin (Ed.), *Population, human resources development* (Vol. 2, pp. 691–750). Quezon City, Philippines: University of the Philippines Press and the Center for Integrative and Development Studies.

Battistella, G. (1998). The Migrant Workers and Overseas Filipinos Act of 1995 and migration management. In B. V. Cariño (Ed.), *Filipino workers on the move: Trends, dilemmas and policy options* (pp. 81–113). Quezon City: Philippines Migration Research Network.

Battistella, G., & Paganoni, A. (Eds.). (1996). *Asian women in migration.* Quezon City, Philippines: Scalabrini Migration Center.

Beltran, R. P., & Javate-de Dios, A. (1992). *Filipino women overseas contract workers: At what cost?* Manila, Philippines: Women in Development Foundation and Goodwill Trading Co.

Beltran, R. P., Samonte, E. L., & Walker, L., Sr. (1996). Filipino women migrant workers: Effects on family life and challenges for intervention. In R. P. Beltran & G. F. Rodriguez (Eds.), *Filipino women migrant workers: At the crossroads and beyond Beijing* (pp. 15–45). Quezon City, Philippines: Giraffe

Books.

Blanc, C. S. (1996). *Balikabayan*: A Filipino extension of the national imaginary and of state boundaries. *Philippine Sociological Review, 44*(1–4), 178–193.

Brown, P. M. (1996). For wedded bliss: Satisfaction of migrant partners of Australian residents. In B. Graziano & A. Paganoni (Eds.), *Asian women in migration* (pp. 123–145). Quezon City, Philippines: Scalabrini Migration Center.

Cabigon, J. V. (1995). Filipino wives in foreign lands. *Philippine Social Sciences Review, 52*(104), 63–75.

Cahill, D. (1990). *Intermarriage in international contexts*. Quezon City, Philippines: Scalabrini Migration Center.

Card, J. J. (1984). Assimilation and adaptation: Filipino migrants in San Francisco. *Philipppine Sociological Review, 32*(1–4), 55–67.

Cariño, B. V. (1994a). Development impacts on professional emigration from the Philippines. Towards an understanding of international migration of women from the third world: The Philippine case. In A. N. Herin (Ed.), *Population, human resources and development* (Vol. 2, pp. 763–784). Quezon City, Philippines: The University of the Philippines Press and the Center for Integrative and Development Studies.

Cariño, B. V. (1994b). International migration from the Philippines: Policy issues and problems. Towards an understanding of international migration of women from the third world: The Philippine case. In A. N. Herrin (Ed.), *Population, human resources & development.* (Vol. 2, pp. 785–816). Quezon City, Philippines: The University of the Philippines Press and the Center for Integrative and Development Studies.

Cariño, B. V. (Ed.). (1998). *Filipino workers on the move: Trends, dilemmas and policy options*. Quezon City, Philippines: Philippine Migration Research Network.

Cheng, S.-J. A. (1996). Migrant women domestic workers in Hong Kong, Singapore and Taiwan. In G. Battistella & A. Paganoni (Eds.), *Asian women in migration* (pp. 109–122). Quezon City, Philippines: Scalabrini Migration Center.

Commission on Filipinos Overseas. (1995). *Handbook for Filipinos overseas.* Manila, Philippines: Author.

Commission on Filipinos Overseas. (2001). *Estimated number of overseas Filipinos (as of December 2001)* [Online]. Available: http://www.cfro.org/statistics

Cox, D. (1997). The vulnerability of Asian women migrant workers to a lack of protection and to violence. *Asian and Pacific Migration Journal, 6*(1), 59–75.

Cruz, V. P., & Paganoni, A. (1989). *Filipino in migration. Big bills and small change.* Quezon City, Philippines: Scalabrini Migration Center.

Fajardo, L. O. (1992). GO-NGO networking for migrant women. In R. P. Beltran & A. Javate-de Dios (Eds.), *Filipino women overseas contract workers. At what cost?* (pp. 73–76). Manila, Philippines: Women in Development Foundation and Goodwill Trading.

Filipino Community of Thailand. (1998, December 6). *Souvenir Magazine for the Centennial Christmas in Thailand.*

de Guzman, A. F. (1993). "Katas ng Saudi": The work and life situation of the Filipino contract workers in Saudi Arabia. *Philippine Social Sciences Review,*

51(1–4), 1–56.

de Jesus, M. L. V. (1982). *Practices in the mental health screening of Filipino overseas workers. Philippine Studies, 30*, 272–282.

Department of Labor and Employment. (1995). *The Overseas Employment Program.* White Paper. Manila, Philippines: Department of Labor.

Go, S. P. (1998). Towards the 21st century: Whither Philippine labor migration? In B. V. Cariño (Ed.), *Filipino workers on the move: Trends, dilemmas and policy options* (pp. 9–44). Quezon City, Philippines: Philippine Migration Research Network.

Heinonen, T. (1996). Connecting family resilience and culture: Recreation and leisure among Filipino-Canadians. *Philippine Sociological Review, 44*(1–4), 210–221.

International Catholic Migration Commission. (1998). *A situational analysis of reintegration needs and response programmes for returned overseas Filipino workers* (Research Project Commissioned by the International Labor Organization Southeast Asia and the Pacific Multidisciplinary Advisory Team). Unpublished Report.

Ishii, Y. (1996). Forward to a better life: The situation of Asian women married to Japanese men in Japan in the 1990s. In G. Battistella & A. Paganoni (Eds.), *Asian women in migration* (pp. 147–164). Quezon City, Philippines: Scalabrini Migration Center.

Javate-de Dios, A. (1992). Japayuki-san: Filipinas at risk. In R. P Beltran & A. Javate-de Dios (Ed.), *Filipino women overseas contract workers. At what cost?* (pp. 39–58). Manila, Philippines: Women in Development Foundation and Goodwill Trading .

Jocano, F. L. (1992). Culture shock: The case of Filipina domestic helpers in Singapore and Hongkong. In R. P. Beltran & A. Javate-de Dios (Eds.), *Filipino women overseas contract workers. At what cost?* (pp. 22–28). Manila, Philippines: Women in Development Foundation and Goodwill Trading .

Kasuga, K. (1991). *A study of Filipino brides, Japanese families and village offices in a Japanese rural community.* Unpublished master's thesis, Tokyo Institute of Technology, Tokyo.

Kobayashi, K. (1997). *Mannual for migrants: Information for living in your community.* Tokyo, Japan: Catholic Diocese of Yokohama Solidarity Center for Migrants.

Lazo, L. S., Teodosio, V. A., & Sto. Tomas, P. A. (1984). Contract migration policies in the Philippines. Geneva, Switzerland: International Labor Office, 1982 as cited in *Working abroad.* Manila, Philippines: Institute of Labor and Manpower Studies.

Licuanan, P. B. (1982). Beyond the economics of overseas employment: The human costs. *Philippine Studies, 30*, 262–271.

Martin, P. L. (1993). Migration and trade: The case of the Philippines. *Asian Migrant, 6*(2), 60-65.

Migrant Workers and Overseas Filipinos Act of 1995. (*Republic Act No. 8042 and its Implementing Rules and Regulations*). (n.d.). Pasig, Philippines: Philippine Overseas Employment Administration.

National Commission on the Role of Filipino Women. (1984). *UPS-CE-NCRFW research on values of rural women in different cultural settings: Implications for education, social and economic policies and development programs.* 9pp.

Osteria, T. (1996). The Filipinos in Japan: Demographic trends and patterns. In W. V. Villacorta & M. R. D. Carlos (Eds.), *Towards a shared future through mutual understanding* (pp. 93–114). Proceedings of the First International Conference on Philippine-Japan Relations. Manila, Philippines: De La Salle University Press and Yuchengco Institute of Philippine-Japan Relations.

Paganoni, A. (1986). *Paano ba ang mabuhay sa ibang bansa?* [Beyond Philippine shores: What is it like?]. Quezon City, Philippines: Scalabrinians.

Perez, A. E., & Asis, M. M. B. (1993). Understanding Filipino migration. *Philippine Social Sciences Review, 51*(1–4). Quezon City, Philippines: College of Social Sciences and Philosophy.

Perez, A. E., & Patacsil, P. C. (Comp.). (1998). *Philippine migration studies: An annotated bibliography.* Quezon City, Philippines: Philippine Migration Research Network.

Pertierra, R. (Ed.). (1992). *Remittances and returnees. The cultural economy of migration in Ilocos.* Quezon City, Philippines: New Day.

Romero, P. (1998, December 2). OFW remittances to hit $1.8B. *The Philippine Star*, pp. 1, 6.

Saito, S. (1977). *Filipinos overseas: A bibliography.* New York: Center for Migration Studies.

Salazar, Z. (1987). The outflow of Filipinos to the Bundesrepublik Deutschland since the 1960's. *Philippine Journal of Public Administration, 31*(4), 463–486.

Samonte, E. L. (1990, November). *Philippine-Japan relations: Can we go beyond economic parameters?* Lecture delivered at the International Education Center, Tokyo.

Samonte, E. L. (1991). Filipino migrant workers in Japan: In search of a better life—The price of a dream. *Philippine Journal of Industrial Relations, 13*(1–2), 75–122.

Samonte, E. L. (1992a, September 2). *Lessons from research and planning programs for the psychological welfare of overseas workers.* Paper presented at the Conference on NGOS/POs: Partners of Overseas Contract Workers, Philippine Overseas Employment Administration, Pasig, Philippines.

Samonte, E. L. (1992b). The psychosocial costs of post-employment of overseas workers. *Philippine Journal of Public Administration, 36*(3), 282–294.

Samonte, E. L. (1992c). Sources of stress and coping mechanisms of Filipinas in West Germany and Holland. *Philippine Journal of Psychology, 25*(1), 20–39.

Samonte, E. L. (1993, August). *The role of psychologists in policy-making regarding overseas contract workers.* Paper presented at the 30th Annual Convention of the Psychological Association of the Philippines, De La Salle University, Manila, Philippines.

Samonte, E. L. (1994a). The acculturation of Filipina brides in Japan and opportunities for intervention. *Philippine Journal of Psychology, 27*(1–2), 43–58.

Samonte, E. L. (1994b, September). *Filipina entertainers in Japan: Issues of survival and responsibility.* Paper read at the UNIFEM Kitakyushu First Conference, Kitakyushu, Japan.

Samonte, E. L. (1994c, September). *Filipinos: Quo vadis*. Paper presented at the 13th International Association of Historians of Asia (IAHA) Conference, Sophia University, Tokyo, Japan.

Samonte, E. L. (1994d). Foreign worker issue: Research findings, research gaps, and implications for policy makers in the Philippines. *Diliman Review, 44*(4), 15–21.

Samonte, E. L. (1995a, July). *Filipino migration: Beyond economics*. Paper presented at the 3rd Legislative Workshop, Nasugbu, Batangas, Philippines.

Samonte, E. L. (1995b, January). *The urgent challenge: Developing migrant workers' socio-psychological skills and competence*. Paper presented at the Asian Migrant Women: Issues and Problems conference, Bangkok, Thailand.

Samonte, E. L. (1996). Filipino-Japanese marriages: A window to new Philippine-Japan relations. In W. V. V. & M. R. D. Carlos (Eds.), *Towards a shared future through mutual understanding* (pp. 130–160). Proceedings of the First International Conference on Philippine-Japan Relations. Manila, Philippines: De La Salle University Press and Yuchengco Institute of Philippine-Japan Relations.

Samonte, E. L. (1997a). Filipino-Japanese couples: Communction variables and marital satisfaction. *Sikolohiya, 1*(1), 1–11.

Samonte, E. L. (1997b, July). *Filipino migrant workers in Hong Kong: Inventory of skills and long-term plans*. Paper presented at the 55th Annual Convention of the International Council of Psychologists, Graz, Austria.

Samonte, E. L. (1998a, November). *Filipino-Japanese families: Challenges toward multiculturalism*. Paper presented at the Fourth Social Sciences Research Lecture Forum, Silliman University, Dumaguete City, Philippines.

Samonte, E. L. (1998b). Filipino migrant workers: Cost-benefit analysis of their sojourn and its implications. In A. B. I. Bernardo, N. A. Dayan, & A. A. Tan (Eds.), *Understanding behavior bridging cultures. Readings on an emerging global psychology* (pp. 77–99). Manila, Philippines: De La Salle University Press.

Samonte, E. L. (1998c, November). *Japanese Nationality Law and Japanese-Filipino children*. Paper presented at the Law and Security of Japan: Impact on the Philippines Conference, College of Law, University of the Philippines, Quezon City, Philippines.

Samonte, E. L. (1999, March). *Filipino values at the threshold of the new millennium*. Paper presented at the International Workshop on The Asian Values and Vietnam's Development in Comparative Perspectives, Hanoi, Vietnam.

Samonte, E. L., & Carlota, A. J. (1989). The mail-order marriage business: A reconsideration of the Filipina image. In A. T. Torres (Ed.), *The Filipino woman in focus. A book of readings* (pp. 77–99). Amaryllis Bangkok, Thailand: UNESCO.

Samonte, E. L., Maceda, C. P., Cabilao, M. I., del Castillo, B. P., & Zulueta, M. P. F. (1995). *Issues and concerns of Overseas Filipinos: An assessment of the Philippine Government's response*. State of the Nation Reports. Quezon

City, Philippines: University of the Philippines Center for Integrative and Development Studies and University of Philippines Press.

Santamaria, F. (1992). Problems regarding family relations and children of migrant workers. In R. P. Beltran & A. Javate-de Dios (Eds.), *Filipino women overseas contract workers. At what cost?* (pp. 69–72). Manila, Philippines: Women in Development Foundation and Goodwill Trading.

Shah, N. M., & Menon, I. (1997). Violence against women migrant workers: Issues, data and partial solutions. *Asian and Pacific Migration Journal, 6*(1), 5–30.

Stasiulis, D. K., & Bakan, A B. (1997). Regulation and resistance: Strategies of migrant domestic workers in Canada and internationally. *Asian and Pacific Migration Journal, 6*(1), 31–57.

Tacoli, C. (1996). Migrating "for the sake of the family"? Gender, life course and intra-household relations among Filipino migrants in Rome. *Philippine Sociological Review, 44*(1–4), 12–32.

Tigno, J. (1993). Migration, the market and society: Issues in Philippine labor flows to Japan. *Philippine Social Sciences Review, 51*(1–4), 57–78.

Vergara, B. M., Jr. (1996). Betrayal, class fantasies, and the Filipino nation in Daly City. *Philippine Sociological Review, 44*(1–4), 79–100.

Wong, D. (1996). Foreign domestic workers in Singapore. In G. Battistella & A. Paganoni (Eds.), *Asian women in migration* (pp. 87–108). Quezon City, Philippines: Scalabrini Migration Center.

Yukawa, J. (Comp). (1996). *Migration from the Philippines, 1975–1995. An annotated bibliography.* Quezon City, Philippines: Scalabrini Migration Center.

Yun, H. A. (1996). Foreign maids and the reproduction of labor in Singapore. *Philippine Sociological Review, 44*(1–4), 33–57.

15

Migration to Australia

Eric E. Rump

In every generation immigrants have brought great enrichment to our nation's life. (Acknowledgement written in 1999 by prime minister, John Howard, and poet Les Murray; cited in Greene, 1999)

Australia's history is a history of immigration. (Lowenstein & Loh, 1977)

THE EARLIEST MIGRANTS

The very first migrants arrived in Australia at least 50,000 years ago, from Asia. The date is somewhat uncertain, and reports based on archaeological work at Jinmium in northern Australia have even suggested habitation over 100,000 years ago (Woodford, 1996). The incredibly ancient dates possibly derived from contamination, by windblown sand, or by flaking from older rock faces. In the rock shelter at Jinmium, ancient rock art, stone implements, and circular engravings were found. Dating was by means of thermoluminescence (Fullagar et al., 1996). Recently, optical and radioactive carbon dating methods have yielded variable and considerably younger estimates, many less than 10,000 years (Roberts et al., 1998). Nevertheless, several other places such as the Malakunanja II site in northern Australia have supported the idea of human colonization of Australia at least 50,000 years ago. Stone Age artifacts found there included silcrete flakes, red and yellow ochres, and a grindstone (Roberts, Jones, & Smith, 1990).

Even more remarkable than these artifacts are the human bones of "Mungo Man," discovered by Alan Thorne of the Australian National University. The bones were excavated at the (dry) Lake Mungo site in New South Wales, and have been dated "in excess of 60,000 years ago" (Dayton, 1999). The area was occupied for many thousands of years, and many other remains have provided ample evidence of the hunter-gatherers' lifestyle. The Aborigines ate rat-kangaroo, the brown-haired wallaby, and fish and shellfish, for instance. Fishnets and traps were used as long as 25,000 years ago (Flood, 1995).

It seems likely that there were a number of distinct early waves of different peoples. For example, the remarkable discoveries at Kow Swamp in Victoria included skeletal remains of at least forty individuals of a very robust type. The large heads had very thick bone, foreheads were receding, and brow ridges were prominent. Despite these archaic features, the burials were recent compared with Mungo Lake, ranging from about 9,500 to 13,000 years ago. These robust people buried their dead with care, one being lain on a bed of mussel shells, and some wore elaborate decorations, such as a headband of kangaroo teeth (Flood, 1995, p. 61).

The Aboriginal people of today contribute much to the cultural life of Australia. They are now recognized as the original custodial owners of Australia, thanks to the High Court decision in the *Mabo* case (Rowse, 1993). Unfortunately, Eddie Mabo from the Murray Islands died before the decision was delivered. Many Aboriginal traditions reflect their very ancient knowledge orally. For example, a myth is told among Aborigines of South Australia about Kangaroo Island, a home of ancestral spirits. Ngurunderi was one such ancestor. When his wives ran away to Nar-oong-owie, Ngurunderi ordered the water to rise up and drown them. They turned to stone and are seen as two rocks off Cape Jervis. The story may well reflect ancient experience; about 10,000 years ago, Kangaroo Island was joined to the mainland, and was inhabited by Pleistocene "Karta" people who left behind many campsites and massive hammer stones and pebble choppers (Flood, 1995, pp. 139–147).

Aboriginal paintings continue other ancient traditions. The Guyon figures painted on rocks in the Kimberley region of Western Australia probably predate the Lascaux cave paintings in France. The figures are thin spirit people of an ethereal kind. Paintings were used to illustrate dream-time myths, to depict food sources, to indicate occupation of a shelter, and generally to maintain traditions (Kupka, 1965). In this century, painters like Margaret Preston recognized the spiritual quality of Aboriginal rock, bark, and body painting (Bambrick, 1994, p. 309). Albert Namatjira became the first famous Aboriginal painter of landscapes (Hall, 1962). Now there are many Aboriginal artists using a myriad of styles (displayed for instance at the Tandanya Aboriginal Cultural Institute in Adelaide), although "dot paintings" are probably the best known genre. For instance, the Australian Arts Ambassador, Heather Kemarre Shearer wrote: "My art is culturally appropriate to being an Arrente woman" (Smolicz, 1998, p. 14).

MIGRATION DURING THE LAST FEW CENTURIES

Exploration

In about 1606, Willem Jansz explored the west coast of Cape York on the Dutch ship *Duyfken*. Shortly thereafter, an English East-India Company ship, the *Tryal*, was wrecked in the Montebello Islands off Western Australia. During the 17th century, the Australian coast (then "New Holland") was steadily charted by such seamen as Abel Tasman, but little was reported to excite the commercial interest of the Dutch East India Company.

The early encounters with Aborigines were a presage of later warfare and mistreatment. For instance, Jan Carstenzoon in 1623 casually mentioned a kidnapping: "So our people seeing their opportunity, caught a black by a string which was attached round his neck and brought him on board" (Newby, 1986, p. 499). William Dampier encountered unfriendly Aborigines in 1699, and reported: "I thought it high time to charge again, and shoot one of them, which I did" (Newby, 1986, p. 501). In this case, Dampier was acting in defense of himself and his men. British interest increased as a result of Captain James Cook's voyages. In 1770, his ship *Endeavour* sailed along the east coast, with a week's stay in Botany Bay. This proved crucial for later settlement, as he claimed New South Wales for the British crown. Two further voyages by Cook in 1773 and 1777 consolidated the charting of the Tasmanian and Australian mainland coasts.

The Penal Colonies

In the mid-18th century, British prisons were overflowing. When the possibility of transporting convicts to Australia arose in the British Parliament in 1785, Sir Joseph Banks stated: "Botany Bay is the only part of this country which I have visited and I am confident that it is in every respect adapted to the purpose" (Hughes, 1982, p. 17). Thus, the first European migrants were convicts transported from Britain, together with their guards (soldiers) and administrators. "During the first forty years of the colony a total of only 57,000 people came including both prisoners and free men and women, and only eighteen percent of them were free settlers" (Lowenstein & Loh, 1977, p. 2).

The first convict settlement began in 1788 at Sydney, New South Wales. Captain Arthur Phillip arrived in the First Fleet with 1,044 people, including 759 convicts. The main purpose was to relieve Britain's overcrowded jails, though a supplementary motive involved keeping out the French and other possible colonial powers. Gradually, soldiers and officials, aided by convict labor, established farms, fishing and other enterprises around the Sydney region. After only 3 years, thousands of convicts were arriving, and there was a plan to send regular shiploads of convicts twice a year. Provisions were also sent from England, but often arrived in poor condition. "It was so worm-eaten that this meant practically nothing. Of 60 lbs of meat issued in one to two messes, 40 lbs was bone, and the remainder was almost too far advanced in putrefaction for even hunger to get it down" (Hughes, 1982, p. 95).

Another large penal colony was established at Port Arthur, Van Diemen's Land (now Tasmania). From 1803 to 1853 a total of about 69,000 convicts were transported from Britain. Most of their crimes were against property (81%), such as petty theft; only 3% were for crimes like murder and rape. Port Arthur prison expanded to become a major industrial complex, with very cheap labor. Nearby, there were a coal mine, a brickworks, timberworks, and farms. One of the specialized jobs was that of flagellator; convicts, particularly if rebellious, were often flogged till near death. For those who did not survive, there was the nearby Isle of the Dead. Despite the terrible conditions, Port Arthur grew to be a thriving township, with over a thousand free migrants, including soldiers and their families, by 1830. Today the story of the settlers' and convicts' lives can be experienced at the site's Interpretive Centre.

A third major convict settlement was established on Norfolk Island, now an Australian territory with a degree of self-government. Captain Cook named the Island after the Duchess of Norfolk in 1774, and described it as a "Paradise" (Clarke, 1986, p. 9). In 1788, shortly after the First Fleet dropped anchor at Botany Bay, 23 carefully selected convicts were transported again to start the prison settlement on Norfolk Island; they comprised 17 men and 6 women, "the best of a bad lot." The youngest, Charles McLennan, had been convicted at age 14 years for "stealing a bladder purse, with a value of one penny, one gold half-guinea, one half-crown, and six pennies" (Clarke, 1986, p. 11). Life for most convicts on Norfolk Island was extremely hard, as can be judged today from the ruins of the underground cells. Six weeks after the landing, the new commandant, Lieutenant Philip King, ordered the first punishment: John Batchelor received three dozen lashes for stealing rum. I personally find these stories moving, as I was born in Norfolk (England). Indeed, Blackbourne Point on the Island was possibly named after a naval officer, David Blackburn, whose distant relatives still live near my birthplace (Neville, 1975).

The first Norfolk Island settlement failed, but later a second settlement was attempted, in order to take the worst offenders from the New South Wales and Van Diemen's Land jails: it was to be "a place of the severest punishment short of death." One commandant became known as "Lasher" Morisset; under his rule, the death penalty became a relief from horror (Clarke, 1986, chap. 12). In 1840, the transportation of convicts was mercifully abolished. Perhaps that convict era has had a lasting effect on the Australian culture. Bushrangers like Ned Kelly are romanticized in art and legend (Bambrick, 1994, p. 306). Convict labor and skills certainly assisted early economic development. Fixed social strata were undermined, as some convicts became prosperous members of society after serving their sentence, giving rise to a relatively egalitarian society.

Migrant Settlers

Eventually, even Norfolk Island was to receive "normal" migrants. Descendants of the *Bounty* mutineers were living on Pitcairn Island with Tahitian Islanders they had taken with them. In 1855, the Pitcairners petitioned Queen Victoria for help, as their tiny island could no longer support the growing community. They were given Norfolk Island, and the following year 193 migrants with surnames such as Christian set forth. To them, Norfolk Island was a wonderland: They saw their first cattle, lavatories, and (to them) exotic fruits and vegetables. Today, this delightful island can still surprise visitors: No air conditioners or gaming machines are allowed, cows have priority on the roads, and goods are still landed from ship to shore on a small dinghy (or two if required).

On the mainland, free settlers began to arrive from 1793 onward. New farming lands were discovered after Blaxland, Wentworth, and Lawson crossed the Blue Mountains to the hinterland of New South Wales in 1813, encouraging more settlers. Indeed, by 1831 the British government financially assisted their emigration, so that 70,000 arrived during the next 10 years. Some of the British migrants needed no assistance, as they were already wealthy. They were granted pastoral leases and became an English "squattocracy." For example, Thomas Macqueen was an English landowner and member of Parliament, who obtained 10,000 acres in the Hunter Valley (New South Wales) in 1823. He sent out mechanics, tenant farmers, and shepherds, and he spent £42,000 on plant and stock. Macqueen himself lived 4 years in Australia and encouraged others to follow (Sherington, 1990, p. 31).

Waves of migration tended to grow as new industries were founded or the economy boomed. To some extent these waves were encouraged by assisted passages, or special contracts such as those for the Kanakas, described later. The gold rushes of the 1850s in Victoria and New South Wales stimulated a large intake, and the total population reached 1 million. In South Australia, the early British colony was based on farming (wheat and wool), with the ideal of religious and political freedom. The early discovery of silver, lead, and copper placed the economy on a more secure footing and encouraged Cornish miners to come (described in a later section).

Following federation of the six colonies in 1901 to form the Commonwealth of Australia, immigration policies became a federal responsibility. For some time, Britain continued as the mainstay for both trade and migrants. To help with industrialization, assisted migration from Britain was increased following federation, growing from 4% of all immigration in 1905 to a peak of 58% by 1911 (Sherington, 1990, p. 96). Gradually, Australia has grown stronger links with the rest of the world, especially the Americas, Europe, and Asia. In the 1920s, the numbers employed in manufacturing increased greatly, and "immigrants probably accounted for 60 percent of the increase" (Sherington, 1990, p. 114).

Just as migration was encouraged during boom periods, it tended to decrease during times of depression. During the Great Depression from 1929, Sherington (1990) noted: "With almost one-third of its own workforce unemployed, Australia could not afford to import even industrial skills" (p. 115). The Depression was often tragic for those who, hoping for a brighter future, did migrate. Many went "on the track" looking for any work. New migrants who did obtain work were blamed for others' unemployment: "The Poms [British migrants] came out here and took our jobs," one recalled.

The period 1949 to 1970 saw a massive influx of about 2.5 million immigrants largely from Europe, who were refugees or taking part in the General Assisted Passage Scheme. These migrants were needed to work on the tunnels, dams, and roads for the Snowy Mountains Hydro-Electric Authority, established in 1949, and similar ventures. Many of the new arrivals first stayed in camps with barrack-style huts and basic furniture, such as Bonegilla in Victoria and Greta in New South Wales. Ila Marosszeky recalled: "Everything was provided, I didn't have to worry anymore." Mostly the men went away to work, returning to the camp at weekends. "On Mondays, all the ladies would queue up outside stores, holding their broken camp beds," laughed Ila (Biggins, 1997, p. 59).

Promotion of population growth remained an objective of government policy for more than 25 years after World War II, during a period of rapid growth and economic expansion. In the immediate postwar years, resettlement of refugees from Eastern Europe was predominant. Thereafter, "the Australian government entered into formal agreements to sponsor migration from a number of European countries, including Germany, the Netherlands, Italy, Greece, and Malta" (Bambrick, 1994, p. 225). As a consequence, those from Italy now form the largest subgroup of the resident population, apart from those born in Australia, the United Kingdom, or New Zealand (Australian Bureau of Statistics, 1999, p. 81). Many came as families; if they were bachelors, they "sent back to Italy for brides" (Dare, 1988, p. 110). "Chain immigration" occurred from particular regions. This happened also with Greek migrants: Ithicans were drawn to Melbourne, Kythenans to Sydney, and so on (Dare, 1988, p. 186). Apart from Athens, Melbourne probably has the largest number of Greek-speaking citizens of any city in the world. Charles Price of Monash University considers that if the whole period of European migration is considered, the German migrants' contribution has been considerable (reported by Way, 2000).

Only White migrants were welcome. "The Immigration Restriction Act of 1901 provided a so-called dictation test. It was designed to exclude any immigrant who because of his color might dilute the white strain" (Dare, 1988, p. 121). During the immediate post–World War II period, Arthur Calwell (Australia's first minister for immigration) maintained a strict "White Australia" policy (Dare, 1988, p. 142).

In 1973, the Whitlam Labor government adopted a policy of nondiscrimination in the selection of immigrants, leading to the admission of more Asians. Later, they were supplemented by the "boat people" from Vietnam. In 1976, a year after the change of regimes in Saigon, a small fishing-boat with five Vietnamese refugees arrived in Darwin Harbor. During the following 5 years just over 2,000 such boat people arrived on the north coast of Australia. Although there was public disquiet at such illegal immigration, the government reacted sensibly by encouraging legal applications for refugee and family-reunion programs. By 1992, about 150,000 Vietnamese and Chinese had been admitted.

SPECIALIZED WORKERS

The following section describes in more detail a few of the specialized groups of migrants who came to Australia during the last 2 centuries, the remaining traces of their lives, and their current contributions to the Australian identity.

At various times since early European settlement, development of Australia's natural resources has required specialist workers. Such workers have been encouraged to migrate to Australia, sometimes alone and sometimes with their families. An outline of some of these interesting groups follows.

Chinese Gold Miners

The discovery of alluvial gold near Bathurst (New South Wales) in 1851, followed closely by further discoveries in Victoria, lead to the first of Australia's gold rushes. Immigration boomed, with the population doubling in 5 years (Bambrick, 1994, p. 171). Among those hopeful gold prospectors were many Chinese. By 1855, there were 8,000 Chinese immigrants in one mining camp north of Ballarat. To stem the flow, the Victorian Legislative Council introduced a poll tax of £10 on every Chinaman who landed in the colony. In 1857, many Chinese migrants landed at Robe (South Australia) to evade the poll tax in Victoria. Robe, being 150 kilometers west of the state border, was the nearest convenient port in South Australia. In 1 year, over 17,000 Chinese passed through Robe on the way to the goldfields, with some being robbed along the walking tracks, and a few being caught and jailed. Today, there are memorials to these transitory Chinese such as the Chinese Cairn erected beside the boat haven in Robe, and the several wells they built along the Coorong tracks.

There was "constant agitation on the part of white settlers to have the intake of Orientals stopped" (Hornadge, 1971, p. 4). This agitation often erupted into violence. "As the gold began to peter out, the White diggers accused the Chinese of unfair tactics, and beat them up, robbed them and, on the slightest excuse, lynched them on the spot" (Folkard, cited by Hornadge, 1971, p. 5). At times terrible riots occurred on the goldfields, with the Chinese miners attacked and their property destroyed such as during the Lambing Flat riots of 1861 (Hornadge, 1971, pp. 8–9). Mine managers at the Lothair Goldmine in 1873 attempted to break a miner's strike by bringing gangs of Chinese miners to work. However, the retaliation by striking miners (mostly Cornish immigrants), who wrecked buildings and attacked the Chinese, forced a retraction by the management. The mine was reopened on the strikers' terms (Hornadge, 1971, p. 11). Even today, surprisingly intense prejudice against the Chinese can be found in Australia (Rump, 1972).

The Cornish Miners

Between 1840 and 1880, many copper miners emigrated from Cornwall (England) to various parts of Australia. The colonies of New South Wales, South Australia, and later Victoria had assisted immigration schemes to attract such workers. In South Australia, copper mines were opening, whereas in Cornwall they were closing. Most of these old mines at places like Burra, Kapunda, and Moonta have been closed since copper prices slumped in 1923, but the shafts and equipment may still be seen. For instance, the engine house and chimney, built of local limestone at Moonta, are very like those built in Cornwall (Faull, 1983, p. 69). The Cornish heritage survives in many ways: place names, like Truro; "Kernewek Lowender" festivals such as the one held on Yorke Peninsula; food, such as "pasties," which are vegetable and meat pies once taken down the mines for lunch; and miners' cottages, some of which are now used for tourist accommodation. As they say: "Has't ee been to Moonta?

No? Then ees never travelled!" (Faull, 1983, p. 109). If you avoid travel, you can still experience Australia's little Cornwall from the wonderful photographs in Philip Payton's (1978) pictorial history. However, it is much more fun to join in the Furry Dance with the 80,000 other visitors during the Kernewek Lowender (Hockley, 1999).

The Afghan Cameleers

Camels were introduced into Australia to help explore and settle the vast arid outback. Burke and Wills used camels in their 1860 expedition from the south to the north of the continent. In the 1870s, the Overland Telegraph Line was constructed from Adelaide to Darwin with the aid of Afghan cameleers. Some came from Afghanistan itself, but many also came from Pakistan and the Middle East. Their skills were invaluable in opening up the country, and then in the provision of transport. About 3,000 "Ghans" were involved in this work, until cars and trains replaced the camels in the 1930s (Cigler, 1986). Even the police at one time used camels in the outback on their patrols. "The combination of a policeman on a camel and a black tracker walking beside him became a trademark" of the arid lands (Cigler, 1986, p. 118).

Although there were never many Afghan migrants, their heritage lives in many forms. In Marree (South Australia), there are families, who are proud of their Afghan ancestors who ran the camel breeding station at one time. They have rebuilt the mosque; the original was built about 1882, the first mosque in Australia (Cigler, 1986, p. 119). Camels roam wild in central parts of Australia and are occasionally rounded up for export to the Near East. Camel races are organized in Marree and near Alice Springs, where I believe Australian riders beat American novices, by tradition. Many of the early cameleers were attracted by city life, and several cities gained substantial mosques such as the one built at Adelaide in 1890. Today, the mosque in the city is a modern, imposing building.

German Migrants and Their Vineyards

By the 1820s, Australia was being promoted in Germany as a desirable haven for those oppressed by population growth and by religious conflicts (Tampke, 1982, p. x). In 1837, surveyor-general Colonel William Light surveyed the area north of Adelaide, which came to be called the Barossa Valley. Meanwhile in Europe, George Fife Angas formed the South Australian Company to promote migration, and discussed the plight of Silesian Lutherans with Pastor August Kavel. In 1842, the first community was established in the valley at a village now called Bethany. Further settlements spread along the valley, with several towns developing, each with its own Lutheran church (or more than one when disputes occurred). By 1891, 7.7% of South Australia's population was of German origin (Walker, 1975). The area was recognized as suited to grapevines, and Johann Gramp planted his first commercial vines in 1847 at Jacob's Creek (Explorer Directory, 1986). One of my favorite wines is called Jacob's Creek. Today, the Barossa Valley is the most prolific wine region of

Australia with many outstanding wineries, bearing such names as Bethany Wines, Siegersdorf, Henschke, Kaiser Stuhl, Karlsburg, and Wolf Blass.

The lives of the German migrants were disrupted by the two world wars in odd ways. Use of the German language was banned, place names were Anglicized, and families were placed in internment camps. Nevertheless, for most of the period of European settlement, German migrants have met with much success and have praised Australian life. Robert Schachner (1912/1982) wrote of his visits, when as "German Bob" he worked in a mine, a woolshed, and a factory: "The principles upon which the Australian laws are based are the only ones capable of solving social conflict" (p. 41). The Australian working man, Schachner wrote, "is always a 'gentleman.' He shows it above all in his behavior towards the opposite sex" (p. 31). Some of its members might not concur! One of the German migrants deserving special mention was Ferdinand von Mueller, baron of Württemberg, some of whose extensive correspondence has recently been published (Home, 1998). He arrived in Australia in 1849 as a pharmacist but established his reputation as a scientific botanist. He explored northern Australia, wrote over 1,500 scientific books and papers, and sent an enormous number of novel botanic specimens to Kew Gardens, then the center of imperial botany. Kew's director was stunned by his zeal, and commented: "His scientific ability is surpassed only by his modesty" (Rothwell, 1999). His memorial consists of the wonderful Royal Botanic Gardens in Melbourne, where visitors may learn of von Mueller's work on the guided tours. Despite his success, he nevertheless felt his life a failure, as he was never able to compile a complete, systematic flora of Australia.

Arrivals from Germany continued during the 20th century, though at a relatively low rate. The total number from 1847 to 1910 was only 55,300 (Cropley, Becker, & Lüthke, 1986). In the 1950s, the rate somewhat increased, and Germans have accounted for nearly 3% of postwar immigrants. Given the growing economic prosperity of Germany and its central position in the European Union, why would they wish to leave for Australia? Cropley et al. (1986) compared 164 applicants for an immigrant visa to Australia with 162 nonapplicants, in Germany. The groups were similar in age, income, and so on, and were asked their views about Germany by means of a 59-item questionnaire. The applicants were found to score relatively high on three factors: narrowness of horizons, limitation of personal prospects, and frustrating burden of deductions. Thus they tended to agree with statements like these from the three factors concerned: "It is impossible to build up anything worthwhile in West Germany any more," "I feel that my personal freedom is too restricted here," "It is impossible to save here." Perhaps their views were based more on hope of green pastures, rather than realistic appraisal of any benefits Australia might offer.

The Japanese Pearl Divers

Some of the most specialized workers to come to Australia were the Japanese pearl divers, whose industry was established at Broome. This is a small port on the northwest coast of Western Australia. Early in the 20th century, about 80% of the world's mother of pearl came from this area, and there were over 400 luggers plying from the port. The industry was disrupted during World War II, when about 500 of the Japanese Australian divers and their crews were interned; and then later when plastic buttons reduced the demand for pearl. However, by 1970 Broome was producing over 60% of the world's cultured pearls, this being a much safer method than the earlier deep-sea diving. Its legacy is apparent in Broome's Japanese cemetery, where over 900 pearl divers are buried. An annual Shinju Matsuri Festival honors the dead of Japanese and other Asian migrants.

Kanaka Workers from Pacific Islands

Queensland "squatters" (White plantation owners) lived in style, growing crops like sugarcane, cotton, and bananas. Their luxury was supported by a system of indentured labor, the Kanakas, until this ceased in 1904. To obtain these workers, "blackbirders" sailed to islands in the Pacific and Torres Strait such as Vanuatu and lured men to work in Queensland on low wages, using persuasion, fraud, or occasionally force. From 1847 to 1904, about 57,000 islanders were brought to Australia, to its shame. Most were men, but hundreds of women were brought, too: Those from the Marshall Islands "often fetched $40 each" (Evatt Foundation, 1991, p. 7).

This "migration" was eventually banned by an act of the new Commonwealth Parliament in 1901. Subsequently many islanders were deported. However, "masters of ships commissioned to repatriate the Islanders were not at pains to return the Islanders to their home islands and these Islanders found themselves in yet another strange and inhospitable land" (Evatt Foundation, 1991, p. 9). Those that remained in Australia were considered aliens, and by 1919 they were "totally excluded from the sugar industry" (Moore, 1985, p. 332). Many died in cyclones and in an influenza epidemic; the few hundreds remaining subsisted by farming poor hilly country, and by fishing. Life was marginally easier for the first generation born free in Australia. "A few owned farms, but most remained rural laborers" (Moore, 1985, p. 336).

It is estimated that there are now up to 20,000 descendants of the Kanakas, though this is uncertain as they are not distinguished in the census. Although some have moved to other areas, their greatest concentration remains along the Queensland coast, particularly in the towns of Bundaberg and Mackay. Often regarded as Aborigines by White Australians, the islanders have suffered from discrimination; but they are not eligible for official benefits available to Aboriginal people. The Evatt Foundation (1991, p. 26) recommended that they should be eligible for benefits in relation to housing, education, and so on.

TALES OF HARDSHIP AND OF SURVIVAL

In the early years of European migration, Australian life could be quite primitive when compared to industrialized Europe. For instance, in the 1850s, Cornish miners were camped along the creek in Burra, and even living in caves dug into the banks. Indeed, some of these dwellings comprised four rooms linked by tunnels, with chimneys protruding into the footpaths above (Faull, 1983, p. 44). Examples of these "grotto houses" can still be seen in Burra.

Even these homes were luxurious compared with the abode of the Herbig family. Johann Friedrich Herbig, his wife, Caroline, and their children lived from 1855 to 1860 in a hollow gum tree, enlarged with canvas. The tree still stands near the main road in Springton, South Australia, where photographs of the family and its history are displayed. The family had 16 children, though only 2 while living in the tree.

The early migrants who managed to build a house might still suffer hardships. In "a migrant's lament," Listemann (1851/1982) recounted his efforts to establish a market garden at Fullarton. (This is now a suburb of Adelaide, next to my own district.) He started with a small hut, whilst his family lived in the city, until he had built a timber house. However, he found the clay soil hard to dig, the distant well often became dry, crops withered in the sun, and worst of all, the neighbor's cows frequently broke the fence to invade his greener pastures. "I was convinced that staying on any longer would ruin us all," he wrote, and the family returned to Germany on the first available barque.

My own family's migration was relatively easy in the 1960s, as I had visited Australia before, and I had a secure position at the university. Even so, it was an unfortunate start when we found that our family of two parents and three children were accommodated on the liner *Arcadia* in a small cabin with only four berths. On arrival, we became rather ill and were assured that this was merely "homesickness." We discovered the actual cause after a week, on the day prior to leaving our temporary hotel accommodation. Plumbers arrived to repair the gas leak in the cooker: We had been suffering from gas poisoning. Of course, homesickness can be real, too. In a poem titled "But I Want to Run Away," Nitu Banerji (1994) elegantly described the pull of India when he is in Australia; it began "I want to go there all the time. But I want to run away when I am there."

Many postwar migrants did not go initially to the luxury of a hotel but rather to a migrant camp. Janina Rozanski (born in Poland) came to Australia in 1949 and was sent first to Bonegilla camp and then Cowra camp where her daughter Janina was born. She was meant to be called Helen, but the registrar confused the mother's name for the intended baby's name, so Janina it was. Later, mother Janina and her children were reunited with her husband at Woodside Migrant Camp, near Adelaide. "But they were still building these rooms before we came and the workers had never done any cleaning after themselves, so it was ankle deep in wood shavings and bits of plaster" (Rozanski, 1994, p. 12). She thought, "My God! What have I done? Why did I come?" Years later she reflected that she now belonged in Australia: "I would not live anywhere else" (Rozanski, 1994, p. 13).

Hardships experienced in more recent times may seem pale when compared with those in earlier times. Nevertheless, trauma can leave lasting memories, especially during childhood. An Adelaide friend, now a successful professional man, recalls arriving in Australia with his parents as a 12-year-old in 1957. He had developed "mumps" on the ship from England and was isolated in the ship's hospital. On docking, he was transferred directly to the Northfield Hospital in Adelaide, still isolated from his family. Before being reunited a few days later, he was scrubbed with disinfectant. His next traumatic memory derived from his first day at a private school. He arrived in a pristine new school uniform, equipped with an English-style shoulder satchel for books. Unfortunately, at that time the Australian boys used handheld schoolbags. The head teacher, making no comment, led the "new chum" to the school-assembly yard, where the child was paraded for the amusement of his peers. He felt very alone, exposed, and different.

Some particularly poignant stories of hardship and survival relate to children, especially orphans. Nearly 10,000 orphans were sent from Britain to Australia between 1947 and 1957. Some of these children were not in fact orphans but rather were born to unmarried mothers or into poor families who could not care for them. Moreover, some were pitifully separated from siblings after arrival in Australia, and many were told untruthfully that all their relatives were dead. "The history of child migration in Australia is in many ways a history of cruelty, lies and deceit" (Bean & Melville, 1989, p. 111).

The Christian Brothers ran one major religious organization that cared for orphans. By the time of the Second World War, the brothers had four large orphanages operating in Western Australia. They functioned as such for some decades, but two of them were changed to agricultural colleges in the 1960s and the other two were closed in 1983. As orphanages, they were often plagued by a lack of funds, discipline problems, and the extra difficulties of disabled children, but they attempted to provide schooling, trade skills, and apprenticeships (Coldrey, 1993).

Regrettably, it has become clear that several of the children suffered severely from the actions of a few of the brothers. An official report in 1938 noted that one brother "is impetuous in punishing....he says he finds it difficult to restrain himself when annoyed" (Coldrey, 1993, p. 397). The later accounts of the boys themselves were more vivid. For instance, Colin Reidy recalled: "I ran away that night and got half a mile down the road and along comes a Brother on a horse and picked me up. I was put into a cold shower and flogged for three hours" (Bean & Melville, 1989, p. 118). There were also many accusations of sexual interference with boys, but "denial by a Brother accused usually meant his word against that of a boy. This usually resulted in warnings to the Brother and no further action" (Bean & Melville, 1989, p. 399). It is only in more recent times that the long-lasting effects of such physical and sexual child abuse have been realized.

Orphan girls suffered too, according to accounts of the Goodwood Orphanage (Adelaide), run by the Sisters of Mercy. Children "were often subjected to depraved acts rather than Bible studies" (Turner, 1998). Girl migrants were flogged with thick leather straps, and would scavenge for crusts of bread thrown on the floor. Peggy Rush (Gill, 1997, p. 217) recalled "beltings and more beltings."

Those children with their families, even living in migrant camps, had a much more positive experience of Australian life. Krystyna Pindral (1994, p. 58) wrote: "I loved Woodside Camp and had a very happy childhood there. It was a very safe and happy environment." Similarly, a friend of mine who is now retired and sailing on his yacht, has spoken with fondness of his time at Bonegilla camp, near Melbourne. He had already learnt some English on the ship to Australia and did not want to stay in the camp school merely to learn more English. He noticed the local children rode to their school on horseback, so he borrowed a horse and joined them. He quickly adapted to his new home.

Many tales of triumph over adversity are told in Katherine Goode's (1997) book on refugee children in Adelaide. For example, Neary was an adopted girl from Cambodia. There during her fractured early childhood, she had been gored by a buffalo, lost her best friend in a Khmer Rouge rocket attack, and her parents also died in the war. After adoption by an Australian aid worker, Neary enjoyed her new life in Adelaide, with its gardens, lorikeets and nourishing food: "Neary inhaled food as it were air." After she became depressed with thoughts of her previous trauma, Neary regained her smile when she discovered packets of elastic bands. She made jumping elastics so that she could once again play her Cambodian game "Jumping to the Heavens" (pp. 49–60).

Lew Kathreptis (1994) told a delightful story of his childhood in the small Greek community of Adelaide. His mother established a Greek restaurant, but in those days not long after World War II she found that Australian-style steak and chips were more in demand than Greek cuisine. Lew and his brother, however, preferred food prepared in the Greek style, so they cooked their own meals. This led to an interesting career. After traveling in Greece and elsewhere, and sampling different types of cuisine, he returned to set up his own Mediterranean-style restaurant, incorporating Moroccan and Egyptian recipes. Later, he became chef to Australia's High Commissioner in London.

THE CONTEMPORARY SCENE

Clearly, contemporary Australia is culturally diverse. In the 1996 census, 2.6 million people (from a population of about 17 million) spoke a language other than English at home. There were 282 languages, including 170 Aboriginal and Torres Islander languages. Through the 1990s, the proportion of Australians born overseas has been about 23%. Those born in the United Kingdom continue to be the largest group, making up 6% of the population. However, the fastest growing groups are from Asia: Those from Singapore increased by 17% in the 1997–1998 period, and from Indonesia, 15%. Of the 77,000 arrivals between 1997 and 1998, 61% were under the normal migration program; 11% were under the humanitarian program; and the remainder were New Zealanders (who do not require a visa) and children born overseas to returning citizens (Australian Bureau of Statistics, 1999). The planned intake for the year 2000 was a total of 82,000, in four categories: skilled workers, 35,000, family reunions, 32,000, humanitarian (e.g., refugees), 12,000, and special eligibility, 3,000. Some businesspeople, ethnic spokespersons, and politicians consider that the intake should be higher (Way, 1999), and indeed in 2001 an extra 6,000 migrants were allowed to enter (Coorey, 2000).

The top 10 countries now providing migrants to Australia are shown in Table 15.1. Neighboring New Zealand has top spot, no doubt associated with the special Trans Tasman Travel Arrangement with Australia. The United Kingdom is still an easy second. The next most important countries are less obvious: China and South Africa. Of course, both these countries have experienced social unrest in recent years, which might encourage the desire for a more stable environment. For example, Margaret Dreyer (an accountant) and her family moved from Pretoria, South Africa to Adelaide, to escape the "violence in Pretoria:" "People in Adelaide don't realize how fortunate they all are" (Lloyd, 1998).

In the last few years, there has been a large growth in long-term visitors to Australia for educational purposes. Such visitors are mostly young (75% are less than 25-years-old) and usually aim for either secondary or tertiary levels of study. Because such students pay full fees or have scholarships, their entry is encouraged by educational institutions and by commonwealth and state governments. The proportion of long-term arrivals intending to study in Australia has increased from 11% between 1977 and 1978 to 51% between 1997 and 1998 (Australian Bureau of Statistics, 1999, p. 21).

The second main reason given for coming to Australia is for employment (14% of all long-term arrivals). Such migrants are mainly in their middle years (70% between 25 and 44 years old). Employment opportunities are diverse, as exemplified by some of the migrants interviewed by Helen Chryssides (1995): Dorinda Hafner, African cook and author; Gasia Dobrowolska, actress; Tenshi Ayukai, oceanographer; Hao Zhou, operatic tenor. The third main group are people seeking long-term holidays, rather than permanent migration. These people form 9% of long-term arrivals, tend to be young (66% being 20 to 29 years old) and are mainly from the United Kingdom or Japan (Australian Bureau of Statistics, 1999, p. 22).

Table 15.1
Top 10 Countries of Birth for Migrants to Australia
During the Year Ending June 30, 1998

Country	Number
New Zealand	14,723
United Kingdom	9,193
China (excluding Taiwan)	4,338
South Africa	4,281
Hong Kong SAR	3,194
India	2,786
Philippines	2,769
Vietnam	2,311
Bosnia-Herzegovina	2,135
Indonesia	1,917

Note: From Australian Bureau of Statistics (1999, p. 12).

These broad categories disguise the often very personal reasons for migration. Scutt (1993) outlined some of the motives given by women for their travels. Ofelia Lopez escaped from political persecution in El Salvador. Sylvia Hennessy accompanied her Australian husband to Australia, leaving family and friends, in part to escape economic-rationalist cuts to health services and in part to escape anti-Irish attitudes in England. Tui Taurua left New Zealand for Australia partly as a result of the breakdown of her second marriage; she rejoined her first husband (her son's father) for a period in Australia. Such individual motives are not disclosed by bare statistics.

New migrants to Australia tend to congregate in particular areas, as would be true of other countries. The major cities of Melbourne and Sydney are the main attractions. In 1996, residents of inner Melbourne suburbs included about 16% recent migrants (arriving between 1991 and 1996), and residents of inner Sydney suburbs included 12% recent migrants (Australian Bureau of Statistics, 1999, p. 39).

The above account relies mainly on literary sources. Mention should be made of other media which provide a contemporary view of Australian migrants. A documentary film called *The Fifth Continent* was made in 1998 by the Australian Broadcasting Corporation, covering post–World War II migration (directed by Stephen Salgo). One of the film's participants recalled being given a Granny Smith apple on arrival: "It was like baptism into Australia." A video documentary called *Migrants in Australia—An Italian Experience* from Equality Media (1997) told the story of the Patti family who arrived from Sicily in 1949 and dealt with topics like language difficulties, the need for new skills, homesickness, and discrimination. A more extensive source is provided by the New South Wales Board of Studies (New South Wales Education Department) in the form of a three-disc set on CD-ROM called *Making Multicultural Australia*. Information on this resource is available at www.boardofstudies. nsw.edu.au/.

Despite the advantages of continuing migration and official programs encouraging the assimilation of migrants, some Australians wish to restrict their numbers more severely, or their countries of origin. Prejudice may be shown against migrants from southern Europe or those from Asia (McConnochie, Hollinsworth, & Pettman, 1988). Racism may be subtle or blatant and is still experienced by many from non-English-speaking backgrounds. Kee and Hsieh (reported by Sanson et al., 1998) found that about half of Taiwanese students in Australia had experienced discrimination. A Malaysian Australian student reported: "A friend of mine was walking through the university and one of the Aussies spat on her because she was Asian. She felt really bad because she couldn't do anything." A member of the South Australian Parliament, Steve Condous, remembered as a 7-year-old when his Greek-born father was spat on. At school, he himself was abused daily, both physically and verbally (Crabb, 1998).

In recent years the antimigrant attitude of a minority of Australians has been formalized by a new political party called One Nation, led by Pauline Hanson. Initially the party had some small success in a Queensland state election, but this has not translated to significant support in Australia as a whole. Indeed, a 1998 survey of young Australians found that most were opposed to racial discrimination. Seventy-one percent of Year 5 pupils, and 68% of Year 10 pupils, considered that "making sure people of all races are treated equally" was an extremely important issue (Australian Council for Educational Research, 1998).

On the other hand, illegal immigration is of general concern, due especially to the boats from Asia that have been captured off Australian coasts or, in some cases, those that have beached in isolated areas. "Migrant trafficking was one of the world's fastest-growing and most profitable illegal businesses," according to Andreas Schloenhardt (1999) who is studying the topic.

ASSIMILATION AND HEALTH

What factors are associated with easy assimilation in modern Australia, and on the other hand what factors are associated with stress and even ill health in migrants? It is possible to mention only a few of the many studies in this area. As would be expected, assimilation is correlated in a study of British migrants with feeling more Australian, with feeling that the decision to emigrate was correct, having an active vocabulary, and having an assimilated spouse (Richardson, 1974, data for 1966). With men from Latvia, Putnins (1981, p. 60) found that assimilation to Australia was correlated .34 with the personality trait of extraversion.

The health of different migrant groups has been considered in many studies. One of the largest national surveys was the 1989–1990 National Health Survey undertaken by the Australian Bureau of Statistics, involving a random sample of 41,519 respondents aged 15 years or over, reported by Stuart, Klimidis, and Minas (1998). These authors also analyzed data from a 1993 census of mental health in Victoria, involving 922 general medical practitioners reporting on a total of 10,848 patients who consulted them. It was found that a person's country of birth had a significant effect on the prevalence of mental disorder, whether reported by patients or by their doctors. Rates of mental disorder "were consistently high amongst those born in Greece, and low amongst those born in the U.K./Ireland or in South East Asia, compared to the Australian-born" (Stuart et al., 1998, p. 22).

In Perth hospitals (Western Australia), admissions during 1990 to 1992 showed high rates for schizophrenia among Polish and Yugoslavian migrants and for organic psychotic disorders among elderly Dutch and Italian migrants. Nevertheless, there was "an overall normalization of rates of European migrants towards those of the Australian born" (Bruxner, Burvill, Faxio, & Febbo, 1997, p. 541).

Stoller and Krupinski (1973) considered that learning to speak English was the most important factor for non-British migrants to assist assimilation and adaptation. Of course, proficiency in English is crucial in obtaining employment, too (Wooden, 1990, p. 236). However, the ill health suffered disproportionately by particular migrant groups is a complex matter, with both the nature of the illness and the country of origin being important. For example, clinical depression tended to be higher for British and Eastern European immigrants. Krupinski (1975) found, moreover, that age was important; for instance, British migrants aged 10 to 15 years when arriving in Australia were subsequently vulnerable to personality disorders and transient disturbances. Krupinski (1975) also reported a number of social factors related to psychological disturbance within migrant communities in Victoria. These included previous experience of war, being single rather than with a family, and having experienced a decline in work status due to nonrecognition of overseas qualifications. Length of residence in Australia proved a hazard for some groups: British males showed a higher incidence of alcoholism, the longer they had been resident (Krupinski, 1975, p. 56).

In a review of migrant health studies in Australia, Krupinski (1984) indicated many contributory factors. Some were concerned with diseases like tuberculosis contracted overseas or previous traumatic experiences; some concerned characteristics such as dietary and smoking habits; and some concerned the general community, such as working conditions, length of residence, and social supports. For example, work injuries were "markedly over-represented in unskilled migrant workers with poor knowledge of English" (Krupinski, 1984, p. 935). Similarly, Taft (1985) proposed a multidimensional framework for understanding the complex topic of adjustment and satisfaction of migrants. "Whether they considered that Australia would or would not provide such satisfaction was determined by their experience in the first few years after immigration in what could be called a testing period" (Taft & Doczy, 1962, p. 32).

In a comprehensive longitudinal study, Scott and Scott (1989) noted the important mediating effect of the acquisition of cultural skills (p. 88, Figure 5.2). In this study, 307 migrants were interviewed and completed questionnaires in their countries of origin (within Europe or America), and then again in Australia. It was found that "the level of cultural skill is a significant correlate of several kinds of subjective adaptation and role performance" (p. 93). For instance, with a subsample of 90 working migrants, job performance was correlated .27 with diverse cultural experience (p. 87, Table 5.4).

Refugees may be particularly vulnerable to both physical and mental health problems. Research with refugees from the former Yugoslavia in Adelaide suggested that various symptoms could occur, such as insomnia, depression, anxiety, anger, and loneliness (Procter, 1998; Williams, 1997). Various types of social support can reduce the effects of stress and illness, as the extensive work of Cohen (1988) has shown. Research supervised by myself with back pain patients, including Polish migrants in Adelaide, illustrated the benefits of social support: Rated pain severity and hypochondriacal tendencies were lower for patients with companionship, and with friends who provided tangible support (Kramarczuk, 1990).

Social support for migrants may be provided at three levels. First, there is help from the general Australian community; the ability to speak English is most important for access to such social support. Second, the migrant's own cultural community is also vital, particularly during the early stages of resettlement. Across 10 groups defined by country of birth, Kraus (1969) found that the larger the migrant community in New South Wales, the lower was the psychiatric hospital admission rate. The family provides the third level of social support. Ben-David (1995) suggested that support provided by a cohesive family system can be of prime importance in coping with the stress of migration. On the other hand, family conflict, especially intergenerational conflict, may increase problems. Rosenthal, Ranieri, and Klimidis (1996) reported that many adolescent Vietnamese refugees in Australia believed they held less traditional values than their parents. Conflict arising between parents and children may exacerbate serious problems like depression, psychosis and conduct disorder (Williams & Westermeyer, 1983).

A recent paper by Rump, Parker, and Fallo (1999) reported correlations between various aspects of social support on the one hand, and health problems on the other for 45 adult Serbian refugees living with at least one child in Adelaide. Three questionnaires in Serbian translations were used. The General Health Questionnaire (Goldberg, 1981) was used to assess anxiety and insomnia, severe depression, social dysfunction, and somatic symptoms. These scales showed good internal consistency, with Cronbach's alpha values ranging from .80 to .94. Access to social support was measured in several ways, using a General Information Questionnaire. Variables included duration of residence in Australia, ability to speak and read English, contact with relatives, participation in Serbian community activities like sport (Procter & Lynch, 1995), church services, dances, and receipt of support from the Serbian community. Family functioning was examined using the Edinburgh Family Scale (Blair, 1996), to measure enmeshment (the degree to which family members are "highly sensitive to, involved with and dependent on each other" (Blair, 1996, p. 16), and the degree of family conflict.

In general, it was found that health problems were mitigated for those refugees with access to social support. Correlations between health problems and access to Australian community resources were negative and mostly significant. Refugees who had been in Australia for a longer period, and who were able to communicate in English, had fewer health problems. For example, longer residence was associated with less social dysfunction and fewer somatic symptoms (both correlations were $-.47$). With regard to access to Serbian community support, again it was generally true that the higher the participation within the local Serbian migrant community, the lower were reported health problems. For example, participation correlated $-.49$ with somatic symptoms.

Family support was also important. Family enmeshment reduced anxiety ($r = -.40$), social dysfunction ($r = -.46$), and somatic symptoms ($r = -.39$). On the other hand, family conflict was associated with increased anxiety ($r = .45$), severe depression ($r = .51$), and somatic symptoms ($r = .41$). Social support was thus shown to be important in ameliorating various health problems amongst these refugees, at the host community level, in terms of participation in the local migrant community, and as provided by a close family network.

CONCLUSIONS

Australia is a continent of migrants and descendants of migrants. Adventurous clans of Homo Sapiens arrived at least 50,000 years ago from islands to the north, and their voyages across at least 70 kilometers of ocean may well represent one of the first seafaring migrations of our species. Much later, during the last 230 years, waves of migrants from Europe populated the coastal areas of the continent and have forged a strong, industrialized society. Both the early Aboriginal cultures and the later groups from Europe have provided many examples of human exploration, expansion and development. There have thus been many opportunities for the assessment of differences between cultural groups, and the effects of the migration experience itself.

Migrant groups from Europe included people with specialized skills, which they put to use in their new country. This was of economic and social benefit and has provided lasting legacies. These legacies include industries such as agriculture, fishing, and mining; private and public buildings; and less tangible assets such as parliamentary democracy, and styles of food preparation. Even in my small local district of Unley, on Australia Day 2000, as many as 11 varied countries of origin were represented amongst the 20 new citizens at the citizenship ceremony. As many as 60% of Australians are "ethnically mixed," with about 20% having four or more ancestries, according to Charles Price of Monash University (Way, 2000). The thriving mix of cultures has led to robust variation and creativity.

Many modern studies of migrant settlement have shown the main factors involved in successful outcomes, such as participation in the workforce. The employment rate is higher for migrants who speak good English, who have been in Australia for some time, who have tertiary qualifications, and who were granted a visa as a result of business skills or employer nomination (Vanden-Heuvel & Wooden, 2000).

On the other hand, the successive waves of migrants have been associated with problems of various kinds. Racism has been rife in the past, and is still evident to some degree. Illegal immigrants, arriving by air and sea, are disrupting services and posing problems for immigration authorities (McKinnon, 1999). Running detention centers, such as the large Woomera center, cost about $130 million in the year 2000 (Eccles, 2000). Some parts of Australia, such as South Australia, would welcome additional migrants, whereas other places like Sydney are already overcrowded. In rural areas, migrants who are medically qualified are especially welcome to work with outback communities.

With the world's population continuing to grow at an unsustainable rate, pressure will grow for Australia to increase its intake of migrants. Refugees from the many conflicts in Asia and Europe add to the pressure. To many observing from afar, Australia must seem like an attractive, nearly empty, haven. The natural limit is set by restricted water supplies. Even now, growing salinity in both river and artesian systems is a major issue, limiting much further expansion of human settlement.

REFERENCES

Australian Bureau of Statistics. (1999). *Migration Australia 1997-98.* Canberra, Australia: Australian Bureau of Statistics.

Australian Council for Educational Research. (1998). *Schools and the social development of young Australians.* Hawthorn, Victoria, Australia: Australian Council for Educational Research.

Banerji, N. (1994). But I want to run away. In P. Moss (Ed.), *Voicing the difference* (pp. 32–33). Adelaide, Australia: Wakefield Press.

Bambrick, S. (Ed.). (1994). *The Cambridge encyclopedia of Australia.* Cambridge, England: Cambridge University Press.

Bean, P., & Melville, J. (1989). *Lost children of the empire.* London: Unwin Hyman.

Ben-David, A. (1995). Family functioning and migration: Considerations for practice. *Journal of Sociology and Social Welfare, 22,* 121–137.

Biggins, F. (1997). Australia calling. *Australian Good Taste, 2*(11), 56–60.

Blair, C. (1996). The Edinburgh Family Scale: A new measure of family functioning. *International Journal of Methods in Psychiatric Research, 6,* 15–22.

Bruxner, G., Burvill, P., Faxio, S., & Febbo, S. (1997). Aspects of psychiatric admissions of migrants to hospitals in Perth, Western Australia. *Australian and New Zealand Journal of Psychiatry, 31,* 532–542.

Chryssides, H. (1995). *Different light: Ways of being Australian.* North Blackburn, Victoria, Australia: Harper Collins.

Cigler, M. (1986). *The Afghans in Australia.* Melbourne, Australia: Australasian Educa Press.

Clarke, P. (1986). *Hell and paradise.* Ringwood, Victoria, Australia: Viking (Penguin Books Australia).

Cohen, S. (1988). Psychosocial model of the role of social support in the etiology of physical disease. *Health Psychology, 7,* 269–297.

Coldrey, B. M. (1993). *The Scheme: The Christian Brothers and childcare in Western Australia.* O'Connor, Western Australia: Argyle-Pacific.

Coorey, P. (2000, April 4). Skills key to 6000 rise in migration. *The Advertiser* (Adelaide, Australia), p. 11.

Crabb, A. (1998, July 11). They spat at dad and called me dago. *The Advertiser* (Adelaide, Australia) p. 3.

Cropley, A., Becker, K., & Lüthke, F. (1986). Forming the decision to emigrate to Australia: Some recent German experience. *Australian Journal of Politics and History, 32,* 52–62.

Dare, T. (1988). *Australia: A nation of immigrants.* Frenchs Forest, New South Wales, Australia: Child & Associates.

Dayton, L. (1999). Ageing fast. *New Scientist, 162* (2188), 13.

Eccles, D. (2000, March 11). Woomera detainees to double. *The Advertiser* (Adelaide, Australia), p. 37.

Evatt Foundation. (1991). *Australian South Sea Islanders: A report on the current status of South Sea Islanders in Australia.* Sydney, Australia: Evatt

Foundation.

Explorer Directory (1986). *A visitors guide to the Barossa Valley* (3rd ed.). Tanunda, South Australia: Barossa News.

Faull, J. (1983). *The Cornish in Australia.* Melbourne, Australia: Australasian Educa. Press.

Flood, J. (1995). *Archaeology of the dreamtime: The story of prehistoric Australia and its people* (rev. ed.). Pymble, New South Wales, Australia: Angus & Robertson.

Fullagar, R. L. K., Price, D. M., & Head, L. M. (1996). Early human occupation of northern Australia: Archaeology and thermoluminescence dating of Jinmium rock-shelter, Northern Territory. *Antiquity, 70,* 751–773.

Gill, A. (1997). *Orphans of the Empire: The shocking story of child migration to Australia.* Alexandria, New South Wales, Australia: Millennium Books.

Goldberg, D. (1981). *General Health Questionnaire—28.* London: NFER-Nelson.

Goode, K. (1997). *Jumping to heaven: Stories about refugee children.* Adelaide, Australia: Wakefield Press.

Greene, G. (1999, March 24). Outcry on preamble. *The Age* (Melbourne, Australia), p. 1.

Hall, V. (1962). *Namatjira of the Aranda.* Adelaide, Australia: Rigby.

Hockley, C. (1999, May 8). $1m spin-off expected from celebration of Cornish culture. *The Advertiser* (Adelaide, Australia), p. 31.

Home, R. W. (Ed.). (1998). *Regardfully yours: Life and letters of Ferdinand von Mueller* (Vol. 1). Bern, Switzerland: Peter Lang.

Hornadge, B. (1971). *The yellow peril.* Dubbo, New South Wales, Australia: Review Publications.

Hughes, T. S. (1982). *Arthur Phillip.* Cabarita, New South Wales, Australia: Movement Publications.

Kathreptis, L. (1994). *Mediterranean cuisine.* Lecture given as part of a course on comparative cuisine at Adelaide University, South Australia.

Kramarczuk, B. M. (1990). *Pain and associated factors in Australian and Polish groups.* Unpublished master's thesis, University of Adelaide, Adelaide, Australia.

Kraus, J. (1969). Some social factors and the rates of psychiatric hospital admissions of immigrants in New South Wales. *Medical Journal of Australia, 2*(1), 17–19.

Krupinski, J. (1975). Psychological maladaptation in ethnic concentrations in Victoria, Australia. In I. Pilowsky (Ed.), *Cultures in collision* (pp. 49–58). Adelaide, Australia: Australian National Association for Mental Health.

Krupinski, J. (1984). Changing patterns of migration to Australia and their influence on the mental health of migrants. *Social Science and Medicine, 18,* 927–937.

Kupka, K. (1965). *Dawn of art.* Sydney, Australia: Angus & Robertson.

Listemann, G. (1982). From Adelaide: A migrant's lament. In J. Tampke (Ed.), *Wunderbar country: Germans look at Australia, 1850–1914* (pp. 161–173). Sydney: Hale & Iremonger. (Original work published in 1851)

Lloyd, M. (1998, July 15). Adelaide: Love at first sight. *Eastern Courier Messenger* (Adelaide, Australia), p. 5.

Lowenstein, W., & Loh, M. (1977). *The immigrants.* Melbourne, Australia: Hyland House.

McConnochie, K., Hollinsworth, D., & Pettman, J. (1988). *Race and racism in Australia.* Wentworth Falls, New South Wales, Australia: Social Science Press.

McKinnon, M. (1999, November 20). Jumbo route for illegal immigrants. *The Advertiser* (Adelaide, Australia), p. 13.

Moore, C. (1985). *Kanaka: A history of Melanesian Mackay.* Port Moresby, Papua New Guinea: Institute of Papua New Guinea Studies and University of Papua New Guinea Press.

Neville, D. (1975). *Blackburn's Isle.* Lavenham, Suffolk, England: Terence Dalton.

Newby, E. (1986). *A book of travellers' tales.* London: Picador.

Payton, P. (1978). *Pictorial history of Australia's little Cornwall.* Sydney, Australia: Rigby.

Pindral, K. (1994). Krystyna Pindral. In C. Murphy (Ed.), *Boat load of dreams* (pp. 58–62). Adelaide, Australia: United Trades and Labor Council.

Procter, N. (1998). The contribution of social science to mental health nursing in the aftermath of ethnic violence. In M. Alexander, S. Harding, P. Harrison, G. Kendall, Z. Skrbis & J. Western (Eds.), *Refashioning sociology: Responses to a new world order* (Published conference proceedings). Brisbane, Queensland, Australia.

Procter, N., & Lynch, R. (1995). The uses of soccer by Serbian Australians in the expression of cultural identity. In C. Simpson & B. Gidlow (Eds.), *Leisure connections: Proceedings of the Second Conference* (pp. 182–188). Lincoln University, New Zealand: Australian and New Zealand Association for Leisure Studies.

Putnins, A. L. (1981). *Latvians in Australia.* Canberra, Australia: Australian National University Press.

Richardson, A. (1974). *British immigrants and Australia: A psycho-social inquiry.* Canberra, Australia: Australian National University Press.

Roberts, R., Bird, M., Olley, J., Galbraith, R., Lawson, E., Laslett, G., Yoshida, H., Jones, R., Fullagar, R., Jacobsen, G., & Hua, Q. (1998). Optical and radiocarbon dating at Jinmium rock shelter in northern Australia. *Nature, 393*(6683), 358–362.

Roberts, R. G., Jones, R., & Smith, M. A. (1990). Thermoluminescence dating of a 50,000-year-old human occupation site in northern Australia. *Nature, 345*(6271), 153–156.

Rosenthal, D., Ranieri, N., & Klimidis, S. (1996). Vietnamese adolescents in Australia: Relationships between perceptions of self and parental values, intergenerational conflict, and gender dissatisfaction. *International Journal of Psychology, 31,* 81–91.

Rothwell, N. (1999, May 1–2). The original Mr Green. *The Weekend Australian* Review Sec., p. 11.

Rowse, T. (1993). *After Mabo: Interpreting indigenous traditions.* Melbourne, Australia: Melbourne University Press.

Rozanski, J. (1994). Dislocation. In C. Murphy (Ed.), *Boat load of dreams: Journeys of European immigrant workers 1947–1994* (pp. 8–13). Adelaide, Australia: United Trades and Labor Council (South Australia).

Rump, E. E. (1972). Comparing Australia and New Zealand on color prejudice. *International Journal of Psychology, 7,* 39–45.

Rump, E., Parker, A., & Fallo, T. (1999, August). *The amelioration of health problems by social support from family and community, amongst Serbian refugees.* Paper presented at the Culture, Race and Community international conference, Melbourne, Australia.

Sanson, A., Augoustinos, M., Gridley, H., Kyrios, M., Reser, J., & Turner, C. (1998). Racism and prejudice: An Australian Psychological Society position paper. *Australian Psychologist, 33,* 161–182.

Schachner, R. (1982). The workers' paradise. In J. Tampke (Ed.), *Wunderbar country: Germans look at Australia, 1850–1914* (pp. 28–41). Sydney, Australia: Hale & Iremonger. (Original work published in 1912)

Schloenhardt, A. (1999). Trafficking in migrants outpaces the law. *The Adelaidean, 8*(9), 1, 12.

Scott, W. A., & Scott, R. (1989). *Adaptation of immigrants: Individual differences and determinants.* Sydney, Australia: Pergamon Press.

Scutt, J. (1993). *No fear of flying: Women at home and abroad.* Melbourne, Australia: Artemis.

Sherington, G. (1990). *Australia's immigrants 1788–1988* (2nd ed.). Sydney, Australia: Allen & Unwin.

Smolicz, C. (Ed.). (1998). *Multicultural life supplement—First Australians.* Canberra, Australia: Office of Multicultural and International Affairs.

Stoller, A., & Krupinski, J. (1973). Immigration to Australia: Mental health aspects. In C. Zwingmann & M. Pfister-Ammende (Eds.), *Uprooting and after* (pp. 252–268). Berlin, Germany: Springer-Verlag.

Stuart, G. W., Klimidis, S., & Minas, I. H. (1998). The treated prevalence of mental disorder amongst immigrants and the Australian-born: Community and primary-care rates. *International Journal of Social Psychiatry, 44*(1), 22–34.

Taft, R. (1985). The psychological study of the adjustment and adaptation of immigrants in Australia. In N. T. Feather (Ed.), *Australian psychology: Review of research* (pp. 364–386). Sydney, Australia: Allen & Unwin.

Taft, R., & Doczy, A. G. (1962). *The assimilation of intellectual refugees in Western Australia* (REMP Bulletin, No. 10, pp. 1–82). The Hague, Netherlands: Research Group for European Migration Problems.

Tampke, J. (Ed.). (1982). *Wunderbar country: Germans look at Australia, 1850–1914.* Sydney, Australia: Hale & Iremonger.

Turner, J. (1998, August 1). Torture of the innocents. *The Advertiser* (Adelaide, Australia), p. 19.

VandenHeuvel, A., & Wooden, M. (2000). Immigrants' labour market experiences in the early settlement years. *Australian Bulletin of Labour, 26*(1),

50–60.

Walker, R .B. (1975). Some social and political aspects of German settlement in Australia to 1914. *Journal of The Royal Australian Historical Society, 61*(1), 26–27.

Way, D. (1999, April 30). Migration changes attacked. *The Advertiser* (Adelaide, Australia), p. 6.

Way, D. (2000, January 7). Anglo-Celts on the wane, study finds. *The Age* (Melbourne, Australia), p. 6.

Williams, C., & Westermeyer, J. (1983). Psychiatric problems among adolescent Southeast Asian refugees: A descriptive study. *Journal of Nervous and Mental Disease, 171,* 79–85.

Williams, R. (1997). *Report of initial research into the new-arriving communities from the former Yugoslavia and the Horn of Africa.* Adelaide, Australia: Multicultural Mental Health Access Program.

Wooden, M. (1990). The labour market experience of immigrants. In M. Wooden, R. Holton, G. Hugo, & J. Sloan (Ed.), *Australian immigration: A survey of the issues* (pp. 227–292). Canberra, Australia: Australian Government Publishing Service.

Woodford, J. (1996, September 21). Unearthed: Australia's lost civilisation. *The Sydney Morning Herald* (Sydney, Australia), pp. 29–33.

V

The Middle East and Africa

16

Immigration and Emigration: Unique Patterns in Israel

Noach Milgram

FAMILIAR PATTERNS OF INVOLUNTARY AND VOLUNTARY IMMIGRATION

The 20th century has seen more waves of migration than any other. Over 100 million people have left their country of origin due to war, civil unrest, and political or religious persecution since the end of World War II (Westermeyer, 1991). Millions of Germans were displaced from Eastern European countries following changes in national borders at the end of World War II; millions of Muslims migrated from India to Pakistan and millions of Hindus moved in the reverse direction following the end of British colonial rule and the independence of both countries several years later; several million people were forced to flee from one part of the former Yugoslavia to another in the 1990s; and, most recently, Albanians were driven from their homes in Kosovo (Milgram, 1998b).

Some migrations have been voluntary. Throughout the 20th century, people migrated to other countries because of their desire for life, liberty, and the pursuit of happiness. Tens of millions migrated to the United States from Europe and more recently from Asia. Other havens of opportunity in the second half of this century have been Germany for migrant workers from Eastern Europe and Turkey, France for immigrants from Arab-speaking countries, and Canada and Australia for immigrants from many European and some Asian countries.

THE UNIQUE PATTERN OF IMMIGRATION TO ISRAEL

The migration history of the state of Israel is unique because the Jewish state came into existence as a consequence of a unique kind of immigration—a homecoming in fact—that combined both voluntary and involuntary immigration. A brief summary of Jewish history is necessary in order to understand this phenomenon (Ben-Sira, 1994; Kolker & Ahmed, 1980).

A 4,000-year-old Jewish tradition, religious in origin, asserts that the area that hugs the eastern coast of the Mediterranean Sea, between Lebanon on the north, Sinai on the south, and the Arabian desert on the east is the "real" home of the Jewish people and that all Jews who live elsewhere are living "temporarily in the diaspora." Historians confirm that there has been a continuous Jewish presence in what is today Israel throughout this time frame and that there were two periods of demonstrable national independence and sovereignty. The first monarchy dating from Saul and David lasted over 400 years and was terminated by conquest and exile in 576 b.c.e. The second or Maccabean monarchy was established 450 years later and ended with a national disaster of greater proportions than the earlier one, with the destruction of the Second Temple in c.e. 70.

During the long exile, the connection of the Jewish people with the Jewish homeland was sustained by (a) the continuous existence of Jewish communities in Israel throughout this period; (b) daily prayers for the return to Israel and the rebuilding of religious and national life; (c) the practice of religious customs in exile that are linked to the past life and to the anticipated future life in Israel; and (d) the actual return of Jews to the Holy Land, specifically to Jerusalem, Hebron, Tiberias, and Safed from 1500 on.

The Zionist movement, which began 100 years ago, was the first organized, political effort to reestablish Jewish sovereignty in Israel by encouraging the mass immigration of Jews to Israel. The details of this migration are summarized briefly with the use of approximate figures for various periods. The local native Jewish population at the turn of the century numbering some 50,000 was soon outnumbered by Eastern European immigrants whose motivation for coming was idealistic, to establish a nation state for the Jewish people based on socialism. The same phenomenon, newcomers outnumbering old-timers, was to repeat itself several times over: In the 1930s, 300,000 Jews fled Germany during and after the rise of Nazism; after Israel's War of Independence (1948–1949) 700,000 immigrants, the majority survivors of the Holocaust, and the remainder from Arab-speaking countries (e.g., Yemen, Libya, Syria) made their way to Israel, doubling the population of the country; in the late 1950s an additional 200,000 Jews from Arab-speaking countries came to Israel; 100,000 Russian Jews migrated in the 1970s followed by 600,000 Russian and other Eastern European immigrants with the collapse of Communism and the breakup of the Soviet Union.

This immigration pattern is different from that of any other in the world. The only country that has enjoyed comparable waves of immigration is the United States; on the other hand, there was never a time when a wave of new immigrants outnumbered the host native population in the United States. Moreover, when people migrate from their country of origin or homeland to escape persecution or economic hardship and/or to enjoy the psychological benefits of a different way of life (e.g., democracy vs. dictatorship), they may enter the new, host country only if the laws of the land and the standards and quotas of the host country permit their entry. In Israel, by contrast, immigration was always seen as home-coming. A symbolic reflection of this perception is the famous Law of the Return, by which Jews anywhere in the world may enter Israel without restriction and automatically become Israeli citizens. Russian Jews were imprisoned in the Soviet Union in the 1970s and 1980s because they asserted that Israel was their homeland and they wanted to leave the Soviet Union to return home; in many instances, Israeli citizenship was conferred upon them in absentia by Israel authorities while they languished in Soviet prisons.

RESEARCH ON THE ADJUSTMENT OF IMMIGRANT GROUPS TO ISRAEL: PRELIMINARY REMARKS

Numerous adjustment-promoting variables have been investigated over the years. These include any and all of the following: resocialization (Bar Yosef, 1969; Eisenstadt, 1954), internal readiness for change (Eisenstadt, 1967), strength of identification with Zionist ideology, Judaism, the Jewish State, and/or Israeli society (Shuval, 1959; Shuval, Marcus, Beran, & Dotan, 1973), the changing state of the Israeli economy and its impact on newcomers and old-timers (Berger, 1975), a critical mass of fellow immigrants permitting the sustaining of preimmigration cultural and religious patterns in a cohesive self-help community (Ben-Sira, 1994), continuing attachment to versus alienation from the country of one's birth (Kolker & Ahmed, 1980), and attractive countries to which one might immigrate if residing in Israel is perceived as unrewarding (Milgram & Zucker, 1985). Many, if not most, of the earlier, classical studies in the field emphasized the relative strength of the motivations, materialistic versus idealistic, for migrating to Israel, while later research became more comprehensive and is based on various sociological and psychological theories.

COGNITIVE APPRAISAL OF STRESS AND COPING

Two theories associated with cognitive appraisal of threat, loss, and assets appear especially appropriate for predicting and enhancing adjustment to stressful situations such as the stress of migrating to any country, and, in the present instance, to Israel. The conservation of resources theory (Hobfoll, 1989) stated that psychological stress occurs in one or more of the following instances: when resources important to the individual (and by generalization to the community) are threatened with loss, when resources are actually lost, and when resources are invested without consequent gain, hence producing a net loss.

Resources may be assigned to one or more of the following four categories: (a) Objects—material things such as one's home, clothing, means of transportation; (b) conditions—social structures and personal circumstances such as secure work, health, a good marriage; (c) personal characteristics—attributes of individuals such as self-esteem, personal values, and skills; and (d) energies—money, credit, time, knowledge that may be used or exchanged in order to protect other resources. These resources are relatively objective, although people may exaggerate or underestimate the resources available to them. When stressed, people may elect to invest intact resources to replace lost resources or to preserve threatened resources, or to accept losses and invest their remaining resources elsewhere.

The second theory (Lazarus & Folkman, 1984) states that psychological stress is a particular relationship between the person and the environment that is appraised by the person as taxing or exceeding his or her resources and endangering his or her well being. Primary cognitive appraisal is initiated to assess the anticipated threat or actual loss, and secondary cognitive appraisal to assess the resources, personal or interpersonal that are available or may be recruited for coping with the objective stressor and with the debilitating or disruptive emotional reactions (a negative hedonic balance) elicited by the cognitive appraisals. The two theories complement one another, with the former emphasizing what is threatened or lost and the latter emphasizing the discrepancy between the demands of the situation and the resources available to the individual.

This composite model is incomplete without the introduction of two additional cognitive assessments—time-referenced comparative assessment and group-referenced comparative assessment—that affect the coping behavior and the affective balance of people exposed to stressful situations over time in general and, in the present context, to immigrants in particular. Immigrants make time-referenced *comparative assessments* of the past, the present, and the anticipated future. In the early phases of adjustment to the new host country, immigrants compare the present with the past in the country of their origin and derive a balance sheet of losses and gains. In the latter phases of adjustment, immigrants compare the current circumstances of their lives with those of the native population and with the prospects of their closing the gap in the future and becoming well established in their new country. Immigrants also make group-referenced *comparative assessments* of the efficacy of their coping behavior and their achievements vis-à-vis a personal or collective standard (Milgram, 1998a; Taylor & Lobel, 1989). They may compare their adjustment to that of other members of their community, to immigrants who preceded them, or to their own level of aspiration. They make these assessments repeatedly throughout the lengthy period of adjusting to the new host country.

Both kinds of assessments operate in conjunction with the appraisals inherent in the Hobfoll (1989) and Lazarus models (Lazarus & Folkman, 1984) to affect the emotional reactions and the problem-solving behavior of immigrants and their plans to remain or emigrate. These concepts are useful in making a comprehensive assessment of the resource losses, gains, and resource balance in the individual immigrant and in the collective to which he or she belongs (e.g., metropolitan Russian Jews vs. small town Russian Jews, Ethiopian Jews, Jewish immigrants from the wealthy, English-speaking countries, etc.). These cognitive theories have been presented in some detail, because they are applicable to research on many long-term stressful situations including the emigration-immigration process. Studies that illustrate some of the concepts in these theories are summarized below.

RESEARCH ON IMMIGRATION TO ISRAEL:
RELEVANT VARIABLES

The majority of studies on immigrant adjustment were done with the vast Russian immigration that took place over the past 20 years. Few studies were done on those groups that arrived earlier because the meager resources of the fledgling state in the 1950s to the 1970s were invested solely in absorbing the new immigrants. Shuval et al. (1973) investigated a number of immigrant groups and found that the newly arrived Russian immigrants were higher in feeling a bond to the Jewish people and to Israel and were comparable in morale, despite the fact that they were less satisfied with housing, employment, and social relations. They found that the intention of the Russians to remain in Israel was strongly correlated with the strength of identification with Israel, followed by satisfaction with their children's adjustment, housing, and other material instrumental resources. Satisfaction was highest among those Russian immigrants who lived in smaller communities and practiced Jewish religious traditions.

Elizur and Elizur (1975) investigated Russian immigrants who applied for an Israeli passport that would permit them to travel abroad and presumably might utilize this opportunity to leave Israel permanently. They found that those who intended to remain were gainfully employed, in general, and employed in their chosen profession, in particular, and tended to be more observant in religious traditions than those who intended to leave. In addition, these people reported that the most important reason for their migrating to Israel in the first place was to live in a Jewish society. Other important reasons for migrating to Israel were concern for the future of their children and dissatisfaction with life in Russia because of anti-Semitism and the absence of democracy. By contrast, a higher standard of living in Israel was listed as the least important reason given by the sample as a whole. Elizur and Elizur asked their respondents to compare their expectations about Israel with the realities they encountered. They found that these new immigrants had optimistic expectations about life being better in Israel than in Russia but were actually disillusioned as a group by their experiences. As might be expected, those who were more disillusioned were more likely to leave than those who were less disillusioned, and they gave as their reasons their concern for their children's future in general and their children's education in particular.

It is important to note that in this period, the 1970s, admission to the five Israeli universities was highly competitive, with many qualified students unable to enter higher education. As a consequence, there was a government decision to expand the opportunity for higher education by encouraging the universities to accept more students, by encouraging the establishment of regional colleges, and by transforming teachers seminaries into degree-granting colleges. As a consequence of this policy, the number of students enrolled in higher education increased from 50,000 in the 1970s to over 175,000, an increase that is well in excess of the increase in the general population.

In 1976, Leshem, Rosenbaum, and Kahanov (1980) compared Russian emigrants who did not continue on to Israel after leaving the Soviet Union with those Russians who did immigrate to Israel. They found that the latter group placed more emphasis on a Jewish way of life, had more friends and family already in Israel, were more optimistic about finding work in Israel, and were older. The possible implications of age in strengthening the intention to remain in Israel were clarified by the research of Shuval, Marcus, and Dotan (1974). They originally hypothesized that younger Russian immigrants would cope more easily with the many demands of adjusting to a new country—language, employment, social relations with natives. They found this to be true, but these advantages did not translate into higher morale in younger immigrants. Moreover, immigrants over 65 were found to be highest in identification with Israel to begin with and remained so despite a rise in this identification over time in the younger immigrants. The investigators concluded that the Jewish experiences during their childhood of the over 65 age group accounted for their high positive identification with Judaism and the Jewish state, and that these experiences were not available to the younger immigrants in their formative years in the Soviet Union.

Confirmation of the importance of this identification was found in a later study by Shuval (1983). She investigated the adjustment of Russian immigrant physicians and found that those who left the country within 3 years of arrival (approximately 5% of the sample) were younger and came from regions of the Soviet Union in which there were few vestiges of Jewish cultural or communal life.

Farago (1978) investigated the ethnic identity of Russian immigrant students who had arrived in Israel several years earlier. Most regarded their Jewish identity more positively than their Israeli or their Russian identity (88%, 53%, and 27%, respectively), with their Israeli identity more related to feeling at home in Israel than their Jewish identity ($r = .37$ and $r = .20$, respectively). A follow-up study 3 years later (Farago, 1979) confirmed the earlier findings, with the Jewish identity still dominant and a modest shift in favor of the Israeli identity.

A study of recent Russian immigrants who arrived in the late 1980s (Damian & Rosenbaum-Tamari, 1993) revealed that the major factor in their moving to Israel was probably the large number of family members and friends already living there (81%, as compared with family and friends living elsewhere in the West, 33%). Identification with the Jewish people and with the State of Israel was lower than that found in local Israeli reference groups, but interestingly enough, it was more highly correlated with intentions to remain in Israel ($r = .35$) than were any of the other variables investigated. The most important reasons given for coming to Israel were to guarantee their children's future and to live in a Jewish state.

Ben-Sira (1994) did a comprehensive study comparing recent Russian immigrants and a representative sample of Israeli citizens and found that the former group described itself as less Zionist than the latter, although they did not differ appreciably in considering themselves part of the Jewish people and in observing some of the Jewish religious practices.

Two studies were done by this writer on Russian students who immigrated to Israel in the 1990s. The first (Milgram & Bass, 1994) found that the major reason for leaving Russia was to pursue a higher standard of living, followed by fears of anti-Semitism. The major reasons for settling in Israel in decreasing order of importance were (a) better Israel than remaining in Russia, (b) the desire to live in a Western country, (c) the desire to live in a Jewish state. These findings are consistent with the future intentions of this group of students. About half said they intend to stay, 20% to leave, and 30% uncertain (with 50-50 odds). On the other hand, the strongest predictors of the intention to remain in

Israel were, as in previous studies, the desire to live in a Jewish state, as well as the importance of knowledge of Jewish history, religion and Zionism, followed by satisfaction with housing, and depth of one's friendships in Israel. Several variables were significantly related to the intention to leave: The desire for cultural change, having time on one's hands, negative affect, and pessimism about future life satisfactions.

In a second study with Russian university students 4 years in Israel, Milgram, Lazar, and Yakobov (1998) found a similar distribution of intentions with regard to remaining versus leaving Israel. Students with a continuing attachment to their country or origin were more likely to state intentions to leave Israel than students without this attachment ($r = .32$). Conversely, a developing attachment to Israel was related to the intention to stay ($r = .21$), but weakly so. Overall, the strength of the attachment to Russia was weaker than that to Israel, but both were relatively weak. If we scan the findings of the research on the Russian immigration cited above, we note the changing composition of the Russian Jews immigrating to Israel. Immigrants with a strong commitment to Judaism or Zionism were more frequent in the earlier years when exit was denied by the Soviet authorities (Shuval, 1982) and became less frequent in the later years when all were free to leave.

Studies on the adjustment of other immigrant groups are fewer and are less accessible. Milgram and Zucker (1985) assessed the efficacy of a variety of resources in reducing ongoing anxiety and in predicting the intention to remain or to emigrate in recent immigrants, all of them heads of families from English-speaking countries. They found that material resources (employment, housing, financial status) were strongly associated with remaining in Israel, followed by the attractiveness of the viable option of returning to their former country relative to the attractiveness of remaining in Israel. Contrary to prediction, prior activity in Jewish or Zionist organizations and knowledge about Jewish history and about Israel were associated with being in an anxious state of mind during this 1st year of settling when compared to little or no prior activity or knowledge. Apparently the initial contrast between the prior positive, exaggerated, and romanticized expectations of these Western immigrants and their actual experiences as new immigrants was great and induced considerable anxiety relative to those who knew little about the country to begin with and accepted things as they were. The findings of this study are consistent with the relatively low rate of immigration to Israel from Western countries and the relatively high rate of emigration among those who did come from Western countries during the past 50 years. The only exception to these trends in recent years are those immigrants from Western countries who possess strong Zionist as well as strong religious convictions.

There is considerable ongoing research on the difficulties encountered by the Jews who have come from Ethiopia in recent years. The enormous discrepancy between the features of the culture in which they have lived for centuries and the corresponding features in Western society has created obstacles that are slowly being mounted. Ethiopian Jews are dark-skinned and some encounter prejudice at a personal level. When these instances of prejudice become known to the general public, they are decried and the perpetrators roundly denounced. Some of the younger people who came as children or were born in Israel have entered military service, and during combat duty, some young men have died. Their deaths and the public ceremonies performed to honor their memory and to show respect for their community become front page news and occupy prime time on television. Some young people are graduating from institutions of higher education, are competing in the economic market place, and entering political life. A member of the Ethiopian community served in the Israeli Parliament (1996–1999), and others are vying for positions of responsibility in Israeli society.

EMIGRATION FROM ISRAEL: DERELICTION OF NATIONAL DUTY

It is commonplace for people to migrate voluntarily from the country of their birth to another country, and millions do so without apology. Israel, too, has experienced the phenomenon of emigration, with a remarkable difference: Many emigrants express guilt feelings and use defensive maneuvers to neutralize these feelings. Since the establishment of the State of Israel (1948), well over 500,000 have exercised this option and have established long-term, if not permanent, residence in Western countries, especially in the United States. This option did not exist for most immigrants until the 1970s when many Israelis were willing and found that they were able to depart for other (greener?) pastures. The actual number of emigrants is unknown, for several reasons. Israelis travel a great deal, and hundreds of thousands leave and return each year. Many Israelis study or work overseas for a number of years and return; still others have no initial intention to do so but return home when their children reach age 18 and enlist in the Israeli Defense Forces.

In the 1960s and 1970s, social opprobrium was attached to leaving the fledgling state, as if it were a dereliction of duty. The late prime minister of Israel, Yitchak Rabin, used very colorful and derogatory language in the 1970s in referring to those who left Israel in favor of the diaspora ("the exile," any country other than Israel). To this day, emigrants find it necessary to rationalize or apologize for their living outside of Israel. Some insist that they serve Israel better by doing so and provide ingenious reasons to justify their living outside Israel. Others speak critically of the Jewish state, implying that they live elsewhere out of respect for some moral principle. Nearly all assert that they would be on the first plane to return in Israel's hour of need. This writer is unaware of any other country where emigration is both widespread and a lingering source of embarrassment for those who reside elsewhere.

Many of the studies cited earlier documented that those immigrants who are religiously observant and/or strongly identified with Israel, are far less likely to leave Israel permanently. The same generalization applies to native born Israelis. A classical study conducted many years ago by Levy and Guttman (1974) with a large representative sample of Israelis, native born and immigrant, indicated that Israelis with a religious orientation are more certain they will remain than Israelis with a secular orientation, and older people more than younger. These findings on emigration continue to be valid today. The conclusions of two major surveys conducted on Israeli youth prior to military service (Meisels, Gal, & Fishof, 1989; Mizrachi & Gal, 1995) indicate that religious adolescents living in the cities are more certain to remain in Israel than their secular age peers, and adolescents living in religious kibbutzim, or collective communities, more than adolescents living in secular kibbutzim. By way of illustration, the percentages of *potential emigrants* in the more recent 1995 sample are 32% versus 24% for urban secular and religious youths, respectively, and 35% versus 6% for kibbutz secular and religious youths, respectively. These differences are paralleled by corresponding differences in identification with Zionist ideology, and in readiness of the young men to serve in combat units in the Israeli Defense Forces. The recent respective percentages for the latter are 46% versus 64% for urban secular and religious youth, respectively, and 59% and 89% for kibbutz secular and religious youths.

Educational achievement, career aspirations, and the size of the Israeli market place also affect these emigration patterns. Secular Israelis tend to be more highly educated than traditional and religious Israelis and are more able to pursue well paying, prestigious employment opportunities. These opportunities may become relatively scarce in Israeli society as more and more people acquire higher education and with it higher career aspirations. Consequently, there will be a "brain drain," especially among secular academics, professionals, and businesspeople. These predictions are offered with some caution, however, because Israeli society is very dynamic and changing simultaneously in many directions at the same time, so that predictions about future trends are always hazardous.

THE IMPACT OF RECURRENT IMMIGRATION WAVES ON ISRAELI SOCIETY

A pattern of massive waves of newcomers who speak different languages (e.g., Arabic, German, Russian, Amhari [Ethiopian]), differ in formal education, and practice different cultural patterns of behavior is a cause for instability in any society, especially one in which newcomers outnumber the old-timers. Each new wave of immigration was, in fact, regarded with apprehension and distaste by those who came in or descended from an earlier wave. The Sephardic Jews who immigrated primarily from the Arab-speaking countries were and still are more observant in religious practices, less educated, and less familiar with Western culture than are the Ashkenazi- or European-born Jews who preceded them. The small number of Jews from affluent Western countries who elected to migrate to Israel for idealistic reasons in the 1970s and 1980s were welcomed and at the same time resented because they received what appeared to be overly generous incentives to settle in Israel and were competing with the locals for prestigious, well-paying jobs.

The more recent wave of Russian and other East European Jews aroused the ire of most groups: The religious were upset because many new immigrants are not Jewish by time-honored traditions (i.e., having a Jewish mother) and are not interested in or are reluctant to undergo a lengthy conversion procedure that requires months of study of religious laws and a commitment to perform them. Descendants of the secular, socialist founders of modern Israel were upset because the recent immigrants do not appear to show the proper appreciation for their own set of cherished values. All were upset because the Russians are highly educated, industrious, and insist on their share of the political and economic power in the state. Some become upset because they attribute, *erroneously,* to the Russian immigrants three relatively minor, but new, phenomena in Israeli life: homeless individuals, usually alcoholics or mentally disturbed, living in the streets and parks; criminals operating on an international scale; and young women imported to work as prostitutes.

Given recurring destabilizing features in these migration patters, one might expect to find evidence of enormous stress in Israeli society. Unquestionably there has been stress and some strain, sporadic instances of individual violence, and overt and covert evidence of prejudicial behavior on the part of old-timers to newcomers. There has not been, however, a serious breach in Israeli society that is directly associated with immigration. There have been relatively few riots of one migrant group against another, nothing like the violence associated with racial or ethnic groups in other countries (e.g., between Blacks and Whites in the United States, between Turkish immigrants and native-born citizens of Germany, and among Serbs, Croats, and Bosnians in the former Yugoslavia). There are several reasons for the absence of manifest violence or organized discontent on the part of old-timers or newcomers.

First and foremost, there are religious and cultural ties that unite Jews who immigrate to Israel regardless of the diverse cultures, languages, and geopolitical settings in which they were raised. Indication of diversity may be seen in a partial list in alphabetical order of the many countries from which Israeli Jews emigrated: Algeria, Argentina, Canada, Egypt, England, Ethiopia, France, India, Iraq, Italy, Lebanon, Libya, Lithuania, Morocco, Poland, Russia, South Africa, Syria, Tunisia, Ukraine, United States, and Yugoslavia. Conversely, indication of common origins and traditions may be seen in the following partial list: Jews who pray, use prayer books that are remarkably similar in the Hebrew text. They pray in the direction of Jerusalem. They circumcise their children (males). They honor the tradition of helping others less fortunate than themselves, first among their fellow Jews, then among others. These and other behaviors shared by many, if not most, Jews from these many countries and cultures provide an antidote in Israel for the prejudices and hostilities that arise in any society between native born and immigrant groups.

Second, the presence of an external enemy common to all Jewish citizens of Israel encourages a degree of unity. Many Arab leaders and their followers are opposed to a sovereign Jewish state in the Middle East and act in violent ways against Israeli Jews, civilians and military alike. Israelis tend to band together when they perceive a common threat.

Third, migration-initiated prejudice and animosity is defused by competing prejudices and animosities. In the United States, the land of immigrants, prejudice against any one group competed historically with prejudice against others (e.g., Protestants vs. Catholics, Whites vs. Blacks, English speakers vs. Latinos).

In Israel, the competing and overlapping splits between Ashkenazi versus Sephardi, secular versus religious, socialist versus free-enterprise capitalist, and right-wing nationalist versus left-wing universalist ideology serve the same function.

Fourth, the blurring of group membership and identity also defuses tensions. Approximately 25% of the Ashkenazi and Sephardi group members are inter-married. Some citizens change their religious practices, secular Jews becoming more observant and the reverse, and the same for political ideology. As a consequence, Israelis number among their family, friends, and neighbors people who differ from them in a number of potentially schismatic ways.

Fifth, democratic features of Israeli political and military life reduce migra-tion-related group prejudice. The multiparty parliamentary system permits citi-zens to vote for a party that represents their values and their grievances, and to have a voice in the decisions of their government. The even-handed draft of young men from most groups in Israeli life encourages their becoming more tolerant with one another. The selection and promotion of military officers on the base of ability rather than class membership also encourages tolerance.

It would be fallacious to pretend that problems do not exist. A pluralistic so-ciety is developing in Israel, with drastically different life styles ranging from the insistence on recognizing homosexual and lesbian unions to the insistence on perpetuating the patriarchal religious family that was the norm in Jewish life prior to modern times and is the norm today among many Orthodox communi-ties. There is an intellectual climate of tolerance for pluralism, but at the same time there is conflict between the various immigrant and ethnic groups. They compete for economic and political power and strive for the preservation and the promulgation of their way of life in Israeli society. Democracy is one of the ide-als of Israeli society, but its definition and implementation differ from one group to another. Each group uses its interpretation of democracy to justify its de-mands and to delegitimize the demands of other groups.

All speak of the need for national unity in the Jewish state. In this writer's opinion, changes in the demographic profile of the country, progressive rise in the educational level of the people and in their political sophistication, changes in the national election procedures, and structural and functional changes in all three branches of the government will reflect and affect efforts to achieve greater national unity. Will Israel achieve this national unity? Where Israel is concerned, the optimists have always been found to be the realists.

REFERENCES

Bar Yosef, R. W. (1969). Desocialization and resocialization: The adjustment process of immigrants. In M. M. Lisack, B. Mizraki, & O. Ben-David (Eds.), *Immigrants in Israel: A reader.* Jerusalem: Hebrew University Press. (in He-brew)

Ben-Sira, Z. (1994). *Immigration, integration and readjustment.* Jerusalem: Is-rael Institute of Applied Social Research.

Berger, L. (1975). Immigration motivations and structural changes in Israel.

Israel yearbook. Tel-Aviv, Israel: Israel Yearbook Publications.

Damian, N., & Rosenbaum-Tamari, J. (1993). *Follow-up research on immigrants absorbed directly from their country of origin* (Tech. Rep.). Planning and Research Branch, Ministry of Absorption. (in Hebrew)

Eisenstadt, S. N. (1954). *The absorption of immigrants.* London: Routledge & Kegan Paul.

Eisenstadt, S. N. (1967). *Israeli society.* Jerusalem: Magnes.

Elizur, D., & Elizur, M. (1975). *To stay or to leave? The characteristics of leaving among immigrants from the Soviet Union.* Jerusalem: Israel Institute for Applied Social Research. (in Hebrew)

Ezrachi, Y., & Gal, R. (1995). *Perceptions and attitudes of high school students about the army and national security* (Tech. Rep.). Zikron Yakov, Israel: Carmel Institute for Social Research.

Farago, U. (1978). The ethnic identity of Russian immigrant students in Israel. *The Jewish Journal of Sociology, 20,* 115–127.

Farago, U. (1979). Changes in the ethnic identity of Russian immigrant students in Israel (1973–1975). *The Jewish Journal of Sociology, 21,* 37–52.

Hobfoll, S. E. (1989). Conservation of resources: A new attempt at conceptualizing stress. *American Psychologist, 44,* 513–524.

Kolker, A., & Ahmed, P. I. (1980). Integration of immigrants: The Israeli case. In G. V. Coelho & P. I. Ahmed (Eds.), *Uprooting and development* (pp. 479–496). New York: Plenum.

Lazarus, R. S., & Folkman, S. (1984). *Stress, appraisal, and coping.* New York: Springer.

Leshem, E., Rosenbaum, J., & Kahanov, O. (1980). *The dropout phenomenon among Soviet Jewish immigrants* (Tech. Rep.). Jerusalem: Center for Research and Documentation of Jerusalem: East European Jewry.

Levy, S., & Guttman, E. L. (1974). *The desire to remain in Israel* (Tech. Rep.). The Israel Institute of Applied Social Research, Jerusalem: Center for Information. (in Hebrew)

Meisels, O., Gal, R., & Fischof, E. (1989). *Perceptions and attitudes of high school students about the army and national security* (Tech. Rep.). Zikron Yakov, Israel: Carmel Institute for Social Research.

Milgram, N. A. (1998a). Children under stress. In T. H. Ollendick & M. Hersen (Eds.), *Handbook of child psychopathology* (3rd ed., pp. 505–533). New York: Plenum.

Milgram, N. A. (1998b). Victims of war. In A. S. Bellack & M. Hersen (Eds.), *Comprehensive clinical psychology* (Vol. 9, pp. 391–406). Oxford, England: Pergamon/Elsevier.

Milgram, N. A., & Bass, O. (1994). *The intention of Russian immigrant students to remain in Israel: Application of cognitive appraisal variables.* (Tech. Rep.). Tel-Aviv, Israel: Tel-Aviv University, Department of Psychology.

Milgram, N. A., Lazar, S., & Yakobov, R. (1998). *Adjustment and the intention to remain in Israel in new Russian immigrant students* (Tech. Rep.). Ariel, Israel: Academic College of Judea and Samaria, Department of Behavioral Sciences. (in Hebrew)

Milgram, N. A., & Zucker, M. (1985). Congruent stress-preventing factors and anxiety in a long-term stress situation. *Journal of Human Stress, 11,* 184–189.

Shuval, J. T. (1959). The role of ideology as a predisposing frame of reference for immigrants. *Human Relations, 12,* 51–63.

Shuval, J. T. (1982). Migration and stress. In L. Goldberger & S. Breznitz (Eds.), *Handbook of stress: Theoretical and clinical aspects* (pp. 677–694). New York: Free Press (Macmillan).

Shuval, J. T. (1983). *Newcomers and colleagues: Soviet immigrant physicians in Israel.* Houston, TX: Cape & Gown.

Shuval, J. T., Marcus, E. J., Beran, N., & Dotan, J. (1973). *Patterns of adjustment of Soviet immigrants to Israel (Part One).* Jerusalem: Institute of Applied Social Research. (in Hebrew)

Shuval, J. T., Marcus, E. J., & Dotan, J. (1974). *Patterns of adjustment of Soviet immigrants to Israel (Part Two).* Jerusalem: Institute of Applied Social Research. (in Hebrew)

Taylor, S. E., & Lobel, H. (1989). Social comparison activity under threat: Downward evaluation and upward contacts. *Psychological Review, 96,* 569–575.

Westermeyer, J. (1991). Psychiatric services for refugee children: An overview. In F. L. Ahearn & J. L. Athey (Eds.), *Refugee children: Theory, research and services* (pp. 127–162). Baltimore: Johns Hopkins University Press.

17

Egyptian Migrations

Ramadan A. Ahmed

Egypt occupies the northeastern corner of Africa and the Sinai Peninsula. In the north it is bordered by the Mediterranean Sea, in the west by Libya, in the south by the Sudan, and in the east by the Red Sea. Strategically situated at the crossroads between Europe and the Orient and between North Africa and Southeast Asia, Egypt occupies an area of about 386,100 square miles. Of these only 3.5% are normally inhabited, the rest being desert (R. A. Ahmed, 1991). In January 1998, Egypt had an estimated population of 62.5 million including 48.8% females (*Al-Ahram,* 1999b). Egyptian culture has Pharaonic ancestors, Arab fathers, and is of a predominantly Islamic character.

In addition to considerable natural wealth, Egypt has large reserves of oil and numerous mineral resources. However, it suffers from a number of population problems, such as a high rate of population growth (2.9% annually) and a young population (43.5% of the population are 15 years and younger; see Abdel-Rahman, 1996; *Al-Ahram,* 1999b; Al-Quady, 1990); large families (in urban areas, the number of family members tends to be three to four, whereas in rural areas, this number is often six or more); a high mortality rate (in 1991, the combined prenatal, maternal, and infant mortality rate was about 53 per 1,000; Abdel-Rahman, 1996; R. A. Ahmed, 1991); a moderate life expectancy (57 years for males and 59–60 years for females, 54–55 years in rural areas, and 58-60 years in urban areas); a very high illiteracy rate (51–62%); a high rate of unemployment (8.2% of the labor force); a high rate of inflation; and an increasingly uneven distribution of wealth. Population pressures and economic problems have led in recent years to the immigration of many Egyptians to other, wealthier countries.

Egyptians, however, have been known for a very long time as the people who do not like to leave their land. This was the case until the early 1950s (Ewis, 1985). Emigration out of Egypt started in the late 1940s, when a small number of Egyptians began to migrate to European countries such as Italy and

France and to the United States. Among the first wave of Egyptian emigrants were some Egyptian Jews (who moved at first to various Western countries, such as the United States, United Kingdom, France, and Italy, from where some then migrated to the newly established Israel). At the same time, and after the Egyptian Revolution in 1952, a number of Egyptian Christians began to migrate to the Western countries, especially to the United States, Canada, and Australia, and even to Egypt's southern neighbor, the Sudan.

By the late 1960s, the number of Egyptians who had migrated from Egypt was still very small; it has been estimated by some researchers (Ibrahim & Mohieddin, 1993) at about 70,000. This number began to increase and reached about 500,000 in 1973 (Ali & Abou-Zaid, 1996; Ibrahim & Mohieddin, 1993; Leila, 1995). The majority of the Egyptian migrants were headed for the recently independent, oil-producing Persian Gulf States and especially for Saudi Arabia and Kuwait.

During the Anwar Sadat period of 1970 to 1981, and especially after the October 1973 war with Israel, Egypt became increasingly a socially and economically open society. This trend, however, has had a negative impact on many of the poorer Egyptians, who were and still are suffering from problems such as rising prices and insufficient chances to secure work even when educated. Gradually, an increasing gap emerged between the rich and the poor, which also had negative consequences for the daily life of the middle class. An important step toward encouraging Egyptians to migrate was made when the Presidential Law No. 574 was issued on October 14, 1981, which established the Ministry for Migration Affairs and Caring for Egyptians Abroad (MIACEA). Soon after, the General Union for Caring for Egyptians Abroad was established under the auspices of the newly established MIACEA. Since then, the number of Egyptian emigrants has increased significantly.

Recent statistical estimates claim that the number of Egyptian emigrants is now above 3 million to 4 million (Ibrahim & Mohieddin, 1993), among them about 800,000 persons who migrated to Western countries such as the United States, Canada, Australia, the United Kingdom, France, Italy, Austria, Germany and also to some Latin American countries such as Brazil, Argentina, and Mexico (Al-Ahram, 1999a). It was noted that most Egyptian emigrants to the Western countries were well-educated persons including about 4,000 scientists, physicians, engineers, and university staff members (Ewis, 1985).

In this context, Fersoon (1985) and Yaseen (1984) pointed out that approximately 70–73% of the Arab graduate students who went to the United States, Canada, and Europe did not return to their original countries after they had earned their academic degrees. As Fersoon (1985) reported, only 27% of the total number of Arab persons immigrating to the Western countries entered the United States and Canada as legal immigrants. Between 1966 and 1977, more than 6,000 Arab scientists (among whom 4,000 were engineers, 1,000 physicists, and 1000 social scientists; 2,000 of the total 6,000 were Egyptians) immigrated to the United States. This number constituted about 5% of the total number of scientists who migrated to the United States in this period. Other statistics showed that 20% of the Egyptian emigrants to the U.S.A. were engineers, and they made up about 2% of all engineers working in the United States in 1977 (Fisher, 1985).

The rest of the Egyptian emigrants (about 3 million) can be found in various Arab countries, especially the six oil-producing Persian Gulf States: Saudi Arabia, Kuwait, the United Arab Emirates, Qatar, Bahrain, and the Sultanate of Oman, in that order. Since the early 1970s, a large number of Egyptians also immigrated to Iraq. Because of the war between Iraq and Iran from 1980 to 1990, they were much needed in Iraq to replace those Iraqis who had become soldiers. The Egyptians worked in fields such as agriculture, industry, housing construction, governmental sectors, and the service sectors.

During the 1970s and 1980s, many Egyptians had also moved to Libya to help build that country's infrastructure. However, at the end of the 1980s, because of mounting economic difficulties, fewer Egyptians remained in Libya.

A large number of Egyptian migrants to various other Arab countries were farmers/peasants and skilled and unskilled workers (Ewis, 1985). In addition, since the early 1970s many well-educated Egyptians have moved to various Arab countries to work there as teachers, engineers, physicians, and nurses; others worked at the universities. In 1988, the number of Egyptian schoolteachers at the primary-, intermediate-, and secondary-school levels who were working in the Arab countries was estimated at 30,000 (*Al-Watan,* 1988). In this context, some writers have pointed out that the migration of the Egyptians' university staff members to some of the Arab countries constitutes a "brain drain." For instance, in the field of psychology in 1987, it was estimated that about 200 Egyptian Ph.D.-level psychologists were working at Arab universities outside Egypt for various time periods (R. A. Ahmed, 1992).

Abdel-Rahman (1996), Fergani (1988), and Ibrahim and Mohieddin (1993) reported that about 90% of the Egyptian emigrants were between 20 and 45 years of age and that nearly 90% of the emigrants were males. These results support the estimations previously provided by Birks and Sinclair (1980).

It should be noted that among the Egyptians who resided in Arab countries, a considerable percentage were university staff members, judges, and schoolteachers. These were invited by the various Arab countries to work for a limited period of time (4 years for judges and school teachers, and 10 years for university staff members which are typically divided up into two separate periods). Some of these Egyptians, however, decided to stay in the new country after they ended their leave from their original Egyptian institutions (Birks & Sinclair, 1980; Ibrahim & Mohieddin, 1993).

In 1986, the number of Egyptian immigrants to other Arab countries was estimated at 2,250,000 or 4.5% of the overall Egyptian population (Ali & Abou-Zaid, 1996; Ibrahim & Mohieddin, 1993). They resided in the following countries: Iraq (35%), Saudi Arabia (30%), Kuwait (12%), Jordan (7.4%), and Libya (2.7%). In addition, official statistics for January 1998 show that the number of Egyptian emigrants to Arab countries is about 2 million (*Al-Ahram,* 1999b).

Fergani (1984) studied the emigration of Egyptians to the oil-producing Persian Gulf countries and its impact on the development process in the Arab world and made the following conclusions:

- The immigration of Egyptians to other Arab countries represented a type of migration in which people move from a Third World country to other Third World countries. In this context, Egyptians mostly preferred to move to other Arab countries reasonably similar to Egypt in cultural characteristics and level of development.

- The immigration of Egyptians to other Arab countries is usually temporary in nature (except in the case of Iraq), and it differs from the typical pattern of migration by Egyptians to Western countries.

- Although the migration of Egyptians to other Arab countries, and especially to the oil-producing Persian Gulf States, is not forever, the Egyptian migrants make up a highly significant proportion of the labor force in these states, occupying a variety of occupations and professions.

- The migration of Egyptians to the oil-producing Persian Gulf States in particular, and to other Arab countries in general, has undergone many changes during the last 4 decades. The number of Egyptian migrants to these countries varied over time, sometimes decreasing and sometimes increasing. It was also noted that those Arab countries receiving Egyptian or other Arab immigrants adopted many precautionary procedures to counteract the possible negative impact of these immigrants on the native populations, but comparable precautionary procedures were not adopted by the countries from which these immigrants came.

- The number of Egyptians who emigrated to other (especially oil-producing) Arab countries has been much larger than is indicated in the official statistics.

Because of the Iraqi invasion of Kuwait on August 2, 1990, and the ensuing second gulf war from February to March, 1991, more than one-half million Egyptian immigrants to Iraq and Kuwait (and a lesser number of Egyptian residents in the other oil-producing Persian Gulf States) had to return to Egypt (Ibrahim & Mohieddin, 1993).

REASONS FOR IMMIGRATION

It seems that the reasons why Egyptians migrate to Western countries are different from those that motivate Egyptians to migrate to Arab countries. Egyptians immigrating to Western countries frequently wish to change their economic, social, and cultural status, or perhaps their educational and professional levels, establish a new life in the new society, and/or join their relatives who had migrated before them. Although Egyptian law allows Egyptian emigrants to keep their original citizenship and to acquire double citizenship, only a small number of Egyptian immigrants to either Western or Arab countries make use of this possibility. Moreover, Egyptian immigration to Western countries is in most cases accompanied by a belief that it will be forever. As a result of this belief, Egyptian immigrants to Western countries frequently cut their ties with their mother country. Unfortunately, no studies have been carried out to investigate the motives and reasons that lead Egyptians to immigrate to the West.

Fergani (1988), however, noted that in the case of the Egyptians who immigrated either to Arab or Western countries, it was typically an individual decision. It was usually made by the migrant with some limited influence coming respectively from friends, parents, siblings, and spouses.

Several sociological and psychological research studies have been conducted during the last 2 decades to examine the reasons why Egyptians migrate to Arab countries (Abdel-Moety, 1982; Abdel-Rahman, 1996; Abdo, 1989; S. N. Ahmed, 1983; Al-Feel, 1989; Al-Quady, 1990; Birks & Sinclair 1980; Ewis, 1985; Fergani, 1984, 1988; Leila, 1995; Merquis, 1985; Moussa, 1987; Thabet, 1979; Yaseen, 1984). Ewis (1985) reported that among the reasons that led Egyptians to migrate to the oil-producing Persian Gulf States were the following:

- The oil-producing Persian Gulf States have small populations and therefore have experienced a growing need to import labor forces who can work in construction, provide services, teach, and support various governmental sectors.

- Egypt is a country that has an educated labor force exceeding its needs.

- The typical salaries given to the immigrant labor force working in the oil-producing Persian Gulf States were (and are) five to six times higher than those they would have been able to earn in their homelands.

- It had been expected that both Libya and the Sudan (Egypt's closest neighbors) would receive the largest numbers of Egyptian immigrants, but that turned out not to be the case for both economic and political reasons.

In response to an early sociological study, Abdel-Moety (1982) investigated the emigration of rural Egyptians to the oil-producing Persian Gulf States and the social correlates of the emigration. The study was based on the following three assumptions:

- The immigration of rural Egyptians to the oil-producing Persian Gulf States should be seen in light of the economic development patterns that have been occurring in both Egypt and the oil-producing Persian Gulf States.

- Emigration of rural Egyptians (and other Egyptians as well) should be seen in connection with the political and economic climate that governed life in Egypt during the 1970s.

- The widespread immigration of rural Egyptians to the oil-producing Persian Gulf States, which decreased during the 1970s and early mid-1980s, has changed the traditionally negative image of Egyptian farmers who were considered, for hundreds of years, as the people who did not want to move from their land.

Abdel-Moety's (1982) results pointed to great changes in women's traditional social roles, especially within their families, whenever the husbands migrated. This in turn led to considerable changes in the rural communities' conceptions of the woman's role and status (Mohiedden, 1991).

As a result of the absence of fathers stemming from migration, some of the family's functions, including the socialization of children, have been adversely affected. Examples of such negative consequences include increased aggression in children, children's having a poor image of their father, weak father-child relationships, and increased delinquency among the children of migrant fathers.

Research results have also shown that new commercial and consumer activities have appeared in the rural areas as a consequence of migration. This in turn has led to dramatic changes in the attitudes of many agricultural and rural workers toward their places of origin. In most cases, these workers have tried to find other jobs, so that they would get higher wages, work fewer hours, and engage in less heavy labor. Finally, and as a result of the migration of rural Egyptians to the oil-producing Persian Gulf States, values emphasizing hope, productivity, and affiliation have been adversely affected. As Abdel-Moety (1982) noticed, these changes in value systems have had a negative influence on the economic and sociocultural development process in Egypt.

Al-Feel (1989) reported the following reasons as the push factors leading to the immigration of Egyptians to various Arab countries: seeking better salaries and life conditions, improving one's economic circumstances (this was true for both well-educated and uneducated persons), and trying to overcome one's feeling that one is unable to provide the necessary living requirements for one's family.

Al-Quady (1990) investigated the migration impact on the social values of Egyptian farmers by comparing samples of farmers and agricultural workers who had immigrated to other Arab countries with comparable samples of non-migrants. She found that the relationships between fathers and their children as well as general family cohesion had deteriorated in the sample of migrants. The wives of the migrants became more and more involved in family affairs while at the same time the fathers' role weakened. In addition, 37% of her nonmigrant sample responded that they would emigrate if given the right opportunity.

In a similar context, Abdel-Rahman (1996) found that the well-educated Egyptians who had immigrated to Saudi Arabia during the last 2 decades were motivated by the following reasons: desire to have one's own house or flat, to establish a family, and to have an opportunity to secure a suitable job.

THE IMPACT OF MIGRATION

Several Egyptian studies have been carried out by sociologists and psychologists to assess the impact of emigration on both emigrants and nonemigrants, on their families, and on Egypt's overall economic and social situation. Examples of such studies include the reports by Abdel-Maqsoud and Tahoun (1993), Abdel-Moety (1984), Abdel-Rahman (1996), Abdel-Sabour (1987), Abdo (1989), Abdruba (1985), S. K. Ahmed (1992), Al-Faramawy (1990), Ali and Abou-Zaid (1996), Awamat (1985), Buddres (1984), Farag (1985), Ibrahim (1982), Ibrahim and Mohieddin (1993), Merquis (1985), Mohieddin (1998), Moussa (1987), Mustapha and Soliman (1993), Shuraydi (1990), and Youssef (1993).

Studies by Fergani (1984, 1988), Ibrahim and Mohieddin (1993), and Mustapha and Soliman (1993) have shown that money transfers to Egypt by emigrants increased from £E140 million in 1974 to £E2,374 million in 1984 and to £E2,845 million in 1987, which amounted to 3.3 % of the national income.

One example of the importance for Egypt's economy of the money transfers of Egyptian migrants to the oil-producing Persian Gulf States could be found during the gulf war of 1990 to 1991 when more than 1 million Egyptian migrants to these states (especially Kuwait, Iraq, and Saudi Arabia) had to return to Egypt. This caused various economic and social problems in Egypt such as an increase in the unemployment rate and an increase in the number and severity of various social problems.

As for the impact of emigration on the social and psychological well-being of Egyptians, several studies have focused on personality traits, social psychological adjustment, values, and changes occurring in the family structure. Some of the results of these investigations follow.

Two Egyptian studies (Abdel-Sabour, 1987; Abdruba, 1985) investigated the impact of migration on feelings of affiliation in Egyptian immigrants to oil-producing Persian Gulf States. Both studies reported that the respondents experienced intense needs for affiliation and also showed increased feelings of alienation. Moreover, the Egyptian emigrants felt abused by their families and relatives back home to whom they had to send gifts, presents, and money. It should be noted that similar results have been obtained in other studies such as those conducted by Abdel-Rahman (1996) and Mohieddin (1998).

Abdel-Moety's (1984) study of a sample of Egyptians who had been working for a long time in Kuwait revealed that a great number of them were suffering from problems such as dissatisfaction with their salaries and the type and time schedules of the jobs they held, unsatisfactory social relations at their place of work, high housing and living expenses, and excessive expenses for their children's education.

Amawat's (1985) study revealed a positive correlation between increased emigration from Egypt to other Arab countries and the number of problems experienced by the children of the emigrants such as psychosocial maladjustment, cultural alienation, and loss of identity. Similar results were reported by Abdo (1989), who found that most Egyptians working abroad had experienced powerful cultural and social shocks, which later led them to attempt to adjust to the new society's values and traditions. These results are similar to those obtained in Abdel-Rahman's (1996) investigation of Egyptian immigrants to Saudi Arabia.

Buddres (1984), who studied a sample of Egyptian immigrants to the oil-producing Persian Gulf States, found that they were suffering from the following problems: an increased rate of broken homes, a high rate of juvenile delinquency, a high divorce rate, a greater incidence of children showing academic problems, less social contact, and difficulty in having to adopt new and strange habits and cultural concepts. These new and strange habits and cultural concepts were frequently in contradiction to prevailing Egyptian habits and cultural concepts, and they also clashed with the local economic conditions.

In a recent study by Abdruba (1988), it was found that the immigration of Egyptians to other Arab countries is associated with problems such as experiencing feelings of hardship and difficulties concerning one's work; problems adjusting to new behavioral rules; feelings of alienation; conflicts between one's original culture and the new culture; and, finally, maladjustment leading to poor self-esteem and feelings of isolation. These results are similar to the findings of a previous study conducted by Yaseen (1984) on Arab migrants to Western countries.

As for the impact of emigration on families, Farag's (1985) study showed that Egyptian immigrant families were suffering from a decline in social stability and a dramatic decline with respect to values such as cooperation and social integration.

In 1987, Moussa found significant psychological differences between a group of Egyptian wives of immigrants and a similar group of nonimmigrant wives. The first group scored lower than the second group on scales of social adjustment and experienced more personal and social tensions.

Youssef (1993) investigated the social adjustment of Egyptian immigrants at three different educational levels (e.g., uneducated persons, secondary-school and university graduates, and some respondents with master's or doctorate degrees) to Saudi Arabian society. His results showed the following:

- Social adjustment was poor in all three subsamples.

- Factors leading to social adjustment and maladjustment differed according to educational level.

- The immigrants were faced with a variety of problems: When compared with Saudi citizens, the immigrants experienced discrimination with regard to rights, duties, and obligations, and in many cases, the Egyptian immigrants were unable to bring their families to live with them, which led them to experience negative feelings such as loneliness.

A recent demographic study conducted by the Demographic Center in Cairo (*Al-Ahram,* 1998) focused on 1,651 families whose fathers were working abroad. The study showed the following results:

- Most of the Egyptian immigrants were between 20 and 45 years old.

- The immigrants' wives were more likely than their nonimmigrant counterparts to have no more than two children.

- The educational levels of immigrants were higher than those of the nonimmigrants.

- Most of the immigrants and especially those living in the Arab countries reported a preference to stay abroad for no more than 5 years.

- Absence of husbands led to great changes in the family structure and in the roles of family members, especially those of wives. They became increasingly responsible for all aspects of running the household and most family affairs.

In a sociological study, Abdel-Rahman (1996) noted that the educational level of Egyptian immigrants to Saudi Arabia has increased during the last 2 decades. In 1996, 47% of her male respondents and 60% of her female respondents were university graduates. The respondents indicated they preferred to get married at a later age (males were 30–40 years; females were 22–30 years) when compared with the nonimmigrant group. Other results showed that the male immigrants increasingly tended to have only one wife; the rate of polygamy was very low among immigrants when compared with that among nonimmigrants. Mothers of infants in the immigrant families were more likely to prefer artificial feeding over breast-feeding. They also used nursery servants and maids more frequently than the nonimmigrants. Finally, Abdel-Rahman reported great changes concerning the roles of family members and especially those of fathers. The fathers in the immigrant families became increasingly preoccupied with their work, which affected negatively their roles inside the family. As a result, the relationships and interactions within the immigrant families were weakened.

As for the impact of immigration on values, some research studies during the last 15 years have assessed the changes in value systems resulting from emigration to both Arab and Western countries. Examples of these studies include those of S. K. Ahmed (1992), Ali and Abou-Zaid (1996), Ibrahim (1982), and Shuraydi (1990).

Ibrahim (1982) reported that Egyptians working in the oil-producing Persian Gulf States showed a gradual decline in many values and traditions which otherwise have been part of Egyptian society for a very long time.

On the basis of the Allport-Vernon scale assessing values based on Spranger's typology, S. K. Ahmed (1992) investigated the dominant and desired values in a sample of Egyptian families who had returned from Kuwait as a result of the Iraqi invasion. Families were chosen from among those who had spent at least 15 years in Kuwait, and they consisted of fathers, mothers, and children. Results showed that the parents emphasized social, economic, and political values as dominant values, whereas children showed more interest in theoretical and aesthetic values. No differences were obtained between parents and children concerning religious values. The above mentioned results showed that reverse migration caused great differences between the value systems of parents and those of their children, and that these changes did not come as a surprise to the fathers.

In another study, Ali and Abou-Zaid (1996) pointed out that the migration process caused noticeable changes in the personality traits (e.g., increased neuroticism, tension, needs for affiliation, etc.) of the returning Egyptian migrants and also in their social values. It also led many Egyptian workers and employees to abandon their original occupations. These results were in agreement with the results of an earlier study conducted by Merquis (1985).

Some Egyptian studies have assessed the stress experienced by those Egyptian teachers working in other Arab countries. Examples of these studies include those by Al-Faramawy (1990) and by Abdel-Masqoud and Tahoun (1993).

Al-Faramawy (1990) studied 175 Egyptian male teachers working inside and outside Egypt. He found that teachers working abroad reported more stress than their Egyptian counterparts. Abdel-Masqoud and Tahoun (1993) compared the stress levels of 390 male and female Egyptian and Saudi teachers working in Saudi Arabia. Results showed that the stress levels of Saudi male teachers when compared with those of their Egyptian counterparts were significantly higher. However, the Egyptian male teachers working in Saudi Arabia reported significantly more stress than the Egyptian female teachers. In contrast, Saudi female teachers reported more stress than their Saudi male counterparts.

As for problems that Egyptian immigrants in Western countries face, some studies have been conducted mainly by Egyptian and/or Arab researchers residing in the West (e.g., Al-Saffar & Borgà, 1996; Mohieddin, 1998; Shuraydi, 1990). In the paragraphs that follow, the main results of these studies are briefly discussed.

In a study conducted by Shuraydi (1990) to assess the influence of Western value systems on Arab immigrants and their families in the United States and Canada, it was found that the children encountered many difficulties concerning their school performance. Prominent among these difficulties were language difficulties. There was insufficient counseling of immigrant parents, which otherwise could have helped them to solve their adjustment problems in the new society. Shuraydi also pointed out that Arab immigrants in the United States and Canada are facing another difficulty which stems from the new societies: These societies have not yet achieved a suitable understanding of the Arab culture. In my opinion, Arab immigrants in the United States and Canada are themselves partly responsible for that, because they did not make sufficient efforts to introduce their culture to their fellow Americans and Canadians. In addition, it seems that Arab immigrants have failed to adjust successfully to these new societies, and they may therefore encounter a lack of understanding from others.

Al-Saffar and Borgà (1996) studied the use of psychiatric services in a multicultural population in Sweden by collecting data on all psychiatric Swedish-born persons, immigrants from Persia and Arabic-speaking areas of the Middle East (among them some Egyptians), and other immigrants who attended the clinic more than once in 1993. Immigrant groups were overrepresented as patients by 50%. Immigrants were more frequently diagnosed as suffering from somatoform disorders, whereas a personality disorder diagnosis was more frequently established for the Swedes. No group differences were noted regarding psychoses and affective disorders. "Exile strain" was detected most frequently among immigrants from Farsi- and Arabic-speaking areas. It seems, then, that the Persian and Arab immigrants experienced psychosomatic disorders and exile strain, which reflected maladjustment of these immigrants to the Swedish society.

In a recent sociological conceptual study on Egyptian transnationals/transmigrants to the United States, Mohieddin (1998) concluded that they are facing the following challenges:

- Many Egyptian immigrant parents in the United States and Canada do not agree that their children, especially girls, should get married by selecting a spouse from the new society. In many cases, the parents brought their daughters back to Egypt once they reached the age of marriage, and with respect to their sons, the parents encouraged them to choose Egyptian wives.

- It was found that in many of the families, children tended to return to their father's native land, although they were born, had grown up, and had been educated in the United States. One manifestation of this trend among this second-generation was an increasing tendency to learn the Arabic language in order to be able to return "home" in the future.

- Many Egyptian immigrants in the United States (and also in other Western and Arab countries) wish to bring gifts and presents when they visit their relatives in Egypt. The Egyptian authorities are allowing this within certain limits. Some researchers believe that such behavior could have a negative impact on the Egyptian value system and on the local economy as well.

- Since the mid-1980s, some Egyptian emigrants have been interested in investing their savings in Egypt. In this context, the Association for Egyptian-American Businessmen was established several years ago. This association has had a promising impact on the course of the Egyptian economy. It should also be noted that such involvements provide the Egyptian American businessmen with an opportunity to serve as leaders for the rest of the Egyptian immigrants to the United States and Canada. Without such an association, Egyptian immigrants could not easily achieve such a prestigious status either in their new societies or in Egypt.

- Egyptian immigrants in the United States, Canada, and Europe (and also in the oil-producing Persian Gulf States) frequently transfer money to Egypt. Such transfers have played an important role in the Egyptian economy since the early 1980s as was already pointed out.

REVERSE MIGRATION

As we mentioned earlier, many Egyptian immigrants to either Western or Arab countries have returned home since 1985 due to many different reasons (Fergani, 1988). Several Egyptian research studies have assessed the characteristics of "reverse immigrants" (Abdo, 1989; Ahmed, 1992; Ali & Abou-Zaid, 1996). In this section, the main results of these studies are briefly reviewed.

Among the common problems facing Arab migrants to the Western countries are the nonexistence of Arab schools for their children, the paucity of suitable places for praying, and a lack of Islamic cemeteries to bury the dead. In Montreal, Quebec, Canada, for example, where more than 20,000 Arab immigrants reside, there exist no Arab schools at any educational level (Yaseen, 1984).

Abdo's (1989) study of families who returned to Egypt after having spent 15 or more years as immigrants in some oil-producing Persian Gulf States reported that they were facing several social and psychological problems as a result of the wide economic, social, and cultural differences between Egypt and those states. The researcher noticed that facing such problems frequently led to a high degree of social and psychological maladjustment.

Ali and Abou-Zaid (1996) compared various personality traits between a sample of married Egyptians who returned from oil-producing Persian Gulf States after they had worked there for a period of 5 to 10 years and a comparable group of locals. The researcher administered the Group Personality Projective Test (GPPT), Rohner's (1990) personality questionnaire, and a locally devised scale for assessing values. Results showed that the returning Egyptians, in comparison to the locals, scored lower on indexes of happiness, will, and affiliation, and higher on indices of anxiety, care, isolation, and asking for help. As for the performance on Rohner's scale, the returning group received higher scores on the inefficiency and emotional instability scales and lower scores on the aggression scale. These results suggest that the returning Egyptians experienced significant adjustment problems and suffered from reduced feelings of psychological well-being.

CONCLUSIONS

Based on our review of pertinent sociological and psychological studies that have been carried out during the last 2 decades on Egyptian migrants, several conclusions may be drawn. First, according to Ewis (1985), the immigration of Egyptians to other Arab countries and to Western countries took the form of two major waves. The first wave occurred after the 1967 war, in which some Egyptians, mostly well-educated ones, immigrated to such Western countries as the United States, Canada, Australia, the United Kingdom, France, Germany, and Austria. This wave, however, was characterized by very small numbers. The second wave occurred after the 1973 war, which was characterized by an increasing number of Egyptians migrating to other Arab countries and especially to the oil-producing Persian Gulf States, and also (to a lesser extent) to the Western countries. The migration to the Persian Gulf countries reached one-half million in 1973, 1 million in 1974, and 1.75 million in 1978. This migration affected 18% of the total labor force in Egypt.

Second, although immigration of Egyptians to other countries has been a very important phenomenon since the early 1980s, the number of relevant research studies remains very small. Additional and more comprehensive studies are very much needed. For example, although a number of studies have investigated Egyptians who have emigrated to Saudi Arabia, only a very few studies have focused on Egyptians who presently reside or used to reside in Kuwait. Moreover, it appears that the Egyptian government has encouraged the immigration of Egyptians to other countries especially since the early 1980s. However, the negative effects of immigration have so far been insufficiently considered (Abdel-Rahman, 1996; Ibrahim & Mohieddin, 1993).

Third, no exact statistics exist concerning the number of Egyptians who have emigrated to Western or Arab countries. Although some official sources have estimated the number of Egyptian emigrants at 4 million, other official and unofficial estimates indicate that the number of Egyptians residing abroad may be no more than 2 million. In addition, no exact studies or statistics exist on the size of and reasons for reverse immigration (Novel & Novel, 1993).

Fourth, although the money transfers made by Egyptian emigrants have played an important role in the Egyptian economy and amount to 3.3% of the national income, many Egyptian sociologists (Ibrahim & Mohieddin, 1993; Mohieddin, 1993; Novel & Novel, 1993) have reported that these transfers have caused considerable damage to Egyptian's social life and to the local economy as well. For example, the Egyptian rate of inflation increased because of these transfers. Moreover, a great many of these transfers occurred outside legal channels. In addition, many Egyptian immigrants prefer to invest their money in limited activities such as house construction and in the small consumer industry but not in infrastructure projects.

Fifth, many researchers have pointed out that the immigration of Egyptians to other countries, and specifically to the Western countries, leads to an important brain drain that is weakening the country. I may mention in this context the studies conducted by Fersoon (1985), Ewis (1985), and Yaseen (1984), who reported that 70–73% of those Arab graduate students traveling to the Western countries for higher qualification did not return to their original countries.

Sixth, according to the results of the research studies investigating the impact of emigration on Egyptian immigrants in both Western and Arab countries, these new societies have failed to be a melting pot for most Egyptians. One possible reason for this failure, especially in the Western countries, may be found in the observation made by Shuraydi (1990) that American and Canadian societies have failed to achieve a suitable understanding of the Arab culture.

Seventh, the immigration of Egyptians to other countries has frequently had a negative impact on the psychological well-being of the immigrants and their families. Relevant studies have pointed to a decided weakening of important value systems, and a negative change in family structures, functions, and roles. As a result of the father's/husband's absence, the wife becomes more involved in and responsible for the care of the family and its members. Also, the father's absence has often negative consequences for the socialization of his children.

Finally, although many negative consequences have resulted from the migration of Egyptians to Arab and Western countries, some positive consequences of this migration can nevertheless be discerned. In general, and through migration, Egyptians have gained direct contact with other societies, thereby contradicting the old saying that Egyptians do not want to leave their homeland. Egyptian migration, especially to the oil-producing Persian Gulf States, has led to many changes in both the migrants' lives and the lives of the remaining non-migrants in Egypt. For example, the socioeconomic level of the migrants has been markedly raised, the unemployment rate in Egypt has been reduced, and money transfers to Egypt made by migrants to the oil-producing Persian Gulf States have increased from £E140 million in 1974 to £E2.845 million in 1987 (Ibrahim & Mohieddin, 1993; Mustapha & Soliman, 1993). One example of the importance of these transfers to the Egyptian economy could be seen during the 1990–1991 gulf war, when more than 1 million Egyptian migrants to Kuwait, Iraq, and Saudi Arabia had to return to Egypt. This led to several economic and social problems (e.g., an increased unemployment rate, a higher inflation rate).

In the case of the Egyptian migration to Western countries, the following consequences can be mentioned. Some Arab organizations have been formed in the United States and Canada by Egyptian and other Arab immigrants. They are aimed at presenting the Arab culture to these new societies, defending the rights of Arabs, and establishing links among Arab migrants to the United States and Canada. Examples of these organizations include the Union of Arab Graduates from American Universities, which was established shortly after the 1967 war with Israel, and the Union of Egyptian Scientists and Engineers, which was established during the 1970s (Fersoon, 1985). Also of importance is the Association of American-Egyptian Professors (AAEP), which was formed in 1973 by a group of Egyptian professors who had migrated to the United States earlier and who were working there. Since 1974, the AAEP has helped to establish strong connections between Arab migrants and their original homelands by, for instance, establishing scientific and academic contacts with many Egyptian institutions of higher education. Examples of the AAEP's efforts include exchanging staff members, collaborating with Egyptian researchers in carrying out various studies especially in medicine, engineering, and economics, and helping some Egyptian governmental and nongovernmental institutions and sectors to improve their performance through training programs organized and held by the AAEP in the United States and in Egypt (Ewis, 1985).

Also noteworthy is that the migration of Arabs in general and of Egyptians in particular to the Western countries (the United States, Canada, and Europe) has provided them with good opportunities to establish themselves scientifically, academically, economically, and personally. Many of the Egyptian migrants to Western societies have found in these new societies a favorable atmosphere to become experts in their respective fields. Examples include geologist Farouk al-Baz (NASA, in the United States); the 1999 Nobel Prize Laureate in chemistry, Ahmed H. Zewail (in the United States), and the famous surgeon, Sir Magdy Yacoub (in the United Kingdom).

In recent years, the political, economic, and social situation in the oil-producing Persian Gulf States has no longer allowed for these states to support a large noncitizen labor force. As a result, it is expected that many Egyptian immigrants to these states will return home sooner or later. In contrast, the economic situation in Egypt has in recent years witnessed some improvements so that, for example, the government was able to support some 600,000 additional opportunities for work each year (*Al-Ahram,* 1999c).

Nevertheless, the Egyptian government needs to take further measures, both economically and socially, to meet the conditions and situations that are likely to arise when many Egyptian immigrants to other Arab countries (and especially to the Persian Gulf States) begin to return home.

REFERENCES

Abdel-Maqsoud, H. A., & Tahoun, H. (1993). Teachers' psychological stress and its relation to some variables: A cross-cultural study. *Journal of the Faculty of Education* (Ain Shams University, Egypt), *2*(17), 295–333 (in Arabic).

Abdel-Moety, A. M. (1982). *Some social variables related to the migration of rural workers to the Arab Gulf oil-producing states: A pilot study of the motives and the impact of emigration of agricultural labor on an Egyptian village.* Cairo, Egypt: Authority for Family Control and Population. (in Arabic)

Abdel-Moety, A. M. (1984). *Emigration to the Arab Gulf oil-producing states and the social issue: A field study on a sample of Egyptian workers in Kuwait.* Cairo, Egypt: Madobouli Bookshop. (in Arabic)

Abdel-Rahman, M. E. H. (1996). *Social interaction between Egypt and Arab Gulf societies: A study of culture and society.* Alexandria, Egypt: Dar el-Maarifah al-Gammeiah. (in Arabic)

Abdel-Sabour, Y. (1987). *Needs for affiliation and social responsibility and their relationship with attitudes toward schooling in a sample of children of Egyptians working abroad.* Unpublished doctoral dissertation, Assiut University, Faculty of Education, Sôhag, Egypt. (in Arabic)

Abdo, F. (1989). The cultural impact of emigrant families: An educational study. *Journal of the Faculty of Education in Demiat, Mansoura University* (Egypt), *12.* (in Arabic)

Abdruba, S. M. (1985). *Emigration to the Arab countries: Its motives and consequences.* Unpublished master thesis, Ain Shams University, Faculty of Arts, Cairo, Egypt. (in Arabic)

Ahmed, S. K. (1992). The predominant and desired values in a sample of Egyptian families having returned from Kuwait. *Journal of Psychology (Egypt),* *6*(21), 24–38. (in Arabic)

Ahmed, S. N. (1983). The impact of structural changes in Egyptian society on its value system and its development. *Journal of the Social Sciences* (Kuwait), *11*(1), 113–130. (in Arabic)

Ahmed, R. A. (1991). Women in Egypt and the Sudan. In L. L. Adler (Ed.), *Women in cross-cultural perspective* (pp. 107–133). New York: Praeger.

Ahmed, R. A. (1992). Psychology in the Arab countries. In L. L. Adler, U. P. Gielen, & N. A. Milgram (Eds.), *Psychology in international perspective: 50 years of the International Council of Psychologists* (pp. 127–150). Amsterdam, Netherlands: Swets & Zeitlinger.

Al-Ahram. (Cairo, Egypt). (1998, September 16). (in Arabic)

Al-Ahram. (Cairo, Egypt). (1999a, February 9). (in Arabic)

Al-Ahram. (Cairo, Egypt). (1999b, February 25). (in Arabic)

Al-Ahram. (Cairo, Egypt). (1999c, November 12). (in Arabic)

Al-Faramawy, H. A. (1990). Teachers' stress level and its relation with some variables. In *Proceedings of the 2nd Annual Conference on the Egyptian Child: Its Socialization and Caring for it* (pp. 427–451). Cairo, Egypt.

Al-Feel, M R. (1989). Immigration of Arab scientists and the role of the Council of the Gulf States to make use of it. *Annals of the Faculty of Arts, Kuwait University, 9.* (in Arabic)

Ali, A. A., & Abou-Zaid, A. A. (1996). A psychological study of some personality and value variables in a sample of Egyptian workers who returned from abroad. *Journal of Psychology* (Egypt), *10*(37), 176–192. (in Arabic)

Al-Quady, M. A. (1990). Egyptian labor emigration: A field study of the impact of emigration on the social values of Egyptian farmers (peasants). *Journal of the Faculty of Arts, Menoufia University* (Egypt), *1*(1), 53–100. (in Arabic)

Al-Saffar, S., & Borgà, P. (1996). Outpatient psychiatry for a multicultural population in suburban Stockholm. *Abstracts of the 24th International Congress of Psychology,* Montréal, Canada, 16–21 August, 1996. *International Journal of Psychology, 31*(3–4), No. 279–8, p. 193.

Al-Watan. (Kuwait City, Kuwait). (1988, May 18). (in Arabic)

Awamat, G. (1985). Problems and issues facing the education of children of Arab emigrants to Europe, and France in particular. *Arab Journal of Education* (Tunisia), *2.* (in Arabic)

Birks, G. C., & Sinclair, C. A. (1980). *Population and international immigration to the Arab countries: Primary data.* Geneva, Switzerland: International Labor Organization. (in Arabic)

Buddres, J. E. (1984). *Social and psychological impact of the immigration of Egyptians to other Arab countries.* Unpublished master's thesis, Ain Shams University, Faculty of Arts, Cairo, Egypt. (in Arabic)

Ewis, I. (1985). Egyptians' emigration. In A. B. Zahlan (Supervisor), *Emigration of Arab professionals (talents): Research and discussion of the seminar organized by the Economic Committee of West Asia, United Nations* (3rd ed., pp. 231–242). Beirut, Lebanon: Center for Studies on Arab Unity. (in Arabic)

Farag, S. A. (1985). *Rural immigration: A study of their motives and adjustment, and results.* Unpublished master's thesis. Ain Shams University, Faculty of Arts, Cairo, Egypt. (in Arabic)

Fergani, N. (1984). *Emigration to oil: The dimensions of the Egyptians' migration to the oil-producing Arab Gulf states and its impact on the development process in the Arab World.* Beirut, Lebanon: Center for Studies on Arab Unity. (in Arabic)

Fergani, N. (1988). *To earn a living: A field study of the emigration of Egyptians to other Arab countries.* Beirut, Lebanon: Center for Studies on Arab Unity. (in Arabic)

Fersoon, S. (1985). American-Arab professionals and the emigration of minds. In A. B. Zahlan (Supervisor), *Emigration of Arab professionals (talents): Research and discussion of the seminar organized by the Economic Committee of West Asia, United Nations* (3rd ed., pp. 243–265). Beirut, Lebanon: Center for Studies on Arab Unity. (in Arabic)

Fisher, A. (1985). Arab scientific talents in the United States of America. In A. B. Zahlan (Supervisor), *Emigration of the Arab professionals (talents): Research and discussion of the Seminar organized by the Economic Committee of West Asia, United Nations* (3rd ed., pp. 210–230). Beirut, Lebanon: Center for Studies on Arab Unity. (in Arabic)

Ibrahim, S. (1982). *The Arab social system: A study of the social impact of oil wealth.* Beirut, Lebanon: Center for Studies on Arab Unity. (in Arabic)

Ibrahim, S., & Mohieddin, M. M. (1993). Studies on the emigration of Egyptian labor force since the 1970s. In N. Khouri (Ed.), *Immigration movement of labor forces and reverse immigration* (pp. 11–57). International Labor Organization, Arab Regional Bureau. (in Arabic)

Leila, A. (1995). *Youth in a changing society: A retrospective on reminiscence and violence.* Alexandria, Egypt: Dar el-Maarifah Al-Gammeiah. (in Arabic)

Merquis, W. F. (1985). *The impact of the transfer of the Egyptian labor force to other countries on the industrial development in Egypt.* Unpublished master's thesis, Cairo University, Faculty of Arts, Cairo, Egypt. (in Arabic)

Mohieddin, M. M. (1991). Emigration of Egyptian peasants to the Arab countries: An attempt to explain the phenomenon. *Proceedings of the Seminar on Agriculture Affairs, April 28–29, 1991* (pp. 230–244). Cairo, Egypt: Center for Arab Research Studies and Documentation. (in Arabic)

Mohieddin, M. M. (1998, May). *Transnationals/transmigrants: A preliminary conception for studying the Egyptian personality in the United States of America.* Paper presented at the Fifth Annual Seminar of the Department of Sociology, Faculty of Arts, Cairo University, Cairo, Egypt. (in Arabic)

Moussa, M. (1987). *Social and psychological problems of some Egyptian families residing outside Egypt.* Unpublished doctoral dissertation, Ain Shams University, College of Girls, Cairo, Egypt. (in Arabic)

Mustapha, M. S., & Soliman, A. A. (1993). The social and economic impact of the emigration of Egyptian workers abroad. In N. Khouri (Ed.), *Emigration, movement of labor force, and reverse immigration* (pp. 79–109). International Labor Organization, Arab Regional Bureau. (in Arabic)

Novel, M. N., & Novel, E. (1993). A suggested system for information concerning the reverse labor force. In N. Khouri (Ed.), *Emigration, movement of labor force, and reverse immigration* (pp. 179–198). International Labor Organization, Arab Regional Bureau. (in Arabic)

Rohner, R. P. (1990). *Handbook for the study of parental acceptance and rejection.* The Center for the Study of Parental Acceptance and Rejection, University of Connecticut, Storrs, CT.

Shuraydi, M. (1990). Cultural background of the Arabic-speaking students enrolled in governmental schools in the USA and Canada. In L. K. Meleika (Ed.), *Readings in social psychology in the Arab countries* (Vol. 5, pp. 444–451). Cairo, Egypt: General Egyptian Book Authority. (in Arabic)

Thabet, N. (1979). *Emigration to other countries: Its nature, motives, and impact.* Unpublished doctoral dissertation, Ain Shams University, Faculty of Arts, Cairo, Egypt. (in Arabic)

Yaseen, A. M. (1984). *Brain drain: Emigration of Arab talents to technological countries.* Beirut, Lebanon: Dar al-Andlus for Printing, Publishing, and Distributing. (in Arabic)

Youssef, M. H. (1993). The social adjustment of Egyptians working in Saudi Arabia: A field study on a sample of Egyptians residing in Berida City in Saudi Arabia. *Journal of Education, Faculty of Education, Al-Azhar University* (Egypt), *133.* (in Arabic)

18

Migration in South Africa:
A Profile of Patterns, Trends, and Impacts

André J. Pelser

SETTING THE SCENE: MIGRATION IN SOUTH
AND SOUTHERN AFRICA IN THE 1990s

The impact of people's migratory behavior on sociopolitical stability and socio-economic development has been a powerful force for social change throughout the centuries. Our epoch has proved to be no exception. As we begin the 21st century, the scope and impact of migration in southern Africa raises a number of complicated policy issues as new potential sources of conflict emerge alongside it.

Like elsewhere in the world, migration patterns in southern Africa are determined by both "push" and "pull" factors, although the push factors tend to prevail. Ever since the late 19th century, poor economic conditions and prospects have become the most important motivation for migration in the region. Due to a general perception of South Africa as a comparatively stable and wealthy country that offers ample economic opportunities, displaced and impoverished people from southern and lately even central Africa have been gravitating toward South Africa for many years. This process, however, has been occurring on an increasing scale since 1990, when profound political changes in South Africa were launched and gained momentum after the election of a new government in 1994. Gauteng Province, for example, is regarded as the migration center of Africa with its capital, Johannesburg, often being referred to as the "bright light" or "New York" of Africa (Schutte, 1993, pp. 3–4). In many ways, the harsh economic conditions in sending countries have either been triggered or exacerbated by realities such as political instability, civil strife, environmental degradation, and rapid population growth. In both Angola and Mozambique, civil wars have affected millions of people, most of whom are potential migrants.

In the past few years, the question of migration, especially of illegal migration to South Africa, has increasingly become one of the major policy issues that the South African government has to confront. The urgency of the issue is further intensified by the fact that public awareness of and public reaction to the presence of both legal and illegal immigrants in the country have risen notably during the past few years. As historically disadvantaged (Black) South Africans stake their claim to a decent livelihood, they increasingly find that their social environment has turned into a battleground for scarce resources, whether it be employment, housing, or social services. Apart from the creeping xenophobia and growing hostility toward aliens, there are myriad social effects caused by unimpeded immigration to South Africa. For example, in the past few years South Africans had to witness escalating rates in drug trafficking, organized crime, uncontrolled invasion of land, official corruption, and so on.

Thus migration, specifically the social consequences resulting from it, raises a number of complicated policy issues, both for South Africa and its neighboring countries. Part of its complexity for the South African government derives from the fact that migration cannot be categorically approached as either a domestic policy issue or a foreign (regional) policy issue; its very nature, scope and impact in the subcontinent involve elements of both. Therefore, when formulating a policy response, South Africa will have to consider and address both domestic and regional concerns. This may place contradictory demands on policymakers, not only in South Africa, but also in neighboring countries as they face the consequences of migration.

Albeit a central aspect in the issue of migration, the scope of this chapter does not allow for a sound in-depth analysis of those domestic and regional determinants that should be considered when formulating a policy response on migration. Rather, the purpose of this chapter is to briefly deal with various aspects pertaining to the nature and problem of migration in southern Africa in general and South Africa in particular. More specifically, I highlight the impact of migration on the social, political and economic life of South Africa, and also point out some implications for the region.

A TYPOLOGY OF MIGRATION IN SOUTH AFRICA

Given the multifaceted nature of the issue in question, this discussion reflects on the nature and consequences of migration in terms of four prominent categories of migrants in South Africa. Although this classification by no means proposes to be exhaustive or universal, such an approach does at least allow for comparisons. The four categories are (a) legal immigrants, (b) contract labor migrants, (c) illegal immigrants, and (d) emigrants.

Refugees, another category of migrants, will be included in the discussion of illegal immigrants. This reflects the interconnectedness of these two categories of migrants, as well as the fact that the pace of global events has increasingly rendered the distinction between refugees and illegal immigrants superfluous.

Legal Immigrants

South Africa has always been a popular destination for international migrants. In fact, some 20% of South African citizens have historical origins in other continents. A considerable proportion of the 5 million Europeans has roots in the Netherlands, Britain, Portugal, France, or Germany. A further 3 million South Africans have a combination of European, African, and Asian ancestry, while another 1 million can trace their descent to immigrants from India.

According to official statistics, between 1947 and 1990 South Africa has shown net migration losses in only 6 years, totaling a net gain of 674, 000 people (Toolo & Bethlehem, 1995, p. 16). In recent times, global events such as the collapse of the Soviet Union, the fall of the Berlin wall, the escalation of civil unrest in the Balkan region and some Asian states, as well as generally poor economic conditions in various countries worldwide, have led many foreigners to see South Africa as a haven and to seek residence there. In 1993, some South African missions abroad were receiving as many as 2,000 daily inquiries from prospective immigrants (Van Heerden, 1993, p. 35). The number of immigrants to South Africa in 1994, however, was 35% less than in 1993. This can most probably be ascribed to uncertainty surrounding the run-up to the country's first democratic elections in April 1994 and a "wait and see" attitude of many prospective immigrants in the months following the election. In fact, since 1993 South Africa has recorded a gradual decline in the number of documented immigrants (Table 18.1). Apart from political and economic uncertainty, a range of other factors also contributes to this trend. Most important among these are numerous media reports pointing to an escalating crime rate, as well as perceptions of a gradual drop in living standards and social services in South Africa.

Until a few years ago, the number of documented immigrants from other African countries to South Africa has been quite small. Since the first Black majority government took office in 1994, an increasing number of immigrants have been coming from the rest of Africa. A considerable number of these people are entering South Africa illegally from different points in the extensive and porous borders of the country (see below). In addition, growing numbers of professionals and skilled workers from all over sub-Saharan Africa had acquired employment in South Africa, causing a "brain drain" in some of the sending countries.

Table 18.1
Documented Immigration to South Africa, 1990–1996

Year	Immigrants
1990	14,449
1991	12,379
1992	8,686
1993	9,824
1994	6,398
1995	5,064
1996	5,407
1997	4,103
1998	4,371
1999	3,669
2000	3,053

Note: Adapted from Central Statistics (1996), *South African Survey, 1999/2000* (1999, p. 23), and *South Africa Survey, 2001/2002* (2001, p. 141).

Historically, the brain drain from Africa was directed mainly toward the industrialized countries of the northern hemisphere. As such countries started implementing stricter immigration control from less developed countries, South Africa increasingly emerged as a destination for these citizens. The professional quality of many of these legal immigrants is evinced by the fact that in 1991 alone, some 200 medical doctors left Zimbabwe to settle in South Africa and, to a lesser extent, in Botswana (Solomon, 1995, p. 7). This obviously holds serious long-term implications for the economies and social services of South Africa's neighbors. In May 1994, the Zimbabwean government, therefore, announced that it would be taking steps to stop the exodus of medical practitioners to South Africa. Zimbabwe claimed that between 1,500 and 3,000 of its doctors were practicing in South Africa at that stage. (However, the South African Medical and Dental Council stated that according to their records, there were only 269 registered graduates with Zimbabwean medical qualifications in South Africa.) A similar exodus to South Africa is found among university lecturers in Zimbabwe and Zambia and among nurses in Botswana, Lesotho, and Swaziland.

A comparison of professional wages in South Africa and Zimbabwe clearly illustrates the attraction South Africa holds for many migrants. A joint survey by the Human Sciences Research Council (HSRC) in South Africa and a Zimbabwean consulting group showed, for instance, that chartered accountants in South Africa in 1991 were earning more than double the salaries of their counterparts in Zimbabwe. Other comparisons for the same year depicted the following: Computing programmers R47,000.00 versus R19,200.00; pharmacists R53,700.00 versus R30,00.00; medical doctors (not in private practice) R75,000.00 versus R42,000.00; and engineers R64,000.00 versus R35,000.00 (Badenhorst, 1993, p. 19). Looking at a similar comparison between the real wages of skilled laborers in different countries in southern Africa, it becomes quite evident why the economic magnet in South Africa attracts so many people. At the end of the 1980–1989 period, real wages of (mainly Black) workers in South Africa in the nonprimary sectors had increased by 27% compared with real wages in 1980. In Zimbabwe, the comparative figure at the end of this period was only 4%. In contrast, the minimum wage in Mozambique dropped by 47% during the same period, due to a large extent to the civil war in the country.

Not only are professionals from neighboring states settling in South Africa, but some migrants come from as far as Uganda, Ghana, Somalia, and Zaire. The brain drain to South Africa is given added impetus when taking into account that professionals who emigrate from these other countries are often married and their spouses are usually also professionals, resulting in the exodus of more skilled people than is accounted for. The loss of skills generates professional gaps in the often poor sending countries that cannot afford to maintain a higher standard of living for their experts. Of course, there are other reasons why professionals emigrate which have nothing to do with higher salaries. In many instances, a combination of political instability, uncertain conditions of physical security, and poor economic prospects in these countries tends to push people toward a seemingly prosperous South Africa.

Apart from the above motivators, university academics in many African countries are also believed to emigrate for reasons such as inadequate laboratory facilities, insufficient time for research, and poor resources available to engage in postgraduate work and research (Solomon, 1993, p. 16). The University of Zambia in particular has been adversely affected by this process and had to close some departments as a result of staff shortages. This inevitably leads to a decline in standards, as universities start to recruit inexperienced or poorly qualified staff. In Zimbabwe, too, university departments have been threatened with closure or compelled to reduce the number of students due to vacancies in professional posts that remain unfilled. As standards drop further, local expertise becomes even harder to find; the result is that many projects either disintegrate or become entirely dependent on foreign consultants.

A truism of emigration, especially in southern Africa, is that the most gifted people invariably leave; this alone impoverishes already struggling sending countries economically, politically, and socioculturally. In fact, economic impoverishment in these countries is an important factor that assists in maintaining the much debated migrant labor system.

Contract Labor Migrants

South Africa is the heartbeat of a regional economic life that has entwined neighboring countries in a web of relations for almost a century. A vital aspect in these relationships has been the demand for and supply of labor to South African gold, coal, and diamond mines. Contract migrant workers from neighboring states work in South Africa on the basis of a legal contract with an employer in the formal sector, usually the mining industry, although there is also some legal recognition of foreign contract workers on South African farms. These workers are of the same variety as Germany's *Gastarbeiter* or guest workers. As the name suggests, a contract is drawn up between an employer, in this case most often the South African Chamber of Mines, and a prospective foreign laborer. In terms of the contract, the employer undertakes to pay the foreign worker a wage and in return the contract laborer undertakes to work for the employer for a fixed period (usually between 12 and 18 months, but hardly ever for more than 2 years). After the contract has expired, the migrant worker is supposed to return to his or her country of origin.

The large-scale employment of foreign labor by the South African mining industry goes back 150 years when migrants came on foot to work in the Kimberley diamond mines. When the first gold mines opened in the 1890s, labor migration gained momentum. Given the difficulties in attracting local labor to the mines, mining companies came to rely on foreign labor drawn from countries adjacent to South Africa, especially Botswana, Lesotho, Swaziland, Zimbabwe, and Mozambique. Large numbers of labor migrants were also recruited in Malawi. Though many of these foreign workers have spent virtually all of their working lives in South Africa, their boundary crossing is (supposed to be) temporary, never permanent. In fact, the single most important feature of labor migration is the fact that it is circular. After their contractual period in the mines has expired, migrants return home, though the likelihood is that in the course of their lives they will migrate several times. For the duration of their stay in South Africa, they remain temporary residents without their families and without the rights and privileges enjoyed by legal immigrants.

An undeniable reality inherent to the system of migrant labor is that many of South Africa's neighbors—Lesotho in particular—rely on income earned from the export of labor to maintain their economies. Not only did Lesotho contribute more than half of its labor force to South Africa in the 1980s, but at that time it was (and probably still is) regarded as the country in the world having the largest number of its labor force working outside its borders (Hanks & Liprie, 1993, p. 182). The livelihoods of many families in the poorer states of southern Africa depend on the remittances of the labor migrants in South Africa. Any significant reduction in migration of this kind—for instance, as a result of economic recession in South Africa—could have devastating effects on the rest of the region. To a certain extent such an effect has already been felt in Malawi. Migrant labor contracts with Malawi were terminated some years ago due to the danger of the spread of AIDS, which is notoriously rife in that country. However, this was not the only event that resulted in a significant reduction of the number of migrants in South Africa in recent times.

By the early 1970s, almost 80% of the gold mines' labor force came from neighboring states, and on certain mines this proportion rose to 90% (Toolo & Bethlehem, 1995, p. 18). In a dramatic few years in the mid-1970s, a series of events in the region and in South Africa caused the proportion of foreign migrants in the industry to plummet to 38% by 1976. This change was primarily a reflection of two events: Malawian president Hastings Banda's recall of some 120,000 Malawian migrants from South Africa in 1974 following a plane crash that killed 73 miners, and a drop in the Mozambican complement from 97,000 to 35,000 workers in the 3 years after the liberation movement, Frelimo, took power (Crush, 1995, p. 18). Although South Africans primarily replaced these workers, migrants from Lesotho, Swaziland, Botswana, and Zimbabwe helped make up the shortfall. Despite a decline in the proportion and total number of foreign migrant workers in the mid-1970s, the proportion of such migrants rose again during the 1980s to reach 47% by 1992. However, since 1987, and particularly since the strike in August 1987, the industry has lost nearly 200,000 jobs (Davies & Head, 1995, p. 204). The context within which these changes have taken place is a deflated international gold price and the fact that a considerable number of mines in South Africa have passed their peak. In addition, with a number of marginal mines facing closure due to escalating production costs and labor unrest, the Chamber of Mines, among other things, began a program of retrenchments. This was accompanied, in some cases, by the introduction of new technologies as part of a new policy aimed at reducing costs. As a result, recruitment of mine labor by The Employment Bureau of Africa (TEBA)—the organization acting as a recruitment agency for the mines, both in South Africa and in neighboring countries—has decreased from a total of 490,000 workers in 1988 to about 340,000 in 1994 (Rowett, 1995, p. 215). The number of foreign migrants employed in the South Africa mining industry has dropped from 173,884 in 1989 to 130,451 in 1998. This decline is expected to continue in the future.

Despite the fall in numbers of mine migrants, migrant labor remittances remain a critically important source of income and foreign exchange for labor supplying states. In the case of Lesotho, for example, migrant wage remittances accounted for 39% of the rural household income in the mid-1980s. Payments from TEBA to Lesotho totaled R284 million in 1992—an amount equal to 65% of the country's 1990 gross domestic product. In the case of Mozambique, migrant labor remittances provided 15.8% of all foreign earnings in 1992 (Davies & Head, 1995, p. 209).

Apart from the impact of migrant labor remittances on the economies of sending countries, the long-term social effects of labor migration have become more evident over the past 2 or 3 decades. These effects can be clustered to depict the impact of migration on the migrant worker and the family, respectively.

Effects on the Migrant Worker

In analyzing the effects of labor migration on the migrant, it is possible to distinguish between a social-structural and a social-clinical dimension. The *social-structural* dimension pertains to the living conditions of migrants in the mine hostels, whereas the *social-clinical* dimension reflects the psychological and health consequences of the work environment for the migrant personally. In reality, however, these dimensions are part and parcel of a single process.

Poor Living Conditions in Hostels. The migrant labor system has to a large extent become synonymous with what many people regard as miserable living conditions in mine hostels. Once a recruited migrant worker has arrived at his new job, he often enters a cloistered, restricted and tightly regulated world. Migrant workers have traditionally been accommodated in single-sex, regimented, company-owned compounds or hostels, located close to the mine shafts on mine property. Hostel walls and fences exclude outsiders and insulate insiders. In many ways, it is easier to get in than out if you are a miner; the reverse is true if you are a wife, dependent, or family member. The miners' working day and leisure time are controlled by security patrols, computerized surveillance, and tracking systems. In this way, any unauthorized entrance to or exit from the mine premises, passage from one part of the mine to another, or between the surface and underground are prevented. In the past, mine workers have often expressed, as a group or through their union, their dissatisfaction with the dehumanizing effect that living in the hostels have on them. When the then South African government abandoned many of its formal influx control regulations in 1986, it meant that for the first time mineworkers could legally settle with their families in the townships close to the mines and were no longer restricted to single-sex hostel life. However, a large number of mine workers still reside in hostels. Investigations into the living conditions at gold, coal, and diamond mine hostels, respectively, revealed that hostels are seen by many residents as a manifestation of discrimination and the general lack of concern management shows for the well-being of workers (Payze, 1995, p. 59). In the same study, residents also expressed the wish for proper accommodation that matched the standard of living enjoyed by white mineworkers and that allowed the latter to stay with their families. Living conditions in the mining industry have nonetheless improved considerably over the past 2 decades.

Social-Psychological and Health Effects on the Migrant Worker. The life of the migrant mineworker is a difficult one in which the stresses of dangerous underground work are exacerbated by the alienation of living away from family, friends, and home. These strains often have a negative effect on the health of the migrant worker. Research indicates a link between stressful situations like those migrant workers are subjected to and health conditions such as high blood pressure and the development of peptic ulceration, diabetes, and cardiovascular diseases (Molapo, 1995, p. 88). In extreme cases, those mine workers suffering from severe posttraumatic stress due to haunting memories or fear of underground accidents have to undergo extensive therapy.

Probably as a result of their living conditions, migrant workers are particularly inclined to indulge in promiscuous sexual behavior. Hence migrant workers have been identified, alongside long-distance truck drivers and sex workers, as a high-risk group when it comes to contracting and spreading sexually transmitted diseases, especially HIV/AIDS. Chirwa (1995, p. 127) found that some migrant workers of Malawi had as many as 10 sexual partners within the first 24 months of their return to their villages. In a country where it is estimated that one in three adults in urban areas may be carrying the HIV virus, it means that the prevalence of AIDS in Malawi will no longer be confined to urban areas. Because the majority of Malawian migrants come from rural areas, rural women have become increasingly vulnerable to contracting HIV/AIDS with the return of these workers. In February 1988, the South African government repatriated 101 Malawian mining recruits after they tested HIV-positive. One month later the Chamber of Mines stopped importing labor from Malawi altogether. Despite these and other measures to combat the spread of the epidemic, recent figures put the proportion of mineworkers in Southern Africa currently infected with HIV at between 20% and 30% (Horwitz, 2001). Migrant workers have also been found to be almost two-and-a-half times more likely to be HIV-positive that non-immigrant workers. As a result, some contemporary studies began to suggest that in order to find the root of HIV/AIDS in South Africa one need to look no further than the system of migrant labor.

Adding to the above stresses suffered by mine workers are labor and human relations problems. Migrant workers often find themselves in a situation typified by little or no prospect of promotion, threats of retrenchments, boredom, a sense of exploitation by the mining industry, living away from their family, limits on lengths of visits by wives, and excessive expectations and pressure from families back home. In addition, kinship relations place a great financial burden on the migrant worker. His earnings usually have to support several people and households back home—his own, that of his parents, and in some cases an unemployed brother or unmarried sister and their children (Molapo, 1995, p. 95). This is a way of returning favors to the extended family who assist the wives of migrants in the fields all year.

Effects on the Family

The migrant labor system has undoubtedly affected the structure and stability of the family of migrants in South Africa's neighboring states, in the process creating serious social problems. Most prominent among these is a breakdown in the family structure due to the absence of a considerable number of men. As the nuclear family disintegrates, women tend to become more socially and economically isolated. In the mid-1980s, women effectively headed roughly 70% of all rural households in Lesotho at a stage when approximately 4 out of every 10 men were working as migrants in South Africa (Hanks & Liprie, 1993, pp. 182–184). Because of the unreliability of financial contributions from their husbands, these women face a lot of insecurity in their lives. The large number of families headed by women is evidence of the fact that the growing number of mine workers during the 1970s and 1980s led to an increase in the number of extremely poor or destitute people.

Many families and communities in the rural areas (both within and outside South Africa) depend on migrant remittances and deferred pay. Some of these communities have already been cut off from access to mine employment for reasons of political policies (Malawi), civil war (Mozambique), and economic rationalization (Botswana and Lesotho). The retrenchments following the 1987 strikes on the mines, and particularly those associated with rationalization programs in the late 1980s and early 1990s, had their most severe impact on the rural families and communities most dependent on mine wages. With massive unemployment becoming a reality, a mine job became a prized possession. The result was the "career miner" who suddenly found himself in a position where he had to continuously work on a particular mine if he wished to hold on to his job. This has exacted a heavy toll on miners' health and effectively eliminates thousands of new work seekers who could once have counted on a mine job, if nothing else. Mine migrants have become a kind of relatively privileged absentee rural elite in the midst of abject poverty. As Lesotho migrants pointed out, there is only one thing worse than having a mine job in South Africa, and that is not having one (Crush, 1995, p. 25). Consequently, workers were now compelled to spend a considerable part of their lives away from home living in the mine hostels. Already this practice has taken its toll in increased stresses on family life.

The dismissal of thousands of mineworkers, resulting in the loss of a regular income, also created additional problems for family life. For instance, in Lesotho the wives of returned migrants have to seek work or have turned to hawking, brewing, or selling crafts—a situation that creates as many problems as it tries to solve. Most ex-mine migrants felt some embarrassment and diminished self-esteem caused by turning over the role of breadwinner to their wives. Some indeed do not want their wives to work, fearing that it would lead to the breakup of their marriages or that their wives inevitably will take up labor migrancy themselves. Indeed, an increasingly prevalent phenomenon is that it is the wife who heads off to South Africa or a border town to find work. Although she promises to send money and to return as soon as possible, she is likely never to be heard from again (Coplan & Thoahlane, 1995, p. 147). Others make no such promises, but simply inform their husbands that because they had lost their jobs in the mines, they are losing their wives as well. The result is an increase in male-headed single-parent households.

The system of labor migration also has negative effects on children. When male members of working age in a family migrate to South Africa, children of school age frequently must replace the absent labor power. Consequently, boys of school age have a much higher dropout rate than girls, because boys are expected to herd cattle in the absence of adult males. Tension in the family is often accentuated rather than relieved by the return of the husband, because the position of the wife is brought into focus. Although the wife, in the absence of the male, assumes responsibility for the household, it is the husband, through his wage-earning capacity, who controls the major resources for its effective management (Hanks & Liprie, 1993, p. 185).

The Future of Labor Migrancy in South Africa

Although the number of foreign contract migrant workers has fallen since the expansion of the early 1970s, still about half of the gold mine work force hails from outside South Africa. Despite the ambition of many groups to terminate or at least reduce this practice—commonly regarded as a legacy of the apartheid era and exploitative in nature—migrant labor is likely to persist. Due to the entrenched character of migrancy, any major changes to the system will impact widely upon mine workers, their families, their home communities, and the economies of neighboring countries. In fact, the history of migrant labor has proved that political interventions in the system have frequently run up against entrenched powers and stark economic realities. Even in the aftermath of apartheid legislation, there are still many impediments to a significant move away from migrant labor. Among these are management's continuing preference for migrant workers, cost in a time of economic stringency, the fear of creating ghost towns, and the high proportion of migrants occupying skilled positions.

However, like much else in contemporary South Africa, the social and political context for potential transformation of the system of migrant labor has changed dramatically since 1994. Most attention in this regard has been focused on the political attitude of the newly elected government toward migrant labor. The new government has yet to declare itself on the question of the position of foreign workers in South Africa. The adoption of a populist policy that, explicitly or implicitly, aims to reduce the number of migrant workers in the hope of increasing employment opportunities for South African citizens is a definite option. With an average domestic unemployment rate of approximately 37% running up to 60% in some parts of the country, and a government committed to massive and rapid economic and social improvement, many foreign workers have reason to fear that their official days in South Africa are numbered.

Illegal (Undocumented) Immigrants

Although the search for work appeared to have been the most important motivation for migration to South Africa for many decades, legal movement to the mines no longer constitutes the main form of migration to the country. In the recent past, contract labor migration has been dethroned by clandestine and illegal migration, much of which remains largely undocumented. Since the early 1990s, however, a strong relationship has developed between contract migrant labor and illegal immigrants. In this regard, the situation in South Africa resembles that in Europe where foreigners enter the country legally as contract migrant workers and then overstay their contract period. In 1995, for example, some 750,000 people in South Africa were classified as illegal immigrants for overstaying the validity period of their temporary residence permits (Solomon, 1995, p. 6). However, these migrants do not represent the only category of illegal immigrants in South Africa.

Categories of Illegal Immigrants

An undocumented or illegal alien is anybody who enters or remains in South Africa in contravention of the Aliens Control Act and, therefore, resides in South Africa without official endorsement. This includes any person who (a) enters South Africa at a place other than a port of entry, (b) remains in the country without a valid residence permit, (c) acts in contravention of his or her residence permit, and (d) remains in South Africa after the expiration of a residence permit.

Illegal aliens in South Africa belong to two main categories: undocumented voluntary migrants and undocumented forced migrants (or refugees). The two categories are used synonymously by most South Africans and even officially little attempt has been made to distinguish between forced and voluntary migrants up to now. However, because forced migrants are increasingly being considered a separate category by international conventions, it is important that a distinction be made in the South African context as well.

Undocumented Voluntary Migrants. Undocumented voluntary migrants can be categorized as either informal movers or organized movers. Informal movers primarily migrate to South Africa for economic reasons. In most cases, they enter the country illegally from neighboring states such as Lesotho, Swaziland, Mozambique, Zimbabwe, and Botswana and then reside in South Africa on a semipermanent basis. The majority enter the country without any documentation and then try to obtain South African identity documents. Others enter South Africa with valid passports or temporary permits as tourists, students, or migrant workers. They then either try to obtain employment or simply elect to remain in the country when their contracts are terminated or the validity period of their residence permits has expired. Quite often their families, who immigrate illegally, join them.

Organized movers are migrants who illegally immigrate to South Africa on a permanent basis. The largest proportion of these people originates from countries in central Africa, Asia, and the Pacific Rim. They may enter South Africa on either valid or fraudulent passports. Because their methods of entry and employment are more sophisticated and, in many cases, linked to criminal activities, this group of illegal aliens must be seen to constitute the major threat to South Africa.

Undocumented Forced Migrants. In contrast to voluntary migrants who make a primarily individual decision to come to South Africa, forced migrants are refugees fleeing political persecution, civil war, environmental degradation, and economic ruin—in other words, displaced persons who were compelled to leave their country of birth due to circumstances beyond their control. In the past 5 years, southern Africa has hosted an unprecedented number of forced migrants. Ethnic conflict in Rwanda, civil strife and famine in Zaire and Angola, postwar impoverishment in Mozambique, and poverty and famine in Zimbabwe have generated large numbers of nonvoluntary migrants to South Africa.

Despite the legal and technical descriptions of a refugee in various international conventions, distinctions between forced and voluntary migrants are often blurred. Mozambican refugees in South Africa who fled civil war between 1985 and 1992, are a case in point. The some 350,000 refugees who entered South Africa did so clandestinely, without the government's approval. Despite a regionwide effort by the UN Higher Commission for Refugees at repatriating Mozambican refugees in 1993, only about 31,000 Mozambicans in South Africa registered for repatriation (Sinclair, 1996, p. 13). The estimated 320,000 refugees that remain in South Africa, are inevitably regarded as a subgroup of the larger number of illegal aliens and are, therefore, subject to prosecution and deportation.

As the most prosperous country in the region, South Africa will probably always find it difficult to slot foreigners into exact categories of "refugee" or "illegal immigrant." Given the potential for future refugee crises in Africa and thus the probability of increased numbers of forced migrants in South Africa, the government will have to formulate a distinct position on refugees. For the time being, however, it seems refugees are destined to be branded as "illegal aliens" regardless of whether they have legal sanction to stay or not.

Extent and Causes of Illegal Immigration

There are widely divergent estimates of the number of illegal immigrants in South Africa. Although official estimates put the figure at between 500,000 and 4 million, some recent reports have published figures as high as 8 million or 9 million and even 12 million (Capraro, 1997, p. 7; Cohen, 1997b, p. 2; Hough, 1995, p. 14; *South Africa Survey, 1999/2000*, 1999, p. 23). This latter estimate seems unrealistic, as it would mean that approximately one in every four persons in the country is not a South African. A more realistic figure would perhaps be between 3 million and 5 million. The largest proportion of these people come from Mozambique. The rest originate from countries such as Zimbabwe, Zaire, Angola, Malawi, Tanzania, Nigeria, Sudan, Ethiopia, Rwanda, Burundi, Taiwan, and the former Soviet-controlled Eastern European bloc countries.

Since the start of political transformation in South Africa, actions to crack down on illegal immigrants appear to have hardened. Official statistics show that the number of illegal immigrants repatriated almost quadrupled between 1988 and 1995 (Table 18.2). The repatriation statistics for the period 1988 to 1999, therefore, can serve as an indication of the increasing extent of the phenomenon of illegal immigrants in South Africa.

Despite intensive police action and other deterrents, the number of people entering the country illegally is increasing steadily. Some reports state that illegal immigrants are entering the country at a rate of one every 10 minutes (Carim, 1995, p. 221). The South African Police Service estimate that one in five squatters (i.e., people living in informal settlements) in Gauteng Province is an illegal immigrant. Their ranks are continuously supplemented by the approximately 1,200 immigrants who are entering Gauteng every month—people flocking to the "golden city" Johannesburg with aspirations for a better life. This pattern suggests, first, that there is a high level of desperation felt by people in neighboring countries, and, second, that purely repressive measures fail to prevent illegal immigration. Of those apprehended and forcibly repatriated, most simply elect to brave rivers, game parks, or electrified fences in yet another attempt to cross the South African border.

The movement of illegal immigrants into South Africa can first of all be linked to the root causes of refugee movements. Civil war, famine, and drought in countries such as Mozambique, Angola, Rwanda, and Zaire have resulted in a combination of refugees and illegal aliens entering South Africa. In the case of Zimbabwe and Zambia, adverse economic conditions seem to be among the major factors underlying the movement of illegal immigrants to South Africa. In addition to these, certain factors seem to facilitate the inflow of illegal immigrants or at least facilitate avoidance of being detected. A first set of facilitating factors relates to physical factors. This includes long borders with a number of African states, a long coastline, and the high cost of border protection. These constraints are aggravated by political factors impeding the more effective use of electrified fences on the Mozambican and Zimbabwean borders.

A second set of facilitating factors is of a sociopolitical and economic nature. This includes among others the relatively smooth transition to majority rule in South Africa and the perception among immigrants of ample employment opportunities in South Africa. Also, some employers in South Africa have seemingly come to view illegal immigrants as a source of cheaper, more reli-

Table 18.2
Repatriation of Illegal Immigrants, 1989–1999

1989	1991	1993	1995	1999
51,529	61,334	96,554	157,084	183,861

Note: Adapted from Klaaren (1997, p. 4), *South Africa Survey, 1995/1996* (1995, p. 32), *South Africa Survey, 1999/2000* (1995, p. 24), and *South Africa Survey, 2001/2002* (2001, p. 141).

able, and non-unionized labor. A further contributing factor is the increase in informal settlements at the outskirts of urban areas in South Africa, which eases the disappearance of illegal immigrants into the mass population. (It is estimated that up to 60% of South Africans do not have formal addresses.)

Another set of facilitating factors pertains to corruption and fraud in departments such as Home Affairs and Customs and Excise. The increase in forged identity documents (until recently, South African passports were reportedly amongst the easiest in the world to forge) and the fact that not all South Africans have identity documents, are contributing factors in this regard. Given its extent in terms of sheer numbers and the apparent escalation of the problem, it is clear that illegal immigration, in various ways, must have a profound impact on South African society.

The Impact of Illegal Immigrants on South African Society

The presence of illegal immigrants has strong negative effects on the South African economy with respect to aspects such as employment opportunities, health, education, and housing. Politicians, trade unions, and the public at large are increasingly strident in blaming immigrants for undercutting prices, grabbing low-paying jobs and scarce housing, and adding to the crime rate. Little wonder that the presence of illegal immigrants is now being linked to either the success or failure of the government's Reconstruction and Development Plan (RDP). Considering the fact that illegal immigrants cost the South African taxpayer approximately R2.5 billion per year (an amount equal to the estimated budget for the 1999 general elections), this state of affairs must surely have a detrimental effect on the RDP. Illegal immigrants, however, do not only have an impact on the macroeconomy; they also have far-reaching political and social consequences for South Africa.

Impact on the Labor Market. The greatest source of fear concerning the increasing number of illegal workers in South Africa appears to be economic. South Africa's unemployment rate is currently very high, and the country is economically vulnerable. Given this, the influx of large numbers of predominantly uneducated and unskilled illegal immigrants is clearly a matter for concern. Most of these immigrants only perform manual labor and are usually active at the lower end of the labor market. They are employed as casual workers or subcontractors in sectors such as hotels and restaurants, construction, domestic maintenance, and informal trading. Because South Africa itself has a large number of unemployed citizens in the unskilled category, illegal immigrants pose first and foremost a threat to the local unemployed.

The large numbers of illegal immigrants seeking work at the lower end of the labor market have a depressing effect on wage levels. Because these immigrants are prepared to accept lower wages to survive, wages in certain sectors have dropped well below the level at which South Africans are prepared and able to work and to live. Union members thus feel that the presence of foreign workers depresses wages and that local people have decreased access to employment as a result of foreign workers. Many of the illegal immigrants from

African states also enter the informal business sector by hawking artifacts, curios, knitted or crocheted items, and African ethnic print cloth that they bring with them. Because they are able to bring in goods at a seemingly much cheaper rate than local traders can, these immigrants are much resented for their price undercutting activities. They are also accused of not paying import and custom dues.

Arousal of Local Hostility Toward Foreigners. In many ways the post-apartheid South Africa has become an international model for social harmony and reconstruction with its citizens having gained a reputation for tolerance toward one another. Simultaneously, however, South Africa is rapidly gaining a reputation for intolerance toward non–South Africans, particularly those from African countries who enter South Africa as illegal immigrants or refugees. A debate on whether migration from other countries should be encouraged, is indeed rife in South Africa.

Since the April 1994 elections, South Africa has experienced an escalating tide of xenophobia against foreigners in general and illegal immigrants in particular. Studies undertaken by the Human Sciences Research Council (HSRC) in October 1994 indicate that 56% of South Africans believed the government should act more severely against illegal aliens. By February 1995, this figure had increased to 72% (Solomon, 1995, p. 12). This xenophobia is manifested in various ways. In the metropolitan areas of Johannesburg, Durban, and Cape Town, for instance, foreign hawkers have been verbally abused, physically assaulted, and their property damaged or destroyed. According to a 1999 report by the UN High Commissioner for Refugees, attacks on foreigners in South Africa were on the rise—more than 30 refugees and asylum seekers had been killed in 2 years (*South Africa Survey, 1999/2000,* 1999, p. 2). This hostility is rooted in a perception among many South Africans that the presence of foreigners will prevent the needs of local people to be met. The general sentiment is one that echoes the proverb "Charity begins at home": South Africans need to address their own country's problems of housing, health care, and education before they can look at helping foreigners. Clearly the reigning perception is that illegal immigrants place a strain on the country's limited resources, which apparently are now being used to shelter, feed, and heal immigrants. It thus appears to many that illegal immigrants are reaping the fruits of the liberation struggle, instead of the (Black) South Africans themselves.

It is not difficult to trace the sources of this xenophobia. A growing anti-foreigner sentiment is, to a certain extent, propagated on television and in newspapers. Media reports increasingly link illegal immigrants to burning social issues such as unemployment, escalating crime, and the spread of AIDS. In the previous political dispensation, the apartheid system took the blame as the source of Black South Africans' misery. With the advent of a democratic government, illegal immigrants have become the scapegoat for the disillusionment and frustration following the post-apartheid epoch's initial euphoria and high expectations.

The opposite side of the debate focuses attention on the human rights abuses suffered by illegal immigrants. Those belonging to this camp stress the fact that countries in southern Africa made a considerable contribution to the liberation struggle by providing bases for banned organizations and by bearing the brunt of apartheid destabilization strategies. Up to now, the local debate on illegal immigrants has thus been polarized between a moral issue on the one hand and a developmental one on the other. Ultimately, however, policy options will have to be based on a development approach, while simultaneously respecting international agreements and conventions on refugees, rather than relying on xenophobia.

Impact on Crime. The rising levels of crime and violence in South Africa are increasingly being linked to the growing number of illegal immigrants. Too often these immigrants are poverty stricken and, therefore, easily driven to crime. There has reportedly been an increase of 150% in serious crime involving illegal immigrants during the months following the elections in 1994, compared with the same period in 1993 (Van Niekerk, 1995, p. 6). The police have estimated that 14% of all crimes within South Africa involve illegal immigrants (Carim, 1995, p. 222). These crimes generally include arms smuggling, drug trafficking, prostitution, money laundering, and car theft. The very nature of these criminal activities, however, frequently results in other crimes such as rape and murder. Some nationalities have also been identified as being closely associated with or involved in crimes of a specific nature. These are illustrated in Table 18.3.

The involvement of illegal immigrants in criminal activities has an adverse effect on the South African economy in at least two ways. First, rising crime rates and levels of violence reduce investor confidence. Second, state resources that could have been earmarked for RDP projects now have to be channeled into the security apparatus of the state.

Impact on Health and Health Care. Illegal immigrants place enormous strain on the health system (another priority area of the RDP). Clinics in the rural areas of Northern Province and Mpumalanga, for example, are flooded by thousands of Mozambicans, who reside illegally in these areas. The "overuse" of these

Table 18.3
Involvement of Nationalities in Specific Crimes in South Africa

Nationality	Type of Crime
Nigerians	Drug trafficking (in particular cocaine) and money laundering
Zairians	Smuggling of diamonds
Taiwanese/Chinese	Smuggling of abalone and crayfish
Thai/Russians	Prostitution
Angolans	Smuggling of arms
Zimbabweans	Car theft and game poaching
Mozambicans	Smuggling of arms, car theft, and game poaching

Note: Adapted from Van Niekerk (1995, p. 7).

facilities particularly gained momentum after May 1994 when a policy of free health care for pregnant women and children under age 6 was implemented by the newly elected government.

Illegal immigrants from Mozambique are also believed to be responsible for reintroducing diseases such as cholera, malaria, and yellow fever into the northeastern parts of South Africa, where these diseases had been eradicated. Because the majority of illegal immigrants enter South Africa in a clandestine manner, it is not possible to ensure that the necessary health precautions, such as immunization, have been complied with before they cross the border. Several studies have also suggested a causal link between illegal immigrants and the spread of the HIV virus in the country as well as in the region (Labuschagne & Muller, 1993; Solomon, 1995). Many illegal immigrants end up in urban areas without their families; sexual services are thus often purchased. Some illegal immigrants also find themselves in situations where prostitution becomes their only source of income. South Africa borders six other countries and because the government is unable to control the influx of illegal immigrants, there is virtually no control over the spread of HIV/AIDS within South Africa or the region. It is estimated that 21.7% of the South African adult population will be HIV positive by the year 2010, which holds serious consequences for the economy (*South Africa Survey, 1999/2000*, 1999, p. 220).

Impact on Social and Welfare Services. The accelerated process of urbanization in South Africa has caused informal settlements (squatter camps) to grow alarmingly. The increasing influx of illegal immigrants further contributes to the squatter problem, because the majority arrive in South Africa destitute, jobless, and homeless. Poverty-stricken illegal aliens, especially in Gauteng Province are, therefore, settling in large numbers in new squatter camps. It has been estimated that as many as 80% of illegal immigrants live in informal housing settlements and squatter camps (Schutte, 1993, p. 9). Because it is extremely difficult to distinguish between the illegal immigrant and the citizen in a squatter community, illegal immigrants come to benefit from the services and houses provided under the RDP at the expense of the South African taxpayer. Funds that are made available to provide services and to upgrade squatter settlements are intended for South African citizens in the first place, but the influx of illegal immigrants into squatter settlements has undoubtedly had an impeding effect on the RDP. It is furthermore obvious that the presence of illegal immigrants places additional pressure on water supplies, educational facilities, transportation, and even firewood. Other irregularities also occur. Illegal immigrants, for example, do not qualify for social pensions, but they often attempt, by insidious means, to obtain such pensions.

Future Trends of Illegal Immigration in South Africa

In most countries, the proportion of illegal immigrants is estimated at 6% or less of the total population, (e.g., 6% for the United States, 2% for France, and 0.2% for Singapore) (Van Niekerk, 1995, p. 10). Based on a (for many, conservative) estimation of 5 million illegal immigrants, South Africa has already reached the 12% mark with no signs of the influx abating. On the contrary, as long as political instability, economic stagnation, and environmental degradation plague the entire region, South Africa will remain the destination for thousands of people willing to risk their lives in search of a better future. However, with the South African government having signaled its intention to adopt a tough approach, the long-term trend points undeniably toward greater government effort and capacity to control illegal immigration. Increasing public pressure, in all likelihood, will necessitate further measures and more comprehensive policing in order to control the influx of illegal immigrants into South Africa.

Emigration

Despite the fact that international migrants seem to regard South Africa as a popular destination, the number of South African residents who have left the country since the 1970s is estimated to be almost 300,000. In the late 1970s and mid-1980s when political instability and violence were most intense, the number of emigrants exceeded the number of immigrants. Since 1994, South Africa has seen a recurrence of this pattern (Table 18. 4).

Official statistics point at a major exodus of White South Africans in the middle and upper income categories since 1993. The most popular destinations of these emigrants reflect an interest in countries having economic viability and political stability: Australia, Canada, New Zealand, the United Kingdom, and the United States. Though the recorded number of emigrants seems small, the official figures are a gross underestimation of those with professional and technical skills that are leaving without declaring that emigration is their primary intention (Cohen, 1997a, p. 2).

Over the past few years South Africa has indeed experienced an alarming outflow of those possessing professional and technical skills. The international marketability of such skills has encouraged a brain drain phenomenon unprecedented in the history of the country. Such a brain drain is not new to South Africa. What is new, however, is the current rate of outflow at a time when full democracy is in place, supported by a bill of rights. In theory, this should serve to retain and attract those with more skills instead of driving them away.

According to official figures, in 1998 South Africa lost 2,532 people in professional, technical, or managerial categories, while gaining only 873 highly skilled immigrants (*South Africa Survey, 1999/2000*, 1999, p. 280). This amounted to a net loss of 1,659 highly skilled people. The comparative figure for 1997 indicates a loss of 1,924 skilled people in sectors such as education, engineering, accountancy, and health. Because it is mostly recent graduates and people younger than 49 years who are inclined to emigrate, the full impact of this trend will probably only be felt once those with current leading-edge skills go into retirement.

Studies on migration to and from South Africa since 1960 suggest a strong relationship between emigration and political events, including violence and economic instability (Cloete, 1996, p. 23). Currently, all these factors are present in South Africa, pointing to a strong possibility of increased losses of skilled

Table 18.4
Officially Recorded Immigration and Emigration, 1990–2000

Year	Immigration	Emigration	Net Gain (Loss)
1990	14,449	4,722	9,777
1991	12,379	4,256	8,123
1992	8,686	4,289	4,397
1993	9,824	8,078	1,746
1994	6,398	10,235	(3,837)
1995	5,064	8,725	(3,661)
1996	5,407	9,708	(4,301)
1997	4,103	8,946	(4,843)
1998	4,371	8,276	(3,905)
1999	3,669	8,487	(4,818)
2000	3,053	11,309	(8,256)

Note: Adapted from Central Statistics (1996), (Cohen, 1997a, p. 2)
and *South Africa Survey, 1999/2000* (2001, p. 23).

people in the foreseeable future. The current exodus has, among others, been attributed to a crime rate that has been escalating since the 1994 elections. Another contributing factor is the implementation of affirmative action policies and the resulting perception that a pending quota system will block career prospects (Ogina, 1997, p. 12). A drop in living standards, declining health services, and poor education—issues perceived by many South Africans to be the price tag of the new political dispensation—are further reasons often put forward by emigrants.

The population policy for South Africa, tabled in 1998, has among others outlined the main issues to inform a comprehensive policy formulation process with regard to migration (NPU, 1998). One of the aims of such a policy will be to curb the exodus of skilled people from South Africa. Among others this might involve the repayment of educational subsidies, or even some form of "conscription" in the sense of compulsory community service after completion of studies. Medical doctors in particular have already been targeted. Whether such measures in practice will ensure a reverse of current tendencies is doubtful. In fact, it may well have the opposite effect. If such policies are seen as punitive, they may be self-defeating in propelling one-way permanent movement and ensuring a lack of cooperation with a possible recruitment network. Political stability, economic growth, and improved personal safety seem to be the only viable solutions to prevent further unaffordable losses in highly skilled labor power.

CONCLUSION

Ever since South Africa's transition to democracy in 1994, a wave of rising expectations of a better life in the south created a very strong pull effect for migration, especially in other African countries. Adding to this is the fact that neighboring countries, to a large extent, are unable to satisfy the expectations of their citizens, and there is a situation in which, most often, push and pull factors operate together, either simultaneously or consecutively. The prospects for the next few years are thus for increased migration to South Africa, at least as far as the category of illegal immigrants is concerned.

In retrospect it would seem that most of the main types of migration occurring in southern and South Africa have a fairly good potential for becoming a source of conflict. As has been indicated, some of the effects of migration (such as the social and economic impacts of illegal immigrants) can cause instability and thus conflict. Already South Africa is experiencing the initial stages of such a potential (domestic) conflict as public hostility toward illegal immigrants in the country grows. It is mainly through the detrimental impact of both immigration and emigration on the economic life of South Africa and other southern African countries that population movement is conducive to conflict in the region. A complex challenge facing policymakers in South Africa is the formulation of a national policy on migrants and refugees that will take into consideration the developmental needs of the country, the economic position and opportunities of South Africans, as well as the position of South Africa in southern Africa. Addressing this challenge requires up-to-date empirical research on the volume and nature of migration from all regions of the world and from other African countries in particular. It is necessary to know the level of skills and the geographical origin of migrants. The effects of legal and illegal migration on the national economy, social services, family life, and crime need also to be researched extensively—something that, to a certain extent, has been neglected to date.

REFERENCES

Badenhorst, P. (1993). Migrasie: Wat hou Afrika vir SA in? [Migration: What does Africa hold for SA?] *Finansies & Tegniek, 45*(36), 19.

Capraro, I. (1997). Stroom onwettiges raak al dikker [Increasing influx of illegal aliens]. *Die Volksblad,* May 12, p. 7.

Carim, X. (1995). Illegal migration to South Africa. *Africa Insight, 25*(4), 221–223.

Central Statistics. (1996). *Statistics in brief.* Pretoria, South Africa: Author.

Chimere-Dan, O. (1996). Migrants from other African countries in South Africa. *South African Labor Bulletin, 20*(1), 45–47.

Chirwa, W. C. (1995). Malawian migrant labor and the politics of HIV/AIDS, 1985 to 1993. In J. Crush & W. James (Eds.), *Crossing boundaries: Mine migrancy in a democratic South Africa* (pp. 120–128). Cape Town, South Africa: Idasa.

Cloete, G. (1996). Migrasie—'n groeiende probleem vir Suid-Afrika [Migration—A growing problem for South Africa]. *Finansies & Tegniek, 48*(19), 23.

Cohen, R. (1997a). *Brain-drain migration.* Unpublished research paper prepared for the South African Commission on International Migration, Johannesburg,

South Africa.

Cohen, R. (1997b). *International migration: Southern Africa in global perspective.* Unpublished research paper prepared for the South African Commission on International Migration, Johannesburg, South Africa.

Coplan, D., & Thloahlane, T. (1995). Motherless households, landless farms: Employment patterns among Lesotho migrants. In J. Crush & W. James (Eds.), *Crossing boundaries: Mine migrancy in a democratic South Africa* (pp. 139–150). Cape Town, South Africa: Idasa.

Crush, J. (1995). Mine migrancy in the contemporary era. In J. Crush & W. James (Eds.), *Crossing boundaries: Mine migrancy in a democratic South Africa* (pp. 14–32). Cape Town, South Africa: Idasa.

Crush, J. (1997). *Contract migration to South Africa: Past, present and future.* Unpublished research paper prepared for the South African Commission on International Migration, Johannesburg, South Africa.

Crush, J., & James, W. (Eds.). (1995). *Crossing boundaries: Mine migrancy in a democratic South Africa.* Cape Town, South Africa: Idasa.

Davies, R., & Head, J. (1995). The future of mine migrancy: Trends in southern Africa. In J. Crush & W. James (Eds.), *Crossing boundaries: Mine migrancy in a democratic South Africa* (pp. 202–214). Cape Town, South Africa: Idasa.

De Villiers, R., & Reitzes, M. (Eds.). (1995). *Southern African migration: Domestic and regional policy implications.* Johannesburg, South Africa: Centre for Policy Studies.

Hanks, D. E., & Liprie, M. L. (1993). South African migration and the effects on the family. *Marriage and Family Review, 19*(1–2), 175–193.

Hough, M. (1995). Illegal aliens in South Africa: Causes and facilitating factors. *Strategic Review for Southern Africa, 17*(1), 1–25.

Horwitz, S. (2001, April). *Migrancy and HIV/AIDS—A historical perspective.* Paper presented at the AIDS in Context conference. Johannesburg, South Africa: University of the Witwatersrand.

Humphries, R. (1995). Foreword. In R. De Villiers & M. Reitzes (Eds.), *Southern African migration: Domestic and regional policy implications* (pp. v–vii). Johannesburg, South Africa: Centre for Policy Studies.

Klaaren, J. (1997). *Institutional reform and immigration management.* Unpublished research paper prepared for the South African Commission on International Migration, Johannesburg, South Africa.

Labuschagne, G. S., & Muller, M. E. (1993). Population and migration in Southern Africa in the 1990s. *Politikon, 20*(1), 47–53.

Maduna, P. (1995). Illegal immigrants as a domestic issue. In R. De Villiers & M. Reitzes (Eds.), *Southern African migration: Domestic and regional policy implications* (pp. 7–11). Johannesburg, South Africa: Centre for Policy Studies.

Molapo, M. P. (1995). Job stress, health and perceptions of migrant mineworkers. In J. Crush & W. James (Eds.), *Crossing boundaries: Mine migrancy in a democratic South Africa* (pp. 88–99). Cape Town, South Africa: Idasa.

NPU (National Population Unit). (1998). *Population policy for South Africa.*

Pretoria, South Africa: NPU.

Ogina, J. D. N. (1997). International migration and the "brain drain" from Africa. *ISSUP Bulletin, 1*, 1–14. Pretoria, South Africa: University of Pretoria, Institute for Strategic Studies.

Payze, C. (1995). Residents' views in three mine hostels. In J. Crush & W. James (Eds.), *Crossing boundaries: Mine migrancy in a democratic South Africa* (pp. 56–61). Cape Town, South Africa: Idasa.

Rowett, R. (1995). The role of TEBA: Changes and potential. In J. Crush & W. James (Eds.), *Crossing boundaries: Mine migrancy in a democratic South Africa* (pp. 215–217). Cape Town, South Africa: Idasa.

Rule, S. P. (1994). A second-phase diaspora: South African migration to Australia. *Geoforum, 25*(1), 33–39.

Schutte, D. P. A. (1993). Migration: The status quo and prospects for southern Africa. *ISSUP Bulletin, 5*, 1–18. Pretoria, South Africa: University of Pretoria, Institute for Strategic Studies.

Sinclair, M. R. (1996). Unwilling aliens: Forced migrants in the new South Africa. *Indicator South Africa, 13*(3), 14–18.

Solomon, H. (1993). *In search of Canaan: A critical evaluation of the causes and effects of migration within southern Africa, and strategies to cope with them.* (Southern African Perspectives: A working paper series, Centre for Southern African Studies). Cape Town, South Africa: University of the Western Cape.

Solomon, H. (1995). *Population movements into South Africa: Trends, outlook, policies.* (Occasional Paper Series No. 2). Braamfontein, South Africa: Foundation for Global Dialogue.

South Africa Survey 1994/1995. (1994). Johannesburg, South Africa: South African Institute of Race Relations.

South Africa Survey 1995/1996. (1995). Johannesburg, South Africa: South African Institute of Race Relations.

South Africa Survey 1999/2000. (1999). Johannesburg, South Africa: South African Institute of Race Relations.

South Africa Survey 2001/2002. (2001). Johannesburg, South Africa: South African Institute of Race Relations.

Toolo, H., & Betlehem, L. (1995). Migration to South Africa: Problems, issues and possible approaches for organised labour. In R. De Villiers & M. Reitzes (Eds.), *Southern African migration: Domestic and regional policy implications* (pp. 13–36). Johannesburg, South Africa: Centre for Policy Studies.

Van Heerden, G. (1993). Spotlight on South Africa's migration issue. *RSA Policy Review, 6*(7), 30–43.

Van Niekerk, B. (1995). The impact of illegal aliens on safety and security in South Africa. *ISSUP Bulletin, 7,* 1–11. Pretoria, South Africa: University of Pretoria, Institute for Strategic Studies.

Name Index

Subject Index

Page numbers appearing in italics denote pages containing tables.

About the Editors and Contributors

LEONORE LOEB ADLER is professor emerita in the Department of Psychology and director of the Institute for Cross-Cultural and Cross-Ethnic Studies, of which she is the founder, at Molloy College. She is also a member of the Advisory Board of the Institute for International and Cross-Cultural Psychology at St. Francis College. She has edited or co-edited 17 books, published about 75 chapters and journal articles, and presented her research reports and papers at numerous international meetings. She is a fellow of the Advisory Committee of Psychology at the New York Academy of Sciences, of the American Psychological Association's Divisions 1, 35, and 52, and of the American Psychological Society.

RAMADAN A. AHMED is a professor of psychology, Department of Psychology, Menoufia University, Egypt. He obtained his Ph.D. in Cognitive Psychology from the University of Leipzig, Germany. His research interests cover concept development and development of moral judgment cross-culturally, social perception, the psychology of women, and the history of psychology especially in the Arab countries. With Uwe Gielen he edited the first review of Arab psychology entitled *Psychology in the Arab Countries*. At present, he is on leave at Kuwait University, where he is working as a professor of psychology.

BRUCE BAIN was a professor of educational psychology at the University of Alberta in Edmonton, Canada. He was renowned for his works on bilingualism, language and cognition, and ethnic studies. He conducted studies worldwide on the effects of second language acquisition under various social circumstances. He had worked and researched extensively in Asia, and particularly in Hong Kong.

FLORENCE L. DENMARK is the Robert Scott Pace Distinguished Professor Emerita at Pace University in New York, where she served as chair of the Psychology Department for 13 years. A social psychologist who has published extensively on the psychology of women and gender, she has long been an energetic force in advancing psychology internationally, particularly as it concerns the psychology of women and human rights. Denmark has served as the president of numerous professional organizations including the American Psychological Association, the International Council of Psychologists, the Eastern Psychological Association, the New York State Psychological Association, and Psi Chi. She was also a vice-president of the New York Academy of Sciences.

ROGELIO DÍAZ-GUERRERO is emeritus research scientist of both the National System of Scientific Research (SNI) and the National University of Mexico (UNAM). In dozens of books and hundreds of articles, he has made extensive contributions to the psychology of the Mexican, culture and personality, and cross-cultural psychology, including studies in two, three, seven, and 30 nations.

KHAYA N. EISENBERG is a graduate student at Pace University. She will be finishing her Psy.D. in School-Clinical Child Psychology as of September 2002. Her research interests include, but are not limited to, gender and cultural issues and psychology of the media. She has collaborated, and continues to collaborate, with Florence L. Denmark on several social psychology research articles.

THOMAS HYLLAND ERIKSEN is professor of social anthropology at the University of Oslo. He has carried out research on nationalism and identity politics in polyethnic societies, and has published extensively about Mauritius and Trinidad. His other writings include general textbooks and books about migrants and natives in Norway. Among his most recent publications are *Tyranny of the Moment* (2001), *A History of Anthropology* (2001), and *Ethnicity and Nationalism* (2nd ed., 2002).

UWE P. GIELEN is professor of psychology and director of the Institute for International and Cross-Cultural Psychology at St. Francis College, New York City. He is the past chair of the Psychology Section of the New York Academy of Sciences and has served as president of both the International Council of Psychologists and the Society for Cross-Cultural Research. He has been editor of *World Psychology* and of the *International Journal of Group Tensions*. His areas of interest include moral development, international and cross-cultural psychology, and Tibetan Buddhism. He is co-editor/co-author of 12 books, including *The Kohlberg Legacy for the Helping Professions*, *Cross-Cultural Topics in Psychology*, and forthcoming volumes on *Childhood and Adolescence: Cross-Cultural Perspectives* and *Families in Global Perspective*.

HALINA GRYZMALA-MOSZCZYNSKA is a professor of psychology at the Jagiellonian University in Cracow and the School of Social Psychology in Warsaw, where she teaches courses such as Psychology of Religion, Cross-Cultural Psychology, and the Psychology of Migration. Her research focuses on the role of religion in the process of cultural adaptation of immigrants and the response of local communities to refugee reception centers and immigrants. She is a member of many national and international professional organizations and serves on the editorial boards of several professional journals. She has published 6 volumes as well as 45 articles and chapters that have appeared in national and international journals and edited books.

ERICA I. HEITNER received her Psy.D. in School-Clinical Child Psychology from Pace University where she was honored as Outstanding Graduate Student of the Year. Currently Ms. Heitner is working with emotionally disturbed children and adolescents at a residential treatment center in Dobbs Ferry, New York.

LEONIE HERWARTZ-EMDEN is an educational theorist and professor of educational theory in the faculty of social sciences at the University of Augsburg, Germany. Her research interests focus on comparative culture and intercultural research, including projects on the topics of schools and minorities in the USA and Germany, intercultural families, socialization and acculturation of children from migration backgrounds, school culture, gender segregation, and family socialization in girls' schools in Augsburg.

NICOLA A. HOLDER earned her doctoral degree in School-Clinical Child Psychology from Pace University in 2002. She currently works as a staff psychologist with the Child and Adolescent Crisis Intervention Program at North Central Bronx Hospital in New York City. In addition, she is an adjunct faculty member at York College of the City University of New York, where the student population is comprised of largely first- and second-generation immigrants from the Caribbean, Africa, and Eastern Europe.

MELINÉ KARAKASHIAN is a clinical psychologist with practices in Morganville and Old Bridge, New Jersey. Her professional interests include the study and treatment of post-traumatic stress disorder, and the adaptation and adjustment of immigrant Armenians to host countries. She continues to conduct research on Armenian migration and immigration through the centuries in order to understand the elements of resilience that contribute to the preservation of this culture. She has presented and published papers and chapters on post-traumatic stress, the long-term effects of war on children, the effects of the genocide of Armenians, parenting, depression and anxiety in women, and other clinical themes at national and international conferences. She has served as a Fulbright scholar in Armenia.

ROBERT J. KLEINER is currently professor emeritus at Temple University in the Sociology Department and a research associate in the Department of Psychiatry of the University of Oslo. He did some of the early seminal work in community studies in urban environments in which small group theory played a central role in explaining correlations between various social variables and mental illness, and where migration was a focal point. These studies were done in the United States and Norway. He has contributed to the development and evaluation of experimental social therapeutic modalities in which the social and structural properties of communities are selectively used for treatment purposes.

WILSON LOPEZ-LOPEZ is president of the Association for Behavior Analysis—Colombia (ALAMOC-ABA) and is associated with the Konrad Lorenz University in Bogotá, Colombia. His research interests include contemporary behavior analysis and the nature of self-conceptions.

ANTHONY J. MARSELLA is professor of psychology at the University of Hawaii, Honolulu, Hawaii. He has been an active contributor to the research on cross-cultural studies of psychopathology and therapy. Most recently, he has called for the internationalization of the psychology curriculum and the development of "new" psychologies that are applicable to the world's diverse populations and many social problems. Dr. Marsella has published 10 books and more than 150 book chapters, journal articles, and technical reports. He received the Award for Distinguished Contributions to the International Advancement of Psychology (1997) from the American Psychological Association and the Soka University Medal of Highest Honor for contributions to the academy and to international peace and understanding.

NOACH MILGRAM is professor emeritus of clinical psychology at Tel-Aviv University and is currently dean of the Social Science Faculty, College of Judea and Samaria. He has done extensive research on the response of people exposed to diverse sources of threat and injury (war, migration, threats and challenges in daily living) and has published over 100 scientific articles and chapters on these topics.

T. JOSEPH O'DONOGHUE received his Ph.D. in International Studies from Catholic University. He began his research into violence in Northern Ireland while serving as United States Fulbright Scholar at University College Cork. He had earlier served as Fulbright Scholar at the University of Tokyo, where he completed *The World of the Japanese Worker*, in which he analyzed the historic role of Japanese workers in establishing Japan as a global economic power. He recently was invited by the University of Limerick to complete a similar book, *The World of the Irish Worker*, as Fulbright Scholar at that University. He is the recipient of outstanding faculty awards at the City University of New York (CUNY) and at Hofstra University.

MARY A. O'DONOGHUE is professor emerita of psychology at Molloy College, New York State. She has a M.A. in general psychology from Montclair State, N.J. and a Ph.D. in clinical and school psychology from Hofstra University, N.Y. She is a New York State licensed psychologist who has presented papers at a number of professional conventions of regional and national psychological organizations.

BARNABAS I. OKEKE is currently senior research and information analyst in the Office of Mental Health and Mental Retardation of the Department of Public Health of the City of Philadelphia. His research interests center on the issue of the interaction between theory and research, the advancement of the Field Theory approach to science, and the African Law of Opposites, which are the cornerstones of the development of science. He has developed innovative approaches and models for analyzing social science data in cross-cultural research. He has also authored and co-authored numerous publications, and presented papers at regional, national, and international meetings.

ANDRE J. PELSER is associate professor of sociology at the University of the Free State in Bloemfontein, South Africa, and senior research associate at two research centers at the same institution. Pelser's research and teaching activities are focused on the intersection of population studies and environmental issues, as well as survey research and opinion polls. He has authored, co-authored, and compiled more than 80 publications in the form of books, chapters in books, articles, and research reports. He has rendered consultancy services to various national and international institutions, organizations, and agencies. Some of his latest research activities center on the potential for conflict as a result of increasing water scarcity in developing nations, and the impact of environmental degradation on health and development in South Africa.

GEVORG POGHOSYAN is director of the Institute of Philosophy and Law of the National Academy of Sciences of the Republic of Armenia, President-founder (since 1992) of the Armenian Sociological Association (ASA), and a member of the International Academy on Problems of Nature and Society. He is the author of 5 monographs and about 100 articles in scientific magazines. Many bulletins, newsletters, maps, and CDs have been issued under his edition. He has contributed as an expert, speaker, and participant to numerous international meetings of non-governmental organizations (NGOs) on issues of conflict resolution, human rights protection, and migration, as well as the development of NGO legislation in the countries of the Southern Caucasus.

ERIN DYER RING holds her Ph.D. in Developmental Psychology. She works as psychological and educational consultant for developmentally delayed children. She also holds a certificate in Disaster Management, Humanitarian Assistance, and International Peacekeeping from the University of Hawaii. Her research interests include human development in cross-cultural and international contexts, specifically the psychosocial and developmental well being of refugee children and their families.

JAIPAUL L. ROOPNARINE is Professor of Child Studies at Syracuse University. He received his Ph. D. from the University of Wisconsin. His research interests include father-child relationships across cultures, early childhood education in global perspective, and Caribbean immigrant families and schooling. His books include *Caribbean Families: Diversity Among Ethnic Groups* and a forthcoming volume entitled *Families in Global Perspective.*

ERIC E. RUMP is a senior lecturer in psychology at the University of Adelaide, Australia where he teaches various topics in cross-cultural psychology over the four years of the undergraduate program. He is a fellow of the Australian Psychological Society and has been a member of the South Australian Psychological (Registration) Board. He has published numerous papers in several fields, including perception, personality, creativity, developmental, occupational and clinical psychology, aesthetic preferences, eating behavior, and social attitudes. The cross-cultural research has involved collecting data from Australia, New Zealand, Poland, Italy, Greece, and Sri Lanka, in collaboration with several colleagues.

V. NELLY SALGADO DE SNYDER is director of community health and social welfare of the Mexican National Institute of Public Health, Center for Health Systems Research. She has published over 70 journal articles, books, and book chapters in the areas of mental health and quality of life in the context of Mexican migration to the U.S. from rural communities. She is a member of both the Mexican Academy of Scientific Research and the Mexican Sistema Nacional de Investigadores and has been designated Leader of the Mexican Section of the Migrant Health Core Group of the United States-Mexico Binational Commission. Additionally, Dr. Salgado de Snyder is a fellow of the American Psychological Association, a Fulbright fellow, and was recently designated New Century Scholar by the Fulbright Program, Health in a Borderless World.

ELENA L. SAMONTE is a professor with the Department of Psychology, University of the Philippines and heads the Industrial-Organizational Psychology graduate program. She has done extensive work in cross-cultural research particularly in the areas of migration, stress and coping, cross-cultural marriages, and nation perception. She is a past president of the Psychological Association of the Philippines and serves as a consultant for various government organizations as well as for the private sector. She has been the recipient of numerous scholarships and research awards and has been a visiting professor/researcher/scholar in Asia, Europe, and North America.

PAUL G. SCHMITZ is a member of the Department of Social- and Personality Psychology at the University of Bonn, Germany and is also a member of the advisory board of the Institute for Cross-Cultural and Cross-Ethnic Studies at Molloy College. He is active in several international organizations, such as International Association for Cross-Cultural Psychology (IACCP), the International Society for the Study of Individual Differences (ISSID), the European Association of Personality Psychology (EAPP), and the German-Japanese Society for Social Sciences. Dr. Schmitz is co-editor of *the Cahiers Internationaux de Psychologie Sociale*, he participates in the postgraduate-program DEPSA (Diplôme Européen de Psychologie Sociale Appliquée), and teaches cross-cultural psychology at French, Portuguese, and Spanish Universities.

MEERA SHIN was born in Seoul, Korea, and received her Ph.D. from Syracuse University in the Department of Child and Family Studies. She is now an assisant professor in the Department of Early Childhood and Family Studies at Kean University. Her research interests include parent-child relationships in Asian families and multicultural early childhood education.

TOM SORENSEN is currently professor of psychiatry at the University of Oslo. For many years, he has been working with Robert Kleiner and Odd Steffen Dalgard on a series of field experiments concerned with the treatment of chronically disturbed patients in various community contexts. Since 1988, he has provided the leadership in developing a new field of "community psychiatry," in which communities are evaluated with respect to their intrinsic properties that raise or lower the risk of metal disorder, i.e., turning attention to the natural community contexts in which behavior occurs and changing the communities accordingly. He has written numerous theoretical papers and has provided the leadership for a number of field studies in process or being designed.

DEBORAH A. STILES is professor of education at Webster University and a licensed psychologist in St. Louis, Missouri. She has conducted research projects with adolescents in the countries of Norway, Mexico, South Africa, Singapore, the Netherlands, Switzerland, Iceland, and the U.S.A. She received a Fulbright Award for her research with immigrant and refugee adolescent girls living in Norway and a Messing Award for her research on schooling and early adolescent development in Singapore. She is interested in cross-cultural human development, sports psychology, and the psychology of art. She is currently writing a book with Judith L. Gibbons on adolescents from 20 countries.

SEISOH SUKEMUNE, a professor emeritus at Hiroshima University, Japan, is now teaching at Mukogawa Women's University Graduate School of Clinical Education, Nishinomiya, Japan, and at Bunkyo Gakuin University Graduate School of Humanity, Tokyo, Japan. He has played a prominent role in the International Council of Psychologists and participated in numerous psychology conferences around the world.

AGNES YINLING YU is a Canadian psychologist born in Hong Kong and educated in Hong Kong, Mexico, and Canada. Her current interests are in Expressive Arts Therapy. Her practice and research have focused on cross-cultural and inter-cultural studies, minority studies, cognitive studies, and adjustment issues among immigrant populations in several continents. The late Bruce Bain and Agnes Yu were partners in research studies in Hong Kong.